Just Awakening

Just Awakening

Yogācāra Social Philosophy in Modern China

JESSICA X. ZU

Columbia University Press
New York

Columbia University Press
Publishers Since 1893
New York   Chichester, West Sussex

Library of Congress Cataloging-in-Publication Data
Names: Zu, Jessica X., author.
Title: Just awakening : yogācāra social philosophy in modern China / Jessica X. Zu.
Description: New York : Columbia University Press, [2025] | Includes bibliographical references and index.
Identifiers: LCCN 2024034271 (print) | LCCN 2024034272 (ebook) | ISBN 9780231216036 (hardback) | ISBN 9780231216043 (trade paperback) | ISBN 9780231561105 (ebook)
Subjects: LCSH: Yogācāra (Buddhism) | Mahayana Buddhism
Classification: LCC BQ7494 .Z86 2025 (print) | LCC BQ7494 (ebook) | DDC 294.3/92—dc23/eng/20240814

Cover design: Milenda Nan Ok Lee
Cover art: *Mushroom Mantra* by Charwei Tsai. Courtesy of the artist.

GPSR Authorized Representative: Easy Access System Europe, Mustamäe tee 50, 10621 Tallinn, Estonia, gpsr.requests@easproject.com

DEDICATED TO THE WRETCHED OF THE EARTH

Contents

Preface ix

Introduction: Changing Referents 1

PART I

When Dharma Meets Darwin 29

1. Lü Cheng and the Birth of Yogācāra Social Philosophy 31
2. Karma, Evolutionism, and Buddhist Social Consciousness 51
3. Karma, Science, and a Just Society 70

PART II

Liberation Buddhology 95

4. Buddhability as Humanity 97
5. Bodhisattva of Democracy 123
6. Scholarship for Salvation 148

Not a Coda: Bending the Arc Together 177

Notes 187

Bibliography 239

Index 257

Preface

Everything arises dependent on causes and conditions. I feel honored and privileged to be part of the process of making this book, *Just Awakening*. My entry into this process started with a puzzle. Born and raised Pure Land Buddhist and trained in theoretical physics, I have always code-switched among multiple, incommensurable paradigms of knowing the self and the world. On the one end of the spectrum is the scientific paradigm of one objective world, independent of human subjective experiences. On the other end is the Yogācāra paradigm, in which every sentient being engenders its own lifeworld, including mountains, rivers, physics, mathematics, and projections of other minds. I initially believed these paradigms were wholly incompatible with one another. Yet I knew that many scholars of modern China had attributed the Yogācāra revival to its compatibility with science. To gain some clarity on this paradox, I started a new project at Princeton University in 2013.

My first moment of clarity occurred on April 23, 2015, after a talk on Yogācāra by William (Bill) Waldron. Stephen F. (Buzzy) Teiser raised a question, which I paraphrase as "*Ālayavijñāna* and common karma seem to be so intersubjective and thus easily applicable to social theories. Do you happen to know any such applications?" The ensuing discussions with Buzzy, Bill, and Jonathan Gold stirred up a tsunami in my brain. Waves of faces and names associated with modern Yogācāra movements swelled up in my consciousness: Zhang Taiyan, Ouyang Jingwu, Liang Shuming, Monk Taixu, Lü Cheng, Han Qingjing, Wang Enyang, and so many more. A common thread among these diverse intellectuals appeared to me: they all employed some Yogācāra concepts for seeking justice and building a new world.

Many people helped me on this arduous research journey. While I cannot name everyone in this limited space, they live in my heart. My gratitude first goes out to the communities of practitioners who lovingly produced, circulated, and preserved the texts studied in this book. I regret that I can name only a few: Xiao Yongming at Jinling Sūtra Press, who shared with me many archived and unarchived texts; Setsuko Noguchi, who helped me access the archives at Musashino University; Notto Reidai Thelle, who assisted with my research in Areopagos's missionary archives; and Swati Ganguly, Sumedh Ranvir, Abhijit Banerjee, and Ajay Kumar, who helped me access Viśva-Bhārati's archives housed in the Tagore Museum and Cheena Bhavana.

My deep appreciation also goes out to mentors, friends, and colleagues at Princeton who read earlier drafts and offered abundant support. Buzzy Teiser not only sparked my initial interest in this research direction but also routinely offered actionable advice. I am deeply grateful to Jonathan Gold, our local Yogācāra philosopher, who patiently guided me through scholarship on Buddhist philosophy and readings of primary texts in Tibetan. Equally important, Janet Chen, with her research focus on the urban poor in modern China and her scholarly commitment to "root for the underdogs," always reminded me to stay true to my scholarly duty: finding out the facts and uncovering the overlooked perspectives. Jacqueline (Jackie) Stone, whom many of my cohort regard as a living bodhisattva, inspired me with her thorough scholarship and her careful illustration of how doctrines and histories were entangled at unexpected moments. I'm deeply grateful to the Center for the Study of Religion at Princeton, whose fellowship in 2019–2020 offered me valuable opportunities to learn, write, and build professional networks across disciplines. Jenny Wiley Legath also deserves a shout-out: she first suggested the term "socio-soteriology," which is now central to my methodology. I'm also deeply indebted to all my colleagues in the Department of Religion, East Asian Studies Program, Center for the Study of Religion, and Writing Center at Princeton.

My colleagues at University of Southern California played a key role in furthering the research and writing of *Just Awakening*. Many colleagues read early drafts of my manuscript, chief among them Mengxiao Wang, Jessica Marglin, Duncan Williams, Lori Meeks, David Albertson, and James McHugh. In October 2023 the Department of East Asian Languages and Cultures organized a manuscript workshop for me, which enabled me to dive more deeply into my main arguments with Jay Garfield, Dan Lusthaus, Bettine Birge, Joshua Goldstein, Sonya Lee, and many others. Special thank also goes to Rebecca Lemon, who offered warm encouragement and timely support for the production of this book. I am also grateful to the students in my upper-level undergraduate course on Buddhist modernism and my graduate seminar on Buddhist philosophy of mind, who suffered through my many failed attempts to explain Yogācāra social philosophy without jargon. I'm indebted to the University of Southern California's administrative support staff. In addition to granting me leave in 2023–2024 so I could complete a fellowship at the University of Notre Dame, the University of Southern California offered me another semester off in fall 2024 so I could sprint to the finish line.

This book was also made possible thanks to the unending support I received from the scholarly community more broadly. In 2017–2018, the generous support of the Robert H. N. Ho Family Foundation and the American Council of Learned Societies made my research trips to China, Japan, and Norway possible. More than financial support, the Ho/ACLS fellowship initiated me into a global community of scholars of Buddhist studies. In particular, I had the good fortune to meet Susanne Kerekes, who is now my partner in crime in advancing our ambitious project, "Buddhism of the 99%." In 2023–2024 the Notre Dame Institute for Advanced Studies' external faculty fellowship provided me precious writing time to finish this book. The institute's vibrant intellectual community opened my eyes to many more areas of research and encouraged me to think more deeply on issues of ethics, poverty, and democracy. My friend Huijun Mai at the University of California, Los Angeles, offered incisive comments on parts of the manuscript. My friends in the "first-book club," Sean Han, Minjung Noh, Susanne Kerekes, and a few others, suffered through many drafts of my book chapters and book proposals. I'm also deeply grateful to my editor, Stephanie Scott, who has been working with me since 2018 and whose numerous edits and suggestions have made me a better writer every time. The book was also made better by comments and suggestions received after I presented different parts of the manuscript at numerous conferences as well as the Five-Colleges Buddhist Studies Faculty Seminar in fall 2023, facilitated by Lei Ying at Amherst College and organized by Andy Rotman at Smith College, and the Philosophy of Religions workshop at the University of Chicago in fall 2024, facilitated by Upāyadhī and organized by Danica Cao.

This book is also the outcome of the unwavering support from the editor of religion and philosophy at Columbia University Press, Wendy Lochner, and her team. Wendy offered much professional advice with unparalleled patience and responsiveness. I am also grateful to the reviewers of this manuscript, whose incisive comments sharpened my arguments and improved the manuscript's readability. Equally important, Charwei Tsai, my favorite artist, graciously allowed me to use her *Mushroom Mantra* as the cover for this book. In addition, chapter 1 of this book was published in *Journal of Global Buddhism*, an open-access journal.

This research changed me and my relations with the self, the society, and the world. As Octavia Butler powerfully said, "All that you touch you change, all that you change changes you." Research is a dependently arising process of entangled influences. I no longer think that Yogācāra and science are inherently incompatible. Rather, I believe incommensurable paradigms are neither the same nor different but mutually enriching through actions, interactions, and consequences of actions. Compatibility, commensurability, belonging, community, and society must be made and sustained through nonviolent, repeated, and motivated actions of attention and care. I hope *Just Awakening* can play a small part in this ongoing project of building a better, more just future for everyone.

Now, a few words about conventions, transliterations, and abbreviations. Throughout this book, a term's Chinese characters and pinyin are marked with a "Ch" to denote its linguistic origins only when the term has multilingual equivalents: for example, "revolutionizing consciousness" (Ch: *zhuanyi* 轉依; Skt: *āśrayaparivṛtti*; Tib: *gnas yongs su 'gyur pa*), where "Skt" stands for Sanskrit and "Tib" stands for Tibetan; but compare this with "remote objective basis" (*shu suoyuanyuan* 疏所緣緣), with its Chinese rendering alone. Tibetan terms are transliterated using the Wylie system. The diacritics of Sanskrit and Pāli terms are maintained because Lü Cheng's use of them is highly technical and often idiosyncratic. I do not italicize commonly known terms such as "dharma" and "nirvāṇa" or "śrāvaka," used to contrast with the "Mahāyāna" path of liberation. In citations in Japanese and Chinese in the bibliography, I provide the ideographs, transliterations, and translations. The notes carry ideographs and transliterations only.

Just Awakening

Introduction

Changing Referents

Dear Honorable Journalist,

Your journal has a long-established reputation for your goal of reforming literature (*gaige wenxue* 改革文學), which often touches upon poetry and theater. Young readers have been inspired [by your journal] profoundly. Truly magnificent! Truly magnificent! In my humble opinion, while it is indeed important and proper to reform poetry and theater, fine art—the one that parallels poetry and theater in art—especially needs to be revolutionized (*geming* 革命). . . .

If the enterprise of aesthetic education has fallen into this [sorry state of affairs], alas, the corruption of fine art in our country is the most severe today. Frankly, we must urgently revolutionize [fine art and aesthetics].

Where does the path of revolution begin? [I] say, first, [we shall] clarify and explain the scope and essence of fine art so that commoners understand what makes fine art aesthetic.

Second, [we shall] clarify and explain the transmissions and principles of painting, sculpture, and architecture since the Tang dynasty so that commoners understand the fine art of our country. [interlinear note]: *Since the Tang dynasty, because of the spread of Buddhist teachings, our country's sculpture and architecture were considerably reformed. Unfortunately, no one has studied this [aesthetic reform].*

Third, [we shall] clarify and explain the transformation of Euro-American fine art and the reality of various new schools today so that commoners understand the trends and directions of fine art.

Fourth, based on studies of the true essence of fine art, [we] cross-examine the right and wrong [claims about] various kinds of fine arts in the East, the West, the New, and the Old. In this way, [this knowledge] could assist those who aspire [to practice] fine art to find [their aesthetic] calling and thereby further develop [their aesthetic calling].

If all the above questions are thoroughly studied, then the society knows the true path of aesthetics, which [will] freshen the audiovisual [inputs of the commoners]. Gradually, [the society's] taste and desire will be transformed. Then there will be no need to dispel the ones [who propagate and practice] vulgar customs. In this way, the [tangible] effects of aesthetic education are not difficult to actualize.

Advocating for these enterprises is merely in the realm of public discourses. However, today's customs are frivolous, human relations are disoriented, and those who dominate public opinion are mostly going along with [the vulgar views]. Only your journal can plan far and wide, especially regarding the questions of art. If your journal can exert some effort to carry on the extra responsibility of initiating an aesthetic revolution, then you will truly become the Italian *Poesia* the second. And the benefit your journal engenders will, for sure, not be limited to one people or one time.

I have rashly shared my humble opinion. I look forward to [your] clear instruction.

Yours truly,
Lü Cheng
December 15, 1918[1]

This spirited reader's letter to the flagship journal of the May Fourth anti-imperialist movement, *New Youth*, was sent during the throes of the New Culture Movement that is often deemed a watershed moment in the making of modern China. Written by a largely unknown art teacher named Lü Cheng 呂澂 (1896–1989), the letter called for an "aesthetic revolution." The editor of *New Youth*, Chen Duxiu 陳獨秀 (1879–1942)—a renowned progressive thinker and later a cofounder of the Communist Party of China (established in July 1921), promptly published the letter and broadcasted his unreserved support for such an aesthetic revolution.

Soon afterward, Liu Haisu 劉海粟 (1896–1994), a renowned artist and educator, invited Lü Cheng to join his academy and work together to revolutionize art and art education. Lü accepted this invitation and moved to the cosmopolitan city of Shanghai in September 1920. There the once-unknown art teacher not only introduced a wide range of Western aesthetics to Chinese readers but also published several essays and monographs that laid the foundation for the academic discipline of aesthetic studies in modern China.[2]

Lü Cheng would soon be recognized as the most erudite Buddhologist of modern China.[3] At the time of this letter, Lü was already proficient in Japanese, English, and French. He was also able to read German with the help of Japanese translations. His language skills provided him direct access to the riches of Western thought. A few years after he moved to Shanghai he expanded his already impressive knowledge of languages. He acquired research proficiency in Sanskrit, Pāli, and classical Tibetan, enabling him to incorporate cutting-edge philological methods into his Yogācāra (the school of consciousness-only) studies.[4]

Today, Lü's Buddhological achievements, though mostly unknown to Western academics, are well respected within Buddhological circles. However, Lü's multilingual edition of an abridged Buddhist reader, *Zangyao* 藏要 (The Essentials of a New Buddhist Canon; henceforth, *Essentials*), remains understudied despite its high standard for textual-philological criticism.[5]

Aesthetic Revolution 美術革命

What prompted Lü to give up his thriving career as a respected aesthete in 1923? What about Yogācāra prompted Lü to devote the rest of his life to studying it? This book traces Lü's intellectual quest to use art to make activism irresistible, which over time metamorphized into a project of using Buddhism to make revolutionary nonviolence unstoppable. Transforming Yogācāra spiritual exercises into resources for an unstoppable project of revolutionary nonviolence necessitated Lü's invention of a new social philosophy, which I term Yogācāra "socio-soteriology."

As a bifocal, diffractive lens, socio-soteriology brings two siloed sets of human inquiries into mutual scrutiny. The "socio" aspect of socio-soteriology in *Just Awakening* investigates how Lü theorized collective liberation as a co-awakening to social justice, which would in turn promote viable actions to establish a just society. The "soteriology" aspect investigates the philosophical underpinnings of Lü's social revolution and explores how he retooled the soteriological exercises and philosophical arguments of the school of consciousness-only to theorize both justice and liberation as recurring, motivated patterns of actions and coactions (collective actions) that would surely lead to co-awakening.

Socio-soteriology spotlights a thus-far overlooked metamethodological dilemma that many humanists and social scientists have struggled with and that has yet to be adequately addressed in both Buddhist studies and sinology: namely, how to study incommensurable worldviews. This issue is particularly vexing for scholars of modern Yogācāra because all the modern Yogācārins studied in this monograph actively engaged with the pressing issues of their time—for example, what makes us human in a scientific world (free will or something else) and how to live together peacefully with other humans, other species, and insentient beings.

And yet the modern Yogācārins rejected the modern épistémè because core Yogācāra teachings deny two basic modern consensuses: we live in one and the same world, and we are independent individuals.[6] The Yogācāra system rejects any ontological subject/object dualistic structure and deconstructs the two pillars of the modern épistémè—subjectivity and objectivity—into aggregates of mental actions, events, and processes.[7] As such, Yogācāra philosophy undermines the fundamental premises of the mainstream academic research paradigm, that is, postpositivism that takes the existence of one shared objective world and stable subjective observers as self-evident truths.

To flesh out these metamethodological complexities and their relevance to the present study, in the remaining space of this introduction, I first sketch the fault lines in this metamethodological dilemma. Revisiting the 1980s Euro-American scholarly war over research paradigms in the social sciences, the first section suggests a new referent with which to comprehend how Lü's socio-soteriology in the 1920s serves as a quintessentially incommensurable research paradigm outside the Euro-American academic orbit. The next section introduces the basic Yogācāra worldview, a worldview that rejects the notion of one objective world, posits multiple lifeworlds, and dismantles any naturalization of social kinds, including objectivity and subjectivity. Then the third section outlines how the postpositivist academic standard of objectivity could be replaced with what I term the "Yogācāra three Cs," i.e., intersubjective corroboration, causal (karmic) efficacy, and coherence.

Competing Research Paradigms and Changing Referents

The human world has long been keenly aware of the limitations of the individual's parochial ways of knowing, as evidenced by adages such as "Fish can't see water," "If all you have is a hammer, everything looks like a nail," the ancient metaphor in *Zhuangzi* about a "frog in a well" that epitomizes epistemic narrowness and arrogance, and the famous question in *Zhuangzi*, "You are not a fish, so how do you know what fish enjoy?"[8] Scholars in the humanities and social sciences are particularly invested in finding viable pathways by which individuals can escape the confines of the modern épistémè. As practitioners of qualitative research have long pointed out, ontology (the study of the nature of reality) is inextricably entangled with epistemology (the study of how we know), methodology (of how we gain knowledge), and axiology (of what is valuable for us to know and how we become moral people). Ontology, epistemology, methodology, and axiology together give rise to a bounded research paradigm.[9] In my use, research paradigm pluralizes the all-encompassing épistémè. Loosening up épistémè to allow multiple coexisting paradigms in this way encourages a *dévisagement réciproque* (reciprocal scrutiny), reconfigures what is thinkable in each paradigm, and enables mutual reflections of one's own situatedness and propensities.[10]

Given the current knowledge-production practices that engage with multiple, equally compelling, and thereby competing research paradigms, it is no longer possible to follow the well-established disciplinary practices of Buddhist studies and sinology, that is, extracting putative objective knowledge about Buddhism or China using textual-critical methods within the postpositivist paradigm and pretending critical theories do not matter in these analyses.[11] Equally important, given the incommensurable ontology of Yogācāra, scholars of modern Yogācāra need to lean into the difficulty of confronting a competing research paradigm and to not only *learn about* Yogācāra sociosoteriology but also *learn from* it.[12]

To better learn from incommensurable worldviews demands scholars change referents. Changing referents, at its core, reflects a long-standing humanist inquiry into how we should and can learn from the other, from the foreign, and from the unfamiliar. In my use, changing referents requires reflexively and systematically learning from other cultures' research paradigms, not merely as raw materials to enrich contemporary academic conversations but rather as theoretical resources to de-parochialize current academic practices of knowledge production.

Changing referents is possible, and there are historical precedents for doing so. As powerfully argued by Leigh K. Jenco, Chinese thinkers in the nineteenth and twentieth centuries intensively theorized and systemized effective ways of engaging with foreign knowledge and of learning from incommensurable worldviews, as seen in the vast body of writings on *bianfa* 變法, which Jenco translates as "changing referents."[13] In recent decades, many scholars have taken up this project of changing referents in their own right, as seen in the aforementioned Foucauldian épistémè, the thriving studies on competing research paradigms, and the fields of postcolonial studies and decolonial studies.[14]

Building upon this rich kit of tools with which to decenter modes of knowing and perceiving prevalent in the Global North, I argue that changing referents must start with systematic inquiries into the ontological, ethical, epistemological, and methodological premises of other cultures. In other words, a change of referents necessitates both proficiency in and openness to multiple incommensurable research paradigms.

Just Awakening narrates the quest to break free from and replace the modern épistémè, a quest that has been advanced by the Chinese Yogācārins since the 1920s. This sense of urgency for changing referents fed upon the widely perceived sense of crisis and doom, as aptly captured by the phrase "protecting the nation and preserving the race" (*huguo baozhong* 護國保種) popularized in the late nineteenth century, but it was eventually wielded in a battle about what counts as knowledge and what kinds of knowledge need to be produced to save China and the world.

I find Norman K. Denzin and Yvonna S. Lincoln's call to diversify the scholarly repertoire of research paradigms most useful for appreciating this ongoing epistemological struggle. As a bounded system of four mutually dependent sets of human inquiry—ontology, epistemology, methodology, and axiology—a research paradigm constitutes the conditions of possibility for certain kinds of knowledge production.[15] Take the postpositivist paradigm as an example. A postpositivist sees the ontological commitment to the ideas of one objective world and a stable subject to be self-evident truths. Consequently, their epistemological benchmark is that the researcher sets aside their own cultural, historical, and personal biases to recover the putatively objective meaning of a text, which is taken to be the authorial intention.

Note that for different disciplines, this putatively objective reconstruction of authorial intent follows different sets of norms and practices. As incisively pointed out by Tao Jiang, philosophers and sinologists imaginatively construct different kinds of authors. On the one hand, sinologists investigate the actors who produced the texts and hence construct their research objects as "historical authors." On the other hand, scholars of Chinese philosophy construct "textual authors" and reverse engineer the "textual intent" that emphasizes the integrity of the text as it has been received and interpreted by a certain tradition.[16] Although Jiang's theorization focuses on Chinese philosophy and sinology, I find this distinction equally valid for exploring the contentions between Buddhology (philology) and Buddhist philosophy. In Buddhist studies, the dominant epistemology is largely one of objectivist investigation, which calls for setting aside one's own subjective impositions. Both philologists and philosophers follow their respective disciplinary norms and practices to construct their respective objects of study, namely authorial intent vs. textual intent, and consider the possibility of reverse engineering a coherent "intent" as relatively unproblematic.

The prefix of "post" indicates the broad consensus that an individual scholar is always limited by their own positionality. In this context, putatively objective knowledge can only be revealed through the collective efforts of scholars in the field to investigate novel claims based on established disciplinary norms and practices. Relatedly, this epistemology requires that one knows the world objectively. Informed by these ontological and epistemological commitments, scholars have assembled robust sinological, philological, historical, and Buddhological toolboxes. What is valuable to know in this postpositivist paradigm is the objective knowledge about the texts and the people who produced and transmitted them. The only path by which to become a moral researcher is to train oneself to become more and more objective.

Under this postpositivist paradigm, the core scholarly value of impartiality is easily confused with the ontological claim of objectivity. Thanks to the presumptively clear boundary between the subjective and the objective, the former notion, impartiality, disinterestedness, or fairness, is in the realm of axiology, bound up with subjective value judgment and conscious human action. In contrast, the latter notion, objectivity, is a metaphysical given in the postpositivist paradigm. Because of the unexamined premise of a naturalized duality in this paradigm, a mind-independent objectivity and a private subjectivity, any human action or conscientious value consideration is automatically considered illustrative of personal capriciousness, randomness, or bias and is rendered, by extension, untrustworthy.

In the Euro-American academia, the positivist mode of knowledge production was powerfully challenged with the emergence of critical theory in humanities in the 1970s and the paradigm wars in social sciences in the 1980s.[17] Both of these new intellectual communities proposed and practiced many mutually incompatible paradigms. To appreciate how far outside the Western academic orbit the research paradigm proposed by Lü falls, it is useful to position Lü's Yogācāra research paradigm relative to the competing paradigms shown in table I.1.[18]

As shown in table I.1, while the mainstream postpositivist paradigm presumes an objectivist epistemology, the countercurrents of critical theory, postcolonial studies and feminist studies by and large presume a subjectivist epistemology. More recently, possibly motivated by the desire to overcome the fragmentation caused by reifications of multiple subjective positionalities and their corresponding worldviews, some feminist philosophers and practitioners of indigenous research paradigms have called into question this naturalized subjectivity and proposed an epistemology in which realities are coconstructed

TABLE I.1. Competing Research Paradigms

	Postpositivism	*Critical theory, postcolonial studies, indigenous research paradigms, etc.*	*Lü's Yogācāra socio-soteriology*
Ontology:What is reality?	Critical realism: "real" reality only imperfectly and probabilistically apprehendable	Virtual reality shaped by social, political, cultural, and economical factors; or constructed realities	Multiple perceptible, karmically entangled lifeworlds, neither one nor two
Epistemology:How do we know?	Modified dualist/*objectivist*, critical tradition/community findings	*Subjectivist*/value-mediated/created findings	Neither subjectivist nor objectivist; intersubjective corroboration, coherence, causal (karmic) efficacy
Methodology:How do we find out?	Falsification of hypotheses; critical multiplism; *qualitative* and quantitative methods	Dialogical; dialectical; *hermeneutical*	*Diffractive analysis*; identification, examination, and modification of anchoring processes
Axiology:What is worth knowing? How do I be a moral researcher?	Reality, objective knowledge, truth, authorial intent	Social justice; the epistemic advantage of the subaltern, etc.	*Karma-informed, action-oriented moral reasoning*; relational accountability
Academic status	Mainstream	Flourishing in humanities and other qualitative research fields but in general seeking recognition and input	Outside the current academic orbit of knowledge production; mainstream in many Buddhist communities

by both the subjects and objects.[19] Yet none of these known research paradigms goes as far as Yogācāra has: Yogācāra is a paradigm of knowing that not only rejects the subject/object divide but also diffracts the naturalized abstractions of subjectivity and objectivity in terms of the more concrete anchoring processes of actions, coactions, and consequences of actions.[20]

Epistemology is inevitably bound up with axiology. Since the 1990s, qualitative social scientists have argued that researchers in the humanities and social sciences can no longer uncritically present themselves as disinterested observers but must be keenly aware of their own positionality: researchers are in fact "interpretative bricoleur[s]." The reason for this, according to the social scientists, is evident. Given the existence of multiple, competing, and incommensurable research paradigms, the myths of a single truth and a single conventional paradigm of knowing no longer hold. Because all truths are "partial and incomplete" and "we occupy a historical moment marked by multivocality, contested meanings, paradigmatic controversies, and new textual forms," researchers "must understand the basic ethical, ontological, epistemological, and methodological assumptions of each and be able to engage them [competing research paradigms] in dialogue."[21]

What is at stake, for qualitative researchers, is both pragmatic and metamethodological. It is pragmatic because the differences between paradigms and perspectives "have significant and important implications at the practical, material, everyday level." For example, feminist researchers and critical race theorists have not only greatly reshaped the academic world to make it more inclusive, but they have also created new possibilities for doing public scholarship, such as producing knowledge for cultivating "social justice and a revolutionary habitus" and for employing "critical social science, a combination of structural and poststructural analysis, the denial of neutrality in scholarship, and the incorporation of . . . 'counter narratives' to speak back against dominant discourses."[22]

At the meta level, rather than mourn the loss of a universalized truth, qualitative researchers see this process of increasingly multiplying and diversifying paradigms as emblematic of "an age of emancipation, freedom from the confines of a single regime of truth, emancipation from seeing the world in one color."[23] More concretely, opening oneself up to multiple social ontologies and research paradigms constitutes a crucial step in correcting the "ontic injustice" that frames many contemporary conversations about gender, race, and other social kinds. As powerfully argued by Katherine Jenkins, ontic injustice highlights that "social kinds can be such that individuals who are socially constructed as members of those kinds can be wronged *by the very fact* of being socially constructed in that way" and that it is "*ontic* because the wrong operates through social ontology, and *injustice* because the wrong is a consequence of our collective social arrangements," irrespective of any individual's good or evil intentions.[24] Informed by this insight, an alternative way of studying social ontology becomes possible: instead of assuming that "our social practices should be guided by the social kinds that currently exist," we should "first ask what that reality is like, specifically, whether it is just or unjust." For Jenkins, recognizing this possibility of ontic injustice has the potential "to disrupt various problematic framings" and "paves the way for an alternative approach" that can more "more conducive" to liberation.[25]

Just Awakening builds upon these thriving debates on research paradigms and their implications for the potential of experiencing liberation from injustice and oppression. It demonstrates that emancipation will only be actualized when researcher-bricoleurs step outside the Euro-American academic orbit, consider competing research paradigms from Asian knowledge systems, and ultimately change referents. To this end, this book introduces a Yogācāra research paradigm that emerged through the multifaceted encounters of Buddhism, science, philosophy, and the social sciences in modern China and that can further this goal of humanistic emancipation.

Against One World: Multiple Lifeworlds

Scholars of Buddhist philosophy have long been attracted to the Yogācāra worldview, partly because it is fundamentally at odds with mainstream academic epistemology.[26] That said, incompatibility with the modern worldview does not make the Yogācāra system incomprehensible or incommunicable. In fact, many scholars have found this épistémè of knowing and perceiving not only defensible and compelling in its own right but also incisive in its critique of the taken-for-granted premises that underpin the mainstream mode of knowledge production.

To begin, the Yogācārin worldview issues a powerful challenge to objectivity.[27] If all that we know and all that we can ever know as humans is inevitably mediated by consciousness, then how do we know there is an objective world outside consciousness? How do we know the notions of "objectivity" and "one shared world" are not mere fictions of the perceiving and constructing consciousness?[28] For readers who find this position astonishing, it might be helpful to read this Yogācāra critique alongside a similar critique that the renowned analytic philosopher Willard van Orman Quine started to work on in 1931 but only put in writing in 1951: "But in point of epistemological footing the physical objects and the gods *differ only in degree not in kind.* Both sorts of entities enter our conception only as *cultural posits. The myth of physical objects* is epistemologically superior to most in that it has proved *more efficacious* than other *myths as a device for working a manageable structure into the flux of experience*" (my emphasis).[29]

Against the prevailing wind that aims to transform mind-dependent social kinds into mind-independent natural kinds, or what is considered "physics envy" in the social sciences, Quine put forth a seemingly radical claim that even the natural kinds are "cultural posits" and that the differences among cultural posits rest in their causal "efficacy." This epistemic view finds remarkable parallels in the Yogācāra three Cs, which will be elaborated in the next subsection. The point of this cross-cultural comparison is not to suggest that Yogācāra is similar to Quine's holism but rather to show that, in the early twentieth century, objectivity as the benchmark of knowledge was questioned on multiple fronts across the East/West divide. The Yogācāra critique was one of many such philosophical fronts, albeit an ignored one.

Once they had done away with the objectivity standard, the ancient Yogācārins pushed further by questioning the existence of one shared world. In making this point, the Yogācārins relied on an extensive philosophical analysis of the concept of *loka* in Sanskrit. Rejecting the notion of one world does not necessarily imply admitting a multiplicity of independent but parallel worlds or some multiverse, as portrayed in popular perceptions of string theory. In fact, as incisively argued by Sonam Kachru, "We cannot treat the world, that is, as a totality or mereological unity, nor may we ground it in anything unitary, such as the mind of God, or some insentient cosmological principle."[30]

In answering the question of what there is, the Yogācāra paradigm considers *loka* a notion of lifeworlds, where subjective experiences and objects are inevitably entangled.[31] Every sentient being, during one of their lifetimes, creates their own lifeworld through their own stream of consciousness, otherwise known as *ālayavijñāna*. But this stream of consciousness is the result of lifetimes of interactions with other sentient and insentient beings and thereby cannot be considered the result of the action of a single agent.

The absence of a single agent suggests that the lifeworlds of one stream of consciousness cannot be isolated from other lifeworlds of other streams of consciousnesses. In fact, the longue durée processes by which all lifeworlds are causally connected to form a stream create what Kachru terms a "cosmological individual."[32] The notion of a cosmological individual highlights the *continuity* grounded in causal processes, replacing the need for ontological identity to ground continuity. Similarly, the causal processes also ground the possibility of individuation of different *ālayavijñānas*.

At the same time, *loka* can also refer to a shared physical context, which, under the Yogācāra paradigm, is created by the collective actions of many *ālayavijñānas*. Returning, then, to the key question of what there is, if there is neither one world nor a multiverse, the alternative answer offered by Vasubandhu (ca. 4 CE) is that "the constitutive variety of worlds is the result of action on the part of sentient beings," which Kachru paraphrases as "a complex function of dynamically open-ended processes."[33]

For me, multiple lifeworlds are neither one nor many but are causally or karmically entangled. To better make sense of this complex nondualistic worldview, contemporary readers might benefit from considering the German concept *Umwelt*. Umwelt was popularized by Ed Yong's 2022 nonfiction book *An Immense World*, in which Yong likened the Umwelt to a "sensory bubble," a "perceptual world" constituting "the part of those surroundings that an animal can sense and experience." One example Yong gives is a tick, whose quest for blood predetermines that its perceptual world mainly consists of "body heat, the touch of hair, and the odor of butyric acid that emanates from skin." This is not a matter of willful ignorance: the tick "simply cannot sense" differences like green trees, red roses, the blue sky, or white clouds that matter to human beings.[34] Even so, this limited tick Umwelt is causally connected to all mammalian Umwelts because ticks need mammalian blood for survival.

The limited scope of the tick lifeworld suggests that the human perceptual world is similarly bound by the human sensory bubble. But for us humans, it feels "all-encompassing" just because "it is all that we know" and all that we can ever know. Of course, all that we know and all that we can ever know does not mean the human Umwelt is "all there is *to* know." This illusion of all that we know means that all there is to know is a profound illusion that every minded creature shares.[35]

Like the zoologist Jakob von Uexküll, who first coined the notion of the Umwelt, ancient Yogācārins were keenly aware that what we can perceive is dependent on our sensory faculties and each species has its own similarly structured sensory bubble. Yet unlike von Uexküll, ancient Yogācārins went to the extreme by pointing out the inevitable variability of every cosmological individual's sensory organs in each lifetime. In doing so, they remind us that even within a species or for one stream of consciousness across multiple lifetimes, there is no such thing as one and the same shared sensory bubble. Rather, every individual in each lifetime has their own perceptual lifeworld, and individuals' lifeworlds are irreducible to one another, hence incommensurable, that is, without common measure. But through an elaborate theory of karma and its consequences, the Yogācāra thinkers also posited that all lifeworlds of all sentient beings in all their lifetimes are karmically connected. Precisely because of the karmic entanglements of different lifeworlds, incommensurability does not lead to incommunicability. On the contrary, a sense of one shared world can be established and maintained through karmic connections, that is, recurring, motivated actions, coactions, and consequences of actions—a point emphasized by all modern Yogācāra social philosophers studied in this book.

Replacing Objectivity: The Yogācāra Three Cs

Tossing out objectivity as the gold standard of knowledge does not mean accepting the absolute relativism of everything goes. In fact, rejecting objectivity as the sole arbiter of what counts as knowledge calls for a more robust investigation of the nature of reality and the entanglement of knowing and consciousness. In their reflexive inquiries, the ancient Yogācārins offered robust epistemological standards. What counts as valid knowing and valid knowledge in Buddhist epistemology has a long and hotly contested history.[36] The Yogācāra three Cs—intersubjective corroboration, causal (karmic) efficacy, and coherence—are the epistemic standards deployed by modern Chinese thinkers. The three Cs are by no means the only modern rendition of this ancient epistemology. They are relevant particularly in the context of appreciating the modern Chinese critique of the colonial épistémè.

Coherence is a widely accepted epistemic standard in Indian philosophical debates. The standard of coherence is implied in Vasubandhu's *Viṃśika* (*Twenty Verses*), a well-known Yogācāra treatise. For example, in verses 1–4, Vasubandhu offers an answer to four objectivist challenges to the coherence of the consciousness-only position: If there is no external object, why can one perceive a definite space-time of an object/event, why can different sentient beings reach intersubjective agreement (or why are mental contents not held privately by one stream of consciousness but can be shared among different minds), and why can mental objects have causal efficacy? In the commentary after verse 6, Vasubandhu questions the coherence of the objectivist position: "What reasons do you have not to admit that the relevant causal process is an entirely mental process of a change, one initiated by the former actions of those beings? In particular, *why speculate about the material elements?*" (my emphasis).[37]

Here, Vasubandhu powerfully challenges his opponent's position: how does his opponent know the so-called mind-independent material elements in his theory are not mere speculations? To drive home the incoherence of other realist and materialist schools, in verses 11–15, Vasubandhu points out the many instances of incoherence in the Vaiśeṣika notion of mind-independent yet momentarily arising and disappearing elemental events (Ch: *jiwei* 極微; Skt: *paramāṇu*; Tib: *rdul phra rab*).[38] Clearly, coherence is an epistemic standard widely accepted by all parties to this debate in *Viṃśika*.

As for the epistemic benchmark of causal (karmic) efficacy, it is a widely accepted Buddhist notion that what makes something or some event real enough is the thing's or the event's karmic efficacy, that is, the ability of something or some event to cause or effect other things or events. More concretely, in *Viṃśika*, Vasubandhu employs the argument of causal efficacy to defend the position of consciousness-only. For example, in verse 4ab, Vasubandhu points out that wet dreams happen not because of actual physical intercourse but because of other mental causal processes such as *vedanā* (affect, feeling; one of the five *skandhas*/aggregates).[39] Immediately after verse 4ab, Vasubandhu presents his argument for "the case of the guards in hell" not as really existing beings but as the fruitions of the karmic seeds in the mental streams of hell beings.[40] Here again, the gist of the argument is that hell beings experience torture by the hell guards. These experiences of suffering are real not because hell guards are material or objective existences but because they arise from the results of the hell beings' own past karmic seeds. The standard of being real enough rests not on the real existence of hell guards but instead upon tangible karmic effects.

The most complex epistemic benchmark is intersubjectivity. Yogācāra rejects the notion of one shared world and in its stead proposes multiple, incommensurable, yet karmically connected lifeworlds. As has been recognized by many scholars of Yogācāra in recent years, in Buddhist soteriology, intersubjective experience takes on paramount significance. Scholars have demonstrated how Yogācāra thinkers such as Vasubandhu, Dharmakīrti, Xuanzang, and Kuiji developed a constellation of concepts related to shared or similar karma to explain the perception of shared experiences of one external world and the experience of other minds.[41]

Nevertheless, few scholars have considered the deeper problem of intersubjectivity caused by Yogācāra's admission of multiple incommensurable lifeworlds.[42] Given the limited scholarly examination of this thorny issue, in the following chapters, instead of presenting a comprehensive argument, I highlight a few modern attempts to replace objectivity with a Yogācāra notion of intersubjectivity employing Chinese Yogācāra terms such as *prasiddha* (*jicheng* 極成; intersubjective agreement), *adhipati* (*zengshang* 增上; activating and amplifying influence), and *huzheng* 互證 (intersubjective verification). All these concepts require the persons to mutually recognize the conscious existence of other persons, which convey a sense of transpersonal or cross-lifeworld communications as a prerequisite for producing intersubjectivity. For now, it is enough to know that Yogācāra rejects common objective ways of perceiving. For example, in verse 15 of *Viṃśika*, Vasubandhu rejects the differentiation of *pramāṇa* (ways of perceiving) and *pramā* (the perceived). When nothing can be privileged as the measure and nothing can be objectified as the measured, a Yogācāra epistemic standard grounded in intersubjective karmic connections can be developed into a reasonable alternative epistemic benchmark.

Socio-Soteriology and Diffractive Analysis

Building upon the metamethodological reflections of the previous sections, *Just Awakening* calls for a diffractive approach to studying Buddhist philosophy, which I term "socio-soteriology," and alternatively, "liberation Buddhology."[43] Broadly speaking, socio-soteriology highlights the crossbreeding of Buddhist soteriological exercises and social philosophy, while liberation Buddhology foregrounds the entanglement of Buddhist soteriology with postcolonial movements.

More than a neologism, socio-soteriology invites scholars to diffract the formations of Buddhist modernism into two interlocking anchoring processes that shed light on differences that mattered to the Buddhist thinkers themselves: how to theorize a just society and how to deploy Buddhist soteriological tools to liberate modern society from all its shackles. Liberation Buddhology, in contrast, highlights the perceived liberative potential of Buddhological knowledge. A change of referents is crucial because, quoting Rafal Stepien's methodological reflection: "while an ethically indifferent, intellectually hermetic disengagement from the pressing problems of worldly suffering may make sense to an armchair philosopher, the attribution of such an abstracted attitude to *modern Yogācārins*, avowedly and actively involved . . . in the soterially motivated project of alleviating and ultimately eradicating suffering, is not only textually unjustified but tantamount to a radical misreading of their entire religiosophical mission."[44]

To better appreciate processual thought in modern Yogācāra, a diffractive methodology is needed. Just like a crystal that separates vibrations of different wavelengths into interference patterns, paradigmatic diffractions require scholars to consider how to diffract their own theories and practices into anchoring processes so as to cast light on the interlocking patterns of knowledge production and to reveal differences that matter to the ameliorative project of producing knowledge for a better future.[45]

I prefer the metaphor of diffraction because it better captures a well-known Buddhist way of reasoning: dependent arising. For example, when contemplating no-self, one common reasoning strategy is to view the self as arising from five collections (Ch: *wuyun* 五蘊; Skt: *pañca-skandhāḥ*; Pāli: *pañca-khandhā*) of psycho-physical processes. One might say that this method diffracts the perceived pattern of a stable personhood into its five streams of aggregated karmic interactions. My use of diffraction does not mean to exclude discussions of Buddhist reductive methods. In fact, both diffractive and reductive methods are central to the Buddhist soteriology. For example, the contemplation of the foulness of the body is primarily about reducing the body into its constitutive parts of hair, skin, bones, and so on.

Rather, I prioritize the diffractive methods to broaden philosophical discussions about Buddhist knowledge system and to accentuate the rich aspects of processual thought and reasoning tactics that have been underrepresented in existing studies of Buddhist philosophy. A closer examination of the evidence presented in the ensuing chapters reveals that the processual worldview took center stage in the revival of Yogācāra in modern China.

Buddhist Process Philosophy and Karma/Action-Oriented Ethics

Diffractive methodologies work well only within the bounds of processual thought. The core argument of this book is that modern Yogācāra philosophers refashioned premodern Yogācāra into a processual *social* philosophy. While Alfred North Whitehead (1861–1947) is widely recognized as the father of the modern school of process philosophy, process thoughts have existed throughout history and around the globe.[46] All processual thinkers, whether Parmenides, Heraclitus, the Abhidharma philosophers of Buddhism, Yogācāra philosophers, Confucius, or contemporary scholars, argue that there are sound reasons and solid evidence to take the processual aspects of nature, experience, cognition, and action as the fundamental features of reality. Furthermore, as incisively argued by Peter Hershock, Buddhist "karmic-relational ontology" fundamentally departs from Whiteheadian process ontology because mainstream Buddhist traditions theorize multidirectional causal relations whereas Whitehead imagines linear causal relations traceable to an ultimate origin: God.[47]

While a philosophically informed intellectual history of *how* non-European process philosophies such as Abhidharma (often dubbed Buddhist psychology), Yogācāra (frequently compared with Berkeleyan idealism, Sigmund Freud's theory of the unconscious, and Edmund Husserl's phenomenology), and Madhyamaka (often likened to deconstructionism) conditioned the Western processual turn remains to be written, *Just Awakening* sheds light on several thus far unrecognized exchanges between pre-Whitehead process thinkers, chiefly John Dewey and Henri Bergson, and the rise of Yogācāra in modern China.[48] Recognizing the dearth of research on Buddhist social philosophy and non-Western process philosophy, I avoid extensive discussion of modern Western process philosophy.[49] Rather, I center the perspectives, concerns, and rationale of modern Chinese Yogācāra philosophers.

As a first step, I weave together the threads of three recently published processual philosophical frameworks to suggest some useful vocabulary and effective bridge concepts that could be useful for introducing these Buddhist social philosophies to English-speaking academia. The lens of process philosophy is helpful because it aptly captures the modern and contemporary developments in Yogācāra thought. Existing scholarship primarily approaches Yogācāra from the lens of idealism or phenomenology because of the interest in the structure of consciousness in premodern Yogācāra texts.

In contrast, many modern Chinese Yogācāra thinkers, to resist the concerted effort of the state and social sciences to reify mind-dependent social kinds as if they were natural kinds, drew from the ancient tradition to theorize social kinds as distinct from the natural kinds and to suggest that they thereby must be studied with a Yogācāra research paradigm. Indeed, modern processual thoughts have deep historical roots. As incisively argued by Vincent Eltschinger, a through line in the Buddhist critique of caste from the early Pāli discourses such as *Aggañña Sutta* and *Assalāyana Sutta* to later Buddhist treatises by renowned philosophers such as Āryadeva (fl. third century CE), Dharmapāla (530–561), Dharmakīrti (fl. sixth or seventh century CE), and Candrakīrti (c. 600–650), is the consistent deployment of the "*étiologique et processuelle*" (etiological and processual) explanation to dismantle the Brahmanical naturalization of caste differentiation and the Brahmanical pride and whose line of arguments had evolved, by the seventh century CE, into "*une conception processuelle et dynamique de la société*" (a processual and dynamic conception of society).[50]

While scholars still debate whether premodern Buddhist traditions developed their own cogent philosophy of a just society, I suggest here that we start with two more fundamental questions: What counts as "a political theory?" Can a philosophy of nonviolence count as a sociopolitical theory? After all, the main critique Johannes Bronkhorst makes of the lack of Buddhist political philosophy rests on his observations that the Buddhists had no concrete advice to offer to kings and monarchies in their mission of conquest or legally sanctioned use of everyday violence until the rise of Tantric Buddhism.[51] Bronkhorst assessment suffers from a long-standing epistemic bias that presumes complex society must have a ruling elite and status hierarchies maintained by violence.[52]

Following in the footsteps of another group of scholars who see the Buddhist message of nonviolence and quest for equality grounded in interdependence as a sociopolitical philosophy of complex egalitarian society, *Just Awakening* argues that twentieth-century Chinese Yogācāra thinkers developed a defensible processual social philosophy that weaved together many of the premodern threads.[53]

Because process philosophy in modern Buddhism remains relatively unstudied, the following theoretical framework is only meant as an initial exploration of the broader projects laid out by Johanna Seibt, focusing on three claims and their intersection with the Yogācāra quest for social justice:

Claim 1: The basic assumptions of the "substance paradigm" (i.e., a metaphysics based on static entities such as substances, objects, states of affairs, or instantaneous stages) are dispensable theoretical presuppositions rather than laws of thought.

Claim 2: Process-based theories perform just as well or better than substance-based theories when applied to familiar philosophical topics identified within the substance paradigm.

Claim 3: There are other important philosophical topics that can only be addressed within a process metaphysics.[54]

In modern China, many thinkers engaged with the first claim. The most common Buddhist critique of the imported "substance paradigm" was related to the notions of the atomic individual and objectivity. As for the second claim, many Yogācāra thinkers subsumed Western sciences into Yogācāra karmic theory and reframed the scientific inquiry of how things are to the investigation of how causal processes perpetuate or change the perceptible worlds. With regard to the third claim, here lie the richest resources offered by modern Yogācāra for theorizing a *processual social philosophy* by rejecting the postpositivism that equates the social kinds with the natural kinds and by positing a processual theorization of what constitutes social kinds (mind-dependent kinds), what constitutes a just society, and how to build democracy.

Chinese Yogācāra thinkers benefited greatly from both Buddhist phenomenology and the prevalent anti-ontological attitude in the Chinese philosophy of living. As François Jullien powerfully argues, while Greco-European ontological thought primarily concerns the question of *l'être* (to be), the main inquiry in Chinese antiontological thought is *vivre* (to live). This philosophy of living is undergirded by a *caractère processuel* in *dao* 道 (the way).[55] Although the bigger and more historical question of to what extent some of the Buddhist philosophical traditions be understood as antiontological, processual thought remains unexplored, in *Just Awakening*, by prioritizing this processual character of living, I showcase how the premodern threads that have congealed into "*une conception processuelle et dynamique de la société*" were further deployed into a social philosophy that functioned to dismantle the substance metaphysical underpinnings of mainstream Western theories and offered a different paradigm of collectivity or togetherness as neither one nor two but karmically connected.[56]

While processual thought is ancient, the notion of processual social ontology is new. It is a branch of social ontology recently proposed by Jason Ānanda Josephson Storm. Frustrated with the unreflexive deconstructive scholarship that has led many humanities projects into a sinkhole where nothing can be said, Storm looked to Buddhism for a way out. Inspired by the Madhyamaka concept of *niḥsvabhāva* (lack of self-nature or interdependence), Whitehead's process ontology, and reflexive sociology, Storm proposes that scholars examine all social entities as processes and investigate the causal schemas that anchor the seemingly stable properties of social kinds.[57] At the risk of stating the obvious, this focus on the causal schemas and processes also aptly describes Eltschinger's study of the premodern Buddhist philosophical critique of casteism.

As for theory of action and coaction, I build upon Mercedes Valmisa's pathbreaking study of the Chinese philosophy of action. In her monograph, Valmisa incisively points out that the process of acting itself is the most fundamental inquiry in all of Chinese philosophy. Valmisa takes coaction to be a key characteristic of the Chinese conception of adaptive agency that presumes neither "a purely individual agent" nor "a fully external world separated from the agent's inner realm." Instead, "all actions are collective events."[58]

This coaction paradigm of agency resonates uncannily with Wendi L. Adamek's interpretation of a medieval Chinese Buddhist group's practices in terms of "agency of relations." Like the coaction paradigm, in the mainstream Buddhist theory of action, the experience of agency is an "effect of the momentum of aggregated processes" and the object is a "functional correlate of the continuum of aggregated processes."[59] In contrast to Valmisa's theory of coaction, "copoiesis" is the term Adamek uses to characterize the acts of a joint process of creation. In this book, I use copoiesis and coaction interchangeably as a means to highlight the significance of processes, actions, and interdependence/relations in Buddhist democratic theories.

Both the theory of coaction and the agency of religions imply a new mode of moral reasoning most often appropriated in support of a processual worldview that I term "karma/action-oriented ethics." As powerfully argued by Francisca Cho, extant scholarship often misconstrues karma as metaphysically misguided hocus-pocus, failing to see beyond the confines of Western ontology, and thereby overlooks the soteriological and pragmatic functions of karma in guiding experiences and redirecting actions, which Cho terms "karma as speech-act."[60]

Action-oriented ethics differs from what David Wong terms "relation-centered" and "autonomy/rights-centered" moral reasoning.[61] This is because the action-oriented approach to ethical dilemmas takes momentary experiences and actions as the starting point and construes relations and rights as stases dependently arising from recurring actions. It requires a reflexive appreciation of one's experiential immersion in the human imagination and activates the imagination to guide one's reasoning in evaluating possible moral actions. Every action changes both the relations and the entities in this paradigm. This action-oriented moral reasoning stems from the diffractive method that trains the actor to identify recurring patterns of actions and coactions underpinning seemingly stable features, which are in turn informed by a processual worldview.

A Biographical Sketch of the Philosopher

Because its chapters are driven by argument instead of chronology, this book assumes a basic familiarity with Lü's major life events. For those who are unfamiliar with him, a biographical sketch of the philosopher is in order.[62] Born into a well-off family of small industrialists and landowners in 1896, Lü grew up in rural Jiangsu Province, which had been the hotbed of Chinese Buddhism since the sixteenth century. Lü's birth name was Zhongwei 鐘渭, and he received a mostly modern education in the cities of Zhenjiang, Changzhou, and then Nanjing in Jiangsu Province. In 1914 during his Nanjing years, influenced by both his eldest brother, the renowned artist, social reformer, and educator Lü Fengzi 呂鳳子 (1886–1959), and his own interest in Buddhist classics that sprouted during his high school years, Lü visited Jinling Sūtra Press, which had been established by the father of modern Chinese Buddhism, Yang Wenhui 楊文會 (1837–1911). At Jinling Sūtra Press, Lü met his future master-cum-mentor, the renowned Yogācāra scholar Ouyang Jingwu (1871–1943). Ouyang quickly recognized Lü's acumen in philosophy and philology and from 1914 to 1916 employed Lü to assist him in collating Buddhist texts.

In October 1917, when World War I was approaching its end, Lü went to Japan to study aesthetics. He studied in Japan only eight months before returning to China in May 1918 together with many other Chinese student-activists to protest Japan's encroachment on Chinese sovereignty. The Chinese language press in Japan had recently leaked documents related to a series of secret military pacts, including the text of the Sino-Japanese Joint Defense Agreement, which granted Japan numerous military privileges within Chinese territory in the name of fighting the common enemy, the Germans. Upon hearing of this leak, Chinese students in Japan organized widespread protests and many decided to return to China to organize protests across China. Indeed, the May 1918 protests in Japan are widely acknowledged as a rehearsal for the watershed event that was the 1919 May Fourth Student Movement in China.

From May 1918 to 1923 Lü mainly taught and wrote on aesthetics and gained broad recognition among students and progressive thinkers. As soon as Lü returned to China, Ouyang invited Lü to join his project of establishing the China Inner Learning Institute (Zhina Neixue Yuan 支那內學院), the institute to which Lü would later devote thirty years of his life. At the time, Ouyang's project had the support of leading reformers and intellectuals such as one of the lesser-known leaders of the late-Qing Self-Strengthening Movement, Sheng Zengzhi 沈曾植 (1850–1922); the late-Qing reformer-cum-Yogācārin Zhang Taiyan 章太炎 (1869–1936); and the educator of modern China, Cai Yuanpei 蔡元培 (1868–1940), who was the president of Peking University—the university at the epicenter of the 1919 May Fourth Student Movement. However, instead of joining Ouyang in Nanjing, in September 1918, Lü found a paid job teaching arts and crafts in a middle school in Changzhou. It was at this time that Lü changed his name to Lü Cheng.

On December 15, 1918, a mere seven months after he had returned to China from Japan, Lü wrote the letter to *New Youth* that appears at the beginning of this introduction. This letter catapulted him to the center stage of the New Culture Movement and enabled him to join other like-minded revolutionaries in Shanghai to toil for an aesthetic revolution in 1920. During his time as an aesthete, Lü engaged in several public and private debates about aesthetic education, revolution, Bergsonian creative evolution, and Yogācāra. Lü's public letters, private communications, monographs on aesthetics, and related essays penned by his peers together with relevant reports in newspapers and periodicals form the bulk of the primary materials in part I of this study.

The year 1922 was pivotal for Lü as he gradually transitioned from promoting an aesthetic revolution to developing his Buddhological project of revolutionizing consciousness. In October 1921 Ouyang again invited Lü to join his project of establishing the Inner Learning Institute. By July 1922 Ouyang had finally raised enough funds to open the doors of the institute. Lü joined him as the provost and worked there till 1952 when Lü was forced to close down the institute. Having relocated from Shanghai to Nanjing, from 1922 to 1923, while acting as provost of the institute, Lü taught art and aesthetics at various middle schools and art schools. Meanwhile, he also wrote and published a few more monographs on aesthetics. After 1923 Lü fully devoted his life and energy to his Yogācāra studies.

Lü's reputation as a scholar of aesthetics helped attract progressive students to the Inner Learning Institute. Even though the registered students at the institute did not exceed forty in any given semester, the students, like Lü, were all keen to study Yogācāra to revolutionize China and transform the world. Through his connections with students at the institute, Lü gained crucial support (e.g., by acquiring dictionaries as well as key Tibetan and Sanskrit texts) enabling him to learn Sanskrit, Pāli, and classical Tibetan on his own. He mastered all three classical languages in three years. Meanwhile, with Lü's multilingual expertise, Ouyang was able to produce a rich collection of high-quality scholarly editions of key Chinese Buddhist texts. These texts were published in stages and were later collected under the title *Essentials*.

Although both contemporaneous observers and today's scholars have seen the institute as a purely scholarly (a.k.a., nonreligious) enterprise, a cursory reading of both the institute's regulations and students' memoirs reveals that the daily life of the institute was suffused with many seemingly religious practices such as maintaining a vegetarian diet and engaging in daily meditation. In the handful of photos of the institute, it is evident that the institute also marked important events with ceremonies. For instance, students paid respect to the newly acquired Tibetan Buddhist canon by dressing in white (or light-colored) robes. In 1937 Lü relocated again with the institute to flee from the invading Japanese army.

Another watershed year in Lü's life and career was 1943. Ouyang passed away in February of that year, and Lü was soon elected to lead the institute in Ouyang's footsteps. In October 1943, Lü started his own training program, *Five Disciplines of Buddhist Learning* (*Wuke foxue* 五科佛學; henceforth, *Five Disciplines*), many of which were based on Lü's scholarly editions collected in *Essentials*. These lecture notes and outlines, together with *Essentials* and the multilingual base texts that Lü drew from, are the focus of the philosophical investigation in part II of this book. Complementing them are Lü's post-1949 publications, drafts of edited dictionary entries, unpublished research notes housed by today's Jinling Sūtra Press in Nanjing, and the publications of the China Inner Learning Institute housed by Cheena Bhavana (the China Institute) at Viśva-Bhārati University in West Bengal, India.

When Japan surrendered in 1945, Lü cut short his ambitious training program, finishing only one of the three training cycles that he had envisioned. He shouldered the main responsibility for relocating the institute back to Nanjing. After 1949, when the Communist Party established its rule in China, Lü moved to Beijing, where he apparently trained future scholars of Buddhist studies, worked with others to produce a dictionary of Chinese Buddhism, and transitioned from a Buddhist revolutionary to a pure scholar. However, in the publications leading up until the onset of the Cultural Revolution (1966–1976), he continued to write about how to transform the self and the society through Buddhist learning, albeit coded in Marxist terminology. During the Cultural Revolution, compared to other scholars of similar stature, Lü did not suffer much. He had to return to his hometown, his extensive research library mysteriously vanished into thin air, he could no longer do any research, he stopped writing, and he might have suffered malnutrition. But he was never severely beaten or sent to a labor camp.

After the Cultural Revolution Lü never regained the intellectual acumen necessary to conduct multilingual research. He relocated to Tsinghua University in Beijing, where his third son and his family cared for him until his peaceful passing in 1989. According to private conversations with his surviving relatives, Lü lived a regular life. He kept a simple vegetarian diet, meditated daily, and read a bit whenever he had the energy. In the 1980s he frequently talked with his former colleagues and former students who collected, edited, and then, in 1991, published *Selected Writings on Buddhist Studies by Lü Cheng* (henceforth, *Xuanji1991*).[63] *Xuanji1991* is now partially digitized online as a branch of CBETA (Chinese Buddhist Electronic Texts Association). But only the Buddhological essays are made available while his more "political" essays such as "Just Awakening and Renunciation" (zhengjue yu chuli 正覺與出離) remain undigitized.[64]

The Flow of the Argument

Just Awakening unfolds in two parts: a philosophically informed intellectual history and a historically contextualized philosophical analysis. My integrative approach connects history and philosophy in different ways. Taking cues from the Yogācāra research paradigm that denies a neat separation of historical facts and philosophical abstractions, part I demonstrates how historical contingencies shaped the formation and reception of core notions of socio-soteriology, and part II reveals how philosophical innovations emerged through the intention to address pressing and seemingly intractable social dilemmas.

More concretely, part I traces the earliest encounters between Yogācāra and social Darwinism in modern China. It investigates the historical forces that gave rise to Yogācāra socio-soteriology and maps out the landscape of Yogācāra social theories. Chapter 1, "Lü Cheng and the Birth of Yogācāra Social Philosophy," examines Lü's early career as an aspiring revolutionary. Lü's 1919 call for an "aesthetic revolution" led him into a phase of intensive study focused on Euro-American aesthetics. Then Lü's revolutionary fervor led him to Yogācāra. In 1921, when many thinkers were dismayed by the terror of World War I and disillusioned by Darwinist racial wars, Lü introduced Yogācāra causal theory as the antidote to social Darwinism, scientific materialism, and Bergsonian creative evolution. Lü's proposal marks the first intentional creation of a Yogācāra social philosophy.

However, Lü's philosophical innovation did not happen in a vacuum. To sustain his endeavor there had to be a wider network of support for the production of such new knowledge. Lü and his colleagues at the China Inner Learning Institute spent the next three decades gathering Buddhist prints and manuscripts, hard-to-find dictionaries, and Western Buddhological studies; engaging in intellectual discussion and readings; conducting academic research; and producing and globally circulating their own academic journal, *Neixue* 內學 (Inner Learning) as well as other publications, as witnessed by Cheena Bhavana's collection in India today. Hence, chapters 2 and 3 extend the horizon of investigation to the wider social conditions that stimulated the Chinese appetite for Yogācāra-informed social visions.

Chapter 2, "Karma, Evolutionism, and the Birth of Buddhist Social Consciousness," upends the received wisdom that has pigeonholed the rise of Yogācāra in modern China as a "Buddhist" movement. While neither denying the key contributions of Buddhist intellectuals such as Yang Wenhui (1837–1911) and Nanjō Bun'yū 南条文雄 (1849–1927) nor downplaying the impact of the reintroduction of lost Chinese Yogācāra treatises from Japan to China, I shed light on the broader historical forces that were set in motion by Yan Fu's 嚴復 (1854–1921) translations.

The available evidence shows that when Yan translated two social Darwinist texts, T. H. Huxley's *Evolution and Ethics* (1893) and Herbert Spencer's *The Study of Sociology* (1873), he unwittingly popularized Yogācāra-informed doctrines among the reformers, revolutionaries, and progressive literati. More concretely, when Yan wrestled with the foreign notions of race and nationality as collective hereditary traits, Yan employed the Yogācāra-inflected term *zhongye* 種業 to make sense of individuality, collectivity, and heredity. Later, to shore up support for his new interpretation, Yan equated *zhongye* with the well-established Yogācāra concept *yezhong* (業種; karmic seeds) and thereby conflated two Yogācāra technical terms—*gotra* (family, lineage) and *bīja* (seed), both of which are rendered in Chinese as *zhong*—and merged them with the social Darwinist notion of racial and national heredity in *zhongye*. Thus, Yan's *zhongye* is best translated as "Yogācāra national karma," which integrates the Yogācāra path of liberation with a social theory for the survival of a nation. When the translated discourse of "the survival of the fittest" metamorphosized into the rallying call of "Protecting the Nation, Preserving the Race" (*huguo baozhong*), *zhongye* qua Yogācāra national karma melded Dharma and Darwin into one path.

Chapter 3, "Karma, Science, and a Just Society," analyzes four garden-variety Yogācāra socio-soteriologies that dotted the lush intellectual landscape of modern China, which have thus far been excluded from scholarly considerations of sociopolitical theories. Specifically, I foreground three shared features in these theories. First, these Yogācāra social theorists rejected the ontological dualism of objectivity and subjectivity. Instead, they launched a Yogācāra counterargument: that the conception of "objectivity" is a convenient fiction, like the illusory self/subject, conjured up by human consciousness to serve the special interests of certain groups. Second, they redefined science to focus not on the ontological question of "what things are" but the phenomenological inquiry of "what casually explains the perceptible world." Some also proposed that scientific findings could be systematically distinguished from false claims by the Yogācāra three Cs. Third, by subsuming objectivity and science into the Yogācāra causal framework, they released theorizations of human agency from the Christian epistemic well of free will and refashioned agency as the potential and efficacy of aggregated karmic processes distributed across the field of causes and conditions. These thinkers, by acknowledging humankind's radical interdependence, offered more control over the outcomes of human actions and broadened the scope of human imagination to create more harmonious and effective social structures.

In part II, "Liberation Buddhology," I foreground three intersecting streams of Lü Cheng's Yogācāra socio-soteriology, highlighting the social practices encoded in Lü's revolutionary nonviolence. To be sure, Lü Cheng was a renowned Buddhologist. Nevertheless, when scholars connect the dots between his revolutionary youth and his mature scholarship, it becomes evident that Lü's scholarly achievement only served to actualize his vision of a just society. As evidence presented shows, continuing his youthful quest for an aesthetic revolution as a mature scholar, Lü Cheng in the 1940s repurposed the Yogācāra soteriological toolbox as the chief means to build up Buddhist civil society organizations, which are assembled through voluntary participation, governed by democratic deliberation, and cohered by the shared goal of co-liberation. Because he centered Buddhological studies in this socio-soteriological project, I term his project "liberation Buddhology."

Three features of Lü's liberation Buddhology warrant scholarly attention. Each chapter in part II homes in on one feature. Making a new society must start with a new vision of the nature of humankind. Therefore, chapter 4, "Buddhability as Humanity," explains why Lü turned the cherished belief of relying on Dharma instead of humans on its head and advocated for relying on humans instead of Dharma. The key to making sense of this reversal for Lü is investigating the meaning of being human. The evidence reveals that, for Lü, the foundation of the humanities rests on Buddhability, a shorthand for the Mahāyāna belief that every sentient being has the potential to become a buddha. This new humanity holds the key to appreciating Lü's socio-soteriology. For him, the ultimate goal of liberation is transpersonal or intersubjective buddhahood, a conceptualization that allowed Lü to redesign the Buddhist path as practices of co-liberation. Thus, Buddhability-cum-humanity offers a valuable opportunity to denaturalize mainstream beliefs about human agency and invite deeper reflections on why and how equality needs to free itself from the "birdcage" of individuality and instead ground itself in interdependence.[65]

Chapter 5, "Bodhisattva of Democracy," sheds light on Lü's reformulation of civil society as a series of recursive, motivated, organizational coactions. The weight of evidence demonstrates that Lü weaved together Yogācāra rules of engaging in liberative conversation and bodhisattva precepts into a set of regulations for democratic deliberation. Rather than mimic Western ethics' focus on autonomy, individual rights, and social contracts, he revived the long-lost spirit of action-oriented republicanism embedded in early Indian monasticism; redefined community as motivated, organizational behavior patterns grounded in compassion and interdependence; and then retooled these rules for building Buddhist civil societies. Lü's Dharmic democracy marks not only a new phase in Buddhist social thinking but also suggests the possibility of noncoercive democracy.

Chapter 6, "Scholarship for Salvation," foregrounds another organizational behavior pattern of Lü's liberation Buddhology—social epistemology. As argued in part I, Lü rejected so-called objectivity as a viable epistemic principle in knowledge production. The evidence in chapter 6 reveals that Lü also replaced the touchstone of objective epistemology with the Yogācāra three Cs and simultaneously refashioned knowledge production as a social practice for the purpose of democratic co-liberation, thereby anticipating the argument made by historians of science such as Naomi Oreskes and Helen E. Longino that scientific knowledge is social knowledge. Thus, Lü's liberation Buddhology is best understood as a social epistemology and a meta-model of transformative interrogation (*rig par byed pa*). I hope that this exercise of recovering Lü's social theory offers a new way to talk about the concepts of revolution, liberation, and democracy.

I also hope that my exploration of these forgotten encounters motivates more inquiries into how these so-called non-Western traditions might structure applicable sociopolitical theory and thereby diversify contemporary discussions of how the world could be otherwise. In keeping with this goal, instead of a traditional conclusion, the last chapter, "Not a Coda: Bending the Arc Together," sketches a set of similar socio-soteriologies in today's North America that take some of their inspiration from those of twentieth-century China and reflect the further development of Buddhism as liberative praxis for post-racial worldmaking.

PART I

When Dharma Meets Darwin

When Dharma met Darwin in twentieth-century China, many elites were seeking rescue from the perceived cultural death of China. The theory of karma and rebirth offered a core narrative structure that facilitated many creative responses to the unfolding cultural destruction, enabled many imaginative theorizations of cultural rebirth, and thereby played a key, albeit overlooked, role in orienting modern China's path to changing referents. The three chapters in part I zoom in on the multiple, serendipitous encounters of Yogācāra with social Darwinism and tease out the broader social forces that gave birth to a compelling social philosophy—Lü's Yogācāra socio-soteriology.

1

Lü Cheng and the Birth of Yogācāra Social Philosophy

> The ultimate social meaning of art is to awaken the empathetic accord in people's mind-heart. Building upon [this awakening], [people] can establish another kind of just and reliable society.
>
> 藝術最高的社會意義，便是喚起人心裏感情的一致，
> 從那上面另外建設一種正當的並且確實的社會.
>
> —Lü Cheng, 1922

As the epigraph to this chapter, taken from an essay by Lü Cheng, suggests, Lü aimed to use art to awaken the empathetic connections among human beings for the purpose of establishing a just and reliable society.[1] Lü's early forays into Western aesthetics paved the way for his lifelong endeavor to reinvent Buddhist soteriology as a way of building an ideal society without the pitfalls of excessive materialism and rampant individualism.

Lü's transition from aesthetic revolution to Buddhist soteriology reveals much about the lure of Yogācāra in a scientific world. Consciousness-only philosophy proved a compelling theory of social evolution that opened up new means of formulating both sides of the imported individual–social antinomy. In Lü's interpretation, ancient Yogācāra intersubjectivity was a fertile ground from which various constructed dichotomies of the social and the individual, objectivity and subjectivity, as well as the external world and the inner psyche, could arise. Thus, in Lü's eyes, the Buddhist path of liberation, specifically the doctrine of nonduality and the spiritual exercises necessary to reach that nonduality, could offer a viable path out of the modern impasse resulting from constructed binaries. After launching a potent philosophical and moral critique of Darwinist competition, Lü turned to the well-equipped Yogācāra soteriological toolbox to initiate a social evolution-cum-revolution by transforming consciousness (Ch: *zhuanyi* 轉依; Skt: *āśrayaparivṛtti*), opening a divergent paradigm revolution not as an event but as processes of adapting and cohering new situations and new conditions.

By unpacking the entanglement of the idiosyncratic rhetoric of revolution and Yogācāra in Lü's early career, I want to deploy the lens of socio-soteriology to diffract constructed binaries such as "conservative" and "radical," "secular" and "religious," into their respective anchoring processes of social concerns and liberative praxis.[2] Rather than deconstruct secularism, I heed Amartya Sen's call to "scrutinize and re-examine habitually accepted priorities, and the reasoning behind them" in accepted discourses about secularism and to break open the secular paradigm to consider other ways of structuring the self, the world, and social arrangements.[3]

Revolution of the Mind-Heart

From its inception, Lü's revolution was an antirealist critique of the rise of a capitalist consumer culture. In his 1918 letter to *New Youth*, Lü identified his revolution as a revolt against the commercialization of art. Lü saw revolution as a moral awakening that enables the common folk to appreciate the universal beauty. In Lü's revolution, once the commoners gain access to such universal beauty, they will naturally know how to differentiate right and wrong and commit themselves to proper cultivation. The outcome of this moral awakening-cum-revolution, in Lü's vision, was an ideal society held together by a renewed aesthetic appreciation.[4]

Lü's vision stood out as a revolution sustained by rigorous studies and proceeded in measured steps. While this may contradict the common perception of revolution as a violent political revolt, it is undeniable that such optimism for profound psycho-social transformation was in sync with the May Fourth crucible of cultural renewal. Indeed, one central strain of thought during this time was a reappraisal of the 1911 overthrow of the Qing dynasty. The 1911 Xinhai Revolution had been followed by decades of violence and trauma: ceaseless battles among warlords, incompetent governance, callous treatment of the poor, and human-made atrocities exacerbated by regional floods, droughts, famines, plagues, and other natural disasters. Violence seemed to beget more violence. In this climate of unending violence and chaos, many intellectuals looked elsewhere for cultural means to invigorate the Chinese mind.

Many firmly believed that real revolutionaries were in it for the long haul, toiling for gradual spiritual invigoration over short-lived political band-aids. Aesthetics, for Lü Cheng and many May Fourth youth alike, was one of many promising avenues for cultivating a new social consciousness and nurturing a new form of upwardly expanding communal life, where upwardness was defined in opposition to the traditional moral order while retaining the traditional notion of human perfectibility.[5]

Against this backdrop of widespread disillusionment about political reform and a yearning for a deeper cultural renewal, the import of Lü's revolution became evident: in one of many competing yet mutually reinforcing subcultures of May Fourth, Lü pioneered a revolution of the mind-heart (*xin* 心). The goal of this revolution of the mind-heart was to eradicate social corruption with art, aesthetic attitudes, sustained education, and lifelong learning. When he wrote the letter to *New Youth* he was still an unknown art teacher in a high school in Xuzhou, a town three hundred miles south of Beijing and three hundred miles north of Shanghai.[6] But he nonetheless dared to propose a total revamping of commercialized society through art and comparative study.

Lü used a well-known avant-garde moment, futurism, to make his case to the editors and readers of *New Youth*. Futurism gained its name from the Italian poet Filippo Tommaso Marinetti's *Manifesto del futurismo* (Manifesto of Futurism), which was published in 1909. As is well known, futurism was an enduring modernist movement that rejected anything old and celebrated youth, speed, machinery, and industry.[7] The futurists reinvented every imaginable medium, including poetry, performance, film, industrial design, painting, sculpture, and architecture. To urge the editor to "shoulder the responsibility of initiating aesthetic revolution" (*yin meishu geming wei jize* 引美術革命為己責), Lü prophesied a bright future for *New Youth* as the Chinese counterpart of *Poesia*, the poetry magazine that first published *Manifesto del futurismo*.[8] Lü's analogy not only worked well with *New Youth*'s self-presentation but also portrayed a future of powerful impact for the periodical. The periodical's editor, Chen Duxiu, answered Lü's call to action with his full support for aesthetic revolution.

Lü fused aesthetics with ethics and beauty with truth. He prescribed a long and difficult revolution, one that would only be achievable through scholarly endeavors. Many features of this blueprint persisted in his later effort to initiate a Yogācāra revolution of the consciousness. Instead of laying out a utopian vision, Lü recommended a methodology to search for shared aesthetic principles. For Lü, "the path of revolution" (*geming zhi dao* 革命之道) began with inquiries into and illustrations of the scope and essence of aesthetics (*chanming meishu zhi fanwei yu shizhi* 闡明美術之範圍與實質), entailed a search for "the truly authentic [evaluations] of right and wrong" (*zhenzheng zhi shifei* 真正之是非), and enabled "the [larger] society to understand the true path of aesthetics" (*shehui zhi meishu zhi zhengtu* 社會知美術之正途).[9] Lü laid out four steps of this revolutionary path, whose focus was conducting rigorous comparative studies of aesthetics from the past to the present and across different cultures in order to identify the mainstream and thereby reveal principles of right and wrong. This moral concern would take center stage in his lifelong endeavor to transform the world.

The surprising purchase of Lü's idiosyncratic definition of revolution in *New Youth* unsettles the taken-for-granted definition of revolution as a violent overthrow of the status quo and uncovers a forgotten alternative revolution erased from Chinese official history. In Lü's revolutionary vision, the essence of a fundamental change of destiny required taking responsibility for the shared past and accepting responsibility for engendering a new world as it should be. Taking responsibility for what is given necessitates an in-depth observation of the current situation. To this end, Lü singled out two modern vices that required immediate action. One was the "profiteering" (*sushi wuli* 俗士鶩利) of art as embodied in the commercialization of paintings of maidens; the other was the proliferation of homespun art institutions and shallow magazines flaunting themselves as champions of aesthetic education. Lü sounded the alarm that, without an aesthetic revolution and under the spell of the materialistic society, "the commoners' aesthetic sensibility would completely deviate from the right path of cultivation" (*hengren zhi meiqing, xi shi qi zhengyang* 恆人之美情，悉失其正養).[10] In short, Lü defined revolution as a moral awakening. He maintained this idiosyncratic vision until 1949 when he read Mao Zedong's works and admitted that "only then had [I] gained deeper understanding of the meaning of revolution" (*duiyu geming de yiyi caiyou jiaoshen de renshi* 對於革命的意義才有較深的認識).[11]

Nevertheless, Lü's revolutionary path stood out because he refrained from offering a panacea to cure China's modern vices, instead proposing a collective path to search for a solution together with all those who were willing to practice careful scholarship. Having taken on the responsibility for engendering what should be, the first step for Lü was to diagnose. Lü pinpointed the main culprit of China's modern depravity as "superficial learning and arbitrary judgment" (*qianxue wuduan* 淺學武斷) that led to the proliferation of "teachings of specious analogies" (*sishi er fei zhi jiaoshou* 似是而非之教授) and "comments based on piecemeal knowledge" (*yizhi banjie zhi yanlun* 一知半解之言論).[12] Lü wanted his readers to see that to cure such a root problem, one must follow the path of moral awakening assisted by diligent studies.

Lü's letter to *New Youth* not only catapulted him to the center of the New Culture Movement but also won him unexpected admiration. The renowned avant-garde artist Liu Haisu, having read Lü's letter, invited Lü to join his Shanghai Art Academy, the hub of the new art movement in modern China.[13] Once there, Lü not only obtained an influential platform with which to advance his revolution but was also initiated into a vibrant network of like-minded reformers. As the chief editor of *Meishu* 美術 (*Fine Arts*), the leading journal of Liu Haisu's academy, Lü turned its focus from artistic practices and techniques to aesthetic theories. He also started a series of lectures in Shanghai, a widely recognized materialistic city that was simultaneously the hub of new international religious establishments and new Buddhist movements at the time. Lü later edited and published these lecture notes as books, which became the earliest academic monographs on aesthetics in modern China. Meanwhile, the community of the Shanghai Art Academy also decisively shaped Lü's intellectual outlook and social theory.

The newly imported analytic category "society" engendered many debates among Chinese thinkers. Key among these debates were the ontological status of the social: What constitutes a social entity? What are the metaphysical sources of social reality? At first glance, the Chinese debate was shaped by European discourses and centers on the following questions: What is the ontological status of social groups (*qun* 群)? Is a social group distinct from the collection of its individual members? The debates about social ontology in Europe at the turn of the twentieth century largely focused on the antinomy of the individual and the social.[14]

However, more attentive readers will notice that the Chinese debates on social ontology took on a different focus than those of their European counterparts. In the 1920s and 1930s there was a vibrant debate about matter (*wuzhi* 物質) and mind (*jingshen* 精神) that was indicative of the larger philosophical showdown between materialism (*weiwu zhuyi* 唯物主義) and idealism (*weixin zhuyi* 唯心主義).[15] This context rendered it inevitable that debates about social ontology in 1920s China would address the tension between idealist and materialist interpretations of the social kinds. The outcome of this philosophical showdown is well known: Marxism and historical materialism won. Consequently, social kinds came to be equated with natural kinds, that is, social categories are considered mind-independent and determined by material conditions and causes. Under the shadow of historical materialism, antirealist social ontologies were soon erased from the Chinese collective memory.

The Social Function of Aesthetics: From Empathy to Intersubjectivity

During his time at the Shanghai Art Academy, Lü's interpretation of aesthetics took a decisive turn toward social philosophy. The seeds of moral awakening in his 1919 letter gradually sprouted into a well-developed antirealist philosophy of what constitutes a just society. Lü's antirealism is most clearly expressed in a 1920 essay expounding on Theodor Lipps's psychological study of aesthetics. In this essay, Lü argued that both aesthetic empathy (*mei de tongqing* 美的同情) and aesthetic antipathy (*mei de fanqing* 美的反情) are based on empathetic exchanges (Ch: *ganqing yiru* 感情移入; German: *Einfühlung*), which in turn are grounded in the artist's personality (*renge* 人格).[16]

During his years at the Shanghai Art Academy, Lü gradually merged the concept of the artist's personality with the concept of "an aesthetic life" (*mei de rensheng* 美的人生) in which aesthetic empathy is the key to enabling a mutually appreciative collective expansion of multiple lives, "just like the blossoming wildflowers in the mountains, growing in the same air and the same soil" (*zhengxiangshi shanjian yipian yehua kai, zai tongyi de kongqi li, tongyi de turang shang* 正像是山間一片野花開, 在同一的空氣裡, 同一的土壤上).[17] In other essays during the early 1920s, Lü further argued that empathy grows out of both an appreciation of things *as is* and a recognition of the desire for life inherent in all sentient beings.[18]

This recognition of life is later linked to "just awakening" (*zhengjue* 正覺) in a 1922 essay that further expanded the 1919 notion of *zhengyang* 正養 (right cultivation) into a path of spiritual-social transformation.[19] Lü's aesthetic attitude readily calls to mind what Judith Butler, one hundred years later, would characterize as "an egalitarian imaginary that apprehends the interdependency of lives." He did not doubt that only deep contemplation could nurture this empathy. He trusted that only by genuinely appreciating all conscious existences, including those of other humans and animals, could one fully develop one's own human potential. Moreover, on multiple occasions, he prophesied that only by outwardly expressing this upwardness (defined as the opposite of selfish tendencies) could one transform a society ensnared in cold-hearted calculations of chances of survival. In this sense, Lü ushered in an astonishingly forceful theory of nonviolence, which presaged Butler's argument that any effort to build a just society must "follow from interdependency as a condition of equality."[20]

Lü's social turn grew out of his readings of the French philosopher Jean-Marie Guyau's (1854–1888) sociology of aesthetics. Borrowing from this talented young philosopher, Lü argued that art and aesthetics, by definition, must employ intersubjective empathy to expand sociality (*neng jizhe ganqing kuoda shehuixing de, jiushi yishu* 能藉者感情擴大社會性的, 就是藝術).[21] In Lü's paradigm the heuristic goal was not to enable more creativity but to engender a turn away from one's petty ego and to instill a love for all living forms. Only when humans broke free from the birdcage of individualism and only when all lives were imagined to be grievable, Lü prophesied, could fully dynamic and expanding living experiences become possible. Lü termed these living experiences "an aesthetic life."[22]

Scholars of religious studies will recognize an uncanny resonance between Lü's aesthetic resonances and Durkheimian collective effervescence, a simultaneous coming-together that enables a community to think transcendentally as one. Unlike ritual in Durkheimian sociology, artistic creation functioned to bind people together in Lü's social ontology. Indeed, this semblance rests upon a common thread. Both thinkers owed their initial theorization of the social totality to Guyau. It is well known that Durkheim's first documented conception of a social oneness came from his critique of Guyau's *L'irréligion de l'avenir: Étude sociologique.*[23] Similarly, Guyau sparked Lü's initial theorization of social dynamics in its totality.

This convergence of interests stemmed from their rethinking of the meaning of revolution. Both Durkheim and Lü rode the tide of a rethinking of communal living in the wake of violent political overthrows. In the 1880s—after the failure of the 1848 revolution, the ensuing monarchist rule of Napoleon III, and the 1870s reestablishment of republicanism—many French thinkers, Guyau and Durkheim included, sought to establish a stronger solidarity than that which could be achieved by social contract and individual rights.[24] As sympathizers of the French Revolution, both Guyau and Durkheim reconceived religion as the sum of all social relations in their struggle to theorize stronger, nonindividualist bonds for building republicanism.

In early twentieth-century China, the multifaceted French Revolution was seen alongside the Enlightenment ideals and social Darwinism. In particular, the term "revolution" was already associated with the logic of global capitalism that saw revolution as a fruit of the Enlightenment, as the unfolding of the progress of the human mind, and, most important, as part of the discourse of civilization that positioned nations and peoples along an evolutionary timeline.[25] Consequently, to justify the Chinese revolution, many intellectuals employed the logic of social Darwinism.[26] Hence, during the May Fourth era, revolution merged with evolution, both of which were justified in terms of reason, scientific realism, material wealth, and economic progress.

Against the mainstream approach of justifying evolution-cum-revolution on scientism and material progress, Lü redefined (r)evolution in terms of intersubjective resonance that would bring people closer and transform them through intersubjective empathy. While Durkheim had faith in the objective reality of social facts, for Lü what unites human beings into a oneness was *not* an objective outside. Instead, Lü believed that both objective existence and subjective experience were manifestations of beauty and truth, a dynamic totality that could only be assembled by purposeful actions to establish intersubjective accord. In this sense, Lü's oneness conveys a sense of togetherness maintained by coactions.

To theorize an intersubjective social oneness without presuming a dichotomy of mind and matter, Lü had to gather diverse Western philosophies into one. In imagining a social totality, Lü was inspired by Guyau's 1887 work *L'art au point de vue sociologique*.[27] In this book, Guyau first identified common bases between aesthetics and ethics and then argued that the purpose of art is to create sympathy among members of a society.[28] To theorize intersubjectivity with a firmer philosophical ground, Lü appropriated strands of thought from Theodor Lipps. In Europe and North America Lipps is well known for having theorized empathy as a main epistemic means of perceiving other humans as independent consciousnesses, primarily due to his influence on the Freudian theorization of the unconscious and his indirect impact on the rise of Husserlian phenomenology.[29] Lipps's Japanese commenter Abe Jirō (1883–1959) contributed to this scholarly legacy by focusing on the function of Lippsian empathy in eliciting emotional responses from artwork and nature.[30] Lü Cheng's reading of Lipps departed from both Lipps's authorial intent and that of Japanese translators-cum-interpreters. Instead, Lü appropriated Lippsian empathy through Guyau's lens and deployed this Lippsian concept to establish the possibility and ensure the endurance of intersubjective accord.[31]

What undergirds Lü Cheng's propensity to read Lipps and Guyau as social theorists was his desire to build a social totality without falling into the mythical binary of mind and matter. Lü strived to find a shared aesthetic principle to bridge the divide in the study of beauty between the subjective (Lippsian psychological approach and Bergsonian *élan vital*) and the objective (Guyau's sociological approach).[32] Echoing Guyau, Lü claimed that—as shown in the epigraph to this chapter—"the ultimate social meaning of art is to awaken the empathetic accord in people's mind-heart. Building upon [this awakening], [people] can establish another kind of just and reliable society." In sum, Guyau inspired Lü to imagine a society in its totality. Lipps provided Lü a ready-to-hand tool to assemble lasting social relations grounded in aesthetic empathy.

The Social Function of Translation: Assembling an Intersubjective Oneness

Unsatisfied with Lippsian empathy, Lü experimented with a different mechanism for assembling intersubjective oneness: aesthetic translation. Rather than defining translation as a movement from a target language to a host language, Lü theorized translation as a concerted and purposeful act of consciousness that renders universal beauty and social oneness perceptible to all. Taking the physicist Helmholtz's theory of color out of context, Lü claimed that "with regard to nature, artists employ their unique languages and writings to transpose and translate it" (*yishujia zhi yu ziran gu geyong qi dute zhi yuyan wenzi er xiang yiyi ye* 藝術家之於自然固各用其獨特之語言文字而相迻譯也).[33] In other words, Lü believed that all artistic creations are merely subjective transformations of nature and every artwork is self-expression, through and through. More important, in Lü's theorization, art itself is a process whose sole objective was to translate universal beauty into unique aesthetic languages comprehensible to commoners.

It is important to recognize that for Lü universality was no longer an ontological category but instead a process of ceaseless conscious copoieses of translation-cum-self-expression. This understanding of oneness as dynamic processes enabled Lü's later fusion of revolution with evolution and social ontology with Buddhist soteriology. In Lü's translation theory, not only art itself but also art criticism ought to be the task of the translator. Lü promoted this theory in a series of letters written in October 1921 and published in the May 1922 issue of *Fine Arts*. In these letters, he argued that the task of art criticism is two-pronged. First, "true critique is an aesthetic creation" (*zhenzheng de piping bianshi yizhong meishu de chuangzuo* 真正的批評便是一種美術的創作).[34] Therefore, criticism was not about evaluating artwork. Instead, "art critics translate existing artistic creation into literary creation" (*pipingjia jiang yiyou de meishu chuangzuo fanyi cheng wenzi de chuangzuo* 批評家將已有的美術創作翻譯成文字的創作). Second, the social function of art criticism is to deepen commoners' appreciation of artwork (*pipingjia biding zhanzai zuojia he minzhong zhongjian cai you yiyi . . . shi minzhong mingbai zhe zuopin de jiazhi youwu* 批評家必定站在作家和民眾中間才有意義 . . . 使民眾明白這作品的價值有無). He further argued that "art critics must be sufficiently cultivated so to enable empathy to arise in every aspect. . . . Only empathetic elucidation is true criticism" (*pipingjia yao you chongfen de xiuyang neng rongde gefangmian de tongqing shengqi . . . weiyou tongqing de shuoming caishi zhenzheng de piping* 批評家要有充分的修養能容得各方面的同情生起 . . . 唯有同情的說明才是真正的批評). In Lü's paradigm, art criticism as translation was meaningful precisely because its in-betweenness promised communal cohesion, bridging the minds of artists with the masses through aesthetic empathy.

In contrast with mainstream social scientists' theorization of society governed by objective laws, Lü imagined a social oneness assembled through aesthetic principles and manifested through the intersubjective copoiesis of aesthetic translation. For Lü, the social function of artists, art critics, and artworks is to awaken aesthetic sensibility in the commoners.

Borrowing from the famous architect of the aesthetic movement, Walter Pater (1839–1894), Lü defined aesthetic sensibility as "the power of being deeply moved by the presence of beautiful objects."[35] Lü valued Pater for his persuasive theorization of art as a pure psychological experience. As a leading advocate of aestheticism who championed "art for art's sake," Pater carved out an art realm purely grounded in subjective occurrences and independent from the objective world.[36] To be sure, Pater never intended his theory to establish a social oneness. On the contrary, Pater theorized artistic sensibility to champion individuality. Nonetheless, this purely experiential explanation of beauty proved a convenient tool for Lü to free aesthetic appreciation from the confines of an objective outside and to establish the validity of intersubjective accord.

Lü argued that the responsibility of establishing intersubjective accord should be shouldered by not only artists and art critics but also commoners. Extending Pater's aesthetic sensibility to the realm of the social, Lü posited that when commoners develop aesthetic sensibility, they become connoisseurs (*jianshang zhe* 鑑賞者).[37] Lü further argued that when a connoisseur appreciates beauty through sensibility, the temperament of the artist is then reproduced in the connoisseur's consciousness. This reproduction then expands the connoisseur's perceptual world. In Lü's social ontology, the true value of artwork and aesthetics lies in their social copoieses, as artists enable the expansion of personality through the aesthetic experience of artwork (*zuojia de renge quan chongxian zai guanzhe yishi li, guanzhe de renge he ta ronghe gengjia kuoda—zhe haoshuo shi yishu de yizhong shehuixing, yishu de zhenzheng jiazhi bianzai zhe shangmian* 作家的人格全重現在觀者意識裏，觀者的人格和他融合更加擴大—這好說是藝術的一種社會性，藝術的真正價值便在這上面).[38] Consequently, Lü posited that a community emerges through repeated occurrences of intersubjective translation.

Against Natural Piety: Enchanting Social Relations with Aesthetic Empathy

Lü challenged May Fourth intellectuals who saw realism and nature as the saviors of China. He questioned whether faith in realism and the edifying power of nature could lead to a viable path out of China's crisis. Lü made public his critique of realism when he was recruited by Li Shicen 李石岑 (1892–1934), the editor of the well-known periodical *Minduo* 民鐸 (People's Bell). Li wanted Lü to comment on the renowned May Fourth thinker and the modern educator of China Cai Yuanpei and his aesthetic education. Cai demanded not only that institutionalized religion be replaced by aesthetic education but also that religious beliefs be verified by science and explained in observable terms.[39] Against the increasing sway of realism as exemplified by Cai, Lü denied the viability of replacing spiritual cultivation with art education and argued that true aesthetic education should aim to actualize an aesthetic human life.[40]

Lü was convinced that natural piety, as embodied in one's emotional experiences of both nature and human-made environments such as art museums, art exhibitions, theaters, and music halls, was merely a perception contaminated by petty ego, which was itself an unconscious habit that expands a person's possessive desires (*zhanjuyu bianxiang de kuozhang* 佔據慾變相的擴張). Lü argued that uncritical trust in nature represents another ignorant entanglement of this Darwinist world, leading to an "actual society" (*xianzhuang shehui* 現狀社會) that is organized based on a few persons' possessive desires. More than a blanket rejection of all desires for life, the focus of Lü's criticism was the systemic issue of unequal access to power that the philosopher Olúfẹ́mi O. Táíwò incisively characterized as "elite capture," wherein a social system allows "the advantaged few [to] steer resources and institutions that could serve the many toward their own narrower interests and aims."[41] For Lü this elite capture produced a corresponding "actual human life" (*xianzhuang rensheng* 現狀人生) that is fundamentally at odds with the aesthetic life.[42]

To emphasize the imperative to break with this actual life, Lü distinguished between two kinds of creativity that were at odds with each other: one generated by egoistic desires in everyday life, and the other a nonindividualist account of social equality sprung from an aesthetic attitude grounded in deep appreciation of all living beings.[43] For Lü, this deep appreciation of all living beings implied both equality and freedom because all the other life-forms (interdependent upon the conventional self) have their own meaning of existence (*zi yeyou gezi cunzai de yizhong yiyi* 自也有各自存在的一種意義), and only by constituting others into a part of one's own life through copoiesis and interconditioning can one expand life itself and create limitless freedom.[44] Again, Lü's vision of aesthetic revolution finds uncanny resonances with Judith Butler's new imaginary of a social equality premised upon interdependency because "each is dependent, or formed and sustained in relations of depending upon, and being depended upon," a core insight in creating a social life of "equal conditions of livability" and in conceptualizing a "social freedom as defined in part by our constitutive interdependency."[45] In stark contrast to Cai, who internalized the discourse of the survival of the fittest, realism, and individualism and prophesied that religion ought to be replaced by art education as human civilization progresses, Lü saw Darwinism, realism, and individualism as a cage that one must break out of by cultivating an aesthetic spirituality.

Aesthetic spirituality, for Lü, functioned to restore moral agency to social interactions, which readily calls to mind many Marxist philosophers' call to change the world.[46] Lü argued that aesthetic educators must "engage in social reform" (*qu congshi shehui gaizao de yundong* 去從事社會改造的運動).[47] Lü chose to respond publicly to Cai's project because he deemed Cai's proposal ineffective for revolutionizing consciousness. In the same October 1922 essay, Lü explicitly denounced Cai's natural piety by pointing out the impossibility of "building up various pleasant environments and waiting quietly for the natural transformative effects [of these environments]." In Lü's eyes, artwork in its material form was merely one aspect of the transcendent totality of an aesthetic life. Moreover, artwork owed its existence to universal beauty. Lü argued that natural piety could only naturalize and expand one's possessive desires, dull one's sense of moral deliberation, and thus abet arrogance.

In questioning natural piety, Lü radically reframed the mind/matter duality in terms of an ontologically primary intersubjective empathy. Lü argued that empathy grows out of both a profound understanding of beings as such and a categorical acknowledgment of all sentient beings' will to live. From this empathy, the social emerges. Lü wrote,

> The foundation of a society is empathy. . . . Therefore, when encountering people, things, and the natural world with an aesthetic attitude, [one] thoroughly understands their essence without exception. Because of one's acknowledgment and affirmation of their desire for life, empathy arises. And then, social phenomena emerge.
>
> 社會之根柢在於同情 . . . 故從美的態度以遇人物自然，莫不一一洞徹本質，而自其生之要求，以為肯定，得起同情，而成社會現象.[48]

In one sentence, Lü redefined social oneness as a never-ending coaction of creating intersubjective accord and empathic resonances.

In line with his 1919 call for revolution, Lü argued that aesthetic education must begin from a moral-cum-aesthetic awakening. One could not rely on nature or beautiful objects for this fundamental transformation. Lü posited that, to begin living an aesthetic life, one must embark upon a self-conscious path of purifying the mind-heart. In this sense, Lü considered himself a revolutionary: his theory proposed both a turn away from the naturalized Darwinist calculations of self-interest and a turn toward the aesthetic life by purifying consciousness. Although Lü did not explicitly engage with the Marxist critique of capitalism, his redefinition of social oneness aimed to challenge the uncritical acceptance of natural piety and to disrupt the logic of selfish calculations exemplified in the capitalist expansion of possessive desires.

Taking seriously Lü's processual theorization of social evolution-cum-revolution gives scholars a valuable opportunity to uncover a salient undercurrent flowing against realist theorizations of other possible futures. Indeed, Lü was merely one of many critics of evolutionism who were nurtured by the influx of Western thought but found inspiration in Buddhist soteriology to reenchant realism, scientism, and evolutionism with collective spiritual progress.[49]

The Rise of Moralized Bergsonism and "Scientific" Yogācāra

To understand the rise of a "scientific" Yogācāra and Lü's later reformulation of a Yogācāra evolution-cum-revolution, we first need to understand the rise of Bergsonian creative evolution as a critique of social Darwinism in modern China.[50] Lü's unconventional view of science and evolutionism emerged through his debate with Zhang Taiyan on the interpretation of Yogācāra and Bergsonism. This debate was primarily carried out through a series of essays and letters published in different periodicals ed. Li Shicen from late 1920 to early 1921. During this debate, Lü elaborated on his conviction to reenchant social relations with beauty and truth and to awaken a universal moral agency.

While the increasing sway of Cai Yuanpei's aesthetic education spurred Lü's critique of realism and scientism, the increasing traction of the Bergsonian vogue in May Fourth China intensified Lü's critique of philosophical solipsism. As persuasively argued by Alex Owen, Bergson's philosophy of intuition has striking parallels with the fin-de-siècle rise of occultism that sought to valorize transcendent self-realization, to advance the experience of the self as inherently spiritual and potentially divine, and to conceive of reality as forever exceeding the reach of the rationalizing mind.[51]

The Bergsonian philosophy of life played a crucial role in stimulating a new wave of Chinese vitalism, as seen in the rise of New Confucianism and the infatuation with the Yogācāra-inflected phrase "the myriad dharmas are only consciousness."[52] However, both the Bergsonian philosophy of the occult self and the Chinese vitalist revalorization of self-consciousness render them vulnerable to the charges of philosophical solipsism.[53]

In many aspects, the Chinese fascination with the occult self revealed a widespread dissatisfaction with scientism and social Darwinism. In the 1920s, when many intellectuals started looking for alternatives to social Darwinism, the Bergsonian philosophy of life gained sway.[54] Many Buddhist intellectuals disliked that social Darwinism posits passive subjects who are subordinated to the mechanization of life. They understood social Darwinism as a prescriptive moral system of science rather than a description of natural processes.[55]

This shared moral concern overdetermined the Chinese reception of Bergson. Bergson rejected natural selection as the driving mechanism of biological and social evolution. Instead, he theorized an evolution motivated by *élan vital*, a "vital impetus" that is an innate human creative impulse. Although in fin-de-siècle Europe Bergsonian *élan vital* bore a distinct relationship to ancient animal occultism, probably thanks to Bergson's fascination with seances and other paranormal phenomena, it satisfied European bourgeois sentimentality precisely because Bergson's concoction of a supra consciousness effectively displaced the analytical power of the intellect as a valid means to access "life as a whole."[56]

However, in their rejection of materialism and scientism, many Chinese admirers of Bergsonism slipped into another trap—philosophical solipsism. They interpreted Bergson's critique of science and rationality through the lens of Confucian sentimentality. For example, Bergsonian intuition was first translated as *zhijue* 直覺 in 1918. *Zhijue* soon became equated with Confucian self-cultivation and therefore was considered an authentic means to access innate knowledge independent from rationalization.[57] Some Chinese intellectuals found Bergsonism appealing, partially thanks to this moralization process, but most crucially for its resonance with Chinese philosophy of living. Bergsonian evolution soon enthralled many Chinese intellectuals, and there were plans to invite Bergson to give lectures in China in December 1921.[58]

Lü was dragged into the debate on Yogācāra and moralized Bergsonism in 1921.[59] Li Shicen recruited Lü to this debate by requesting that Lü comment on Zhang Taiyan's comparison of Yogācāra and Bergsonism. Zhang Taiyan attempted to use "science" to "prove" the truth of Yogācāra. For Zhang Taiyan, the resemblance of *ālayavijñāna* (storehouse consciousness, about which more later) to the Bergsonian vital impetus and intuition provided "scientific" evidence to validate Yogācāra epistemology.

There were two main camps in this debate. Lü Cheng and Liang Shuming (1893–1988), a renowned philosopher, saw an unbridgeable difference between Bergsonism and Yogācāra.[60] Zhang Taiyan and Li Jinxi (1890–1978), another renowned May Fourth intellectual, argued for the equivalence of the Bergsonian vital impetus with the Yogācāra storehouse consciousness. However, both only read Yogācāra and Bergson in translation and both approached Yogācāra through the lens of Chinese Buddhist hermeneutics.[61]

As early as 1917, Zhang Taiyan had already started a systematic comparison of Bergsonism and Yogācāra.[62] Zhang's first public proposition appeared as part of this larger project. This was a January 5, 1921, letter from Zhang to Li Shicen, which Li abridged and titled "Experience and Analysis" (*shiyan yu lixiang* 實驗與理想).[63] In this abridged letter, Zhang equated empiricism (*shiyan* 實驗) with the Yogācāra epistemological category *xianliang* (Ch: 現量; Skt: *pratyakṣa*) and likened analysis (*lixiang* 理想) to *biliang* (Ch: 比量; Skt: *anumāna*, commonly translated as "inference").[64] In Yogācāra epistemology, *pratyakṣa* and *anumāna* are two mutually exclusive modes of knowing, and both have a long-contested history of interpretation.[65] In the eyes of the aspiring Buddhologist Lü Cheng, Zhang's crude comparisons committed the fatal sin of creating specious analogies.

Although by contemporary standards Bergsonism could hardly count as science, in the late 1910s and early 1920s philosophical methods still occasionally outweighed experiments and the logic of falsifiability.[66] A relevant anecdote helps us understand the contested perceptions of science at the time. At a 1920 cultural event, the physicist Albert Einstein ran into Bergson. During this short encounter, Bergson harshly criticized Einstein's 1916 publication on general relativity, accusing Einstein of mixing metaphysics with empirical science. In 1921, when the Nobel Prize committee deliberated on Einstein's award, they decided that because of Bergson's public critique of Einstein's theory of time it would be more justifiable to recognize Einstein for his relatively less controversial—albeit much less influential—work on the photoelectric effect.[67] Zhang Taiyan was not alone in classifying Bergsonism as scientific.

Initially this debate was a private one. Lü Cheng critiqued Zhang Taiyan through epistles mediated by Li Shicen. Li published these letters in January 1921 in *Xuedeng* 學燈 (The Lamp for Learning). Once dragged into the public arena, Lü Cheng was compelled to participate further. Li organized a special issue on Bergson in December 1921 in the *People's Bell*, where Lü published his one and only essay on the topic of Bergsonism and Yogācāra. Li continued to publish Lü's and Zhang's letters in the *People's Bell* until January 1922.[68]

Moral Agency Lies Neither Inside nor Outside

Despite the prima facie focus on the Yogācāra doctrine of storehouse consciousness and Bergsonian vital impetus, Lü's participation had a deeper motivation. A closer analysis of the letters reveals that Lü's first goal was to establish a rigorous comparative method as the foundation for awakening commoners' aesthetic sensibility. His second goal was to put forth a different social theory to explain collective progress, one that would be grounded in Yogācāra causal enframing (*weishi yuanqi* 唯識緣起) and would posit a universal moral agency as the sole driver of social evolution.[69]

Moral agency, for Lü, lay in the intersubjective—that is, the agentive seeds in storehouse consciousness—not in the impersonal objective world or in some mythical interior psyche. By articulating his criticism of both Zhang Taiyan and Bergson, Lü Cheng sharpened his theorization of an agentless moral agency. Lü was convinced that, to guarantee that one was moving toward collective emancipation, one must take seriously one's own limitations and rely on comprehensive comparisons to expand one's intellect. Only then could one harness the power of the universal moral agency as the driving force of a collective march toward an aesthetic society. To miss the soteriological function of Lü's philosophical investigation would be to impose present disciplinary categorizations on early twentieth-century China when the boundaries between philosophy, Buddhology, and soteriology were still contested.

Lü clearly stated his motive in his reply to Li Shicen: to avoid mixing seemingly similar ideas, especially when the truth was still beyond reach. Lü said, "The theorists shall not use seemingly alike concepts to precipitate further confusion" (*gu lishuozhe buke gengyi yixi fangfu zhi tan, zhuanxiang hunhuo* 故立說者不可更以依稀彷彿之談, 轉相混惑).[70] At first glance Lü seems obsessed with the accurate interpretation of ancient doctrines. However, careful readers will recognize Lü Cheng's consistent attentiveness to analytical methods in both his call for aesthetic revolution and his quest for deciphering the true messages of the Buddha. In an age overwhelmed by imported Western thought, Lü Cheng relied on rigorous methods as the vessel with which to keep oneself afloat during the tempest of proliferating false analogies. In this debate, one finds an essential characteristic of Lü's scholarship that shaped his lifelong comparative studies: his careful provision of textual evidence in its original language.

One must read the endnotes of these letters to appreciate Lü Cheng's insistence on accessing writings in their original languages. In the special issue on Bergson with twelve contributors, only three—Bergson's Chinese translator Zhang Dongsun, Bergson's biographer Yan Jicheng, and Lü Cheng—cared enough to read the French original.[71] Lü's introduction to Bergsonism was brief but to the point.[72] Likewise, in articulating Yogācāra doctrines, Lü Cheng was careful to list all textual sources to substantiate his claims. Lü's careful approach is in stark contrast to that of Zhang Taiyan, who rarely referenced primary texts to support his claims. One of Lü Cheng's main critiques of Zhang was that most of

Zhang's interpretations contradicted canonical Yogācāra sūtras and treatises penned by Xuanzang 玄奘 (602–664) and Xuanzang's disciple Kuiji 窺基 (632–682).[73] Lü argued that Zhang's invention of specious analogies, given Zhang's lack of scholarly due diligence, should not be valued by scholars.[74]

This debate also reveals the seeds of a Yogācāra social evolutionism. Lü Cheng was keenly aware of the pitfalls of joining this debate: randomly comparing two thought systems out of context could hardly bear scholarly fruit. Nevertheless, to dispel the proliferation of false equivalences, Lü chose to engage. Out of numerous possible reasons that one could marshal to dispel random associations, Lü focused on three. These three points provide valuable information on why Yogācāra became newly relevant for Lü and like-minded Buddhist revolutionaries.

First, Lü reframed the perceivable world in terms of Yogācāra causal theory. He extensively described three irreconcilable contradictions between Bergsonian etiology and Yogācāra dependent-origination. Antirealism lay at the center of Lü's soteriological project. Lü Cheng argued that "the very reason that Mahāyāna Buddhism set up the concept of storehouse consciousness was to dispel the mistaken belief in a really-existing objective world and to establish the truth of consciousness-only" (*kuang dacheng zhi li zangshi suoyi zheli shijing wancheng weishi zhiyi* 況大乘之立藏識所以遮離實境完成唯識之義).[75] Experts on Yogācāra philosophy will immediately recognize the soteriological ramifications here. For Lü, establishing consciousness-only (*weishi* 唯識) entailed the simultaneous destruction of two mistaken views that deemed either external objects (attachment to dharma) or internal sensory organs (attachment to the self) as really existing (*shijing* 實境). Thus, it becomes evident that Lü Cheng did not reject Bergsonism per se; he only denied the analytic efficacy of Bergsonian etiology and rejected the validity of Zhang's method, which used Bergsonian "science" to "prove" the truth of consciousness-only.[76] In Lü's mind neither Bergsonism nor Zhang Taiyan's Yogācāra could lead China out of its modern crisis.

Indeed, Lü stressed that Yogācāra causal enframing, which explains all processes in the entire perceptual world in terms of seeds and their causal efficacy, was the most accurate description of how things evolve:

> The cause is the potential in storehouse consciousness that could cause a dharma to rise. This [potential in storehouse consciousness] is called seeds. Conditions are all other already arisen dharmas. Only seed could cause its own fruit.
>
> 因即藏識中能生其法之功能. 所謂種子. 緣即諸餘已現起法. 種子但能各生自果.[77]

Throughout history, many Yogācāra masters have posited that moral agency lies in the karmic seeds stored in *ālayavijñāna*, not in an interiority of the self or in any objective world. In the Yogācāra paradigm, there are eight kinds of consciousness. The first five can be intuitively equated with the consciousnesses associated with the five senses (seeing, hearing, smelling, tasting, touching). The sixth consciousness entails a wide range of psychological functions, including but not limited to perception, emotion, intention, and, most important, deliberation and discernment. But the seventh and eighth consciousnesses are the unique interpretations of Yogācāra philosophers. The eighth consciousness, often called storehouse consciousness (*ālayavijñāna*), contains all karmic seeds. In contrast, the seventh consciousness manufactures the illusion of a subject/object divide in mental processes.

For Lü, the path of collective liberation relied on the learner's conscious discernment (which relies on the functions of the sixth consciousness) of false analogies and on the ascertainment of the correct interpretation. In contrast, Zhang prescribed a soteriological path that followed the Chinese Chan tradition, whose fundamental teaching is that liberation is a matter of taming and stopping the functioning of the sixth consciousness (*fuduan yishi ze zangshi zixian* 伏斷意識則藏識自現). Lü not only criticized Zhang's soteriology as a misreading stemming from what he deemed the abiding Chinese Chan misconception (*miushuo* 謬說) but also further insisted that "this [sixth consciousness] is the only place where learners can put forth their effort [to realize the truth of consciousness-only]" (*xuezhe zhuoli zheng weici shi lai* 學者著力正惟此是賴).[78]

While Lü prioritized conscious discernment of the human mind-heart as the path out of the Darwinist jungle, Zhang followed the Bergsonian dismissal of the reasoning intellect and saw the sixth consciousness as antithetical to liberation. In doing so, Zhang challenged the mainstream Yogācāra theory of how all eight consciousnesses relate. In the mainstream paradigm, the sixth consciousness is always present.[79] And liberation is a matter of purifying the self-grasping and object-grasping aspects in cognitive activities. When Zhang suggested that Bergson must have directly experienced *ālayavijñāna*, Lü Cheng considered his statement a speculation.[80] In Lü's eyes, Zhang and Bergson's shared causal story was a prima facie etiological intuition without conscious discernment. This jettison of reason and analysis, Lü believed, could only intensify one's egotistic grasping and lead one further into a solipsistic trap.

Lü's second refutation concerned the ontology of nature and was tied to the question raised in Lü's debate with Cai Yuanpei on whether nature has any liberating potential. While Bergson imbued both plants and animals with moral agency, Lü considered plants and nature in general as mere manifestations of consciousness. Bergson tried to bridge the mind and matter dualism by asserting that all matters are streams of vibrations. Under this rubric, what distinguishes animals and plants is mobility: plants can survive without moving (photosynthesis), but animals must chase streams of vibrations as food. Despite the apparent similarities between streams of vibrations and streams of momentarily arising and disappearing consciousness, the streams tell entirely different causal stories. Bergson reduced the evolutionary trajectory of every plant and animal to one common origin, a thinly veiled theological concept, and put plants and animals on equal footing.

Lü was convinced that Bergson had wrongly identified plants as agentive.[81] In the Yogācāra system, nature arises dependently from the lifeworlds of sentient beings. Therefore, for Lü, plants were mere appearances in the five consciousnesses engendered by shared agentive seeds in storehouse consciousness. Lü Cheng faulted Bergson for having mistakenly ascribed transformative agency to insentient beings, thus undermining the sole source of moral agency, namely the agentive seeds in storehouse consciousness.

Third, Lü took issue with Bergsonian memory, which Lü judged to be lacking analytic efficacy and thereby void of liberating potential. Scholars of Buddhist philosophy will immediately recognize memory as a central concern of Yogācāra thinkers. Because Abhidharma Buddhists consider consciousness as momentarily arising and disappearing and assume annihilation is self-evident, explaining the apparent continuity of memory is a thorny issue for defenders of no-self. Indian idealists argued that a continuous memory proves the existence of a real self. To defend the doctrine of no-self, Yogācāra masters invented storehouse consciousness as a stream of momentary karmic impressions, that is, seeds, to explain the perception of a continual memory without an enduring self. In contrast, Bergson took for granted that memory was the very reservoir of durations in life, extending life from past to future.[82] For Lü Cheng, this naïve assumption of duration not only lacked explanatory power but was also too crude to have any analytic efficacy. Lü likened it to the Chan doctrine of one thought (*yixin* 一心), which contains many arisings and disappearances of karmic seeds. Lü believed that to hold onto this composite illusion was to miss the opportunity for actual realization.

To sum up, Lü rejected Bergsonism because he saw Bergson's life force as another failed attempt to escape the Darwinist jungle. In contrast with Bergson's Chinese supporters who moralized Bergsonian intuition, Lü rejected Bergsonism because it could not lead to collective liberation. Either way, Bergsonism was not received on its own merits but rather served as a springboard for Chinese intellectuals to launch their own renewals.

The Birth of a Socio-Spiritual Evolutionism

This debate revealed a crucial step in Lü's transition from aesthetics to Yogācāra. It was the first time that Lü linked the evolution of life with Yogācāra causal theory. This debate also paved the way for Lü's later reframing of social (r)evolution with Yogācāra soteriology. During the debate, Lü experimented with comparative hermeneutics to clarify his point and convince others. Although Lü failed to garner broader support, his careful arguments in this debate established Lü's authority as a Yogācāra scholar. This debate reveals that like many Buddhist intellectuals at the time Lü was convinced that Buddhist knowledge was the best vehicle for achieving collective emancipation.

Thus, this public debate on seemingly obscure Yogācāra doctrines marked a watershed moment: the rise of Yogācāra as a socio-soteriology. Lü and Zhang's debate played a key role in introducing Yogācāra as an alternative evolutionary theory to the May Fourth generation thanks to the broader readership of the *People's Bell* and the journal's sustained effort to introduce various evolutionary theories to Chinese readers.

When contextualized within the intellectual horizon of the *People's Bell*, Lü's Yogācāra provided a powerful alternative to both Western evolutionary theories and Bergsonian vitalism. Lü saw Yogācāra causal enframing as the only antidote to the two extremes that were the roots of all modern depravity: realism, as embodied in science and social Darwinism; and philosophical solipsism, as embodied in sinicized Bergsonism. Once Lü Cheng, Zhang Taiyuan, and Li Shicen introduced Yogācāra alongside the global flow of evolutionary theories, the ancient doctrines of Yogācāra took on a new afterlife in the May Fourth era.

2

Karma, Evolutionism, and Buddhist Social Consciousness

To gain a well-rounded understanding of the implications of Lü's Yogācāra socio-soteriology, it is necessary to revisit a set of earlier serendipitous encounters of Yogācāra with social Darwinism and sociology at the end of the nineteenth and turn of the twentieth centuries that primed the intellectuals for the promises of Yogācāra socio-soteriologies. At the end of the nineteenth and turn of the twentieth centuries, Yogācāra met social Darwinism and sociology in China. These encounters set in motion the merging of Yogācāra soteriology with modern sociology and lay the groundwork for Yogācāra socio-soteriologies to gain traction. Both momentous encounters occurred when Yan Fu translated two English-language texts into Chinese in 1895 and 1903, respectively T. H. Huxley's *Evolution and Ethics* (1893) and Herbert Spencer's *The Study of Sociology* (1873). In these translations, Yan Fu strived to integrate the scientific épistémè into the traditional moral paradigm of the Heavenly Principle and thereby invented the socio-soteriological paradigm of the "heavenly process" (*tianyan* 天演).[1] The first translation married the Orientalist reading of individual karma with the Darwinian theory of natural selection, and the second conflated a Yogācāra-inflected karmic theory with the Spenserian notion of survival of the fittest.

It is well known that Yan Fu's translations introduced the concept of race to a wider circle of Chinese intellectuals and opened the floodgate to imported imaginaries of racial ontologies and racial hierarchies.[2] Indeed, pseudoscientific racism found many admirers among Chinese intellectuals who looked to the West for models of a strong China. Chief among them was Zou Rong 鄒容 (1885–1905), who penned an influential 1903 booklet, *Gemingjun* 革命軍

(*The Revolutionary Army*), that galvanized the 1911 Xinhai Revolution by advocating for the genocide of the ruling Manchu race.[3] Mysteriously, after the Han Chinese toppled the Manchu-ruled Qing empire in 1911, no genocide of the Manchus came to pass.

While it is impossible to know why racial cleansing did not happen, there are ample cases in which Chinese intellectuals moved away from their early admiration of social Darwinist racist ideology by engaging with Yogācāra. One apt example is Zhang Taiyan, the interlocutor of Lü Cheng in their debate on Bergsonism and Yogācāra in 1921 and 1922. In 1903, Zhang wrote an enthusiastic preface to *The Revolutionary Army* and was imprisoned with Zou Rong. During his three-year imprisonment, Zhang immersed himself in the study of Yogācāra and later theorized a just, peaceful utopia grounded in a Yogācāra processual holism. Extending the rich scholarship on Zhang's Yogācāra political theory, *Just Awakening* turns its analytic gaze to Yogācāra social philosophy itself, which helped many thinkers shift from the mentality of racial wars and toward a pluralist worldview.[4]

My analysis here expands upon the Durkheimian insight that religion is an essential force that creates and continuously reproduces the society in which it exists.[5] Although the modern Yogācāra worldview could not have emerged without a series of political crises, colonial domination, and anti-imperialist struggles, the political milieu alone can neither account for its complexity nor explain its trajectory. Rather, the modern Yogācāra worldview, as an innovative mode of being, knowing, and experiencing the self and the world, held sway among many progressive Chinese intellectuals because it conjured up a social imaginary in which not only could Buddhism coexist harmoniously with cherished modern ideas and practices such as science and democracy but also all peoples could flourish together, their differences enriching this collective flourishing.

The significance of recovering this modern Yogācāra worldview is twofold. Historiographically, doing so sheds light on a past that has been rendered invisible by the secular paradigm but has nonetheless crucially shaped China's experience of becoming modern. Philosophically, it provides a comparative vantage point from which readers can clearly see that Western concepts such as those of race, the atomic individual, and society as a group of individuals held together by a social contract are parochial: they do not make sense outside of the post-Enlightenment Euroatlantic context, just as a fictional character does not make sense outside the cultural contexts of the fiction. Rather, each imported concept analyzed in this chapter was created anew by grafting it onto similar yet distinct Buddhist ideas. Along with the Buddhicization of these ideas, a Yogācāra-inflected socio-spiritual horizon emerged.

To shed light on these repressed memories, I provide here a fine-grained analysis of how Yogācāra concepts became entangled with social Darwinism, sociology, and the political survival of China and, crucially, how these serendipitous encounters prepared a fertile ground for the birth of the modern Yogācāra worldview and the concomitant making of Yogācāra social theories. Indeed, with the aid of two key translations by Yan Fu, the ancient doctrine of karmic seeds was gradually transformed into the doctrine of Yogācāra national/racial karma. I use the terms "national" and "racial" interchangeably in this study because Yan Fu never presented these two concepts as mutually exclusive, as shown in his frequent use of phrases such as "national demise and racial extinction" (*wangguo miezhong* 亡國滅種) and "protecting the nation, preserving the race" (*huguo baozhong* 護國保種).

Yan Fu, the Chinese Spencerian

Born in 1854 in Fu Zhou, Fujian Province, a port city known as a crucial part of the Chinese Maritime Silk Road, Yan received a modern education decades before the Qing government abolished the civil service exam in 1905. At the time modern Western education was a disappointing alternative path because the exclusion from the civil service exam meant no official career in the future.[6] In 1877 the government sent Yan to England to study naval technology. However, once there, he turned his attention to statecraft, politics, jurisprudence, economics, and sociology. After the Qing empire's humiliating 1895 defeat by Meiji Japan in their struggle to control the Korean Peninsula, Yan Fu translated many Western political and social works by leading thinkers such as T. H. Huxley, John Stuart Mill, Herbert Spencer, and Adam Smith into classical Chinese.

In Chinese collective memory, Yan is seen as the first to introduce the Chinese people to evolutionary thinking, including its doctrines of natural selection and survival of the fittest. Yan saw this evolutionary thinking as the secret to Western wealth and power. These Western secrets of domination sparked the 1911 Xinhai Revolution whose supporters toppled more than two thousand years of dynastic rule and established the first republican Chinese state.[7] Yet in his later years Yan not only opposed republicanism but also turned increasingly to Western spiritualism and the Chinese practice of spirit-writing.[8]

Most relevant to the current study, Yan's Western training, his belief in Daoism, and his familiarity with Buddhism cohered into a mysticism that shaped his reinvention of imported ideas within the Chinese repertoire. Like their

European counterparts who continued to be fascinated with the supernatural despite claims of disenchantment, Chinese progressives like Yan Fu deployed traditional worldviews to shape their acts of knowledge production and social organization.[9] Importantly, in many of his translations, Yan experimented with Buddhist terms to convey Western ideas for the purpose of building a stronger modern China.[10]

A careful examination of Yan's Buddhicization of imported concepts enables scholars to explore the broader implications of Yan's neologism.[11] Indeed, Yan Fu's grafting of evolutionism onto Buddhist repertoire engendered an innovative socio-spiritual horizon in which Yogācāra, social Darwinism, and sociology functioned as a hotbed for the rise of Yogācāra social theories.

In addition to bringing the social Darwinist discourse of the survival of the fittest to modern China, Yan introduced race as a political ideology to the Chinese revolutionaries.[12] For Yan and like-minded Chinese intellectuals, race, rather than being a scientific or biological category, was a political idea in the technical sense of the term. Borrowing Eric Voegelin's insight, "A political idea does not attempt to describe social reality as it is, but it sets up symbols . . . it is not the function of an idea to describe social reality, but to assist in its constitution."[13] Zou Rong's call for racial cleansing of the ruling Manchu race is a prime example of how race functioned as a political idea to create a new social reality in which the Chinese people were bifurcated into the "enslaved" Han race and the "enslaver" Manchu race.

Karma and Evolutionism in the Euroatlantic World

Two more pieces of background information are needed before analyzing the rise of Yogācāra racial/national karma in China: the Western academic knowledge about collective karma and the encounters of karma and evolutionism outside China. These two aspects are intertwined. The earliest encounters between Buddhist karma and evolutionism happened in colonial India, England, and postbellum America, largely thanks to the popularization of Buddhism in Euro-America. Propelled by the tide of colonial information, a tremendous number of cross-cultural encounters occurred. These encounters generated new ideas and churned up surprising interpretations of familiar notions. Among these novel interpretations were various modern afterlives of the age-old pan-Asian idea of karma.[14]

Despite the impact of this widespread idea, the history and philosophy of collective karma in Buddhism remain understudied to this day. Up until two decades ago, the scholarly consensus in European and Anglophone Buddhist studies was that collective karma was a modern corruption and the authentic Buddhist karma was about individual responsibility. These systematic misreadings were only recently debunked by Jonathan S. Walters in his 2003 seminal essay "Communal Karma and Karmic Community in Theravāda Buddhist History."[15] Walters conducted an extensive survey of both Pāli sources and secondary literature on this issue and coined the term "sociokarma" to capture his sevenfold topology of the social dimensions of karma. Similar studies on non-Pāli Buddhist literature have yet to be conducted. Equally important, in 2011, Hisao-Lan Hu critically reconstructed early Buddhist teachings of karma into a social ethics of "interconditionality" of all beings, actions, material presence, and sociocultural contexts.[16]

In 2020, a group of scholars worked across disciplines to address this longstanding neglect.[17] Three of their insights are especially relevant to the current inquiry into modern Yogācāra social philosophy. First, the debate between individual and collective karma dates back to the earliest strata of Buddhist literature. By the fourth to fifth century CE, when Yogācāra thinkers like Vasubandhu were theorizing collective karma as part of the consciousness-only worldview, collective karma had morphed into "cosmo-sociokarma" to account for both the perceptions of materials existences and social dynamics. Second, in Chinese Buddhist literature, there is ample evidence that Buddhist practitioners utilized sociokarma cluster concepts for resolving family issues, maintaining communal harmony, and gathering support for public projects such as building roads, bridges, and temples.[18] And third, there is good evidence to show that, in modern and contemporary Buddhist cultures, sociokarma cluster concepts are widely employed by practitioners to find purpose, seek justice, build community, and anchor their moral compasses in a rapidly changing world.[19]

Informed by this knowledge about the state of the field, this section examines two episodes that are relevant to the birth of Yogācāra social theory in modern China: T. H. Huxley's (1825–1895) individual karma and the Theosophical concept of collective karma. I single out these two episodes not because they are the earliest but because they are the most relevant for understanding the fusion of Yogācāra karmic theory with evolutionism. These two earlier encounters form a necessary backdrop to appreciate the significance of the encounters of Yogācāra karmic theory with evolutionism and sociology.

Both Huxley and the Theosophists shoehorned the Buddhist nondualistic karmic worldview, a worldview informed by the theory of dependent arising, into the Western-constructed ontological categories of the individual agent and racial hierarchy informed by the Great Chain of Being. Huxley's *Evolution and Ethics* presents an unmistakably Orientalist reading of karma as individual responsibility.[20] Drawing on the writings of leading Buddhologists, namely, T. W. Rhys Davids (1843–1922) and H. Oldenberg (1854–1920), Huxley portrayed karma as a sort of energy-like magnetism that is firmly attached to a singular agent as the agent undergoes their cosmic transmigration life after life, echoing more clearly the Theosophical understanding of karma than Rhys Davids's.[21] While Huxley applauded the Buddha for his ethical theory grounded in impersonal karmic laws without a personified God, he saw karma and its corollary of cosmic transmigration as part of a naïve, incomplete, or even false evolutionary story that had been superseded by his own "scientific" evolutionary theory of human nature and society.[22] As part of the British discovery of Buddhism, Huxley's Orientalist reading of karma as an individual trait has been repeatedly validated by scholars as orthodox because it fits nicely within the secular subtraction story of how rationality gradually replaced superstition.[23] Huxley's misreading of karma has contributed to the long-standing modern misconception of Buddhism as apolitical and a private matter of individual spirituality.

In contrast to Huxley's since-normalized reading of individual karma, the Orientalist reading offered by the Theosophical Society has been seen by both contemporaneous colonial scholars and today's mainstream academia as an aberration because of its notion of collective karma and its political ramifications. Indeed, after living in South Asia for years, the founder of the Theosophical Society, Helena Petrovna Blavatsky (1831–1891), wrote freely of "national karma" and human spiritual evolution, which is often conceived of as the evolution of root races.[24] The Theosophical notion of root races follows the mainstream schema of the Great Chain of Being.[25] Blavatsky's invention of racial/national karma harnessed the appeal of both Western raciology and the modern Indic interpretation of evolutionism with Hindu karma.[26] Blavatsky posited that karma is a material substance that is shared by all the members of a race just like some traits are hereditarily passed on, without variation, from generation to generation. Because national karma merges traditional karmic theory with Western raciology, some later disciples went even further and combined the Theosophical concept of karma with radical politics to promote socialism.[27]

Viewed in this light, it is evident that both Huxley's individual karma and Blavatsky's collective karma are undeniably modern Orientalist myths. Yet curiously, most early studies focus exclusively on criticizing the Theosophist invention as an aberration, leaving the impression that Huxley's Orientalist reading is more legitimate or less Orientalist than Blavatsky's. For example, in his encyclopedia entry on karma and rebirth, Wilhelm Halbfass dismisses the

Theosophical conception of "national karma" as an "invention" and claims that the concepts of collective karma never existed in canonical Buddhist sources.[28] Today, in Richard Hayes's online course on Buddhist philosophy, participants can find a detailed refutation of the concept of collective karma, in defense of the "canonical" and thereby "objective" portrayal of individual karma.[29]

While an in-depth study of the diverse modern adaptations of karmic theory must wait for another occasion, this brief discussion reveals that both academics and practitioners in the Euroatlantic region have long been reducing the pan-Asian concept of karma to a dualistic fiction of the individual against the collective. Boxed into this parochial Euroatlantic fiction, Buddhist sociopolitical theories, if they are allowed to exist at all, can only follow one of two paths: one that conforms to Western individualism and another that conforms to Western racism.

However, if scholars turn their attention to the Asian-Pacific world, a different picture emerges. As shown in the next section, Yan Fu, in translating Huxley's *Evolution and Ethics* and Spencer's *The Study of Sociology*, fused the Buddhist concept of caste, the idea of Yogācāra karmic seeds, and Western racial heredity to invent a unique notion, *zhongye* 種業, which I translate as "Yogācāra national/racial karma." In and of itself, Yan Fu's concept of *zhongye* may seem misguided to scholars well versed in Yogācāra terminology. Nevertheless, it is a curious fruit borne of the late Qing literati's desire to appropriate Buddhism for the purposes of protecting China and preserving the Chinese race.[30] As a crossbred idea, it served as the first bridge between Yogācāra and evolutionism. These bridge concepts paved the way for later, more sophisticated, nondualistic theorizations of sociokarma and should be credited as such.

Zhongye as Yogācāra Individual Karma

The first recorded encounter of Yogācāra with evolutionism occurred in 1895 when Yan Fu translated Huxley's *Evolution and Ethics*, titled *Theory of Heavenly Process* (*Tianyan lun* 天演論) into Chinese. In this "translation," Yan Fu gives the familiar term *zhongye* 種業 a nontraditional meaning by contrasting it with the Buddhist concept of *zhongxing* 種姓 (caste/birth/family; Skt: *gotra/jāti/kula*) and by conflating it with the Yogācāra concept of *yezhong* 業種 (karmic seeds; Skt: *karma-bīja*) as well as the common Indic term *jiemo* 羯磨 (a transliteration of *karman*, a declination of karma).[31] Yan Fu then uses *zhongye* to interpret Huxley's Orientalist reading of individual karma.

Indeed, Yan is keen to distinguish Buddhist "individual" karma, which Yan conflates with Yogācāra karmic seeds, from the imported concept of society—that is, nation/race—that Yan interprets as *zhongxing*. Without much appreciation of the prevalent nondualistic teachings in Mahāyāna Buddhism, in different drafts and publications, Yan consistently distinguishes Orientalist individual karma from the collective, hereditary traits labeled as *zhongxing*. For Yan, *zhongxing* represents a cross-cultural conception of shared characteristics passed on from parents to future generations (*fumu zisun dai wei xiangchuan* 父母子孫代爲相傳). According to Yan, the Buddhist karma is different from this collective heredity because it asserts that "everyone has afterlives. There is no need [to pass on character traits from parents] to children and grandchildren" 人有後身不必孫子.[32] In this translation, Yan sees *zhongxing*-cum-race as the collective held together by hereditary traits. He distinguishes this collectivity from the Buddhist emphasis on personal responsibility by noting that Huxley's Orientalist reading of karma ensures that one's own actions generate karmic seeds and that these seeds follow individual agents throughout their transmigrations, life after life, until they are able to liberate themselves (*zidu* 自度).[33]

Yan subsequently links *zhongye* with Yogācāra-inflected notions of *yeshi* 業識 (karmic consciousness), *zhongzi* 種子(seeds), and *xunxiu* 熏(薰)修 (the practice of perfuming). I call the terms *yeshi*, *zhongzi*, and *xunxiu* Yogācāra-inflected notions because they are not exclusively used in classic Yogācāra texts. Rather, they appear frequently in pre-Yogācāra and non-Yogācāra texts such as *Rice Seedling Sūtra* (Skt: *Śālistambasūtra*; Ch: *Daoganjing* 稻稈經; T.709) and *Heap of Jewels Sūtra* (Skt: *Ratnakūṭa-sūtra*; Ch: *Baojijing* 寶積經; T.310) as well as post-Yogācāra East Asian commentaries on Abhidharma (e.g., T.1821) and the *Śūraṅgama Sūtra* (e.g., T.1799), and in Chan Lamp Records (e.g., T.2076).[34]

Yan Fu's use of *zhongye* appears to be heavily influenced by Yogācāra doctrines. He seemingly conflated the term with the well-established Yogācāra doctrine *yezhong*. To the best of my knowledge, when Yan cited this term in his translation, he was not aware of it as a specific Yogācāra term. In fact, in a different draft, he cited an indigenous text, the *Śūraṅgama Sūtra* (T.945), as the canonical support for his choice.[35] In Chinese canonical scriptures, the character *zhong* in *zhongye* is typically used as a unit counter to demonstrate different kinds of karma. Hence, *zhongye* frequently appears in context as *zhongzhong ye* 種種業 (various kinds of karma) or *shizhong ye* 十種業 (ten kinds of karma). In some cases, the term also appears together with concepts such as *gotra* (*zhongxing* 種姓), as in *fozhong ye* 佛種業 (the [untainted] enterprise of the Buddha [family]).[36] Irrespective of how *zhongye* is used in canonical sources, in his modern interpretation, Yan Fu consistently equates *zhongye* with other canonical terms as *jiemo*.[37] And more important, Yan equates *zhongye* with *yezhong*—a term that first appeared in the early Indian Abhidharma literature and is mostly known to Chinese readers because of its centrality to Yogācāra philosophy. To be sure, in core Yogācāra texts, *zhongxing* and *yezhong* are used in tandem, where *yezhong* 業種 are employed to explain the detailed karmic mental processes in each sentient being's mental stream that give rise to the group characteristics of *zhongxing*.[38]

Importantly, at this stage, Yan clearly separates *zhongye*-cum-Yogācāra-individual-karma with the notion of race or nation, which he renders as *zhongxing*. The use of *zhongxing* opens the door to later projections of Yogācāra readings onto these imported dualistic categories. In early Chinese translations of "race," *zhongxing* appears as one of the choices, albeit far less frequently than the now well-accepted term *zhongzu* 種族. Historically, *zhongxing* emerged as the Chinese translation of the Brahmanical concept of caste long before the systematic documentation of sustained philosophical confrontation between Buddhists (including Yogācārins like Dignāga, Dharmapāla, and Dharmakīrti) and non-Buddhists appeared at the end of the Gupta empire (ca. 319–ca. 550 CE). However, in medieval East Asia, *zhongxing*'s meaning was deeply influenced by the Yogācāra soteriological classification of *five gotras* (families).[39] This influence is due to a related, and heated, debate on Buddha nature, a pan-Asian Buddhist doctrine.[40] By the early twentieth century, the Chinese translation of "nation" had already converged to *minzu* 民族, though sometimes *zhongzu* was also used. While *minzu* is an uncommon term in Buddhist scriptures, *zhongzu* is used frequently and interchangeably with *zhongxing* to indicate a group linked by their karmic connections, such as the buddha family, the bodhisattva family, or the *śrāvaka* (hearer) family, in which each embodies a particular soteriological path, with the śrāvaka path ranked lower than the others. Thus, the conflation of *zhongxing* with the imported concept of nation/race in Yan Fu's translation reveals the complex processes by which imported racial thinking was grafted onto the existing Chinese adaptation of the Indian casteism.

In unpacking the diverse historical uses of these three terms, *zhongye*, *yezhong*, and *zhongxing*, I find that Yan's conflation of *zhongye* and *yezhong* marks the first recorded, albeit inadvertent, encounter of Yogācāra with evolutionism. Informed by these three themes, readers can better appreciate the far-reaching implications of this brief encounter. Thus far, most scholars have periodized the beginning of the Yogācāra revival in modern China with Yang Wenhui's historical meeting with Nanjō Bun'yū in Great Britain in 1886 and have attributed the main driver of this revival to Yang's later reintroduction of lost Yogācāra treatises with Nanjō's help.

The evidence presented here uncovers another force that contributed to the rise of modern Yogācāra: Yan Fu. Yan's merging of Yogācāra karmic seeds with evolutionary theories brought this obstruse school of Buddhist philosophy to a much wider circle of late-Qing reformers and revolutionaries who were eager to strengthen China and protect the Chinese nation/race. While Yang Wenhui reintroduced lost Chinese texts of Yogācāra from Japan, Yan Fu's *Theory of Heavenly Process* produced a generation of Chinese intellectuals ready to receive Yang's rediscovered Chinese Yogācāra texts.

Zhongye as Yogācāra National/Racial Karma

The metamorphosis of *zhongye* from Yogācāra individual karma to Yogācāra racial/national karma happened in Yan Fu's 1903 translation of Spencer's *The Study of Sociology* (1873), titled in the Chinese language as *Qunxue yiyan* 群學肄言 (Reviews of and comments on the study of groups). This translation is widely recognized by scholars as the birth of sociology, or *qunxue* 群學, in modern China. Unsurprisingly, this translation is also the site of the birth of a Buddhist social consciousness, although a self-aware Buddhist social consciousness-only arose later in the 1920s when sociology became part of the Republican China's state apparatus. In translating Spencer, Yan used *zhongye* to capture Spencer's conceptualizations of national/racial character and the nature of a people/nation/race. Consider the passage in which Yan's effort to paraphrase Spencer's raciology gives rise to *zhongye* as national/racial karma:

> [Spencer] For, in the ease of these most-involved of all movements, there is the difficulty, paralleled in no other movements (being only approached in those of individual evolution), that each factor, besides modifying in an immediate way the course of a movement, modifies it also in a remote way, by changing the amounts and directions of all other factors. A fresh influence brought into play on a society, not only affects its members directly in their acts, but also indirectly in their *characters*. Continuing to work on their *characters* generation after generation, and altering by inheritance the feelings which they bring into social life at large, this influence alters the intensities and bearings of all other influences throughout the society. [my emphases]
>
> [Yan Fu] 夫宇宙萬物，皆動以致變，獨羣之爲動，與他物殊。必求其似，其人身之天演乎？ 一外力之用事也，效不獨見於其近也，且將見於其遠者，不獨自爲變也。且取他力之並行於其中者，而左右疾徐之，故國家著一令立一法，不獨民之行事從而異焉，性情好惡從而殊焉，乃至積力之久，且相轉而爲種業。及乎種業之成，則民之愚智善惡，若根夫天性，而羣之百爲，與夫天時地利之端，凡民力之所裁成，皆從之而爲異。[41]

> [My translation of Yan Fu's Chinese translation] The myriad things in the universe are all movements that lead to changes. However, the movement of the group is different from the movements of other things. If one must find parallels, then the [closest analogy] is the cosmic unfolding of the individual. The varied consequences of one external force are not only manifested in the immediate surroundings but also reach far and wide. It is not limited to change in oneself. Furthermore, if one factor is impacted by another form, then many related factors also gradually change accordingly to the left and to the right. Thus, when a nation-state establishes one regulation or one law, not only the citizens' actions but also their nature, emotions, and preferences are transformed accordingly. The effects of the force [of the different actions and transformed nature, emotions, and preferences] accumulate over time, mutually influencing one another and then becoming *zhongye*. When *zhongye* is formed, a citizenry's intelligence and morality become like a cosmic nature. Consequently, the group's numerous actions combine with natural conditions; everything that is tailored by the citizenry's power will change because of [this *zhongye*].

In my English translation of Yan Fu's Chinese translation I leave *zhongye* untranslated to underscore how it took on the additional meaning of national/racial karma. To be sure, Spencer was deeply influenced by the myth of the Great Chain of Being, and his use of "brute" readily calls to mind the Aristotelian ontological other—the "barbarians."[42] In Spencer's reviews and comments, "race" is used to refer to a wide variety of concepts that are now categorized differently, including species (such as "the human race" in contrast to "animal species"), race (such as "the Teutonic race," "the inferior race"), and tribal groups (such as "the historic races").

As a forgotten founder of Western sociology, Spencer was interested in collectivity and the laws that govern common characteristics, following the positivist paradigm first set up by Auguste Comte.[43] Spencer frequently discussed the characteristics or traits of a race, a society, or a social group. In the quoted passage, Spencer's "character" refers to the collective traits of a population that have been developed through both collective actions and hereditary transmission.

Yet Yan used *zhongye* to convey the sense of the shared character of a society regulated by a state. Thus, in this translation, *zhongye* accrues the additional meaning of national karma, wherein causal connections are built upon the accumulated, collective actions of a nation-state. In another instance, Yan used *zhongye* to translate "national characters." Yet in three other instances, Yan used *zhongye* to translate "racial characters," wherein the causal connections are built upon heredity. In still another case, *zhongye* was used to translate "species traits," also grounded in heredity.[44] Irrespective of the multiple shades of meaning that Yan Fu attempted to convey with the term *zhongye*, this translation marks the first encounter of Yogācāra karma qua *zhongye* with Western sociological categories.

Soon afterward, thanks to the far-reaching impact of Yan's translations on the Chinese Revolution, *zhongye* became a widely used term. According to Lei Ying, some of the leaders of new literature, such as Lu Xun 魯迅 (birth name Zhou Shuren 周樹人) and his brother Zhou Zuoren 周作人, took up this term to make sense of "the history of humankind."[45] Yet intellectuals well versed in Buddhist literature, chief among them Liang Qichao 梁啟超, Zhang Taiyan, and Liang Shuming 梁漱溟, quickly switched to canonical Yogācāra terms such as *gongye* 共業 and *tongye* 同業. Probably because of Yan Fu's confidence in equating *zhongye* with Yogācāra karmic seeds and partially due to Yan Fu's choice of *zhongxing* (whose meaning has a deep Yogācāra imprint) to translate race/nation, *zhongye* qua racial/national karma became mistaken for a canonical Yogācāra doctrine.

To be sure, when I say that *zhongye* qua racial/national karma was mistaken for a Yogācāra doctrine, I am not denying the existence of Yogācāra collective karma. Yogācārins developed a rich philosophical toolbox of concepts—concepts that include but are not limited to shared karma (*gongye* 共業), similar karma (*tongye* 同業), indirect *ālambana* (*shu suoyuanyuan* 疏所緣緣), and *adhipati* (*zengshang yuan* 增上緣)—to explain and defend collective, intersubjective karmic influences.[46] Nor am I claiming that the Yogācāra toolbox of collective karma has never been used to classify individuals into ontologically distinct groups. In fact, Yogācārins can hardly be considered anticaste heroes: many of their proposed *zhongxing* classifications, though not directly used to justify casteism, have long been used to defend the ontological category of *icchantikas* as a group of sentient beings who will never be able to achieve buddhahood.[47]

I flag *zhongye* qua racial/national karma as mistaken neither to dismiss its historical significance nor to establish an "orthodox" Yogācāra. Rather, the goal is to draw scholarly attention to a much broader and much more complicated issue that warrants further study: namely, how the Western concept of race was reproduced in modern China with the assistance of a preexisting Buddhist repertoire whose multifaceted connections with the scholastic tradition of consciousness-only ushered in a new socio-spiritual worldview in which Yogācāra and evolutionism morph into each other.

With his invention of *zhongye* qua national/racial karma, Yan elevated the status of long-forgotten Yogācāra scholasticism among progressive intellectuals when China was on the cusp of revolution. Yan Fu's new lexicon initiated the colliding of two horizons wherein Yogācāra and social theory arrived at the same time on the same scene. These colliding horizons would soon fuse with the newly established analytic category of society. The establishment of this category primed the soil for the sprouting of the Buddhist social consciousness to resist the gaze of the state. This resistance further cleared the way for the spread of Yogācāra among Chinese intellectuals.

The Birth of Buddhist Social Consciousness

Before examining the wide variety of Yogācāra social theories, one more piece of background information is needed: the rise of society as an independent category during China's tumultuous twentieth century. Domestically, the Xinhai Revolution in 1911 officially ended more than two millennia of dynastic rule. The ruling ideology of the Confucian moral universe was also brought to the brink of collapse. Although China nominally became a republican nation-state (*gonghe guo* 共和國), in reality, for the next two and a half decades various warlords vied for dominance and fought numerous regional and national battles. Internationally, the impending threat of colonization by Western powers seared deep into the Chinese collective consciousness the instructive lesson of survival of the fittest, a discourse initiated by Spencer yet received as Huxley's most impactful message. Yet the ghastly destruction of World War I (1914–1918) also brought forth an anxiety about the impending collapse of Western civilization and a deep yearning for peaceful coexistence (*gonghe* 共和). Intellectually, since the signing of various unequal treaties in the nineteenth century had opened the floodgates to Western commodities, many Western ideas and theories also came to proliferate in the Chinese intellectual landscape.

Floating in the sea of Western goods and ideas, uprooted from Confucian morality, many intellectuals turned to Buddhism for resources with which to imagine and theorize a future of peaceful coexistence of all peoples and all cultures. This shared yearning sustained the Buddhist revival, including the revival of Yogācāra.[48] At the height of the New Culture Movement (Xinwenhua yundong 新文化運動, 1915–1920s), a movement that fueled the anticipation for a national debate about the nature of social facts and sociality among Chinese intellectuals and state bureaucrats, came the birth of Buddhist social consciousness.

The birth of Buddhist social consciousness was connected with the rise of society as an independent category of analysis, especially in terms of the imported sociology that stemmed from founder of positivism Auguste Comte's

(1798–1857) social physics. I am not saying that in premodern China Buddhist communities never engaged with social issues; there are many studies of Buddhist economics, Buddhist statecraft, and commoners' uprisings inspired by Buddhist visions.[49] Neither am I dismissing the importance of the late Qing tendency to use Buddhism for administering this world (*jingshi foxue* 經世佛學). Indeed, as convincingly argued by Gong Jun, when many late Qing literati eagerly excavated Buddhist scriptures for inspiration and spiritual support of their reform and revolution, they conveniently overlooked their own superficial knowledge and naïve, incoherent conflation of Buddhism with Western science.[50] In many ways, Yan Fu's invention of *zhongye* qua racial/national karma is an apt example of how late Qing scholars, out of their fervor to save China and the world, superscribed imported Western concepts such as freedom, democracy, and equality onto Buddhist terms.

Rather, by "Buddhist social consciousness," I highlight a nontraditional pattern of intellectual engagement: in early twentieth-century China, given the nation-state's need to justify its secular rule with data and statistics, society became firmly established as a pillar of the rising positivist paradigm of knowledge production.[51] When society, and by extension social facts (i.e., anything related to social groups, social kinds, and collective behaviors), became an independent category, many intellectuals came to feel dissatisfied with positivism. For them, these imported social theories were built on sand, namely, the unexamined notion of the individual as a unitary, free agent. As evidence presented thus far reveals, this deeply felt discontent with the Western antinomy of the individual against the social engendered a self-conscious theorization of humanity and society grounded in Buddhist paradigms of knowing.

One prominent example is Wang Xiaoxu's 王小徐 (1875–1948; also known as Wang Jitong 王季同) commentaries on society and philosophy. As an established mathematician and successful engineer, Wang advocated for Yogācāra and deemed it a higher science.[52] Wang promoted Yogācāra philosophy because he considered all social issues to have arisen from mistaken ontological notions. For example, in his 1932 essay "A Comparative Study of Buddhism and Science," he claimed that "at the heart of the social problem mentioned above are philosophical problems."[53] Wang was referring to the myriad social sufferings resulting from capitalism, socialism, materialism, unfair social structures, and the like. The essay, which represents Wang's unique take on Chinese society, was prefaced with three competing notes, the first two were penned by two prominent leaders of the New Culture Movement, the educator of modern China, Cai Yuanpei and the champion of "total Westernization" (*quanpan xihua* 全盤西化), Hu Shih (1891–1962); and the third by the lesser-known intellectual Guan Yici 管義慈.[54]

As clearly seen in Wang's scholarship, rather than adopt the conflict thesis of religion and science advocated by Cai Yuanpei, Hu Shih, and Guan Yici, Wang saw Yogācāra as a new paradigm of producing knowledge and the goal of knowledge production as the establishment of a more just society, an urgent issue in view of the impending eruption of World War II.[55] In fact, Wang went so far as to fault Western materialism and its related scientific methods as the source of the social problems that led to the clash between capitalism and communism. In a later essay self-published in 1936 at the height of the German and Japanese fascism and titled *Makesi zhuyi pipan ji fulu—foxue lichang* 馬克思主義批判及附錄—佛學立場 (A critique of Marxism and appendixes: The Buddhist perspective), Wang reiterated these points, clearly preferring Marxism over fascism or capitalism but criticizing all three social philosophies with a new twist. He now argued that compared to Aristotelian syllogism and Hegelian and Marxist dialectics, Buddhism offered more thorough dialectics (*chedi de bianzhengfa* 徹底的辯證法).[56] For Wang, philosophy and sociology were entangled, and all social problems could be resolved if one analyzed them through a Yogācāra paradigm of knowing.[57]

Discussions about Buddhist social consciousness spread beyond intellectual circles like Wang Xiaoxu's. One apt example is the modern afterlife of a folkloric love story featuring the Buddha's assistant Ānanda and the outcaste maiden Prakriti. This story was made into a dance drama by Rabindranath Tagore (1861–1941) and a modernist Peking opera by the Chinese playwright Qingyi Jushi 清逸居士 (?–1931) and performed by the Peking Opera singer Shang Xiaoyun 尚小雲 (1900–1976).[58] In the love story's modern afterlives, the Buddhist anticaste consciousness is retooled as a social critique of either the Indian caste system or Chinese patriarchy.

However, this Buddhist social consciousness was not mere talk. Midlevel bureaucrats also participated in this trend of using Buddhist soteriology to resolve social issues. For example, in 1920s cosmopolitan centers such as Beijing and Shanghai, one often found Buddhist preachers educating the incarcerated.[59] Nor was this Buddhist social consciousness limited to elite practitioners. In fact, many commoners found mundane, daily Buddhist practices such as chanting the Buddha's name and maintaining a vegetarian diet appealing precisely because they perceived themselves as able to save the world from impending calamities, a phenomenon I have elsewhere termed "poor people's philanthropy."[60]

My argument thus stands in stark contrast with existing scholarship in both Chinese and English. The scholarly consensus in Chinese-language scholarship is that the modern Chinese Buddhist revival marked a continuation of traditional classics studies (*jingxue* 經學) or one wave in the vast tide of Qing evidential research.[61] Unlike the English-language scholarship that thus far has examined modern Chinese Buddhism through the lens of Western impact and Asian response, Chinese scholarship characterizes modern Buddhism as a continuation of traditional Chinese culture.[62] While deepening our understanding of the multiple threads that connect modern Buddhism to both its past and the West, both camps have yet to investigate a core element of Buddhism that led to its unprecedented revolutionary fervor: the modern experiment to actualize Buddhist spiritual equality as social equality.[63]

I argue that a key factor in Buddhism's modern transition was the social turn in Buddhist soteriology: a self-conscious challenge to the positivist mode of knowledge production combined with a concerted effort to deploy the message of spiritual equality in the ancient Buddhist soteriological toolbox to build a just society and to resolve perceived or real social problems. *Just Awakening* restores the historical significance of the epistemological battle over the key question whether knowledge about the social should be produced following the positivist or Buddhist research paradigm. My central methodological intervention in this book, then, is to demonstrate that many features of modern Buddhism can be effectively investigated through the lens of sociosoteriology. In particular, I ask what kinds of Buddhist soteriological tools have been adapted to address what sorts of social issues, by whom, and for what purpose.

If this intense revolutionary fervor were only seen in modern Chinese Buddhism, I would happily concede that it was merely a local response, be it due to the influence of late-Qing evidential research or some special features related to the cultural context. But even a cursory investigation of modern Buddhist movements proves otherwise. In fact, this revolutionary fervor has been espoused by many modern Buddhist intellectuals and activists globally. Late nineteenth-century India saw its own Buddhist revival brim with figures full of revolutionary consciousness: the anticaste Tamil Buddhist movement led by Pandit Iyothee Thass (1845–1914);[64] the Marathi Buddhist scholar and Marxist historian Dhammanand Kosambi (1876–1947), who had extensively studied Buddhism and Marxism;[65] the Buddhist studies scholar (and admirer of the sixth-century Yogācārin Dharmakīrti), Indian-independence activist, and accomplished novelist Rahul Sankrityayan (1893–1963);[66] the founder of the Indian Socialist Party's popular platform and admirer of the renowned founder of Yogācāra Vasubandhu (4–5 CE), Acharya Narendra Dev (1889–1956); and the politician turned Dalit Buddhist leader B. R. Ambedkar (1891–1956).[67] In modern Korea, the understudied Buddhist reformers Han Yongun (1879–1944) and Paek Sŏnguk (1897–1981), like many of their Indian counterparts, preached the compatibility of Buddhism, science, and social justice.[68] In modern Japan, the renowned Nichiren Buddhist and Marxist activist Girō Seno'o (1889–1961) employed Marxist language to reform Buddhism.[69] In Southeast Asia, decades before the rise of Dhammic socialism advocated by the renowned Thai Bhikkhu Buddhadāsa (1906–1993), the Irish sailor and migrant worker turned Buddhist monk and anticolonial activist U Dhammaloka (born William Colvin in 1850s Dublin) rallied Buddhists across Asia, challenged the power of the British Empire, and scandalized the colonial establishment of the 1900s.[70] Moreover, collaborations between Buddhists and Marxists in Burma and Cambodia have existed since the colonial era.[71]

Equally importantly, none of these Buddhist reformers were working alone. There were frequent intra-Asian travels and communications. In the Chinese Buddhist periodicals, there were frequent reports about Dongya fojiao dahui 東亞佛教大會 (East Asian Buddhist Conference), Shijie Fojiao dahui 世界佛教大会 (World Buddhist Conference), and Shijie Zongjiao dahui 世界宗教大會 (International Conference of World Religions) from the 1920s to 1940s. These conferences were held around the globe: in Japan, Korea, Yangon (Burma), Geneva, Honolulu, Washington, and New York, among other locations. There were also frequent reports about Western Buddhist converts and worldwide vegetarian movements as well as Buddhist reforms and movements in Burma, Thailand, Sri Lanka, and India in Chinese, Japanese, and Bengali Buddhist periodicals that I studied. While an extensive study of the history and philosophy of these myriad modern radical Buddhist movements as well as their mutual influences is beyond the scope of this book, the questions raised by socio-soteriology may help to reveal wider patterns and probe the assumptions that lie dormant behind received narratives and scholarly constructs.

The evidence presented here shows that the late Qing tide of Buddhism for administering the world worked in tandem with several intersecting global forces: the dissemination of Darwinism and social Darwinism, the increasing institutionalization of sociology, the rise of the positivist research paradigm, the concomitant rise of society as an independent category, and, possibly, the global processual turn as seen in the popularization of Buddhist concepts such as karma, no-self, and compassion. All of these local and worldwide flows converge into a vortex and bring forth an unprecedented Buddhist social consciousness that resulted in a fresh and distinctly Buddhist way of knowing, perceiving, and relating to the world.

From this Buddhist perspective, the meaning of being human and the manner of peaceful coexistence are closely related to the Buddhist terms of spiritual equality, interdependence, and karma. Note that Buddhist social consciousness, as a new pattern of intellectual engagement, does not indicate a nontraditional social reality. In premodern China there were many kinds of grassroots organizations outside the control of the imperial court. In fact, scholars recognize that long before the rise of the nation-state there existed many local self-governing communities. These communities formed a "cultural nexus of power" that sustained a public realm that resembled what Jürgen Habermas termed "the public sphere."[72]

What I am highlighting is an entangled history of the birth of modern Buddhism: a history of multiple interlocking causes and conditions. Early on, late Qing literati projected their own revolutionary fervor onto Buddhism and appropriated Buddhist repertoire for understanding imported concepts. This revolutionary Buddhism engendered a colliding of horizons, fusing political ideas such as the nation-state, race, and other Western notions such as democracy, social contracts, and civil society with the Buddhist discourse of liberation. Later, in the Republican era, unlike in the late Qing era when Buddhism was seen from perspective of the state, many Chinese thinkers reverted this gaze.

Thus began the era of seeing society and revolution with Buddhist eyes. The thinkers self-consciously employed Buddhist philosophical tools to theorize humanity and sociality. Despite the fundamental differences between the two camps—one using the Qing evidential method to appropriate Buddhism and the other using Buddhist soteriological terms to imagine a just society—they aimed at similar outcomes: to save China from colonial powers and to form autonomous social organizations as the foundation of a hopeful future of peaceful coexistence.[73]

From Buddhist Social Consciousness to Yogācāra Social Theory

These crisscrossed encounters highlight the promise of socio-soteriology to refocus scholarly attention on the question of how indigenous philosophical systems challenged imported ideas and offered meaningful alternatives to theorize the self and the world. As I argue in the later chapters, validated by the late Qing trend of Buddhism for administering the world and invigorated by the quest for a just society, many intellectuals started to consciously theorize the nature of social relations and the role of human beings into unconventional forms of interconditionality and relationality from a Buddhist perspective.

Instead of uncritically applying imported theories, these thinkers employed Buddhist analytical repertoires to expose the limitations of social contract theories, to dispel the enchantment of doctrines like the survival of the fittest and Western individualism, and to break open new possibilities for rearranging social relations. They also proposed their own Buddhisized (*fohua* 佛化) social ontology.[74] In many respects, this quest to Buddhisize the world seems more congruent with the early Buddhist quest to "contain" rather than completely eradicate "inequalities in society" and to offer the commoners, losers, and victims of violence "the provision of succor rather than the acquisition of power."[75] While many scholars have rightly interpreted this trend of Buddhicization as a means for Buddhists to justify their own relevance in the modern world, the evidence here suggests another important yet overlooked aspect: namely, that Buddhism offers both incisive critiques of Western social ontology and a tantalizing vision of how the world could be otherwise.

3

Karma, Science, and a Just Society

"Neither the subjective self nor the objective universe is real." That conclusion is the mastermind of Buddha Dharma.

「主觀的我和客觀的宇宙都不是真」那個結論是佛法的主腦.

—Wang Xiaoxu, 1931

While Lü Cheng's proposal marked the beginning of a new form of Yogācāra philosophy, he was by no means alone in his ideas. Many other thinkers proposed similar Yogācāra socio-soteriologies. At the heart of their proposals lay a paradigmatic contention that rejected both the subjective self and the objective universe as ultimately true, as seen in the epigraph to this chapter by Wang Xiaoxu, a renowned mathematician, successful engineer, and self-taught Yogācāra philosopher, in the 1931 preface to his pamphlet *A Comparative Study of Buddha Dharma and Science*. By likening a statement negating both subjectivity and objectivity (typically deemed as an object) to an active agent of "mastermind," the epigraph itself deconstructs the subject-object duality. A decade later, in 1942, when the Japanese army was wreaking havoc in mainland China and in the former British, French, and American colonies in Southeast Asia, Wang republished this pamphlet. His decision was guided by the belief that World War II was the tragic outcome of flaming greed and misanthropy around the globe and that only the spread of Buddha Dharma could serve as a timely antidote.[1] The core of Wang's critique of modern depravity and his quest for a just society was paradigmatic: he deemed the key culprit to be the corrupt Western paradigm of knowledge production grounded in a mistaken dualistic reification of subjectivity and objectivity.

Four types of Buddhist socio-soteriology (see table 3.1), like Wang's contention, drew from the Yogācāra research paradigm and envisioned a just society grounded in no-self, interdependence, and compassion. Strictly speaking, none of the philosophers studied in this chapter were trained in the discipline of philosophy. Neither were they self-taught Buddhologists like Lü. Some did not even know much about Yogācāra. Yet every thinker analyzed here intuitively or consciously drew from the nondualistic ways of knowing in Yogācāra to go beyond the epistemic well of postpositivism and to effectively address the pressing social question of their time: How to establish peaceful coexistence (*gonghe* 共和)?

Because the thinkers' proposals unsettled some cherished yet unexamined beliefs about humanity, relationality, and secularism, more than serving as an intellectual novelty, these proposals deserve to be treated as philosophy, where philosophy is broadly defined as "how things hang together."[2] These modern Yogācārins presaged a recent attempt to go beyond ontological categories of the social, namely, processual social philosophy.[3]

Process philosophy investigates what causally explains the perceptible world instead of how things ontologically are.[4] By shifting away from the ontological questions and toward causal processes, these Yogācāra sociosoteriologies not only anticipated Katherine Jenkins's call to reject the "ontology-first approach" in contemporary Euroatlantic discussions about social justice but also enrich our social imagination and enable deeper cross-cultural conversations about the collective future of the planet.[5] Equally important, these Yogācāra social theories together put forth a different paradigm of secularism. Instead of a subtraction story that eschews religious connections altogether, Yogācāra social theories offer an additive story of becoming secular because they call for reflective scrutiny and "symmetric treatment" of all traditions and communities and seek to guarantee every citizen's right to worship or not worship while maintaining and showcasing their philosophical roots in Buddhist traditions.[6]

These four types of theory were grafted onto three Yogācāra doctrines and one misreading. The three Yogācāra doctrines are karmic confluences (*gongye* 共業 or *tongye* 同業), Yogācāra intersubjective karmic influences, and *ālayavijñāna*. The misreading, which I term "universalized *ālayavijñāna*" (see table 3.1), is a popular interpretation of *ālayavijñāna* as a universal, processual oneness, influenced by similar terms in indigenous Chinese texts such as the *Śūraṅgama Sūtra* (T.945), *Awakening Faith* (T.1666), and the Chan rhetoric.

Instead of a comprehensive analysis of these four types of Yogācāra social theory, I will focus here on three philosophical issues central to the Chinese debates on sociality: first, how to avoid the two extremes of idealism and materialism; second, how to theorize human moral agency in a deterministic, scientific universe; and third, how karmic interconditionality and an action-oriented ethics could engender a nonviolent and just society. For all three issues, it is important to keep in mind that the most basic sense of karma is

TABLE 3.1. Four Types of Yogācāra Social Theory

Yogācāra doctrine	*Central ideas*	*Main advocates*
karmic confluence	society $=$ the confluence of past karmic tracks of each person karmic laws $\geq$ scientific laws $\cong$ social laws	Yinguang, Yuanying, Taixu
intersubjectivity	society $=$ collaborative, mutual actions and consequences karmic laws $\geq$ natural sciences $\neq$ social sciences social facts $\cong$ intersubjective karmic actions	Wang Enyang, Lü Cheng
ālayavijñāna	society $=$ the sum of all *ālayavijñāna*s karmic laws $\geq$ natural sciences and psychology psychology $\geq$ social sciences	Wang Xiaoxu, Yinshun
universalized *ālayavijñāna*	society $<$ universalized *ālayavijñāna* karmic laws $\cong$ scientific laws $<$ social laws	Zhang Taiyan, Li Jinxi, Cai Yuanpei

Note: $=$ "is identical to"; $\geq$ "is greater than or equal to"; $\neq$ "is not equal to"; $\cong$ "is approximately equal to"; $<$ "is smaller than"

action and that, in Chinese culture, karma can refer to the conditions, causes, and consequences of action whose precise meaning must be unpacked in a case-by-case manner.

These four types of Yogācāra social theory reconfigure what is thinkable in social philosophy in three ways . First, philosophers like Wang Xiaoxu rejected the underexamined materialist and idealist ontologies of Western sociology, reconceived of subject/object duality as the consequence of deluded mental processes, and proposed solutions to stop the karmic processes that lead to the recurrence of such dualistic patterns of seeing the self and the world.

On the one hand, Chinese Yogācārins rejected the notion of an external, objective world devoid of human interests and concerns. These thinkers retooled Yogācāra arguments to reject materialism (*weiwu zhuyi* 唯物主義).[7] Materialist substance metaphysics, in their eyes, formed the ill-conceived ontological foundation of the natural sciences as well as the social sciences, including areas of interest such as Durkheimian sociology and Spencer's and Huxley's social Darwinism. For these modern Yogācārins, the moral consequence of this mistaken view that there is material wealth to be gained was Darwinist competition. This competition fanned the flames of colonial invasion and racial wars.

On the other hand, Chinese Yogācārins rejected the ontological notion of an internal, subjective world that humans can directly access through introspection. These thinkers thus also retooled the Yogācāra line of inquiry to refute idealism (*weixin zhuyi* 唯心主義).[8] Idealist substance metaphysics, in their eyes, substantiated the misguided ontological foundation of both Bergson's creative evolution and some forms of New Confucianism (Xinrujia 新儒家). For some Buddhist intellectuals, Bergsonism and New Confucianism overreacted in their rejection of materialism and went to the other extreme of mistaking the mind for an actually existing substance. This idealist position was hard to defend because critics recognized that it would easily lead to philosophical solipsism.[9] Either way, in the Yogācāra processual worldview, the inherent moral defect of Western social theories is evident: such theories validate moral egoism from both sides of the subject/object divide, taking it to be a self-evident truth that there are material benefits that merit competition and selves worthy of violent protection.[10]

Second, after dismantling the Christian-influenced notion of free will and the untenable ontological premises of the sciences and social Darwinism stemming from the paradigm of Great Chain of Being with God sitting on top, the modern Yogācārins found themselves having to make a convincing argument for the Buddhist notion of an agentless agency without jettisoning the sciences.[11] The trail of clues leads us to believe that they redirected their attention from the ontological question of what building blocks constitute the observable world, which takes for granted the binary of an "objective" observer and "substantial," "mind-independent" things to be observed, to the Buddhist diffractive question of what causally explains the workings of the perceptible world. According to the Buddhist perspective of personhood as five aggregated karmic processes, human agency is not the capacity of individuals to initiate change but the potential of recurring karmic processes to influence the directions of change.[12] The Chinese critics rightly sensed that, by granting social facts and collective behavior their own ontological existence, Durkheimian sociology provided little room for human moral agency outside of social context.[13] They also questioned the soundness of social Darwinism, which tended to reduce human agency to the mechanical calculation of material loss and benefit. By reframing both agency and science in the processual paradigm, that is, as recurring patterns of aggregated karmic processes, these thinkers carved out a space for appreciating human agency as patterns or propensities of relations and actions engendered by agentive karmic seeds stored in the *ālayavijñāna* of each mental stream.

Third, these thinkers offered a plausible explanation, devoid of the ontological baggage accompanying Western social theories, of why socially constructed or mind-dependent categories such as groups and institutions could engender tangible consequences in the perceptible human world. For these Yogācārins, modern science was fundamentally flawed because it uncritically equated what things are (ontology, or the science of being) with how things work (causal efficacy).[14] Positivist social theories erred further by reifying mind-dependent social kinds and social facts as if they were mind-independent natural kinds. Going beyond this twofold mistake of naturalizing subjectivity and objectivity, they drew from Yogācāra causal theory to defend the conventional *correctness* of mind-dependent categories for their capacity to bring forth tangible karmic consequences for the self, others, and the world.[15]

Seen from this perspective, ontological distinctions between the subjective and the objective do not offer special explanatory power for questions such as how to live a good life or how to build a livable future. Furthermore, social contract theories, by naturalizing the individual as a singular, unitary agent and by validating moral egoism as the "natural" starting point of moral concern, lock the individual and the collective into an eternal antinomy.[16] The consequences of this antinomy, in the eyes of these modern Yogācārins, were dire: it bound individuals and groups in relentless struggles. To undercut these fatal fictions, the thinkers adopted a pragmatic stance and posited that mind-dependent categories such as individuals, groups, and communities were conventionally efficacious because they were engendered and sustained by recurring patterns of actions, coactions, and consequences of actions. They then offered an alternative theory of how more egalitarian karmic interconditionality could lead to more freedom, more equality, and world peace.[17]

Karmic Confluence Gets a Yogācāra Mark-up

In the 1930s, threatened with Japanese invasion and plagued by natural disasters, a new trend of understanding society as karmic confluence emerged in China.[18] This vision of society-cum-karmic-confluence is noteworthy for two reasons. First, according to this vision, karmic society is cocreated by a democracy of the karmic tracks of all its members, where no one person (whether the ruler or the ruled) can monopolize karmic merits or retributions. In this way, the vision reverts the premodern social imaginary of a dualistic codependence of the ruler and the ruled into a nondualist, equitable social imagination of interdependence. Second, in contrast to the dangerous fictions of Darwinist racial wars or the antinomy of the individual against the social, this vision of society-cum-karmic-confluence narrates a nonviolent, noncoercive story of how to avoid conflicts and live peacefully together. I find these karmic tales remarkable because they push the boundary of what is imaginable and proposed a nonhierarchical means to build a complex society of equality, freedom, and justice.

These Buddhist thinkers offered their accounts of equality and justice by using two terms interchangeably: *gongye* 共業 and *tongye* 同業. As evoked in the passages analyzed in this section, both *gongye* and *tongye* mean karmic confluence. By "karmic confluence," I mean the parallel plays by each person's similar karmic past that lead to similar karmic outcomes in the present. One often-cited example by Republican-era Buddhist thinkers was the collective karma of killing: every Chinese person had eaten meat and caused the death of animals in their past (including past lives), and these similar karmic tracks now brought to fruition similar experiences of death caused by war or disaster.

In and of themselves, this notion of collective karma most likely implies a sense of coincidences engendered by similar karmic pasts instead of karmic interactions among different streams of consciousnesses.[19] This is because in these narratives past actions, such as eating meat or killing animals, are mostly presented as mundane daily behaviors that can be done alone, without joint effort.[20] There is no indication that the members of a country knew of one another in the past. There is no indication of whether those who have cotransmigrated as a social unit to suffer the ongoing war had, in the past, jointly killed another group of sentient beings who themselves had cotransmigrated to punish their past killers.

The use of collective karma as karmic confluence does not mean that the thinkers denied shared karmic responsibilities due to joint actions. Rather, it means that when talking about the collective karma of war and disaster, the thinkers speculated that collective karma is the karmic confluence of all personal primary karmic responsibilities. Personal karma (*ziye* 自業 or *bieye* 別業) bears primary responsibility (*zhengbao* 正報) because it is predicated on one's own actions. As for shared karmic responsibility due to joint actions, for example, karmic responsibility distributed among family members due to their shared economic life (e.g., a butcher's children might suffer shared karmic retribution due to their father's karma of killing animals for meat), the thinkers saw it as a secondary/remainder responsibility (*yubao* 餘報).

In the 1930s, karmic confluence emerged as a frequently evoked explanation for the ongoing wars.[21] A perusal of Republican Buddhist periodicals and newspapers shows that before the 1930s, mentions of *gongye* and *tongye* were infrequent and limited to doctrinal discussions. However, in the 1930s, threatened with the prospect of a Japanese invasion and in the aftermath of the September 18 Incident in 1931 (Jiuyiba shibian 九一八事变), when the Japanese Kanto army attacked Shenyang, and the January 28, 1932, Songhu Battle (Songhu zhanzheng 淞沪战争) when Japan attacked Shanghai, many Buddhists invoked the rhetoric of the shared past karma of killing animals as the chief cause.

More than an opium of the masses, the discourse of collective karmic tracks is remarkably secular because it allowed Buddhists and all those who adopted this karmic worldview to imagine the world as a karmic collective of the common folk, regardless of religious affiliation, gender, race, or any other group label. For example, in his 1933 speech "Zenyanglai jianshe renjian fojiao" 怎樣來建設人間佛教 (On how to build Buddhism in the human world), Monk Taixu 太虛 (1890–1947), the father of Humanistic Buddhism (Renjian Fojiao 人間佛教), commented that to avoid natural disasters and human calamities everyone must do good and cultivate virtue because *gongye* is the mental creation by the majority of people (*gongye shi duoshuren xinli gongtong suozaocheng zhi ye* 共業是多數人心理共同所造成之業).[22] Here, Taixu's use of *gongye* conveys a sense of the convergence of karmic tracks determined by individuals' similar karmic pasts. The notion of a collective future is built upon the summation of all the karmic tracks.

Similarly, in his 1936 lecture on protecting the nation, Monk Yinguang (1862–1940) asserted that national disasters were caused by the karmic retribution of all national subjects and called on commoners to engage in mundane, pious actions to build a better future together:

> As for today's calamities, they all result from our collective karma. If everyone could chant Amitābha and do good, then our collective karma could be transformed. Thus, our misfortunate fate could be dissolved. . . . Hence, we know that national catastrophes could also be avoided if the commoners could chant Amitābha with sincerity.

> 蓋今日之災難，皆是大家共業之所招．若人皆能念佛行善，則共業可轉，而劫運亦消矣 . . . 故知國難亦可由大眾虔懇念佛挽回之也.[23]

In stark contrast to the call to arms inherent in the rhetoric of the Darwinist struggle for survival, Yinguang's message of protecting the nation was decisively nonviolent. In addition, chanting Amitābha with sincerity also indicates that, for Yinguang, the karmic future of the nation could be modified by the sum of every virtuous action, if enough commoners performed enough good acts. I have argued elsewhere that Yinguang's use of *gongye* suggests a new sociopolitical imagination of the nation as a karmic society.[24] Yinguang's use of nation as karmic confluence differs from what Jonathan S. Walters terms "political karma," which refers to the joint actions taken by a political group, such as "the populations of imperialist or genocidal polities" who, Walters writes, "should be reborn into the postcolonial societies where they experience the poverty or other forms of suffering they created during previous lives."[25] Further proof that Yinguang's *gongye* is closer to karmic influence is his belief that even if chanting Amitābha could not stop the unfolding national disasters, such virtuous actions could at least stop personal adversity, a common trope in Buddhist miracle stories.[26]

Yet Yinguang was not alone in imagining the nation as a karmic society and in striving to resolve social conflicts through nonviolent pious actions. Around the same time, Monk Yuanying 圓瑛 (1878–1953) also repackaged his 1920s exhortation of not killing, releasing life, and keeping a vegetarian diet that he had advocated for when preaching the *Śūraṅgama Sūtra* by adopting a new moral frame of similar karma. This new moral frame linked wars with the past karma of killing in a similar manner (*tongzao shaye zhiyin* 同造殺業之因).[27] Like Yinguang, Yuanying saw war as collective retribution for the past killings similarly executed by every person.

These karmic stories demonstrate the remarkable rise of a new notion of karmic society. This vision of a karmic society reveals an additive secular paradigm that is worthy of scholarly analysis. First, the karmic paradigm drastically shifted the focus of discussion on what counts as a just society. The basic premises of many Buddhist conversations on this topic are nonviolence and voluntary association. This is because these Republican Buddhist leaders imagined the country as a karmic society cohered by the karmic confluence of all its members. In this social imagination, the country does not resort to institutionalized coercion such as that enacted by the army or police to ensure its survival. This was in stark contrast to the coercive secular discourse of the nation-state as a political entity whose existence is premised upon military power, legal regime, and state control. Here also lies a shared feature of the modern Buddhist social consciousness: justice cannot be brought forth by violence and thereby any theorization of a just society must be sustained by nonviolent, noncoercive means such as karmic consequences.

Second, this karmic society is a democracy of individual karmic tracks, which underpins the requirement for the symmetric treatment of all individuals in terms of policy and law, regardless of religious affiliation. In contrast to the premodern Buddhist political imagination in which the ruler's overflow karma determined the collective well-being of the ruled, in these modern discourses, the nation's collective future was determined by every commoner's karmic past and could be transformed through everyone's pious actions of doing good, keeping a vegetarian diet, and chanting Amitābha.

For a self-conscious theorization of socio-soteriology, we must look to Taixu's oeuvre. In 1925, Taixu proposed his own social theory in a short essay titled "You zhizhi de zhongzhong guoji zuzhi zaocheng renshi hele guo" 由職志的種種國際組織造成人世和樂國 (Establishing a harmonious, happy country in the human realm by building various international organizations based on professions and aspirations).[28] In this essay, Taixu shifted the debate about society from the secular discourse of individualism to the Buddhist discourse of karma and articulated how a just society could arise from common karmic seeds.[29]

Taixu based his theorization on the renowned seventh-century scholar-monk and Yogācāra master Xuanzang's *Cheng Weishilun* 成唯識論 (Establishing consciousness-only; henceforth, *CWSL*), a composition in which Xuanzang critically analyzed ten Indian Yogācāra masters' treatises on *Triṃśikā* (Thirty verses; Ch: *Weishi sanshi song* 唯識三十頌) that had been written by the recognized founder of the Yogācāra school, the fourth-to-fifth-century scholar-monk Vasubandhu. One of the key doctrines in *CWSL* is that the observable shared natural world is created by karmic seeds with common characteristics (Ch: *gongxiang zhong* 共相種; Skt: *sāmānya-lakṣaṇa-bīja*; henceforth, shared karmic seeds).

Taixu extended this doctrine to include the newly imported category "society" and thus forged a unique Yogācāra theory of a nonhierarchical, noncoercive, nonelite-centered complex social formations. This is the earliest record of Taixu's Yogācāra social theory. He argued that "the natural world is made this way [by common karmic seeds], so is society" (*qishi jiran, shehui yi er* 器世既然社會亦爾). He elaborated,

> Thus, when one organizes various international organizations based on professions and aspirations, these [organizations] encompass all of the human world. The formation [of these organizations] is grounded in the cosmic law that the shared karmic seeds in the ripening consciousness [i.e., *ālayavijñāna*] collectively engender [these organizations]. [This logic is like] the resonance of sounds, the convergence of Qi, and the getting together of the same kind. In this way, its trajectory is the most natural and its principle the most just. Compared to the [principle] of setting up territories and demarcating borders to form a nation-state, [the two principles] are very far apart in terms of their difficulty vs. easiness and appropriateness vs. inappropriateness.

> 故由一一職業志業等組織成一一國際之團體，個個遍與全人類之世界，乃根據於異熟識中共相種共變世界之天則。聲應氣求，同類相聚，其勢甚順，其理最正；較之隔疆劃界以組為國家者，其難易正反之相去者遠矣.[30]

Three points can be drawn from this passage. First, Taixu intentionally contrasted two notions of the secular nation-state. The first is the country (*guo* 國) as a nonhierarchical, mutually dependent society whose geographic presence could one day spread across the globe. The second is the nation-state as a political entity individuated by the forceful demarcation and military control of its territory.[31] This intentional distinction marks Taixu's vision as a social theory. Taixu's Yogācāra socio-soteriology treats society as an independent unit of analysis and an entity differentiated by its nonviolent, voluntary goals and actions. In Taixu's worldview, a peaceful and happy country (*hele guo* 和樂國) is run solely by international civil society organizations (*guoji zhi tuanti* 國際之團體) such as educational organizations, religious organizations, commercial organizations, agricultural organizations, and industrial organizations, whose membership is based on the noncoercive association of persons with shared aspirations and professional skills. Implicit in this social vision is that all bodies, be it the physical bodies of individuals or the institutional bodies of organizations, are mere thresholds of relations whose individuated forms are maintained through reliable and repeated actions.

Second, to justify his theory of nonviolence grounded in interconditionality, Taixu drew upon *CWSL*'s doctrine of shared karmic seeds as "natural" (*shun* 順) and "just" (*zheng* 正). Implicit in Taixu's social philosophy is the conviction that similar karmic trajectories naturally bring forth formations of a just society. Also implicit in his theory is a critique of the logic of the nation-state whose territory must be defended by institutionalized violence. At the same time, Taixu skillfully weaved together widely accepted premodern metaphors of how humans could harmonize with each other through the copoiesis of stimulus and response into his new analytic category of civil society organizations bound by shared karmic seeds: the resonance of sounds, the convergence of Qi, and the joining of similar kinds of people. Significantly, all three metaphors invoke the strategy of acting along with others in a given field of causes and conditions. None of these metaphors requires an ontological foundation and yet each offers a robust explanation of how a livable future emerges through peaceful coactions that stimulate (*gan* 感) and respond (*ying* 應).[32] Indeed, by adopting an explicit Yogācāra framework, Taixu's additive story of a secular society offers a powerful vocabulary with which to understand how to see nonviolence as natural and just and to reconceive differences as enriching through *ganying*. It also ensures the symmetric treatment of all groups and individuals by considering actions, coactions, and consequences of actions only.

Moreover, Taixu called into question the newly imported distinctions between the natural sciences that analyze the natural kinds and the social sciences that study the social kinds. Indeed, Taixu put *shehui* (which may refer to social kinds such as social groups and social organizations) on the same footing with *qishi* (which literally means the receptacle world but, in this context, refers to natural kinds): both arise from the fruition of shared karmic seeds. At first glance, this theory falls short of its own goal because it does not offer a satisfactory solution to the problem of human agency in a scientific universe. As discussed in chapters 1 and 2, one chief Chinese grievance against social Darwinism, science, and sociology was that if collective behavior and social facts are ontologically determined by scientific laws, then these laws overdetermine that humans are mere automatons controlled by predetermined collective behavior and are thereby deprived of moral agency. Taixu's theory of agency is only problematic if one uncritically accepts the ontological divide between subjectivity and objectivity.

Alternatively, if scholars adopt a processual or relational philosophical paradigm, a mainstream approach in Chinese culture, it becomes evident that for Taixu and like-minded Buddhist leaders, agency emerged through the actions and coactions of aggregated karmic processes in an open-ended field of causes and conditions.[33] Or, to put it differently, instead of unreflexively hewing to the egocentric view of humans as autonomous agents who alone can act, Buddhist intellectuals conceived of agency as a potentiality (shared karmic seeds) to a coaction that is activated when conditions are ripe and further activates other potentialities. In a sense, Taixu's karmic socio-cosmos anticipated Tim Ingold's SPIDER metaphor of the world: instead of an assemblage of actors and objects or bits and pieces, the world is a karmic "meshwork" of entangled pathways, irreducible interplays, interwoven chains of actions and coactions, and coordinated dances of activated potentialities and activating conditions.[34] In contrast to the ANT metaphor, where actors and objects can enter or leave a relation without themselves being changed, in my reading the meshwork metaphor better captures the Buddhist notion of emergent agency because every changing relation changes the perceived actors and objects in this meshwork of copoiesis.

This sort of nonviolent society-cum-karmic-confluence theory gained traction among Chinese of all social strata at the time. Its appeal is understandable. To begin, mainstream process philosophy in traditional Chinese culture made it easier for commoners to accept insentient beings as agentive and to conceive of agency as an emergent feature of coordinated actions. It is also well known that in Chinese culture, the boundaries among the divine, ghosts, the human, the animals, and the natural world are porous and therefore nonhuman agents proliferate in the Chinese spiritual landscape. Furthermore, throughout imperial China, the cosmos was generally seen to care deeply about human affairs and to intervene in the human world through both natural and supernatural means. Consequently, it was intuitive for commoners to accept seemingly objective entities as potential moral agents.[35] An added benefit of this blurring of boundaries is that because of its inbuilt immunity to the essentialist categories, Yogācāra karmic society allows socially constructed categories such as individuals, nations, and ethnicities to have agency (understood as karmic efficacy and propensity) without reifying these categories as absolute. It thereby reveals the peculiarity of the Western impasse of the individual against the collective.

By interpreting scientific laws as intersubjective agreements arising from shared karmic seeds, this form of Yogācāra socio-soteriology extended the traditional Yogācāra causal framework to subsume the newly imported analytic categories of the social and the scientific into its fold.[36] This sort of Yogācāra socio-soteriology provided timely scriptural authority for the reformers who wished to actualize ancient Buddhist spiritual equality into tangible social equality. At the same time, for the progressive intellectuals, it offered a compelling nondualistic, non-violence-based theorization of nation, science, and human agency, outside the dangerous reifications of mind over matter, individual against society, and the survival of the fittest.

I would like to point out that society-cum-collective-karma is worthy of scholarly attention for an additional reason: it demonstrates that the scientific enterprise needs neither to anchor itself to ontological realism nor to presume a mind-independent objectivity, an insight that has gained scholarly attention recently.[37] In this sense, this sort of Yogācāra socio-soteriology marked an attempt to explain both science and society in terms of irrealism, where irrealism is understood as a form of representationalism that sees the postulation of an external world as part of the representations and the claim that there are objects beyond representation as itself part of these representations.[38] Freed from ontological realism, society-cum-collective-karma sufficiently explains why social kinds, as mind-dependent categories, may have tangible consequences: Yogācāra causal theory ensures that these socially constructed categories have real karmic consequences.

Perhaps the only drawback to the notion of society as karmic confluence is its lack of a robust theorization of intersubjective karmic influences. To be sure, scholars well versed in Yogācāra philosophy will notice that intersubjectivity is implied in the Yogācāra notion of shared karma. This is because shared karmic seeds themselves are conceived of as open to intersubjective interventions; for example, pure or impure karmic seeds can be planted by listening to pure or impure teachings. Nevertheless, given its lack of explicit theorization of intersubjectivity, this socio-soteriology is vulnerable to being misread as a Sinicized version of society as the sum of individuals, where each person is individuated by bounded karmic tracks.

Society as Intersubjective Coaction

Can Yogācāra offer a robust social theory grounded in genuine intersubjective interactions? The answer is yes. At least one group of Chinese intellectuals recognized the importance of theorizing social relations as a matter of dealing with other minds. They were the core members of the China Inner Learning Institute. Founded by Ouyang Jingwu in July 1922 in Nanjing, the institute soon became the hub of the Yogācāra revival. Despite its small scale in terms of students and teachers, the institute exerted outsized influence on the modern Chinese intellectual landscape thanks to its rigorous comparative studies, first-rate scholarly editions of key Yogācāra texts, and extensive connections with late Qing literati and progressive intellectuals.

Ouyang envisioned the task of his institute as one of educating leaders for a socio-soteriological project. He encouraged his students as follows:

> The ancients aspired to manifest bright virtue to all under heaven; [to fulfill this goal,] I shall enable all to enter nirvāṇa, which entails extinguishing worldly afflictions and releasing all from suffering.
>
> 古之欲明明德於天下者，我皆令入涅槃而滅度之.[39]

Readers familiar with Confucian classics will readily identify the Confucian overtone in this verse. Indeed, Ouyang's socio-soteriology speaks volumes about the power of Confucianism to function as a "civil religion" and a "habit of heart," embodying the ongoing effort to build a "global civil society which a spiritual dimension drawing from all the great religions of the world."[40] As a civil religion, Ouyang's vision seamlessly integrates Confucian relation-centered ethics, Buddhist spiritual perfectibility, and what Amartya Sen terms "secular symmetry" that was long practiced in Ashoka's Mauryan Empire and Akbar's Mughal Empire.[41] Under Ouyang's leadership, most of the institute's students strived to use Yogācāra doctrines for building a peaceful and just world.

Most notably, this group of thinkers all carefully distinguished intersubjectivity (the social kinds) from objectivity (the natural kinds), although they also vehemently debated among themselves which sorts of Yogācāra doctrines should be used to differentiate social phenomena from natural existence. Like Taixu, Ouyang and his followers saw both objectivity and subjectivity as convenient fictions imposed by a perceiving mind. Yet unlike Taixu, Ouyang believed similar karma had to be combined with intersubjective corroboration (*huzheng* 互證), the latter of which requires intersubjective affirmation of other sentient beings as subjects. In his influential 1921 essay "Buddhism Is Neither Religion nor Philosophy" (fofa fei zongjiao fei zhexue 佛法非宗教非哲學), he explained his secular socio-soteriology as follows.

First, *ālayavijñāna* is a stream of consciousness particular to each sentient being, and every *ālayavijñāna* creates their own cosmos. This Yogācāra rejection of the notion of one world complicates the question of intersubjectivity. Philosophical discussions about intersubjectivity are all premised upon one shared world. In contrast, Yogācāra philosophies, despite many internal debates, all attempt to explain the karmic processes that give rise to the illusion of one shared natural world. In Ouyang's understanding, these particular cosmoses all intersect without obstructions, and what appears to be the same object at a particular place and time is due to similar karma. In this Yogācāra worldview, because of similar karma, even though the particular causal processes of each mental stream's perception differ, an agreement can be reached through intersubjective verification. "Intersubjective verification" here must be understood as the karmic processes that lead to agreements among different mental streams. Ouyang explicitly rejected the notion that there is one object to be known commonly by all sentient beings, "fei gongzheng yi zhi 非共證一知."[42] Ouyang took it to be a self-evident truth that intersubjective corroborations could happen without resorting to external objects.

Other than referring to similar karma, Ouyang never felt the need to specify which Yogācāra doctrines could be used to explain how intersubjective verification between different mental streams could be reached if each mental stream generated and inhabited its own cosmos. For greater detail, we need to examine his students' writings. Because Wang Enyang 王恩洋 (1897–1964) was the coauthor of Ouyang's famous 1921 essay and wrote the latter half on why Buddhism is what the world needs now, let us start with his appendix. In it Wang posed a pressing hypothetical question, calling to mind the Darwinist rhetoric of *huguo baozhong*:

> In today's world, there is only might without right. If everyone learns Buddhism, then would it not lead to the demise of the nation and the extinction of the race?
>
> 當今之世有強權而無公理. 使人皆學佛, 則國不亡, 種不滅乎?

To overcome this existential threat, Wang, like all the Buddhist thinkers studied thus far in this chapter, resolutely proposed nonviolent actions. Echoing Ouyang's socio-soteriological ambition, Wang asserted that "to govern the world, to resist the insult, and to succor (in the wake of) catastrophe, to protect (in time of) danger, these are all the enterprises of bodhisattvas."[43] In this vision, nonviolence does not entail nonaction. Rather, it calls to mind what Judith Butler terms "aggressive nonviolence," "one that emerges in the midst of conflict, one that takes hold in the force field of violence itself."[44] Indeed, Wang Enyang's bodhisattva, like Ouyang's, was that of a fierce activist who sought to not only liberate themselves but also transform society.

Like Ouyang, Wang was keen to distinguish the objective existence from the intersubjective resonances. Yet, unlike Ouyang, Wang left ample evidence for scholars to reconstruct his Yogācāra sociality-cum-intersubjectivity. The rest of this section examines his aforementioned appendix to Ouyang's lecture and his 1924 essay, "Establishing the Doctrine of Consciousness-Only" (Chengli weishi yi 成立唯識義), contextualizing as needed his doctrinal points within the sociopolitical concerns of his complete works. A modern commentary on Vasubandhu's *Twenty Verses*, Wang's 1924 essay is a lucid illustration of key Yogācāra insights with contemporary metaphors and examples.[45]

Briefly speaking, in crafting his Yogācāra social theory, Wang employed indirect *ālambana* (Ch: *shu suoyuanyuan* 疏所緣緣) to describe scientific findings (i.e., intersubjective agreements on seemingly objective existences) and *adhipati* (Ch: *zengshang li* 增上力; amplifying and activating forces) to theorize genuine intersubjective coactions such as the actions between teachers and students and between the killer and the killed. As is well known, in Xuanzang's *CWSL*, the objective basis of perception (Ch: *suoyuanyuan* 所緣緣; Skt: *ālambanam-pratyaya*) is divided into two subcategories, the direct *ālambana* (Ch: *qin suoyuanyuan* 親所緣緣) and the indirect *ālambana*. Historically, these two terms were employed by Xuanzang to explain the existence of seemingly objective objects such as rivers and mountains as well as the existence of other minds.[46] Meanwhile, *adhipati*, in Xuanzang's and Kuiji's use, was an auxiliary explanation of how indirect *ālambana* functions to explain intersubjectivity, or karmic influences among different mental streams.[47] Departing from his predecessors, Wang mapped these two terms to the seemingly objective aspects and the seemingly subjective aspects of the perceptible world, respectively.

Like Ouyang, Wang asserted in his 1921 appendix that agreements about the seemingly objective existence could be reached through intersubjective verification. However, unlike Ouyang, in his 1924 essay on consciousness-only, Wang argued that while the objective aspect of eye consciousness gives rise to direct *ālambana* (i.e., a visual image of a seemingly external object like a river), which can vary according to each sentient being's own karma, the objective aspect of *ālayavijñāna* gives rise to indirect *ālambana* (i.e., a seemingly external object like a river), which is shared among the sentient beings of a species. The reason that this objective aspect of *ālayavijñāna* (the part that gives rise to indirect *ālambana*) remains more or less constant within one's lifetime and is shared among sentient beings of the same species, according to Wang, is because of the power of past karma (*suye* 宿業).[48] Hence, different kinds of sentient beings can collectively experience a more or less stable and similar natural environment. According to Wang, because indirect *ālambana* affirms that the seemingly objective world is not solely determined by one's particular mental continuum in this very lifetime, the doctrine of indirect *ālambana* distinguishes Yogācāra from other idealisms and avoids the pitfalls of solipsism.[49]

During his lifetime, Wang consistently sought to differentiate Yogācāra from Western idealism and solipsism from the angles of both philosophical soundness and social function. For example, in 1951, he penned an essay explicitly refuting George Berkeley's (1685–1753) idealism (*guannian lun* 觀念論) that claims ordinary objects as collections of ideas, asserts objects as finite mental substance, and posits an infinite mental substance: God. In his refutations of Berkeleyan idealism, Wang extensively employed the Yogācārin take on dependent arising. Amid his philosophical refutations, he could not resist making fun of Berkeley's notion of God, saying, "When one falls short of originality, one makes it up with God" (*xibugou shenxian cou* 戲不夠神仙湊) This saying had long been weaponized by progressive intellectuals to disparage what they deemed superstitious. Wang also provided ample examples to demonstrate how Yogācāra karmic theory offers a better explanation of the self and the world than Berkeleyan idealism. For instance, he explained the economic function of paper currency in terms of karmic efficacy and *adhipati*. Ultimately, Wang valued Yogācāra because he saw it as the most suitable philosophy in a future complex society without class and without nation-state: Yogācāra teaches no-self and no-God, combines theory with practice, and integrates compassion with wisdom.[50]

At the same time, although Wang thought that each sentient being generates their own cosmos, he believed indirect *ālambana* provided a plausible explanation for why the same kind of sentient beings (say, humans) could reach intersubjective agreement on their shared natural environments arising from shared karmic seeds. Wang saw this sort of intersubjective agreement (e.g., scientific laws) as formed through intersubjective corroboration mediated by language (*mingyan* 名言). Thanks to indirect *ālambana* and similar karma, Wang's Yogācāra intersubjectivity does not suffer the problem of the inverted spectrum: that is, the hypothetical case in which two persons use the same color vocabulary and discriminations but the colors one perceives (i.e., one's private mental images) are systematically different from the colors that the other person perceives. In Wang's theorization, while *adhipati* gives rise to a shared color vocabulary (which can suffer from the problem of the inverted spectrum), indirect *ālambana* and similar karma guarantee that there exists a commonality of mental images of colors that is not merely linguistic convention but the result of similar past actions.

In Wang's Yogācāra paradigm, scientific laws can be discovered through epistemological checks of intersubjective corroborations, coherence, and causal efficacy without presuming an ontologically real, mind-independent external world. Meanwhile, intersubjective verification underpins the soteriological efficacy of teaching because the Buddha's teaching is independent from any particular mental continuum but can be verified or conveyed through language.

Adhipati functions crucially in Wang's theorization of socio-national karma. Wang theorized socio-national karma on multiple occasions. One of the most representative examples can be found in his 1941 lecture notes, "A General Explication of the *Heart Sūtra*."[51] This lecture was given in Chongqing, Sichuan Province, during the throes of the Japanese invasion and after the Nationalist government had relocated to Chongqing. Here, Wang frequently referenced national karma and ways to ameliorate the unfolding disasters caused by the Japanese invasion. Like the first group of Buddhist thinkers, Wang Enyang frequently used collective karma (*gongye*). Yet unlike Taixu, Yuanying, and Yinguang, whose use of *gongye* can be easily misread as karmic confluence, Wang explicitly interpreted *gongye* as intersubjective coactions. In his speech, Wang defined *gongye* as follows:

> [By means of] connected forces and collaborations, things are established by the masses. It is not something that one can accomplish alone. . . . From the smaller deeds such as sustaining the economic life of a family to the bigger enterprises such as governing a nation and a society, because [those deeds] are impossible for one lone individual to achieve and must be accomplished through the collaboration of all, through collective efforts and mutual assistance, it is therefore called *gongye*.

通力合作，事籍眾成，而非一人所能獨造者是也.... 小之一家庭生活之維持，大之一國家社會之組織. 既非一人所能為，必合全體以成事，共力同濟，故名共業.[52]

This excerpt shows that for Wang, that which undergirded the formation of the nation and society was precisely intersubjective collaborations and mutual assistances. Immediately after delivering these lines, Wang explained that uncommon karma (*bugongye* 不共業), or karma particular to one person, could become collective karma if one's action could, through *adhipati*, influence others' actions. Once again, the benefits of seeing the world through Wang's Yogācāra theory of coaction become clear. This worldview not only avoids the pitfalls of rational egoism (which Wang took to be the root of all worldly problems) and nationalism (which Wang took to be a form of collective egoism that validates and abets individual egoism) but also leads to a livable future that equally affirms all sentient beings' desire for life.[53]

This brief examination of selected passages from Wang shows that Wang's Yogācāra social theory clearly distinguishes natural kinds from social kinds. Wang's social theory explains scientific agreements about natural kinds in terms of indirect *ālambana*. It posits social kinds that arise from genuine intersubjective interactions (such as justice, formations of the nation, and transformations of individual karma into collective karma) in terms of *adhipati*. Significantly, Wang's engagement with social ontology was soteriological: his goal was to build a just world plagued by neither nationalism nor egoism.

However, because society was a new category, there was no clear-cut way to refashion it through the lens of traditional Yogācāra doctrines. This openness generated many debates and led to various ways of theorizing Yogācāra sociality-cum-intersubjectivity. As I discuss in part II, Lü Cheng offered another robust social theory grounded in Yogācāra intersubjectivity. Irrespective of their doctrinal differences, both Wang and Lü saw sociality in terms of genuine intersubjectivity and thereby left enough room to theorize an agentless moral agency in their respective Yogācāra social theories. Whereas in conventional Western academic discussions of agency, the disappearing agent is widely regarded as a weakness of event-causal theories, according to the processual philosophies discussed in this chapter, agentlessness is an antidote to the Darwinist competition and moral egoism abetted by substance metaphysics.[54] Furthermore, like society-cum-karmic-confluence, society-cum-intersubjectivity, by assigning society its own karmic mechanism, provides timely scriptural authority for implementing spiritual equality into institutional equality through nonviolent coactions and noncoercive reform.

Society as an Epiphenomenon of Storehouse Consciousnesses

In contrast to the previous two kinds of Yogācāra social theory discussed, strictly speaking, the proposals studied in this section do not consider society as an independent analytic category. At the first sight, because the commitment to storehouse consciousness is a necessary condition, this sort of socio-soteriology seems harder to accept as a form of secularism than the previous two kinds. However, a closer examination shows that this group of thinkers largely saw Yogācāra as a philosophical position rather than a religious commitment. This philosophical reading of Yogācāra makes it possible to position their socio-soteriology as superscription of secularism.

Although the theories' proponents shared the goals of establishing a just society and world peace, they largely reduced social issues to psychological matters and thereby confined their solutions to the framework that is the individualistic soteriology of purifying the mind. Unlike the previous two groups of thinkers, these thinkers' engagements with Yogācāra were motivated by two of three pressing issues. The first was formulating a nondualist understanding of humanity so to enable peaceful coexistence. The second was examining the role of human agency in a scientific world. None of them meaningfully engaged with the issue of social kinds or social facts. Their theories nevertheless warrant scholarly attention as they extended traditional soteriology to subsume both the natural sciences and social sciences. As such, the theories showcase the possibility of participating in the scientific enterprise without submitting to ontological realism.

Wang Xiaoxu is a representative scholar in this group.[55] In the latter half of his life, he devoted considerable time to studying Yogācāra. Most of his writings offer a critique of scientific materialism and psychologism from the Yogācārin perspective. To be sure, his understanding of Yogācāra did not differ significantly from those of the first two groups. Yet with regard to how Yogācāra doctrines explain seemingly objective and intersubjective existences, unsurprisingly, Wang's interpretation diverged significantly from those of the first two groups. Wang largely saw Yogācāra purification of the heart-mind alone as sufficient to address all social issues. Tending toward psychologizing social issues, Wang's proposed solution to social problems was personal spiritual cultivation.

To begin, Wang agreed with Taixu that seemingly objective existences are produced through similar karma. Thus, Wang's critique of scientism focused on the limitations or unfoundedness of the ontological premises undergirding mind-matter dualism and scientific materialism. Wang argued that scientific laws only apply to phenomena produced through similar karma. By reframing scientific laws as a subset of Yogācāra karmic laws, Wang Xiaoxu manufactured a discourse of science as a branch of Buddhism. He asserted,

> Various sorts of scientific inquiries and the commonsense knowledge that science is based on are nothing more than the karmic confluences produced by the similar karmic tracks in the past lives of all human beings.
>
> 種種科學問題，與其所基之常識，皆不過吾人夙生同業所感之總報而已.[56]

Note that Wang Xiaoxu acknowledged the existence of intersubjective resonances. Like Wang Enyang, Wang Xiaoxu saw intersubjective resonances as coming from *adhipati*:

> However, A's consciousness could also be the *adhipati* of B and enable the fruits of the karmic seeds related to the objective aspect of B's *ālayavijñāna*, e.g., A's speech could be heard by B.
>
> 然甲之識亦能為乙之增上緣，使乙之八識相分由種子成熟而生現行；如甲演說，使乙得聞是也.[57]

Despite Wang Xiaoxu's acknowledgment of intersubjective resonances, unlike Wang Enyang, Wang Xiaoxu did not attempt to assign *adhipati* any additional role in explaining social reality. Instead, he held on to an individualist reading of karma and saw personal cultivation as the only way out of the world's troubles. He claimed that "heaven and hell are not other than what resonates with one's own karma" and therefore personal cultivation is enough to transform both oneself and others.[58]

The chief reason that he insisted on individual karma is not because he rejected the concept of collective karma; indeed, he saw karma as both individual and collective. Rather, he rejected the idealist position that karmic rewards and retributions come from other powers such as deities. For example, Wang claimed that in Christianity and Daoism, there are teachings about deities who distribute karmic rewards and retributions. Wang insisted,

> According to the teachings of the Buddha Dharma, good and bad karmic causes produce their own wholesome and unwholesome fruits. Therefore, deities so-and-so are only *adhipati* of such karmic laws.
>
> 依佛法說，則善惡業因自生勝劣果。某某神不過為其增上緣.[59]

In other words, Wang used individual karmic responsibility to distinguish Buddhism from other religions and used karmic confluence to subsume science into the Yogācāra worldview.

That said, other than criticizing scientific materialism and historical materialism, Wang never explicitly proposed his own social theory. One reason might be that Wang's chief goal was to position Yogācāra as a new paradigm of producing knowledge, in which society or social knowledge is seen as a derivative of karmic connections among different *ālayavijñānas*. The unstated premise is that if everyone follows the Buddhist path and purifies their own mental continuum, society will naturally become peaceful. Among the Chinese Yogācārins, Wang Xiaoxu hewed closest to the imported vision of society as the sum of its individuals.

This line of thought was common among Republican Buddhist thinkers. For example, Monk Yinshun 印順 (1906–2005), another renowned proponent of Humanistic Buddhism who was seen by many as the Dharma heir of Taixu, affirmed a similar interpretation of individual karma. In a short essay titled "Three Principles of Learning Buddhism" (Xuefo sanyao 學佛三要), Yinshun claimed,

> To make the world pure and glorious, the only hope is that everyone does good and avoids evil.
>
> 要世界清淨和莊嚴，也唯有人人能行善止惡，才有希望.

He further asserted,

> If social relations are built according to Buddha dharma, then it necessarily becomes a system of teachers and friends, which is conducive to the spirit of democracy.
>
> 以佛法而構成社會關係，必然爲師友文化體系，適合於民主自由的精神.[60]

Like Wang Xiaoxu, Yinshun saw Buddhist soteriology itself as sufficient to bring forth a just, peaceful, and democratic society. Indeed, to the best of my knowledge, many Buddhist intellectuals took it for granted that once everyone followed the Buddhist ways of knowing and acting, social relations would become harmonious. Social reform was thereby rendered secondary to one's own soteriological pursuit. Other modern Yogācārins such as Han Qingjing 韓清淨 (1884–1949), Zhu Feihuang 朱芾煌 (1885–1942), and Zhou Shujia 周叔迦 (1899–1970) also turned to Yogācāra solely for its soteriological efficacy.[61]

At first glance, this group of thinkers may seem less revolutionary than either of the first two groups. However, a peruse of the thinkers' biographies reveals that many of them engaged deeply with science and revolution before turning to Yogācāra. For example, in 1909, Zhu Feihuang joined the United League (Tongmenghui 同盟會), the underground resistance movement founded by the father of the nation, Sun Yat-sen, and served in the interim Nanjing Republican government after the 1911 Xinhai Revolution. But in 1922, he turned to Yogācāra, studied with Han Qingjing, and wrote a three-million-word dictionary of Yogācāra terms. Zhou Shujia, though he never dabbled with revolution, started his career as an engineer before turning to Buddhism and Yogācāra in the 1930s.

Although these Buddhist intellectuals saw social issues as an epiphenomenon of soteriology, at least some among them such as Wang Xiaoxu cared enough to explain why science does not need ontological realism and why the Yogācāra worldview offers a different social imagination yet still leaves room for both science and moral agency. Even though the belief in a storehouse consciousness seems a precondition, at least for thinkers like Wang Xiaoxu, this commitment was more of a philosophical investment than a putatively "religious" belief and thereby was more open to incorporating other religious beliefs into its fold. Of course, regardless of whether these thinkers participated in revolution or reform, their proposals to build a just society were consistently nonviolent and espoused a secular symmetry.

Society as a Subset of a Universal Oneness

One more group of Buddhist thinkers deserves our attention for their far-reaching impact in popularizing Yogācāra as a sociopolitical theory. In contrast to the previous three groups of thinkers, the Buddhist intellectuals studied in this section could hardly be seen to be Yogācārins or even Buddhists, even though some of them self-identified as such. Notably, all the scholars discussed in this chapter are widely seen as advocates of secularism. Although they shared a keen interest in repurposing Yogācāra philosophy to resolve social issues, they lacked in-depth knowledge of this rich tradition. Unsurprisingly, they often mistook Yogācāra for a form of idealist realism: they questioned the objective existence of material entities yet took for granted that *ālayavijñāna* is a universal existence independent of the individual psyche. Their respective social theories varied but their engagements with Yogācāra were motivated by the same single pressing issue: the role of human agency in a scientific world.

Strictly speaking, because of the thinkers' misreadings of Yogācāra, especially their understanding of *ālayavijñāna* as a form of universal oneness, it is appropriate to classify their theories as Huayan-Tiantai-influenced Buddhist social theories. Zhang Taiyan, Li Jinxin, and Cai Yuanpei, all of whom Lü criticized during the debates about social Darwinism and Yogācāra as analyzed in chapter 1, belong to this group. Recall that all three started as anti-Machu revolutionaries and/or reformers. By the 1920s and 1930s, they all saw Yogācāra as a resource for establishing a just society through nonviolent means such as education and self-cultivation.

In particular, they all conflated *ālayavijñāna* with Bergsonian *élan vital*. These thinkers' interpretations significantly deviated from the mainstream Yogācāra understanding of *ālayavijñāna* as particular to each sentient being and something that must be relinquished after one arrives at the stage of arhat.[62] Their interpretation of *ālayavijñāna* as the universal consciousness most likely stemmed from their reading of the influential treatise *Awakening Faith*, which frequently appears in the commentarial traditions of East Asian Buddhism and explicitly asserts that *ālayavijñāna* can subsume and engender all dharmas.[63]

Zhang Taiyan is a case in point. As discussed in chapter 1, in 1921, the influential periodical *People's Bell* published several special issues promoting social Darwinism and Bergsonian creative evolution. Both Zhang Taiyan and Li Jinxi contributed essays and expressed their views of *ālayavijñāna* as Bergsonian *élan vital*. In the published abridged letters addressed to Lü Cheng, Zhang insisted that Bergson must have directly experienced *ālayavijñāna* because *élan vital* refers to the "physiological impulse, which is precisely *ālayavijñāna*" (*shengli chongdong jishi zangshi* 生理衝動即是藏識).[64] Hence, Zhang was arguably more of a Bergsonian than a Yogācārin. In addition, many Chinese intellectuals like Zhang read both Bergsonism and Yogācāra as forms of idealist monism.[65] In a later issue, *People's Bell* published a letter by Li Jinxi commenting on Zhang Taiyan and Lü Cheng's debate. In his letter, Li supported Zhang's conflation of *élan vital* with *ālayavijñāna* and evaluated Zhang's points as "thorough and incisive talk" (*jingdao zhi tan* 精到之譚). Li further asserted that everything from consciousness to mountains and rivers, from the beginningless past to the endless future, was a manifestation of *ālayavijñāna*.[66]

This kind of idealist reading of *ālayavijñāna* as a universal life force seems to have been quite popular among intellectuals who only had an impressionistic understanding of Buddhism. Cai Yuanpei followed this trend. In his 1932 preface to Wang Xiaoxu's *A Comparative Study of Buddha Dharma and Science*, Cai likened *ālayavijñāna* to Bergsonian *élan vital* and interpreted both as the "flow of life" (*shengming liu* 生命流) or "a form of an original force of life" (*yizhong shengming de yuandongli* 一種生命原動力).[67] However, unlike Zhang Taiyan and Li Jinxi who saw Buddhism, especially Yogācāra, in favorable terms, by 1932 Cai Yuanpei had already positioned himself firmly within the scientific camp.[68] He suggested that Wang Xiaoxu use scientific methods to prove the existence of rebirth, thereby proving that Buddhism is equivalent to "scientific" theories such as Bergsonian creative evolution.

More detrimental than their casual appropriation of Yogācāra terms, this group of thinkers reduced society to a subset of a universal life flow. Consequently, they did not see the necessity of creating an independent social theory outside the paradigms of either Buddhist soteriology (Zhang Taiyan and Li Jinxi) or science (Cai Yuanpei). Instead, they took Yogācāra out of context and placed it within a realm in which they themselves felt competent to make claims. These thinkers also firmly believed in the compatibility of Buddhism and science and trusted that scientific authority alone could distinguish authentic Buddhism from superstition. As such, strictly speaking, none of their theories could be counted as a socio-soteriology.

Ironically, their appropriation of Yogācāra turned into a blessing for the Chinese Yogācāra revival. This is because these thinkers engaged with Buddhism as a potential equal to Western science and philosophy. Given the thinkers' high social status at the time, their misreadings granted Yogācāra a cultural aura it did not have in either the traditional Buddhist world or the newly emerging secular nation-state. In this sense, the thinkers' appropriation of Yogācāra elevated Buddhism in the minds of a generation of students and intellectuals who later became receptive to more sophisticated Yogācāra social theories.

A Nonviolent, Nonhierarchical, Complex Society Is Thinkable

In surveying Lü Cheng's Yogācāra socio-evolutionism in chapter 1, Yan Fu's invention of a Yogācāra national karma in chapter 2, and the four kinds of Yogācāra social theory in the current chapter, we have come full circle. Yan Fu's initial melding of Yogācāra and Darwinism and Zhang Taiyan's misreading of *ālayavijñāna* as *élan vital* worked in tandem to raise the visibility of this ancient Buddhist philosophy among revolutionaries and progressive thinkers. The modern aura of Yogācāra motivated a more serious engagement with Yogācāra as social philosophy on the part of Lü Cheng and his cohorts of students at the China Inner Learning Institute. These early versions led to the proliferation of various Yogācāra social theories proposed by experts and amateurs alike and kindled a yearning among the Chinese intellectuals for a deeper understanding of this ancient tradition. Yogācāra socio-soteriologies exerted a larger influence on the making of modern China than scholars have thus far been willing to recognize.

Methodologically, the lens of socio-soteriology has helped me uncover many incidences in which premodern, pragmatic, soteriological exercises in Buddhism were reinvented by diverse Chinese thinkers with drastically different philosophical orientations to serve the shared goal of building a better future with care and compassion. Indeed, one can identify a common thread between the Chinese Yogācāra thinkers and the non-Chinese pragmatists and feminists: they all saw philosophy as an instrument for social reform. For example, feminist philosophers have long argued for the necessity of engaging with two kinds of academic projects. One is the descriptive that analyzes what is and what has been. The other is the ameliorative that investigates which concepts we should be using given our purpose in those inquiries.[69] In hindsight, the Chinese thinkers studied in this chapter took it as a self-evident truth that the scholarly enterprise ought to be an ameliorative project.

This pragmatic concern was not unique to these Chinese philosophers. For example, William James saw truths as "species of the good" that bridge loyalty to facts and confidence in human values.[70] John Dewey saw philosophy as a form of "criticism of criticisms" and sought to integrate philosophical inquiries into the mission of "education-for-living."[71] Both James and Dewey used philosophical tools to address unresolved but important social inquiries. This convergence is not accidental: in fact, William James had studied Buddhist psychology quite extensively, and at the height of the New Culture Movement, John Dewey taught at Peking University, where Yogācāra studies had started to gain traction among progressive students.[72]

Noticing these parallels constitutes only an initial foray into the worldwide revival of processual thoughts of which Yogācāra socio-soteriologies are a part. Though they suggest a radically different and often counterintuitive way of construing humanity and worldliness, these Yogācāra socio-soteriologies can be cogent, coherent, and compelling in their own ways. They narrate other stories about how we become human, how things work, and most important, how the world could be otherwise.

PART II

Liberation Buddhology

Lü Cheng's ameliorative project of producing Buddhist knowledge for collective liberation had three strands: (1) the psychological structure of Buddhability-cum-humanity that guides the aspiring bodhisattva's moment-by-moment actions in a world devolving into the Darwinist chaos, (2) the institutional structure grounded in *Yoga Bodhisattva Precepts* that encourages the aspiring bodhisattva to lead a courageous life of caring for all sentient beings, and (3) the epistemic structure, which I term "transformative epistemology," which calls for a radical vision of engaged scholarship produced by the academy and communities in partnership. Having emerged at a time when the Chinese moral fabric was breaking down and a new world was struggling to be born, Lü's liberation Buddhology invites readers to meditate together on the ever-pressing questions of how to learn to die as a culture, how to change referents, and how to struggle for a rebirth together.

4

Buddhability as Humanity

The *raison d'être* of humans is that they can become buddhas.
眾生之存在價值，謂其能成佛耳.
Therefore, only humans can be the support for this world.
故勘為世間依止者唯人.
Humans can spread Dharma. Apart from spreading Dharma, there are no other human affairs.
人能弘道，弘道外無人事.

—Lü Cheng, 1943

Making a new society necessarily begins with a new vision of what humans are, can become, and ought to do. As the epigraphs show, Lü redefined the value of human existence as the ability to achieve buddhahood and refashioned human affairs as the actions of practicing and spreading Dharma. In doing so, Lü fundamentally changed the terms of debate on what makes a person human from the ontological perspective of human *being* to the Yogācāra-informed processual view of human *propensity*, whose renewal is effected by the way that the situation (of actions and coactions) tends to lean (French: *pencher*).[1] Simultaneously coming into view was the action-oriented moral reasoning of human interconditioning.[2] Lü's new paradigm of Buddhisized human propensity, which I term "Buddhability-cum-humanity," has broad implications for ongoing discussions about how to build a livable future.[3]

As the first of three core strands in Lü's social process philosophy of building a just, nonviolent society, Buddhability-cum-humanity was Lü's way of engaging with the global debate about how to become modern. Although Charles Taylor has approached the question of being human in modern times by tracing the modern notion of "what it is to be a human agent" in Anglo-European cultures, I broaden the inquiry into humanity by highlighting the overlooked notions of *doing* and *living* in the making of modern China.[4] Indeed, from the renowned philosopher-cum-reformer and the progenitor of Chinese nationalism Liang Qichao's (1873–1929) essay "On New People" (Xinmin shuo 新民說; 1902) to the Chinese Communist discourse on the "New Man," historical actors who wished to reshape Chinese culture, society, and the state integrated into their projects different answers to the enduring question of what makes a person human.[5] While the details of the proposals vary, the core Chinese belief in human perfectibility seems only to become stronger. Lü is no exception to this enduring pattern. By merging bodhisattva ideal with the Chinese model of sages and saints (*shengxian* 聖賢), Lü's liberation Buddhology Buddhisized human perfectibility and offered a highly adaptable psychological framework in which the entire perceptual world of experiences and actions could be evaluated.

Lü's Buddhability-cum-humanity hinges crucially on a curious reversal of a widely accepted doctrine that Dharma is the support (*yi* 依) for the world. As seen in the epigraphs to the chapter, Lü turned this cherished teaching on its head. He matter-of-factly stated that humans, not Dharma, are the support for the world. It is worth noting that Lü made similar statements during his lectures on *Five Disciplines in Three phases* (*wuke sanzhou* 五科三週; henceforth, *Five Disciplines*). To downplay the subversiveness of this reversal, Lü performed sophisticated interpretational gymnastics and cited many Pāli, Sanskrit, Tibetan, and Chinese canonical sources to demonstrate the alignment of his liberation Buddhology with traditional values. I will stitch together these textual threads to present a fuller understanding of the karma-informed, action-oriented moral reasoning in Lü's socio-soteriology.

Five Disciplines and Three Phases: A Sketch

In October 1943, eight months after his teacher Ouyang Jingwu had passed away, Lü became the leader of the China Inner Learning Institute and launched his own training program, *Five Disciplines* (see table 4.1 for the curriculum). In his opening lecture, Lü identified his program as "Yuanxue" 院學, that is, the Institute's Learning. In doing so, he announced his institution-building intention. Lü defined Yuanxue as a revival of the famous monastic learning center in ancient India, Nālandā, where the Chinese monks and translators Xuanzang (602–664 CE) and Yijing (635–713 CE) had studied.[6] In Lü's imagined lineage, Xuanzang and Yijing were the pivotal figures who had brought the complete Buddhist teachings from India to China.[7] Lü also announced the goal of Yuanxue: to launch a bodhisattva enterprise of saving oneself and helping all living beings achieve buddhahood.[8]

> The Lectures of *Five Disciplines* are established according to our late teacher [Ouyang Jingwu]'s treatise *On Teaching*. The aim is to directly point to the essential and the subtle so that one can pursue advanced studies step by step. For this reason, [I] have edited and arranged many texts and divided them into three phases. Each phase is organized under one central theme. If [one] studies them frequently and analyzes them repeatedly, after three to five years, one will surely enter the Dao.
>
> 五科講習乃依先師釋教之說而立，意在直指精微，以階深造，故編次群書，三周區別。周各以一要義貫通，反覆研尋，曆三五載，亦可入道矣.[9]

This passage lays out the Institute's Learning as a soteriological path in three phases. This path must be trod sequentially and with the end goal of entering the Way. It is important to note that Lü designed this directly pointing (*zhizhi* 直指) path to the essential and the subtle (*jingwei* 精微) to be accessible to all in a limited time frame (three to five years) in this very life. Compared to the premodern bodhisattva ideal that demands eons of practices over many lifetimes, Lü's training program represents a fast track.[10]

Lü presented *Five Disciplines* as the root of Yuanxue and a systematic integration of Buddhology into soteriology.[11] At first glance, readers might mistake *Five Disciplines* for a program to train Buddhologists because all of the texts were selected from the high-quality scholarly editions in *Essentials*. However, as shown in the aforementioned quotation, the goal of *Five Disciplines* is clearly soteriological: that is, to orient experiences and guide actions to "enter the Dao." The significance of Lü's systemization of inner learning was immediately recognized by contemporaneous Buddhist intellectuals as "the stroke that dotted the eye of the dragon," an idiom emphasizing the finishing touch on an artwork that gives the work a soul.[12] In both its immediate reception in the 1940s and contemporary academic discourse, Lü's project has been perceived as a return to Buddhism's Indian origin: namely, the monastic and Tantric learning center named Nālandā (ca. 700–1200 CE). This reception is understandable as Ouyang and Lü themselves both asserted that they intended to reestablish genuine Buddhism modeled after Nālandā.

However, when looking beyond the rhetoric of genuine Buddhism, it becomes evident that Lü wove a new tapestry of disciplinary studies from Nālandā's textual remains. As I argue in chapter 6, Lü employed the Nālandā model to build a new intellectual community motivated by the goal of producing knowledge for co-liberation. For now it suffices to note that in 1943, when Lü recounted the intentions of his earlier scholarship, especially his own work *A Brief History of Indian Buddhism*, he claimed that he ended the book with Nālandā because he wanted to underline "the fact that Indian Buddhist

TABLE 4.1. Curriculum of Five Disciplines

	The First Phase	*The Second Phase*	*The Third Phase*
Essential Teaching	*Original Quiescence*	*Revolutionizing Consciousness (Skt: āśrayaparivṛtti)*	*One True-reality Dharma Realm*
Abhidharma	*Dhammapada* *The Heart of Abhidharma*	*An Abhidharmic Reading of the Four Āgamas* *Root Verses of Abhidharma-kośa-bhāṣya* *Root Verses of Mahāyānābhidharmasūtra* *Compendium of Abhidharma*	*Compendium of Dharma* *Treatise on Entering Abhidharma* *Treatise on the Four Noble Truths* *Selections from Kathāvatthu*
Prajñā	*The Diamond Sūtra* *Root Verses of Resources for Bodhi*	*The Vimalakīrti Sūtra* *The Sūtra on the Great Perfection of Wisdom* *The Treatise on the Great Perfection of Wisdom* *Fundamental Verses on the Middle Way*	*The Great Perfection of Wisdom—The Mañjuśrī Chapter* *A Compendium of the Perfection of Wisdom* *Commentary on the Four Hundred [Stanzas of Madhyamaka]* *Jewels in the Hand Treatise*
Yogācāra	*The Great Ornament Sūtra* *Verses Distinguishing the Middle and the Extremes*	*Noble Sūtra of the Explanation of the Profound Secrets* *Bodhisattvabhūmi* *Acclamation of the Holy Teaching* *Compendium of the Great Vehicle*	*Seven Selected Chapters from the Avataṃsaka Sūtra* *Explanation of the Investigation of Objective Bases* *The Jewel-Arising Treatise on Establishing Consciousness-only* *Selections from Establishing Consciousness-only*

Nirvāṇa	*The Sūtra of the Lion's Roar of Queen Śrīmālā* *Treatise on the Nonduality of Mahāyāna Dharmadhātu*	*The Lotus Sūtra* *Mahāparinirvāṇa Sūtra—The Chapter of True Dharma* *Laṅkāvatāra Sūtra* *Stanzas from the Treatise of the Ultimate One-Vehicle Jewel Lineage*	*The Great Cloud Sūtra—The Chapter on the Great Assembly* *The Sūtra on the Invisible Splendor of the Mahāyāna* *Treatise on the Buddha-Stage Sūtra*
Vinaya	*Vaipulya Sūtra of the Pure Vinaya* *Yoga Bodhisattva Prātimokṣa and Karman*	*The Inquiry of the Householder Ugra*	*Collection of Six Perfections Sūtra* *Deeds of the Buddha*
Supplementary Readings	*The Path of Liberation* *Six Doors of Teaching Dhyāna*	*Introduction to Logic* *Flower Ornament Sūtra—The Chapter on Cultivating Compassion*	*Selected Passages from Compendium of Validities* *Sūtra of the Questions of Bodhisattva Ākāśagarbha—The Section on Deciding and Selecting*

Learning ended here [with Nālandā] and Chinese Buddhist Learning started from here [Nālandā]."[13] Lü actualized this earlier claim with his careful design of *Five Disciplines* and meticulous selection of texts. According to Lü's outline, the five disciplines include four disciplines of teaching (*jiao* 教), namely, Abhidharma, Prajñā, Yogācāra, and Nirvāṇa, and a fifth discipline of precepts (*jie* 戒), Vinaya.[14]

Equally important, as seen in the list of supplementary readings associated with each phase, Lü combined trainings in meditation and reasoning into one method to complement the textual learning at each phase. Notably, the disciplines that constitute Lü's program differ from the five disciplines of Nālandā: Hetuvidyā, Abhidharma, Prajñā, Yogācāra, and Vinaya.[15] Lü's blueprint also diverges from Ouyang's curriculum, in which textual studies (*wenzi* 文字) and meditative absorption (Ch: *sanmei* 三昧; Skt: *samādhi*) are two separate categories and teachings and precepts are divided into two bounded yet related forms of training.[16] Lü even claimed that in the earliest Buddhist discourses, there was no distinction between *sūtra* and *vinaya* and that this separation was a later development.[17]

In *Five Disciplines*, textual analysis, meditative training, precepts, and teaching are remixed into five disciplines and arranged into three progressive phases: (1) the first phase, which aims at realizing original quiescence (*xingji* 性寂), (2) the second phase, which focuses on revolutionizing consciousness (Ch: *zhuanyi* 轉依; Skt: *āśrayaparivṛtti*; Tib: *gnas yongs su 'gyur pa*), and (3) the third phase, which brings forth one true-reality dharma realm (*yizhen fajie* 一真法界).

Most pertinent to understanding Lü's innovation of Buddhability-cum-humanity is that in *Five Disciplines*, hetuvidyā (Buddhist logic) is no longer an independent subject but is integrated into the meditative training spread across all three phases in the form of supplemental readings. A new discipline named Nirvāṇa replaced hetuvidyā to become the fifth discipline.

The Discipline of Nirvāṇa

By design, all teachings in *Five Disciplines* converge to a new interpretation of nirvāṇa and cohere in a new discipline called Nirvāṇa. The springboard for this path is original quiescence (the essence of the first phase)—nirvāṇa as cause, that is, the aspect of nirvāṇa that can be accessed by the conditioned. Diverse teachings are consolidated into one path by *āśrayaparivṛtti* (revolutionizing consciousness), the essence of the second phase. The perfection of this path is one true-reality dharma realm (the essence of the third phase)—nirvāṇa as outcome, that is, the unconditioned, ultimate liberation. Note that one true-reality dharma realm, in Lü's paradigm, is nondual, especially regarding the duality of individuality and society. Instead, it connotes something inherent to streams of consciousnesses (*xin xiangxu* 心相續) that is manifested through shared phenomena (*wei gongxiang zhi suo xian ye* 為共相之所顯也).[18] In short, the new discipline Nirvāṇa embodies a transpersonal doctrinal oneness, which is the alpha and omega of the ongoing process of revolutionizing consciousness. The actualization of this doctrinal oneness is none other than one true-reality dharma realm, which calls to mind Lü's intersubjective oneness as an aesthetic society.

In Lü's own words, nirvāṇa marks both the root (*genben* 根本) and the ultimate goal (*guisu* 歸宿) of this bodhisattva path of co-liberation and hence legitimizes the dynamic wholeness of his training program.[19] Immediately after making this claim, Lü Cheng identified the disciplines of Prajñā and Yogācāra as both the pragmatic application (*shijian* 實踐) and the finger that points toward home (*zhigui* 指歸), that is, an experience-based, action-oriented ethical training. As the root cause, nirvāṇa is manifested as the originally quiescent consciousness (*xingji zhi xin* 性寂之心).[20] As the ultimate goal, nirvāṇa is manifested as the achievement of intersubjective buddhahood, which is synonymous with one true-reality dharma realm:

> The fundamental nature of the buddha is the dharma realm. The dharma realm is the realm of nirvāṇa. That is to say, the fundamental nature of the buddha is nirvāṇa. This clarifies why a buddha is a buddha.
>
> 佛以法界為體性，法界即涅槃界，是即以涅槃為體性，乃明佛之所以為佛也.[21]

Here, nirvāṇa itself is reimagined as a path, including both the beginning and the end, both the cause and the effect, enabled by and enabling diverse social and historical configurations in different space-times. Simultaneously, the realm of nirvāṇa, a.k.a. buddhahood, is precisely one true-reality dharma realm that includes all beings (hence transpersonal) bounded by karmic processes and the processes of purification, or a nirvāṇic interconditioning.[22] Readers familiar with the vast literature on the pan-Asian debates about Yogācāra and Tathāgatagarbha might feel that Lü's reading of nirvāṇa is too similar to that of the sworn enemy of Yogācāra (as portrayed in mainstream scholarship on East Asian Buddhism), the Tathāgatagarbha school.[23] To fully capture Lü's position in this complex debate would require an independent book-length study; for the purposes of the current chapter, it suffices to note that Lü stayed within the bounds of a weak *Tathāgatagarbha* reading.[24] His key terms such as original quiescence, nirvāṇa, original purity, buddhahood, and *dharmakāya* (dharma body) all refer to the unconditioned dharma that can be made accessible to commoners through the bodhisattvas' subsequent awareness.

Furthermore, for Lü, the discipline of Nirvāṇa marked both the culmination of Buddhism and the authenticity of the Chinese transmission. On the one hand, he expanded the traditional meaning of buddhahood to include all social and historical configurations and made buddhahood a foundation for a transpersonal and intersubjective oneness. In this way, Lü revealed his social imagination of infinite spiritual co-progress. On the other hand, Lü further substantiated his claim that this "genuine" interpretation of buddhahood as intersubjective oneness was preserved in Chinese Yogācāra thanks only to Xuanzang's effort. He singled out two texts in this discipline of the third phase, *Dacheng miyan jing* 大乘密嚴經 (*The Sūtra on the Invisible Splendor of the Mahāyāna*; Skt: *Ghanavyūha Sūtra*; T.681), which Lü attributed to Dharmapāla, and *Fodi jinglun* 佛地經論 (*Treatise on the Buddha-Stage Sūtra*; Skt: *Buddhabhūmi-sūtra-śāstra*; T.1530), which Lü attributed to Śīlabhadra. Note that both Dharmapāla and Śīlabhadra, according to Chinese Yogācāra traditions, were Xuanzang's master teachers at Nālandā. As captured in table 4.1, Lü asserted,

> These two texts were the final conclusion of Nālandā learning and the beginning of the Chinese translation of Nālandā learning. Xuanzang's learning originates here [from these two texts].
> 又此二籍為那寺講學最後之結論.而為華譯那寺學說之開端.奘師之學即從此出也.[25]

Further, readers can sense the significance of the discipline of Nirvāṇa in how Lü shortened the program when pressed for time. In August 1945, after Japan unexpectedly surrendered to China, Lü and his colleagues made plans to move the Inner Learning Institute back to Nanjing. At the time, Lü was already halfway through the first phase of his program. But present circumstances required that he shorten this three-phase training. After completing all five disciplines of the first phase, he skipped directly to the discipline of Nirvāṇa in the second phase.[26] He finished lecturing on three of the four texts outlined in the discipline of Nirvāṇa of the second phase, aborted the training, and never had the chance to teach it again. Yet the parting words of this abortive program, located in the discipline of Nirvāṇa, gesture toward the heart of Lü's revolutionary nonviolence.[27]

Revolutionizing Consciousness in Three Phases

While the discipline of Nirvāṇa gestures toward the ultimate teaching, the three phases in *Five Disciplines* manifest the path of Lü's Yogācāra socio-soteriology, which is *zhuanyi* 轉依 (Skt: *āśrayaparivṛtti*; Tib: *gnas yongs su 'gyur pa*).[28] This path is firmly grounded in Yogācāra soteriology. The focus in this section is the relationship between this three-phase *āśrayaparivṛtti* and Lü's revolutionary nonviolence.[29]

I translate Lü's use of *āśrayaparivṛtti* as "revolutionizing consciousness" to throw into relief his lifetime endeavor to remake the world through nonviolent strategies such as scholarship, self-cultivation, and transformative epistemology.[30] In Yogācāra classics, *āśrayaparivṛtti*, its Tibetan translation *gnas yongs su 'gyur pa*, and its Chinese translation all referred to a fundamental transformation of the mental basis. In Xuanzang's Chinese translation, *zhuan* 轉 indicates "turn away" or "turn to" and *yi* 依 means "basis" or "support." Whereas the sense of "fundamental" is implied in the Sanskrit and Chinese terms, the Tibetan translation makes it explicit as *yongs su* (totally), which captures more Lü's use of it. My use of "revolutionizing consciousness" is intended to foreground Lü's consistent interpretation of revolution not as a violent political movement but as a fundamental change of attitude toward all living beings and living processes, from his 1920s quest for an aesthetic uprising to the making of the Institute's Learning in 1943 and to the 1950s when he paraphrased *zhuanyi* as a new paradigm (*xin fanchou* 新範疇) of liberation (*jietuo* 解脱), i.e., remaking this world (*zhuanshi* 轉世).[31] Notably, the term *yi* is part of Lü's *siyiren* 四依人, which refers to the four kinds of humans as the worldly support. Reading these two terms together, one can readily recognize the resonance between revolutionizing consciousness and transforming the worldly support. This parallel underscores that *Five Disciplines* is the fruit of the seeds of aesthetic revolution, which matured into a path of co-liberation in three phases (see table 4.1).

The first phase grounds the path of liberation directly in the realization of the original quiescence of consciousness, with nirvāṇa as the cause of liberation:

> The first phase is focused on the original quiescence of consciousness. Once [one] realizes that the [originally quiescent] consciousness exists [at this moment], then this learning happens. Therefore, if there is the [realization of this originally quiescent] consciousness, then this learning exists. It is different from what permeates from the outside. This is called knowing the root.
>
> 初周，主於心性本寂，自覺有此心，而後有此學，故心存則學存，異於外鑠，此之謂知本.[32]

Importantly, Lü saw learning and the meditative realization as interconditioned: if one arises, the other arises. Notably, original quiescence, in Ouyang and Lü's interpretation, was a synthesis of different concepts such as original purity and nirvāṇa in Yogācāra hermeneutics.[33] Knowledge and practice are thus also interconditioned, a point that undercuts the dominant reading of Lü's Buddhology as purely objective scholarship. To substantiate his aforementioned claim, in the rest of the outline, Lü Cheng first equated original quiescence with the early Indian Buddhist claim, "The nature of the mind-heart is originally pure but defiled by guest dust" (*xinxing benjing kechen suoran* 心性本淨客塵所染).[34]

In fact, by performing years of meticulous multilingual comparative analysis, Lü had identified this passage as the foundation of all Buddhist teachings. He integrated this concept into his explications of the five sūtras and seven treatises in the first phase. Lü contended that once one realized this original quiescence, this original quiescence (an unconditioned dharma) would no longer be different from the momentarily arising and disappearing of psychological events in *ālayavijñāna*. By grafting learning onto an unconditioned and originally quiescent consciousness inherent in all living beings, Lü differentiated Yuanxue from other imported education models such as Cai Yuanpei's aesthetic education, which Lü criticized as a form of environmental determinism that served only to perpetuate Darwinist devolution.

Learning is more than acquiring objective knowledge. Lü grounded learning in a path motivated by a moral purpose. On the one hand, this approach calls to mind the contemporary feminist injunction to engage with ameliorative projects in scholarship.[35] On the other hand, because Lü melded the training and textual analysis with meditative insight, this approach reflects a continuation of the Nālandā scholastic-soteriological quest. Lü was confident that this initial realization of original quiescence would inspire one to emulate the sages (*jianxian siqi* 見賢思齊), alluding to the enduring Chinese belief in human perfectibility. At the same time, it hearkened back to his 1920s notion of aesthetic awakening as a means to emulate artists and art critics—that is, the leaders of the joint-awakening enterprise. In 1943 Lü not only reframed the notions of awakening and revolution in Buddhist terms but also argued that if one could maintain this insight of original quiescence without forgetting, then Buddhist learning indeed sprung from searching deep within instead of acquiring external knowledge.[36]

Lü presented this reweaving of scholastic effort and meditative insight in the very first text in his curriculum, *Dhammapada*, a variant translation that parallels the Chinese translation-compilation the *Forty-Two Sections Sūtra*.[37] It is telling that Lü began his program with the Chinese translation of a sūtra outside the four Āgamas.[38] Lü justified his choice by arguing that because the language was plain, accessible, and rich in meaning, the text must be an accurate record of the Buddha's words.[39] However, to unpack the unsaid meanings in Lü's discourse, one must understand two subtexts. First, the *Forty-Two*

Sections Sūtra had long been seen by Chinese Buddhists as an authentic translation, and the very first Buddhist scripture translated into Chinese whose preface records its own transmission history: namely, the legend of how Emperor Ming of Han (28–75 CE) dreamed about the Buddha. Second, the 1750 French translation of the *Forty-Two Sections Sūtra* by Joseph de Guignes is the earliest European translation of Buddhist texts and was believed to be representative of the "original teaching" in early European Buddhological circles.[40]

By starting *Five Disciplines* with an earlier version of this legendary text that was accepted by both Chinese Buddhists and European Buddhologists as fundamental, Lü Cheng made an implicit claim to the legitimacy of both Chinese translations and Yuanxue: only the careful comparative studies of the Chinese translations of *Dhammapada* alongside their extant Pāli and classical Tibetan parallels as well as Sanskrit fragments could uncover the true history of transmitted texts and to extract the genuine principles of the Buddha.[41]

Doctrinally, *Dhammapada* enabled Lü to graft his own interpretation of original quiescence onto what contemporaneous Buddhists and Buddhologists deemed the earliest layer of transmitted Buddhist teaching. He opened his lecture on *Dhammapada* by pointing out that the central tenet of this text is precisely the "originally pure heart defiled by guest dust."[42] Simultaneously, Lü retooled this well-known phrase for establishing bodhisattva learning by presenting "perfuming through hearing" (Ch: *wenxun* 聞熏; Skt: *śrutavāsanā*) as the most proper method of washing off guest dust.[43]

To further tie *Dhammapada* to what he had identified as the foundational tenet—original quiescence—Lü Cheng linked *Dhammapada*'s teaching of original purity to *Bian zhongbian lun* 辯中邊論 (Distinguishing the middle from the extremes; Skt: *Madhyāntavibhāga*; T.1600; henceforth, *MAV*), a multilayered text whose root verses are attributed to Maitreya and whose commentary is attributed to Vasubandhu. *MAV* is a critical text in Lü's discipline of Yogācāra of the first phase. Lü argued that *MAV* reframes the original purity of consciousness in terms of relinquishment (*jimie* 寂滅) and quiescence (*jijing* 寂靜).[44] By borrowing arguments in *MAV*, Lü Cheng mapped out a progression from the earlier limited teaching of original purity to a more developed concept of original quiescence that culminates in the Yogācāra teaching of the perfected nature. As expected of a Buddhologist, Lü buried this argument in an interlinear note:

> The Perfected Nature: In old translations, the perfected is actualized-ness. This is to say it is quiescent by nature. It is not other things that make it quiescent. This is known as its innate nature, which is actualized purity and cleanness.

> 圓成實自性 (舊譯圓成為成就性, 谓其自性本寂, 非餘法使然, 即本性成就清淨之谓).[45]

None of his chosen terms deviates from those used in earlier Chinese translations. Nevertheless, the new conceptual construct of doctrinal unfolding is evident: from *Dhammapada*'s original purity to original quiescence in *MAV*, and finally to the Yogācāra doctrine of the perfected nature. Long before making this claim, Lü had devoted his time and energy to substantiating this invented discourse of doctrinal unfolding by making historical and philosophical connections.

Indeed, he had started this task as early as 1924 when he first wrote about comparative hermeneutics. In this essay, Lü described the significance of the "cross-examination of similar terminologies rendered in different sūtras" (*yijing tongshi zhi bijiao* 異經同事之比較), which required a chronological comparison of all variant interpretations of *ālayavijñāna*, from original purity to *Tathāgatagarbha*, the Buddha nature; to nirvāṇa as the outcome of liberation; and to many other ontological synonyms of the unconditioned dharmas.[46] In 1943 the import of this case study in Lü's 1924 methodological reflections became fully manifested: original quiescence is innate to consciousness, the latter of which also lies at the heart of Lü's curriculum of co-liberation.

While the first phase puts Yuanxue on firm textual ground, the second phase paints a bright future for practitioners on the path: once original quiescence manifests itself in the first instance, consciousness itself will "naturally" propel one toward the unstoppable process of abandoning afflictions and approaching purity. According to Lü,

> This second phase is to exhaust the function of consciousness. Once the characteristics of quiescence become manifest, then true wisdom abundantly swells. Thus, [the process] of discarding afflictions and turning toward purity will surely be set on the track of revolutionizing consciousness and thus become unstoppable.
>
> 次周，盡心之用，寂相著明，則真智沛發，捨染趨淨必循軌轉依而不可遏.[47]

The significance of this passage should not be underestimated. Lü regarded the texts of the second phase as the authentic doctrinal lineage (*zhengzong* 正宗).[48] For Lü, the function of original quiescence was to spark the long-term process of *āśrayaparivṛtti*. However, for one who is still in the afflicted state, the only path by which to arrive at a momentary realization of original quiescence is via the interconditioned copoiesis of perfuming through hearing. According to Lü, once one gained this momentary insight, this originally quiescent consciousness would make the process of revolutionary nonviolence irresistible.

Thusly, Lü Cheng presented the revolution of consciousness in terms of a continuous balancing act between nature and nurture. For him, the basis (Ch: *yi* 依; Skt: *āśraya*) was precisely *ālayavijñāna*. In Lü's interpretation, even though consciousness is quiescent by nature, for one who is currently afflicted, it functions as the basis of all worldly suffering and perpetuates this actual life. Therefore, perfuming through hearing is the only means to create an opportunity of direct realization of this original quiescence. After the initial manifestation of original quiescence, if one continues to hold this meditative insight in mind, then original quiescence itself will guarantee one's continual action of abandoning affliction and transitioning toward nirvāṇa. This process is precisely what Lü deemed "revolution" (Ch: *zhuan* 轉; Skt: *parivṛtti*), an abandoning of the deluded *ālayavijñāna* and a manifestation of the perfected nature that can be momentarily accessed by deluded beings as original quiescence.[49]

In this way, *āśrayaparivṛtti* allowed Lü to naturalize his nonviolent, noncompetitive social evolutionary theory in terms of Yogācāra soteriology. In this training of revolutionizing consciousness, original quiescence and nirvāṇa were presented as a Möbius band. When viewed locally, there are always two sides: the cause that is in the distant past, original quiescence (the unconditioned among the conditioned), and the effect that is in the distant future, nirvāṇa (the unconditioned that is fully actualized). When viewed globally, there is only one side. This global oneness and local duality enabled Lü to justify this new path of co-liberation: because of the oneness of cause and effect, liberation is bound to happen; because of the temporary duality due to the limitedness of mortals, original quiescence is a natural propensity (*ziran zhi shi* 自然之勢) whose revolution is, like a bountiful river (*jianghe peiran* 江河沛然), unstoppable.[50] While the image of a bountiful river as the propensity of kindness has a productive literary life in Chinese culture, in Lü's socio-soteriology, it metamorphosized into a notion of agentless agency, one that invokes the Buddhist agency of relations and aggregated karmic processes. In contrast to the deadly myths of the survival of the fittest that glorified competition and self-interest, the metaphor of a bountiful river augmented Lü's revolutionary nonviolence as an idyllic flow of compassion destined to wash away all worldly suffering.

In the third phase, one clearly sees the social characteristics of Lü's project. Posited as the unconditioned, the essence of the third phase is one dharma realm (*yifajie* 一法界), a.k.a. one true-reality dharma realm, which includes both the material environment (living processes and natural cycles) and the sentient realm (all living beings). According to Lü,

> The third phase is to expand the reach of the function of [original quiescence]. Both buddhas and sentient beings possess this consciousness. Interconnective stimulations and dependent co-arisings rely on the same base and are thus equal. This is called "one dharma realm." The ultimate goal of this learning is to apply great vows without limit and to aspire for the perfection and purification of the whole realm.
>
> 三周，充用之量，佛與眾生遍具此心，交感緣起，依等而相同，謂之一法界，弘願行於無極，期全界之圓淨，斯乃此學之終鵠也.[51]

Here, instead of the apophatic understanding of nirvāṇa as the relinquishment of afflictions, Lü portrayed the fruition of revolutionizing consciousness from the cataphatic perspective of manifesting *dharmakāya*. In Xuanzang's treatise, this *dharmakāya* is equated with one true-reality dharma realm, otherwise known as dharma-realm dependent co-arising (*fajie yuanqi* 法界緣起).[52] It foretells an ever-expanding community of interwoven sentient beings in a distant yet reassuringly bright future, calling forth the metaphor he used during his aesthetic revolution, "a blossoming field in a mountainside" with abundant flowers in all hues of color.[53]

The phrase "interconnective stimulations and dependent arisings" is important for appreciating Lü's innovative refashioning of nirvāṇa as co-liberation. The phrase combines the Chinese processual coaction paradigm of *ganying* 感應 (stimulus and response) with the Buddhist process philosophy of dependent arising.[54] This was not the first time that the two paradigms had been combined to fashion a new form of soteriology. As argued by Wendi Adamek, since sixth-century China, Chinese Yogācārins at Baoshan had been fashioning a practice tradition grounded in the "agency of relations," where "constructions—textual, visual, and reflexive—emerge out of processes of intention and action and in turn have efficacy within these processes."[55] While the paradigms share the important features of formulating an agentless agency and giving relations themselves more agentive force in the mycelial meshwork of actions and coactions, Lü's unique phrase *jiaogan yuanqi* combines the Chinese paradigm of coaction (*jiaogan*) with the Buddhist paradigm of dependent co-arising (*yuanqi*) to drive home the point that the relata or the end points of relations, buddhas, bodhisattvas, human beings, other sentient or insentient beings, are mere outcomes of causally constitutive and interconditioning chains of actions.

Furthermore, Lü's deployment of interconnective stimulations, when read in the context of the predicate "rely on the same base and are thus equal," reveals that Lü retooled both paradigms of agentless agency to build a realm sustained by equalized relations. In contrast to the historical use of both paradigms to affirm the spiritual hierarchies of the buddhas and the commoners, in Lü's program, these karma/action-oriented ethics are mobilized to democratize the path of liberation.

Importantly, conceiving of community in terms of motivated, recursive, organizational coactions redefines the fundamental meaning of community: contrary to the contemporary mainstream view of community as the sum of its members, community, as Lü theorized it, exists in its relationality, be it a joint striving for the interconnective stimulations to manifest one true-reality dharma realm or an ever-expanding process of co-liberation. In this way, a community is similar to a university where students, professors, and administrators come and go yet the university maintains its identity because of motivated, recursive, organizational actions: students learn, professors teach, and administrators grant degrees. Lü's conception of community also echoes Taixu's radical notion of civil society organizations discussed in chapter 3. At the risk of pointing out the obvious, Lü's early quest of using art to make activism irresistible had morphed into a project of using Buddhism to make revolutionary nonviolence unstoppable.

The path interweaves two strands of action into a double helix: the strand of textual analysis works in tandem with the strand of vinaya practice, and the two are fused together by the supplemental method of critical thinking grounded in meditative absorption. Textual study provides interpersonal guidance for vinaya practice, and vinaya practice both purifies guest dust in the consciousness and actualizes soteriological insight gained from the textual analysis. Moreover, textual analysis precedes vinaya: one must know the correct path before putting knowledge into practice. For Lü, to actualize one true-reality dharma realm, one must "study each discipline in turn, know how to decide and select wisely" (*zhuxi geke, shanzhi jueze* 逐習各科, 善知抉擇).[56] As for what counts as "wisely," Lü claimed that worthy teachings always illuminate different means to benefit all sentient beings:

> The ultimate Mahāyāna teachings illustrate the intimate relations between sentient beings and buddhas. They are not separable. They are one dharma realm. Therefore, the closer one approaches the ultimate, the more one becomes involved with sentient beings.
>
> 大乘之究竟在說生佛關係之密切，彼此不離，為一法界，故愈究竟，則愈近眾生.[57]

Like his teacher Ouyang, Lü took it to be a self-evident truth that the core of Mahāyāna teaching is intimate engagement with living beings for the purpose of co-liberation, a merging of social action with soteriological practice.

Buddhability, Humanity, and Intersubjectivity

Precisely because Lü trusted that, at the ultimate level, buddhas and commoners are not two but one, Lü saw Buddhability and humanity as one and the same and claimed that even deluded commoners could be the support for the world. Given the centrality of nirvāṇa-cum-buddhahood in *Five Disciplines*, it is no surprise that most of Lü's claims on this point appear in his lectures on the discipline of Nirvāṇa. As the evidence demonstrates, this reversal of the received doctrine showcases the first central strand by which Lü's épistémè of compassion materialized into institutional configurations. Lü saw Buddhability-cum-humanity as fundamental for building a community grounded in compassion and interdependence, one in which aspiring bodhisattvas, buddhas, sentient beings, and insentient beings are all provisional equilibriums sustained by recurring patterns of copoieses such as vows, purified consciousness, mental afflictions, and imputations. Of course, for Lü, to be closer to the commoners, aspiring bodhisattvas had to act as socially engaged and politically active Buddhists.

Dharmic Humans Are the Support for the World

The idea of a self-governed community of aspiring bodhisattvas hinges crucially on what Lü termed "four kinds of humans as the support [for this world]" (*siyiren* 四依人).[58] As mentioned earlier, this statement of human support directly contradicts the well-known doctrine that one shall rely on Dharma, *not* on humans (*yifa buyiren* 依法不依人). Ouyang first made this surprising reversal in 1941 in his *Instructions for the Institute · On Teaching*. In this short text, Ouyang asserted, "As for the four kinds of support (*siyi* 四依) today, Dharma exists because of human beings. Therefore, one shall rely on Dharmic humans."[59]

Why did Ouyang and Lü promote a doctrine that directly contradicts conventional wisdom? Briefly speaking, Ouyang wished to establish his Inner Learning Institute as the model for a different kind of lay community with strict gender separation.[60] To be sure, Ouyang's claim had historical roots. Many commentaries penned by eminent monks such as Huiyuan 慧远 (334–416), Jizang 吉藏 (549–623), Daoxuan 道宣 (596–667), and Yuanzhao 元照 (1048–1116) promoted this doctrine for different reasons.[61] In addition, this idea is repeated in the influential Buddhist encyclopedia, *Forest of Gems in the Garden of the Dharma* (*Fayuan zhulin* 法苑珠林) compiled in 668, under the section "Various Essentials."[62] All these texts refer to the *Mahāparinirvāṇa Sūtra* as the scriptural support for this provocative claim. Given the precedence, it is not difficult to see that Ouyang may have chosen this obscure teaching to promote a different kind of lay Buddhist organization.

If Ouyang had claimed so only in passing, Lü, in 1943, elevated this provocative claim to the focus of Yuanxue. In his lectures on the *Mahāparinirvāṇa Sūtra—The Chapter of True Dharma*, the second text in the discipline of Nirvāṇa of the second phase, Lü emphasized the significance of the saṅgha jewel (*sengbao* 僧寶) section, where the *Mahāparinirvāṇa Sūtra* claims that the saṅgha jewel refers to the four kinds of humans as worldly support. Lü saw this section of the sūtra as devoted to the discussion of people as the foundation of worldly support, and thus he labeled them "the eternal abiding of the saṅgha jewel" (*sengbao changzhu* 僧寶常住).[63] To be sure, the exact phrase "*siyiren*" 四依人 does not appear in any of the Chinese translations. The closest phrasing is found in a passage in which the Buddha claims that "these four kinds of humans are the support for this world" (*rushi siren wei shijian yi* 如是四人為世間依).[64] However, the notion itself frequently appears throughout this section, as these four kinds of humans are variously rendered as the support for this world, the foundation of refuge, the best among people, and those who can bring joy and happiness to humans and gods alike.[65] In explicating this passage, Lü repackaged this doctrine to justify his experience-based, action-oriented moral training:

> Saṅgha means the assembled disciples, that is, the four assemblies of the Buddha's disciples. They can recite the words of the Buddha and practice what the buddhas practice. The eternity of the saṅgha jewel comes from the eternity of the Dharma jewel. . . . However, by itself, Dharma cannot function [in this world]. To activate [Dharma's] efficacy, one must rely on humans who clarify [Dharma] and instruct [others]. Therefore, only humans can be the support for this world.
>
> 僧谓徒衆，即佛四衆弟子，能誦佛言行佛行者也．僧寶之常，由法寶之常而來．．．．然徒法不能自行，必待人之闡明指示，乃生效用，故勘為世間依止者唯人.[66]

This passage underscores Lü's redefinition of humanity in terms of actions and coactions: in this case, to activate and spread Dharma. First, Lü highlighted that the saṅgha, as a fourfold gathering, included laity. Second, he refashioned the essence of saṅgha based on actions alone: reciting the words of the Buddha and emulating the buddhas' deeds. Third, Lü subordinated the saṅgha jewel to the Dharma jewel, rendering the Dharma jewel the foundation and the saṅgha jewel the activation of True Dharma, calling to mind both Ouyang's use of *tiyong* 體用 (foundation and function) and the copoietic paradigm that allots agency to texts, Dharma, and humans in the spiderweb of karmic processes. Lü concluded this passage by circling back to his earlier redefinition: humans *become* the support for the world only when they *activate* the True Dharma, hearkening back to the agency of relations implied in interconnective stimulations.

As concerns content, the previously quoted passage is an accurate interpretation of the opening in the sixth fascicle of the *Mahāparinirvāṇa Sūtra*, which Mark Blum translates as "there are four kinds of people who capably protect the true-dharma, promote the true-dharma, and keep the true-dharma in their thoughts . . . for they are the support for the world."[67] In the rest of the lecture, Lü Cheng drew upon a wide range of Buddhist metaphors, scriptures, and doctrines to justify his redefinition of the saṅgha jewel as humans voluntarily assembled together to practice and activate True Dharma.[68]

Importantly, the innovation of Lü's Buddhability-cum-humanity becomes evident once the passage is situated within the swelling tide of the "New Man" discourse in modern China. Instead of merely reviving some ancient, genuine Buddhist traditions, Lü employed a Yogācāra causal framework to change the terms of the modern debate about what makes a person human. He openly criticized the Western practice of debasing humans as slaves (*nuli* 奴隸), oxen and horses (*niuma* 牛馬), and flesh cannonballs (*roudan* 肉彈).[69] Published in the 1940s, this passage nonetheless shines a light on a striking condemnation of structural violence (probably widely shared among anticolonialists at the time), which Aimé Césaire in 1950 powerfully called "*colonization = chosification*."[70] Indeed, to both thinkers, the dark heart of colonialism lay in its *thingification* of living beings. Lü's action-oriented ethics and human interconditioning, by centering actions and coactions, offers a compelling path out of the colonial agenda of thingification.

Lü also prioritized the aspirational agency of the Dharmic humans by claiming that aspiration alone distinguishes saints from commoners and commoners from animals.[71] Although in some medieval practices, vows are crucial to accessing the agency of relations, in Lü's socio-soteriology, the volitional power encoded in bodhisattva vows alone activates the interconditioning Buddhability.[72] To become worldly support is not a birthright but a choice. Only through aspirations and actions to embark on the bodhisattva path can one become initiated into the team of worldly support.

Seen from the processual point of view, Dharma and humans are one, not two, in the sense that they both are mere provisional stases in a constantly changing yet mutually conditioning meshwork of events and actions. In his lecture on the chapter titled "Accepting True Dharma" in the *Śrīmālādevī Siṃhanāda Sūtra*, one of the two texts in the discipline of Nirvāṇa of the first phase, Lü explicitly pointed out that the fundamental essence (*genbenyi* 根本義) of this text resides in its unique teaching that fuses Dharma with the Dharma-holders (*jiang fa yu chifazhe dacheng yipian* 將法與持法者打成一片), echoing the epigraphs herein.[73]

Following the logic of process philosophy, Dharma and Dharmic humans are one because they both belong to the karmic mycelium of aggregated actions. The location of agency does not lie in some mythologized individual agents but instead flows in and out of dynamic stases that are conventionally designated as bounded agents such as humans, buddhas, bodhisattvas, or texts but in reality are produced by intentions and actions.[74] For this reason, Lü valued humans and buddhas yet located the ultimate value in the teachings of the *Mahāparinirvāṇa Sūtra*:

> Humans are valuable because they can become buddhas. Buddhas are valuable because they can actualize this Dharma of nirvāṇa. Therefore, the Dharma of nirvāṇa is the most valuable.
>
> 人之所貴, 在能成佛, 佛之所貴, 則在能證此涅槃法, 故涅槃法最可貴也.[75]

Having firmly grounded the sanctity of humanity in one's propensity to become a buddha and resolve to enact True Dharma, Lü sought to prove that even commoners with mental afflictions could be part of the saṅgha jewel. Careful readers will have already inferred that Lü elevated the teachings of the *Mahāparinirvāṇa Sūtra* to minimize the gap between buddhas and humans. Buddhas and humans are both valuable because they can actualize True Dharma. Under Lü's philosophy of living, the difference between buddhas and humans is a time lapse: buddhas have already actualized True Dharma, whereas humans can become buddhas only after their propensity is accentuated by external conditions (*waiyuan zengshang* 外緣增上), where these conducive external conditions are precisely the teachings in the *Mahāparinirvāṇa Sūtra*.[76]

To prove that deluded commoners could be the worldly support, Lü again drew from the doctrinal elements already present in the *Mahāparinirvāṇa Sūtra*. According to this sūtra, the first group of worldly support comprises those commoners who are above worldly affairs but whose consciousnesses are still afflicted.[77] In many commentaries, the remaining groups are mapped onto different saints who have achieved one of the four realizations (*siguo* 四果) or the patriarchs of specific Dharma lineages. However, most extant commentaries agree that the first group of people consists of some sort of commoners, such as Buddhist commoners (*neifan* 內凡) or Buddhist commoners belonging to the families of those who have yet to enter the ten bodhisattva stages but are endowed with understanding and practice (*diqian zhongxing jiexing neifan* 地前種性解行內凡).[78] Building upon the medieval commentarial tradition, Lü renamed the first group of people "commoners with awakened *bodhicitta*" (*youzhi fanfu* 有志凡夫).[79] I translate Lü's neologism as "aspiring bodhisattvas" to highlight these persons' aspirational agency. Lü saw the value of these aspiring bodhisattvas as depending solely on whether they could preach True Dharma. Whether they were laity or ordained clergy, old or young, their observation or violation of some specific monastic precepts was seen as irrelevant.[80]

The social function of these aspiring bodhisattvas is undeniable. They are the saṅgha jewel precisely because they aspire both to achieve buddhahood themselves and to assist others in becoming buddhas.[81] This social function of bringing all to nirvāṇa predetermines another aspect of this new bodhisattva ideal: all aspiring bodhisattvas are voluntary *icchantikas*, or bodhisattva *icchantikas* (*pusa yichanti* 菩薩一闡提).[82] In conventional wisdom, *icchantika* refers to a sentient being who will never be exposed to Buddhist teaching and therefore cannot achieve buddhahood. Throughout medieval China, there were vehement debates on whether an *icchantika* could become a buddha.[83] Xuanzang is well known for his conviction that there exist *icchantikas* who cannot achieve buddhahood in the foreseeable future.[84] In modern China, when Western democratic values became the prevailing wind, Xuanzang's view came to be seen as problematic. To resolve this conflict, Lü redefined *icchantikas* in terms of their great vow to stay in saṃsāra. In doing so, Lü reinterpreted Xuanzang's spiritual hierarchy as a matter of voluntary participation. For Lü, the essential quality of voluntary *icchantikas* was diligence. This quality distinguishes bodhisattva *icchantikas* from those who are lax and heedless, as suggested by the traditional interpretation. Once the characteristics of *icchantika* are reframed in terms of their volition, Xuanzang's categorization becomes provisional, conditioned upon one's willpower. Thus, in Lü's paradigm, all humans, including the traditional *icchantikas*, have the potential to choose a different path and thereby transform themselves into voluntary *icchantikas*.[85]

To further emphasize that buddhahood is open to all commoners to enact, Lü interpreted the Buddha Nature as preordained propensity for awakening:

> Therefore, one knows that afflictions existed in the past but are cut off now and that true wisdom did not exist in the past but is born now. This is the meaning of the transformability of the Buddha nature. However, this transformation has a predetermined propensity.
>
> 故知煩惱昔有今斷，正智昔無今生．此即佛性有轉變之義，而轉變又有一定之趨勢也．[86]

Precisely because of Lü's faith in this destined transformative force of the Buddha nature, in his parting words preserved in his lecture on the *Laṅkāvatāra Sūtra*, the third text in the discipline of Nirvāṇa of the second phase and the concluding text of Lü's shortened lecture series, Lü implored the audience to become bodhisattva *icchantikas*. He concluded that the essence of Yuanxue was thus: whether one becomes a [lazy] *icchantika* or a buddha is entirely determined by one's own [diligence and aspiration]. Therefore, one shall exhort oneself.[87]

In short, Lü democratized the ancient bodhisattva path, rendering it open to all aspiring learners. In his lectures, he sculpted an ideal learner who is skilled in textual analysis and meditative absorptions but is still afflicted by mental defilements. The aspiring bodhisattvas trust their natural propensity toward awakening. Because of their deep insight into True Dharma and their commitment to assist all sentient beings through learning and teaching, they become the worldly support in a troubled time. Because of their conviction, aspiring bodhisattvas are voluntary *icchantikas* who forgo the opportunity to quickly achieve buddhahood yet tirelessly acquire all kinds of soteriological knowledge suitable for assisting different kinds of sentient beings. Thus, Lü weaved different strands of traditional teachings into a new tapestry within which ancient doctrines accrued new relevance and became the very foundation of humanity. This newly minted Buddhability-cum-humanity was crucial to Lü's socio-soteriology that wedded liberation Buddhology and democracy.

Sociality and Yogācāra Intersubjectivity

However, to fuse humanity and sociality in a processual philosophical paradigm, one key component was still necessary: a reformulation of intersubjectivity. Without a convincing theory of how intersubjective exchanges can happen apart from presuming external objects, Lü's socio-soteriology would have been untenable. Without a defensible processual social ontology, Lü's program would have read just like any other individualistic soteriology or an idealist rendering of society as the expansion of an individual psyche, as was analyzed in chapter 3. As evidenced by this subsection, Lü refashioned buddhahood-cum-nirvāṇa as intersubjective oneness by redefining the imported category of sociality in terms of Yogācāra intersubjectivity.

One critical term in Lü's sociality-cum-intersubjectivity is indirect *ālambana*. As was discussed in chapter 3, *ālambana* (objective basis) explains how mental karmic processes are perceived *as if* objectively existing outside consciousness. Indirect *ālambana* is the term coined by Xuanzang to explain intersubjective karmic influences. In Lü's theory, indirect *ālambana* serves as the cornerstone of an intersubjective sociality. Lü's earliest interest in this doctrine became manifested during a 1923 debate at the Inner Learning Institute when his focus transitioned from aesthetic revolution to liberation Buddhology.[88] Recall from chapter 1 that at this early stage when Lü was simultaneously teaching Yogācāra and aesthetics, Lü's goal of aesthetic revolution was to establish an intersubjective oneness cohered by aesthetic empathy and produced through intersubjective and cross-modality (e.g., from auditory to visual) translation.

Whereas in 1921 and 1922 Lü was still patching up different Western aesthetic theories to explain how aesthetic empathy could ground an intersubjective sociality, in this 1923 debate, Lü hinted that he now found Yogācāra intersubjectivity to be a more powerful toolbox to establish this intersubjective oneness. The central question in the fifth research conference in 1923 was whether Thusness (*zhenru* 真如) could be indirect *ālambana*. The debate started when Lü proposed discussing a question posed by another Buddhist revolutionary, Huang Jusu 黄居素 (1897–1986).[89]

In the debate, Lü took pains to prove that Thusness, both in its absolute sense (*shixing zhenru* 實性真如) and its objective aspect (*faxiang zhenru* 法相真如), could be an indirectly perceived object.[90] More important, Lü asserted that Thusness perceived by bodhisattvas who had achieved subsequent awareness (Ch: *houdezhi* 後得智; Skt: *pṛṣṭha-labdha-jñāna*) could be an indirect *ālambana* accessible to deluded commoners.[91] The critical doctrinal underpinning of Lü Cheng's position was that *ālambana* describes what can be grasped as if it is an objective substance, alluding to the Yogācāra critique of objectivity as a convenient fiction.[92]

Lü was alone in holding this position. At first glance, Chen Zhenru, another Buddhist revolutionary, seemed to support Lü's position.[93] Chen claimed that both Huang and Lü were right because absolute Thusness cannot be indirect *ālambana* (thereby affirming Huang's point and misreading Lü's point) and the objective aspect of Thusness can be an indirect *ālambana*. Wang Enyang, another reformer who had developed his own Yogācāra social theory, argued that both Huang and Lü were wrong in that they both mischaracterized the two kinds of Thusness. However, the central thrust of Chen's, Huang's, and Wang's objections was similar: if Thusness as perceived by the subsequent awareness can be grasped by ordinary beings as indirect *ālambana*, then because indirect *ālambana* requires substance, to make Thusness available to be grasped as indirect *ālambana* necessitates equating Thusness with substance, which was a mark of heterodoxy.[94] As outlined in chapter 3, this sort of debate is to be expected whenever a newly imported category needs to be explained in terms of received concepts. Without these internal debates and irreconcilable differences, the Yogācāra tradition would lack depth. Furthermore, because each position can be justified by selective readings of the past and the present, the question of "authenticity" is moot. A more fruitful line of inquiry is to examine the purpose for which each position is proposed.

I argue that Lü Cheng invested heavily in his position because Thusness as indirect *ālambana* is central to theorizing an intersubjective sociality, a cornerstone of Lü's revolutionary nonviolence. In this early phase of the revolution, Lü argued that universal beauty, as perceived by artists and materialized through their artwork, can awaken the innate aesthetic sensibility of viewers and thereby expand the viewers' aesthetic potential. Art critics, similarly, by translating the visual and auditory experiences of beauty into verbal and textual expressions, can inspire future artists and expand the reach of artwork. If only the objective aspect of universal beauty—that is, a shadow—can be indirectly perceived by unenlightened beings, then commoners must experience a miraculous leap to grasp true beauty. Conversely, if other beings can indirectly perceive the universal as expressed through artists' aesthetic sensibility, then commoners can access true beauty through reason and emotional connection with artwork. Seen in this light, Lü arguably insisted that Thusness could be indirect *ālambana* because he hoped that True Dharma, as embodied in the subsequent awareness of the bodhisattva, functioned as an indirectly perceivable object for commoners.

To deny direct access to True Dharma through other consciousnesses is to admit that sacred texts are mere shadows of Thusness in ink, the interpreters of the texts are mere chasers of elusive shadows, and commoners are mere prisoners of Plato's cave. This renders scholarship devoid of salvific efficacy.[95] It is little wonder, then, why Lü insisted that Thusness could be indirect *ālambana*. The result of this debate was underwhelming: all participants agreed to disagree.

But this debate did not end with the conclusion of the conference. The issue was too important to let go. Lü Cheng continued to labor on the "true meaning" of *ālambana*. To prove his point, in his 1927 essay "Guan suoyuan shilun huiyi" 觀所緣釋論會譯 (A comparative exposition of the [Chinese and Tibetan] translations of the *Ālambana-parīkṣa*), Lü Cheng identified all central passages supporting his interpretation by placing a circle beside the relevant Chinese characters.[96] In the second collection of *Essentials* published eight years later, in 1935, in collating Yijing's translation of Dharmapāla's *Ālambana-parīkṣa-vṛtti* (*Guan suoyuanyuan lun shi* 觀所緣緣論釋, T.1168), Lü not only incorporated his 1927 findings but also systematically accentuated the passages that explain *ālambana* as an aspect of consciousness (Skt: *vijñāna*) but one that appears *as if* (*ru* 如) it exists outside of consciousness as substance. He highlighted these passages by rendering other passages lower than these essential lemmas.[97] In particular, to stress the centrality of consciousness-only doctrines, he used a footnote to equate *shi* 識 with *vijñāna* and then linked *shi* with a rephrase of Yogācāra causal enframing. The paraphrase in this footnote implies that even though indirectly perceived objects are termed *zhi* 質 (substance), these substances only appear *as if* they were substances. In reality, they are mere *vijñāna*.[98]

Lü's decade-long comparative study of this doctrine reveals the main tenet of liberation Buddhology: the possibility of collective liberation is achievable only through scholarly pursuit. Because he saw all authentic texts as narrated by buddhas and bodhisattvas with subsequent awareness before being written down, if Thusness could be indirectly perceived, then the texts would no longer be mere shadows in ink and ordinary beings would not be condemned to the eternal cave of darkness. Lü analyzed and compared all these textual interconnections over the years just to prove his 1924 argument that indirect *ālambana* merely describes that which can be grasped as objective support and is, in reality, a manifestation of other mental streams.

In sum, Lü employed indirect *ālambana* to explain how the mental streams of commoners could be enhanced and activated by conducive external conditions. Lü's bodhisattva path requires that True Dharma as experienced by the buddhas and bodhisattvas and as later written down in the *Mahāparinirvāṇa Sūtra* is indirect *ālambana*. Only in this way can the commoners, who have awakened the resolve to practice and spread True Dharma, activate their Buddhability and engage in transformative investigations that allow them to remake the world into one true-reality dharma realm.

A Spiritual Coevolution

Lü endeavored to recast human experiences and actions in the Yogācāra soteriological mold. As the renowned intellectual historian Wang Hui has pointed out, the heart of the May Fourth political imagination is "culture and morality." The core project of May Fourth was to rediscover forgotten yet "natural" patterns (*wen* 文) to stimulate collective transformations (*hua* 化) that would call forth a new political subject and more egalitarian state politics.[99] A key clash at this moment was between the "new" scientific worldview and the "old" Heavenly principle: whereas the new disenchanted everything and every relation into materiality and relations of interests and necessity for survival, the old enchanted all material relations as a matter of the mind-heart and ethicized every piece of knowledge into moral knowledge.[100] This divergence set the scene for a paradigm war: positivist knowledge, objective knowledge against moral, subjective knowledge.

Lü trod a less traveled path, integrating both paradigms into an intersubjective mutual conditioning. After briefly experimenting with aesthetic solutions to the crisis of the Republic, Lü turned to Yogācāra to construct new social patterns that would resolve the modern vices of Darwinist competition, excessive materialism, and rampant individualism. World War I was the stimulus for the cultural turn in the May Fourth era. Lü's suffering during World War II, when he first lectured on *Five Disciplines* while Japanese bombs were raining down on Chongqing, only confirmed Lü's diagnosis of the modern disease and his resolve to stop the tide of the unfolding Darwinist dystopia.

To contextualize Lü based on recognizable Buddhist doctrinal fine points is to willfully ignore the richness of Lü's intervention and the multilayered debates he participated in. By adopting a socio-soteriological lens, we bring Lü's social vision into view. Yogācāra causal enframing provided Lü and many likeminded thinkers with a narrative structure to imagine a different future, that is, a social imagination of nonviolence that would allow its followers to face the reality of cultural deaths with courage and to work for cultural rebirths with care.

The global flow of Darwinism and the philosophy of Buddhism overdetermined that Lü remade the central Buddhist doctrine of dependent arising into a social theory. In the late nineteenth century, when Yan Fu published his translations of Huxley's and Spencer's social Darwinism, he employed Yogācāra-inflected karmic theory to explain modern sociality. In the 1920s, Yogācāra causal theory provided Lü vital inspiration to rethink the notions of humanity and sociality. When Lü reframed Yogācāra causal enframing as social coevolution, intersubjectivity grounded in aesthetic resonances found a new formulation, that is, the dependent arising of one true-reality dharma realm. Without a doubt, Lü's new theorization was driven by the pressing question of his time: how to build a democratic society that transcends the logic of capitalism and that dispels the dangerous monolithic narrative of Darwinist competition. As a result, the ancient teaching of dependent co-arising took a decisive social turn.

To launch his movement of revolutionary nonviolence, Lü defined learning as the chief means. Explicitly equating social engagement with Buddhist learning, he stated,

> If learning exists in the cosmos, then it is Buddhist learning. If genuine human life exists, then it is a human life [in accordance with] the Buddha dharma. Nevertheless, one must acknowledge that [this genuine human life] arises out of one's self-awakening. If one were confined to the Hīnayāna

> teachings and if one were afraid of talking about the [genuine] ego, then one would consider sentient beings as floating duckweed drifting with the wind. Then, who could carry on the myriad deeds of six pāramitās and the limitless enterprise [of releasing all into nirvāṇa]?
>
> 宇宙間有學,則佛學而已,有真正人生,則佛法人生而已.然此出於人之自覺,不可不知也.彼一往拘泥小乘之義,而懼說我者,視眾生有如水面浮萍,隨風飄蕩,六度萬行,無邊事業,複伊誰負之哉.[101]

This passage represents Lü Cheng's impassioned call to revolutionize society through liberation Buddhology. Lü saw collective liberation as starting with textual analysis but aiming for social change. Some scholars of Buddhist philosophy might feel uneasy about Lü's position on the teaching of a genuine ego. Instead of faulting Lü for championing "unorthodox" doctrines, his argument resonates with a recent one put forth by Joseph Walser. Walser analyzed Pāli texts and argued that the historical Buddha (or authors/reciters of early sūtras) preached different doctrines to brahmin and nonbrahmin followers.[102] If this is the case, then it is entirely possible that different early Buddhist communities preserved different sets of teaching, which eventually developed into the schools and traditions we know today. Viewed from this longue durée perspective, Lü's socio-soteriology is only one recent wavelet in the many currents and countercurrents that are lumped together under the umbrella term of Buddhism.

By the end of 1944, when Lü issued this call, the once-incessant Japanese air raids over Chongqing had eased up slightly. In hindsight, one cannot help but wonder how anyone could have continued studying ancient Buddhist texts as the bombs were falling. Yet this short passage reveals Lü's deep conviction that only a Buddhist soteriology could lead all out of the living hell of Darwinist competition. Against the backdrop of wartime terror, for intellectuals like Lü, liberation Buddhology must have seemed not only relevant but also sorely needed.

5

Bodhisattva of Democracy

Can we imagine a just society outside of the tired myth of free individuals' eternal struggle against social constraints? For Lü and many of his colleagues at the China Inner Learning Institute, the answer was a resounding yes. Rather than imagine society as the sum of its members, all of whom are negotiating for rights and resources, Lü revived the early republicanism in Buddhist saṅgha and used it as a model to conceptualize civil society as a set of recursive, motivated, organizational coactions.[1] In line with the refashioning of humanity as interconditioned liberation, which deconstructs Western individualism and then reconstructs a Buddhist personhood enacted through actions, Lü's theory of civil society decenters the dystopian myth of Darwinist competition and retheorizes complex society as provisional stasis engendered by collaborative actions.

Lü's redesign of *Yujia pusajie* 瑜珈菩薩戒 (*Yoga Bodhisattva Prātimokṣa*) served as communal rules for democratic participation in deliberation processes. In this redesign, Lü imbued the ancient term *prātimokṣa* (literally, "toward liberation") with a modern sense of the democratic, nonviolent revolution of consciousness. Concomitant with Lü's redesign was a reorientation of six perfections (Skt: *pāramitā*) as guidelines for proper engagement in activism, which I understand as a Buddhist philosophy of coaction and a karma-informed, action-oriented form of moral reasoning. These two sets of action-based rules identify Lü's theory of humanity and society as a form of processual social philosophy. Careful readers might recall that in the 1920s Lü turned to Yogācāra in search of an alternative to the two extremes of social realism and social idealism. In the 1940s Lü retooled Yogācāra causal theory as a philosophical framework for investigating social kinds such as communities and institutions—*not* in terms of their ontological building blocks, but in terms of their recurring patterns of actions that anchor homeostasis in a world in flux.[2]

The institute's renewal of *Yoga Bodhisattva Prātimokṣa* marked an interesting experiment in actualizing the Buddhist social consciousness into institutional existence. This lay *vinaya* (codes of conduct) renewal reveals the road not taken by many self-avowed revolutionaries: in contrast to political revolutionaries, many progressive thinkers like Lü remained aloof or even suspicious of state power and the ramifications of violent struggles. Like Wang Enyang, Wang Xiaoxu, and Monk Taixu, Lü stayed true to the Buddhist principle of nonviolence and insisted that a just society must foremost be a nonviolent one. This less traveled path is worthy of scholarly attention because it opened up a new potentiality of becoming modern: Instead of the continual spiritual control of the hierarchical saṅgha or endless violent struggles for power, Lü toiled for a lay-led, self-governed, nonviolent, yet socially engaged democracy. Instead of reproducing hierarchical institutions, Lü mapped out an alternative path of spreading ideas and transmitting norms of collective actions to enable different actors to start communities of equal conditions for liberation.

Lü manufactured an unbroken institutional lineage of "bodhisattva vinaya" (*pusa lü* 菩薩律), one that could be traced back to the historical Buddha and that was developed in parallel with the monastic code or "śrāvaka vinaya." Lü's maneuver is astonishing because it contradicted all known scholarship. Historically, the bodhisattva community had never established an institutional presence outside the monastic leadership. It is textbook knowledge that Mahāyāna emerged from early śrāvaka teachings. To legitimize an independent, self-governed bodhisattva community in ancient India, Lü had to employ comparative hermeneutics to manufacture a semblance of historicity.

Lü also reconfigured bodhisattva precepts as the chief means to arrive at the core of Yogācāra soteriology: *vijñānamātratā* (the truth of consciousness-only; Ch: *weishi xing* 唯識性). In doing so, Lü repurposed the épistémè of compassion into a rallying call for activism. And he reframed six perfections as the organized coactions for bringing forth a revolutionary nonviolence aimed at actualizing an aesthetic society, which became Buddhisized as one true-reality dharma realm. In a 1953 essay "Zhengjue yu chuli" 正覺與出離 (Just Awakening and Renunciation), as the first of three lectures on "The Fundamental Issues in Buddhist Learning" (foxue jiben wenti 佛學基本問題), Lü further characterized the path of bodhisattva of democracy as *zhuanshi er chushi* 轉世而出世 (renouncing this world through transforming it), explicitly linking the project of renunciation and revolution or human interconditioning and nirvāṇic interconditioning on a Möbius strip.[3]

Manufacturing an Independent Lineage of Bodhisattva Vinaya

To establish a self-governed bodhisattva democracy outside of monastic control, Lü had to first manufacture an independent lineage of Mahāyāna (synonymous with bodhisattva in this context for Lü) vinaya out of thin air. Then he had to discredit the long-established bodhisattva vinaya taken from the *Brahmā Net Sūtra* and establish *Yoga Bodhisattva Prātimokṣa* as the only authentic lineage of Mahāyāna vinaya. Lü achieved these goals in two of his lectures on the Vinaya discipline in the first phase of *Five Disciplines*. This section of *Five Disciplines* includes three texts: *The Vaipulya (Extensive) Sūtra of the Pure Vinaya* (T.1489; henceforth, *Extensive Pure Vinaya*), *Yoga Bodhisattva Prātimokṣa* (T.1501), and *Yoga Bodhisattva Prātimokṣa Karman* (T.1499).

Lü's textual gymnastics can be periodized to two stages. The first stage occurred from 1924 to 1926, when he developed his idiosyncratic method of comparative hermeneutics (to be discussed in chapter 6) and argued that only by combining historical, philological, and philosophical investigations could one recover the true intent of the Buddha. For Lü, only after one recovered this true intent behind each vinaya rule could one adapt the rule to contemporary situations so as to establish a new community that supports mutual spiritual growth. At this time, Lü still followed the scholarly consensus that Mahāyāna Buddhism arose from early śrāvaka teachings.

The second stage occurred in 1943, when Lü started *Five Disciplines*. This is the time when Lü made the radical claim that bodhisattva and śrāvaka teachings emerged not in sequence but in parallel. Lü employed historical and philological methods to manufacture an independent lineage of Mahāyāna vinaya that was purportedly expounded upon by the historical Buddha in different discourses. Lü surmised that these scattered bodhisattva vinaya rules were first collected by the mythical founder of Yogācāra, the future Buddha Maitreya, and then written down by Asaṅga. Then Lü employed hermeneutics and intertextual analysis to illuminate the superiority of Asaṅga's *Yoga Bodhisattva Prātimokṣa* (i.e., Mahāyāna vinaya) to *Śrāvaka Prātimokṣa* (i.e., monastic vinaya).

In the first stage, Lü paved the way for an independent Mahāyāna vinaya by wresting authority from monks and putting it into the hands of scholars. As I mentioned briefly in chapter 4 and argue later in chapter 6, Lü employed historical, philological, and philosophical methods in the 1920s to refashion the history of Indian Buddhism into an evolutionary theory: he argued that the primitive teachings for śrāvakas matured into Nālandā learning, whose textual seeds were then transmitted and preserved in Chinese Yogācāra.[4] Most relevant to this stage is his 1926 *prātimokṣa* study, which was a comparative study of the code of all monastic precepts.[5] Although coauthored, this 1926 essay was nonetheless the first application of Lü's comparative method that utilized not only primary materials in Pāli, Sanskrit, Tibetan, and Chinese but also secondary literature in English, French, and Japanese. This extensive comparative analysis later became the hallmark of Lü's scholarship.

The political import of Lü's comparative studies is evident: Lü Cheng needed to legitimate his institution-building project without sounding like an apologete. In concluding his essay, he first dismissed Monk Taixu's saṅgha reform as groundless.[6] Then Lü proposed his own blueprint for saṅgha reform. Lü argued that to build a genuine saṅgha anew according to the true intent of the Buddha, one must do the following:

> What is the first step in establishing [a genuine saṅgha]? I say, it starts with vinaya studies. As for the procedure, there should be several stages.
>
> 建立何由始? 曰, 由治戒學始. 分其步驟, 應有數層.
>
> First, search for the root *prātimokṣa*; find the original intent of stipulating these precepts; do not be partial toward any sect; eliminate the confusion caused by sectarian obsessions.
>
> 一, 尋繹根本戒, 得制戒原意, 不偏一家, 以去部執之惑.
>
> Second, understand and cohere various sectarian editions based on the root *prātimokṣa* so to reveal the Dharmic rules of adaptation and implementation in each situation.
>
> 二, 以根本戒會通各家, 見其適應實施之法則.
>
> Third, examine the Indian social realities throughout the history of Buddhist transmission to find the economic principles of harmonious coexistence [of the saṅgha] in a society in the root *prātimokṣa*.
>
> 三, 考校印土歷世佛教實況, 以見根本戒內與世相洽之經濟原理如何.
>
> Fourth, survey and examine the history of our country and the current situation to investigate how to apply this root *prātimokṣa* [in the contemporary world] and to provide a new interpretation.
>
> 四, 再由我國往事及現狀, 考究此根本戒之應用如何, 而加以新解釋.
>
> Fifth, based on the previous [stages of studies], establish saṅgha regulations and truly observe these precepts to establish a foundational *Daochang* of Buddha Dharma.
>
> 五, 由前種種創立僧制, 真正持戒, 以為佛法根本道場.[7]

Two conclusions can be drawn from this passage. First, Lü considered comparative methods the only means to recover the intent of the Buddha. In doing so, he challenged monastic authority in adjudicating authentic or inauthentic interpretations. The second is that Lü was not a traditional Buddhologist like his European and Japanese counterparts who were trained to look for "objective" facts.[8] As clearly stated at the beginning and end of the quoted passage, the goal of Lü's comparative studies was to establish a *Daochang*, which literally means the place of *Dao*. But in Lü's use, *Daochang* entails an institution (both a physical place and a group of people) where the members "truly observe these precepts," calling to mind a "practicescape" that weaves together "related activities pertaining to livelihood, dwelling, and skill" to function as a "niche for individual and community practice of a universalist soteriology."[9]

Lü's scholarship was part and parcel of an ameliorative project: he wished to establish a new community bound by webs of mutual commitment to lead all toward liberation. Indeed, Lü took two steps that extended his October 1922 plan for establishing a seed community for aesthetic revolution. In the first stage of his aesthetic revolution, Lü sought to spread true knowledge of beauty among all. In the second stage, Lü advocated for "initiating social reform movements."[10] This would be done by cultivating leaders who could establish their own seed communities. He then diagnosed the chief vice of the actual society as its webs of possessive impulse. Lü's central social critique of existing sociopolitical systems was that because undemocratic organizations and legal structures institutionalize moral egoism and reify elitism, they must be dismantled through nonviolent means and be replaced with civil society organizations like his seed communities. In 1926 Lü refined his critique of unjust social structures and systems of oppression and looked to Buddhist communal rules for an alternative, and more equitable, complex system. Lü Cheng was invested in establishing a genuine saṅgha precisely because he saw it as an organization motivated by collective actions to cleanse egoistic afflictions together with structural inequalities that abet egoism. He thus linked inner change with social change through karmic interconditioning.

Whereas in the 1920s Lü laid the groundwork for his saṅgha reform by elevating scholarly authority, in 1943, when he began teaching *Five Disciplines*, he put his two decades of comparative studies into practice, but with a more radical goal—manufacturing an independent lineage of bodhisattva vinaya in parallel with śrāvaka vinaya. Readers familiar with the history of Buddhism will immediately see through Lü's agenda. Indeed, historically, the set of bodhisattva *prātimokṣa* (*pusajie* 菩薩戒 or *dachengjie* 大乘戒) has rarely been seen as having any institutional independence. It is well known that even after the fourth century CE, when the Mahāyāna vehicle achieved some sense of institutional boundedness, the Mahāyāna communities still followed the so-called śrāvaka vinaya (*shengwen jie* 聲聞戒), which is equivalent to monastic vinaya in Lü's use.

To complicate the issue further, the messy translation history of vinaya fused communal codes and rules for personal conduct into one word, *jielü* 戒律. Traditionally, *jielü* has had two broad senses. The first is a translation of vinaya (code of conduct; also translated as *lü* 律). The core of any vinaya is a set of rules called *prātimokṣa* (*biejietuo* 別解脫, *suishunjietuo* 隨順解脫). This collection of rules is often referred to as the *Prātimokṣa Sūtra* (*Boluotimucha jing* 波羅提木叉經 or *Jiejing* 戒經), where "sūtra" means the connecting thread rather than the Buddha's discourse. The second is a translation of *śīla* (moral discipline) or *sikkhāpada* (*xuechu* 學處). Both *śīla* and *sikkhāpada* have been translated as *jie* 戒. Despite the clear distinctions between vinaya, *prātimokṣa*, *śīla*, *sikkhāpada*, and other technical terms in Indic languages, in their Chinese translations, different senses of communal codes and personal moral guidelines are fused into one, especially when discussing Mahāyāna/bodhisattva vinaya.

A more generous reading of Lü's claim might suggest that he made this claim based on some earlier Mahāyānist effort to reestablish a genuine saṅgha.[11] This suspicion is confirmed by Lü's 1953 essay "Just Awakening and Renunciation," where Lü paraphrased a passage from *Mahāyānasūtrālaṃkāra* (*Dacheng zhuangyan jinglun* 大乘莊嚴經論) and made a more radical claim: the two systems (*xitong* 系統) of the śrāvaka vehicle (*shengwen cheng* 聲聞乘) and the bodhisattva vehicle (*pusa cheng* 菩薩乘) developed in parallel from the historical Buddha's teaching, and despite the occasional vehement disputes (*jilie zhenglun* 激烈爭論) between them, they nonetheless acknowledged the original parallel existences of each other (*liangcheng de yuanlai bingcun* 兩乘的原來並存).[12] For Lü, not only did bodhisattva vinaya came directly from the "original" Buddha's words, but also the whole system of bodhisattva teaching maintained its boundedness and distinction from the śrāvaka system.

Despite this tenuous historical evidence, Lü gathered enough traces to weave them into a coherent discourse with a shimmer of historicity. This manufactured discourse served as a powerful tool for reinventing the historical bodhisattva vocation as a self-governed community of aspiring bodhisattvas. This institution-building intent is clearly seen in the first vinaya text of Lü's *Five Disciplines*, titled *Extensive Pure Vinaya*. The text explicitly uses the term "bodhisattva vinaya" (Pusa pini 菩薩毘尼) to present itself as a set of communal code for bodhisattvas and then goes on to explain the superiority of the bodhisattva communal codes over the "Śrāvaka Vinaya" (i.e., monastic vinaya).[13]

Equally important, in Lü's lecture notes, he meticulously highlighted the institutional aspect of bodhisattva precepts. For example, he sectioned the relevant passages as "Chapter on Explicating Vinaya" (*jielüpin* 解律品), where he used *lü*, the code of conduct that includes communal rules, to position bodhisattva vinaya not as a complementary set of rules for monastic communities but as communal codes for bodhisattva groups. Thereby, he effectively presented bodhisattva vinaya *as if* it were an independent lineage of transmission.[14]

Lü buttressed his seemingly outrageous claim with sophisticated textual gymnastics. In his scholarly edition of *Extensive Pure Vinaya* in the third collection of *Essentials*, Lü explicitly linked the section on bodhisattva vinaya to the chapter on additional vinaya learning (Skt: *adhiśīla*; Ch: *zengshang jiexue* 增上戒學) in *She dacheng lun* 攝大乘論 (*Mahāyāna Compendium*; Skt: *Mahāyānasaṃgraha*; T.1594; henceforth, *MSg*), a Yogācāra classic.[15] Lü Cheng established this link between *Extensive Pure Vinaya* and *MSg* through meticulous textual analysis. First, Lü pointed out that Asaṅga had cited a vinaya text in his treatise, which Lü identified as *Extensive Pure Vinaya*. However, the vinaya text that Asaṅga cited had a different title, *Pinaiye jusha fangguang jing* 毗奈耶瞿沙方廣經 (*Vinaya Ghoṣa Vaipulya Sūtra*). Lü noticed this difference but employed a trick to explain it away. He identified a variant translation of *Extensive Pure Vinaya* titled *Jitiaoyin suowen jing* 寂調音所問經 (*The Inquiries of Jitiaoyin*). According to Lü, "Ghoṣa" is a variant translation of "Jitiaoyin" (the name of a famous king, meaning "the sound that tranquilizes and tames [afflictions]").[16] Then Lü argued that the vinaya text that Asaṅga cited in *MSg* is precisely the bodhisattva vinaya section of *Extensive Pure Vinaya*. For me, this evidence is flimsy. In all these versions, the bodhisattva chapter tends to be brief and mentions only the general superiority of three collections of precepts. Without any concrete reference, such as a particular metaphor or specific quotation, it is impossible to say anything conclusive about whether *MSg* quotes *Extensive Pure Vinaya*.

Criticizing Lü's scholarship is beside the point, given that Lü's self-proclaimed goal was not a positivist project but an ameliorative one—learning from the past to see how to establish a new kind of community. Lü believed that once this textual link had been established, he could borrow Asaṅga's high regard for *Vinaya Ghoṣa Vaipulya Sūtra* to establish the authority of *Extensive Pure Vinaya*, which would in turn give credibility to his newly invented Yogācāra bodhisattva path premised upon equal conditions for liberation.

Once this link was established, Lü then employed the Mahāyāna tropes of belittling śrāvakas to promote the comprehensiveness and self-containment of this new Yogācāra bodhisattva path. Lü Cheng believed that this path for Yogācāra bodhisattvas was comprehensive because bodhisattva vinaya, which can alternatively be termed "three categories of pure precepts" (Ch: *sanju jingjie* 三聚淨戒; Skt: *trividhāni śīlāni*), combines the śrāvaka practices and monastic vinaya in the first of the three categories, the precepts for the maintenance of restraint (Ch: *she lüyi jie* 攝律儀戒; Skt: *saṃvara-śīla*) for all seven groups of Buddhist practitioners. These groups include the *upāsakas* and *upāsikās* (commonly known as laymen and laywomen) who observe the five precepts, the *śikṣamāṇās* (Ch: shichamona 式叉摩那) who observe six or ten precepts, the novice monks and nuns, and the fully ordained *bhikṣus* (monks) and *bhikṣuṇīs* (nuns).

Lü borrowed the specific rhetoric of comprehensiveness seen in the phrase "three categories of pure precepts" from well-known scriptures such as *Da zhidu lun* 大智度論 (T.1509) and *Shizhu piposha lun* 十住毘婆沙論 (Skt: *Daśabhūmikavibhāṣa*; T.1521), both attributed to Nāgārjuna in the Chinese transmission. In doing so, Lü erased the traditional leadership role of ordained clergy and put laypeople and monastics on the same institutional footing.

The recycling of this well-known rhetoric also transformed his Yogācāra bodhisattva path into a path of social engagement because the other two categories of pure precepts provide a robust doctrinal basis for social activism. Both sets of precepts exhort learners to conduct all virtuous deeds—whatever works for goodness (Ch: *she shanfa jie* 攝善法戒; Skt: *kuśalā-dharma-saṃgrāhaka-śīla*)—and to grant mercy to all sentient beings—whatever works for the welfare or salvation of living beings (Ch: *she zhongsheng jie* 攝衆生; Skt: *sattvārtha-kriyā-śīla*).[17]

Once he had established the all-comprehensive and socially engaged nature of this new path, Lü turned his attention toward justifying the institutional independence of this bodhisattva community. Lü achieved this goal by highlighting the community's collective soteriological goal and comprehensive soteriological toolkit. Significantly, Lü Cheng did not reject monasticism per se. Instead, he strived to establish alternative yet equivalent group dynamics that would (1) guarantee each member's voluntary and equal participation in deliberations on issues concerning the bodhisattva community and (2) prompt the members to collectively shoulder leadership responsibility toward the larger society in the joint soteriological project.

The quest for equal participation is best captured in Lü's lectures on *Yoga Bodhisattva Prātimokṣa* and the corresponding *Proceedings [for Conferring Bodhisattva Prātimokṣa]*. Two aspects of Lü's view warrant further attention. The first is Lü's preference for a historical narrative about the formation of bodhisattva vinaya. The second is the equal application of rules in *Yoga Bodhisattva Prātimokṣa* to both the laity and monastics. This provision for lay-monastic equality is in stark contrast to the hierarchy of monastics supervising the laity presented in the *Brahmā Net Sūtra*.[18] As I will demonstrate, both aspects are indicative of the concrete steps taken by Lü to establish a communism of soteriological knowledge.

Establishing this historical narrative necessitated Lü's use of rigorous methods as a means to extract soteriological knowledge. Lü Cheng dismissed the validity of the *Brahmā Net Sūtra* that made the Buddha preach, in one setting, all bodhisattva precepts and the proceedings for conferring precepts. To a certain extent, the genre of the Mahāyāna sūtra predetermined the *Brahmā Net Sūtra*'s ahistorical narrative. As is well known, most authors of Mahāyāna scriptures suffer from the inferiority complex of their words not-being-the-words-of-the-Buddha.[19] To sidestep this problem, authors of Mahāyāna scriptures often employ mythical settings and present these texts as a record of what has been said by supramundane buddhas. The *Brahmā Net Sūtra* adopted these time-honored Mahāyāna hermeneutics. It opens with the historical Buddha emitting miraculous light in the deep *dhyāna*. It then has the Buddha transport the assembly to the presence of the mythical Buddha Vairocana. Later in the narrative, it presents the full set of bodhisattva precepts as preached by the primordial Buddha Vairocana. Dismissing the myth in the *Brahmā Net Sūtra*, Lü discredited the sūtra's ahistorical authentication strategy.

To justify his contrasting myth of a historical bodhisattva community, Lü needed a historical narrative about the birth and formation of bodhisattva precepts, in parallel with the development of monastic vinaya. Thus, in his lectures, Lü emphasized that *Yoga Bodhisattva Prātimokṣa* and its *Karman* constitute a collection of different precepts and procedures that the Buddha preached on different occasions and that Bodhisattva Maitreya collected later into one text. This narrative mirrors Śrāvaka Upāli's recitation and the eventual collection of monastic precepts in the first Buddhist Council of 500 Arhats. Recall that in 1926 Lü had already begun his mission of extracting the principles of vinaya for establishing local communities.[20] In 1943 Lü put his two decades of scholarship into action.

In his lecture notes, Lü promoted structural equality between the bodhisattva community and the śrāvaka community. This is clearly seen in Lü's arrangement of the four grave offenses (Skt: *pārājika*; Ch: *tashengchu* 他勝處 or *boluoyi* 波羅夷). For example, in his collation of *Yoga Bodhisattva Prātimokṣa*, in the footnotes, Lü carefully pointed out all instances of the phrase "Resembling Śrāvaka Precepts" (*xiangsi shengwen jie* 相似聲聞戒).[21] In *Essentials*, Lü's intentional promotion of the bodhisattva vinaya as parallel to the monastic codes was relegated to the footnotes, whereas in his 1943 lectures on *Five Disciplines*, this intention was made explicit.

As shown in table 5.1, a key feature in this rearrangement is that Lü explicitly linked the purification of the mind with institutional regulations, causing the rearrangement to demonstrate remarkable structural resemblance to his aesthetic revolution. Furthermore, he arranged the four grave offenses of both *Yoga Bodhisattva Prātimokṣa* and *Śrāvaka Prātimokṣa* in parallel, in accordance with how they had been set up to eliminate the three root mental afflictions (greed, anger, ignorance) for two kinds of communities and two paths: the bodhisattva and the śrāvaka.[22]

Lü's gymnastics to create an independent textual transmission of bodhisattva vinaya followed the steps that Lü had laid out in his 1926 essay. First, Lü

TABLE 5.1. The Four Grave Offenses

	Tan 貪 (*Greed*)	*Dao* 盜 *Stealing* (*Greed*)	*Chenhui* 嗔恚 (*Anger*)	*Wangyu* 妄語 *Lying* (*Ignorance*)
瑜伽菩薩戒 *Yoga Bodhisattva Prātimokṣa*	*Zizan huita* 自讚毀他 Praising oneself, undercutting others	*Linxi caifa* 慳吝財法 Displaying stinginess in wealth and Dharma	*Fennao youqing* 忿惱有情 Showing anger and irritation with sentient beings	*Sishuo bangfa* 似說謗法 Preaching specious teaching and slandering Dharma
Shengwen jie 聲聞戒 *Śrāvaka Prātimokṣa*	*Yinyu* 淫欲 Having sex	*Buyuqu* 不與取 Taking what is not given	*Sha* 殺 Killing	*Weizheng weizheng* 未證謂證 Claiming enlightenment that has not yet been achieved

insisted that everything must trace back to the words of the Buddha. He then pointed out that all the bodhisattva points of learning (Ch: *xuechu* 學處; Skt: *śikṣāpada*) were first scattered among various sūtras that the Buddha had preached under different circumstances, just like monastic codes were first preached depending on the occasion. He subsequently noted that Bodhisattva Maitreya undertook the project of compiling all these scattered points of learning into one chapter in *Yogācārabhūmi*, thereby referring to the following passage from the Yogācāra classic:[23]

> As for the bodhisattva points of learning, the Buddha discussed them according to occasions in various discourses. . . . Now, they are collected in this underlying matrix of the bodhisattva piṭaka.

> 菩薩學處，佛於彼彼素呾纜中隨機於散說. . . . 今於此菩薩藏摩呾理迦，綜集而說.[24]

Instead of using an earlier translation of Yogācāra precepts *Bodhisattvabhūmi-sūtra* (Ch: *Pusadi chi jing* 菩薩地持經) attributed to Tan Wuchan, Lü Cheng harked back to Maitreya through Xuanzang's seventh-century translation. Attentive readers by now will see Lü's consistent maneuver to use Xuanzang and Yijing as the pivots for legitimizing Chinese Yogācāra: they had translated all essential teachings of Nālandā, considered the peak of Indian Buddhist learning, into Chinese. Thus, Lü's manufactured lineage of bodhisattva vinaya coincided with his imagined Yogācāra lineage: the historical Buddha→Bodhisattva Maitreya→Nālandā learning→Xuanzang's and Yijing's translations→the China Inner Learning Institute.[25] This manufactured lineage provided Lü with a justification for establishing a valid modern polity embodying the spirit of Buddhist democracy.

To justify the authenticity of Maitreya's authorship, Lü imbued the Indian term "the underlying matrix" (Ch: *benmu* 本母; Skt: *mātṛka*, *mātarī*) with the modern concept of intertextuality. In doing so, he dislodged the issue of authenticity from the historicity of the person Maitreya. Rather, Lü redefined authenticity as intertextual practices. Lü's use of this strategy prefigures Hidenori S. Sakuma's argument that Yogācāra authorship is a marker of doctrinal affiliation rather than individual properties.[26] Homing in on the intertextual practices of *Yogācārabhūmi*, Lü first claimed that what Maitreya had compiled was not only firmly grounded in the underlying matrix of Mahāyāna sūtras but also itself served as an underlying matrix for many later treatises. According to Lü,

> In the treatises, if these [passages] are cited by other treatises, then they are mātṛka.
>
> 論議中有為餘論所本者即為本母.[27]

For Lü, the authenticity of Maitreya's authorship lay in the text's intertextual connections, both in terms of what it cites and how it is cited by later texts: this network of intertextuality supports the identification of a doctrinal system that can be traced back to Maitreya. To be clear, Lü's definition of the matrix seems to have been his own invention. Lü understood the underlying matrix as a relationality embedded in a mycelial meshwork of textual connections, in the sense that if a treatise was quoted by some later treatise, then the quoted treatise would become an underlying matrix for the later treatise. In this way, Lü repackaged *mātṛka* as the Buddhological notion of intertextuality.

Lü further employed this invented mātṛka-cum-intertextuality to defend the authenticity of the compilation of *Yogācārabhūmi* in general and the collection of Yogācāra bodhisattva precepts in particular. He first pointed out that Maitreya's compilation of this vinaya text was neither randomly done nor hastily put into a book but was modeled after an earlier compilation in *Baoji jing* 寶積經 (*Heap of Jewels Sūtra*; Skt: *Ratnakūṭa-sūtra*).[28] Then he asserted that only saint scholars like Bodhisattva Maitreya could undertake such an enterprise. Because he considered the text to be buttressed by the sainthood of Maitreya and the authentic teachings in the *Heap of Jewels*, Lü claimed that one must take this unparalleled bodhisattva vinaya seriously. To further cement the centrality of *Yoga Bodhisattva Prātimokṣa*, Lü Cheng asserted that the rigorous mātṛka-cum-intertextuality of this edition rendered it the clearest and most succinct. For Lü, intertextuality dislodged the authority of oral transmission (i.e., tying authority to the historicity of the hearers/śrāvakas) and reestablished authority through intertextual conventions (i.e., locating authority in the written words).

To understand how this mātṛka-cum-intertextuality worked to authenticate Lü's bodhisattva lineage, scholars must examine Lü's expositions of the *Heap of Jewels Sūtra—Mahākāśyapa Chapter.* First of all, among different translations of *Heap of Jewels Sūtra*, he chose *Moheyan baoyan jing* 摩訶衍寶嚴經 (*The Sūtra of the Great Jewel Ornament*; Skt: *Mahāratnapratimaṇḍitasūtra*; T.351; henceforth, *Great Jewel Ornament*). This is the text that he edited and included in the third collection of *Essentials*. In *Five Disciplines*, he paired it with a chapter from *Yogācārabhūmi* that he considered to be commenting directly on *Great Jewel Ornament.*[29] This pairing created an intertextual link and equated the bodhisattva practices in *Great Jewel Ornament* (which may or may not have direct links with *Yogācārabhūmi*) with the explications of bodhisattva vinaya in *Yogācārabhūmi*. With this "discovered" link, Lü was able to claim that Yogācāra bodhisattva precepts are indeed the underlying principles of the bodhisattva practices explicated in all editions of *Heap of Jewels Sūtra*, cementing the authenticity of the Yogācāra school onto the earlier and more broadly accepted genre represented by *Heap of Jewels Sūtra.*

Once Lü had established the historicity of the Yogācāra interpretation that all previous bodhisattva practices were included in various transmissions of *Heap of Jewels Sūtra*, Lü sought to strengthen the link of soteriology with sociality as well as inner cultivation with social reform. He asserted that Yogācāra bodhisattva practices rely on "innate endeavor, contemplation of the innerworkings of the consciousness (*xin* 心), independent of other causes; unlike śrāvakas' reliance on the [objectified] words of the Buddha for liberation."[30] With this statement, Lü presented mātṛka-cum-intertextuality as the textual trace of the intersubjective consciousness that underpins the authenticity of a Yogācāra bodhisattva lineage.

To establish the historicity of an independent bodhisattva lineage, Lü Cheng also had to explain away the fact that, in early Mahāyāna Buddhism, all Mahāyāna monastics were ordained in śrāvaka vinaya traditions. His explanation, again, repeated well-known Mahāyānist rhetoric. He argued that past bodhisattvas took part in the learnings of the śrāvakas only to demonstrate their skill-in-means and inclusiveness: śrāvaka learning was only one part of what they vowed to learn and hence the all-encompassing bodhisattva vow further demonstrated the superiority of the bodhisattva vehicle.[31]

Despite these exaggerated claims, Lü's scholarship reveals a concerted effort to establish an independent bodhisattva institution buttressed by a bounded textual and institutional lineage of Mahāyāna vinaya. Once Lü had manufactured a historicity of bodhisattva vinaya's institutional independence, he sought to design rules of conduct for this new kind of community. By designing these communal guidelines, Lü proposed his own processual social philosophy, which opened up a new horizon from which to see communities not as the sum of individual agents but as mycelial networks of mutual commitment, reciprocal actions and relations, voluntary associations, guides for self-governance, and the shared goal of co-liberation.

Dharmic Democracy: Civil Society as Motivated, Organizational Coactions

Scholars agree that the historical Buddha was not a prince and the Shakya clan was most likely a republican state with some sovereignty.[32] When T. W. Rhys Davids pointed out these inconvenient facts in his 1903 *Buddhist India*, the idea of Buddhist democracy caught on among many Indian revolutionaries and Buddhist anticolonialists alike, largely because one of the pretexts for British colonizers denying India independence was the Orientalist claim that Indians could not govern themselves democratically. To this day, however, no study has mapped out how inchoate monastic republicanism gained a new afterlife as Dharmic democracy, thereby escaping the dualistic impasse between capitalism and communism across modern Asia. Nor has any study considered its vast unexplored connections with processual social philosophy.[33]

Lü employed Yogācāra karmic theory to theorize civil society as motivated, organizational coactions. Rather than pigeonhole Lü's theory of democracy as merely a "religious" vision outside of the public or "secular" discussions about self-governance and the future of humanity, I suggest that we take seriously Lü's processual social philosophy and theory of coaction and include similar kinds of Buddhist democratic theories of nonviolent, noncoercive, complex society. Failing to do so would reproduce the implicit Orientalism of the secular paradigm.[34]

Before analyzing Lü's theory of democracy, I need to clarify the theoretical frameworks of process social ontology and the theory of action and coaction. Process social ontology is a branch of social ontology proposed by Jason

Ānanda Josephson Storm. According to Storm, in the processual paradigm, change is taken for granted, the primary research question also shifts from why and how things change to why and how things can remain stable for a while. Storm invites scholars to investigate what are the broader causal processes that anchor seemingly stable properties of certain social entities.[35] As for the theory of action and coaction, in addition to Valmisa's coaction paradigm and Adamek's model of agency of relations discussed in the introduction, it is also useful to note Tim Ingold's theory of tasking. For Ingold, a task "is not something you do completely from your own free will" but rather "an act to which you submit as indeed you must submit to the world in whose form-giving processes you partake, and from which you draw your very being."[36] In other words, readers can conceive karma-informed, action-oriented ethics as a Buddhist theory of tasking, which underpins Lü's innovative democratic theory of no-self, interdependence, and compassion.

Lü theorized Buddhist democracy in three steps. First, in this explication, "vinaya learning" (*jiexue* 戒學) means the "overarching principles" (*gangwei* 綱維) of all motivated activities in Buddhist soteriology: learnings (*xue* 學) and practices (*xing* 行). He wrote,

> Vinaya learning is the overarching principles that interpenetrate and cohere all learnings and practices.
>
> 戒學乃貫通一切學行之綱維也.[37]

Although *gangwei* has taken on a variety of meanings ranging from the legal code of a country to an outline of a text to the administrators or guardians of disciplines in a monastery, in Lü's idiosyncratic use, *gangwei* signifies the set of rules governing all Buddhist soteriological activities, ranging from personal behaviors to communal affairs, to all business matters related to knowledge production. Some readers might find it surprising that Lü included knowledge production in soteriology. Lü anticipated this reaction. To justify his inclusion of knowledge production in vinaya, Lü reinterpreted the modern sense of learning in terms of the traditional understanding of two core sets of soteriological practices: (1) three learnings (*sanxue* 三學), namely, *śīla* (*jie* 戒), *samādhi* (*ding* 定), and *prajñā* (*hui* 慧); and (2) six perfections, namely, *dāna* (gift), *śīla* (moral discipline), *kṣānti* (forbearance), *vīrya* (vigor), *dhyāna* (contemplation), and *prajñā* (wisdom). Note that *śīla*, or *jie*, ranks first among the three learnings and the second among the six perfections. In Lü's paradigm, three learnings represent the learning aspect of *xuexing* 學行, and six perfections represent the practical aspect. He elaborates:

> In Buddha Dharma, there are learnings, which are always called three learnings. Among [three learnings], vinaya learning is the first. In Buddha Dharma, there are practices, of which six perfections are the ultimate. Among [six perfections], the first four, namely, donation, moral discipline, forbearance, and vigor, are all subsumed under vinaya [learning].
>
> 佛法有學, 恆稱三學, 而以戒學居首. 佛法有行, 六度最勝, 而前四度施戒忍勤, 統攝於戒.[38]

Thus Lü elevated vinaya learning as the compass guiding all Buddhist soteriological task. Using vinaya learning as the pivot, Lü integrated the scholarly production of knowledge with the soteriological goal.

More concretely, vinaya learning organizes and guides social actions. Lü subsumed the first four of six pāramitās—*dāna*, *śīla*, *kṣānti*, and *vīrya*—into vinaya learning. All four serve as guidance for one's social or interpersonal actions. Donation entails actions of generosity. Moral discipline entails ethical actions. Forbearance, in the Chinese context, entails acceptance or equanimity when facing insult. Vigor entails a strict work ethic. This reinterpretation of vinaya learning as the organizing principles of social action permeates Lü's explications of his selected canonical sūtras and śāstras (treatises). For Lü, vinaya learning alone governed all Buddhist socio-soteriological knowledge production and activation.

Lü put forth two central arguments in his explication of *Extensive Pure Vinaya*. First, he argued that the outcome of this bodhisattva path is different from that of the śrāvaka one: buddhahood vs. arhatship. As discussed in chapter 4, Lü saw buddhahood as intersubjective oneness, and this rendered bodhisattva vinaya as the guideline for all actions leading to co-liberation.

Second, Lü prioritized bodhisattva vinaya because it merged the two processes of purifying the mind and building institutional-social equality into one Möbius band. He claimed that the śrāvaka vinaya merely "constrains behavior," whereas the springhead of bodhisattva vinaya is the originally pure consciousness (*shixin benjing* 是心本淨) and therefore the function of bodhisattva vinaya is to guard one's consciousness.[39] The significance of this manufactured dichotomy should not be underestimated. In chapter 4 I discussed why Lü began *Five Disciplines* with the Chinese equivalent of *Dhammapada*. The doctrinal lineage that Lü manufactured is that the teaching of the "originally pure heart defiled by guest dust" dovetails well with the Yogācāra soteriological strategy of "perfuming through hearing" to wash off guest dust and thereby justifies the foundational tenet of Lü's system—original quiescence. In the discipline of Vinaya, Lü made a similar argument based on the guidelines of coactions. He then traced the support for the two previous claims to the well-known *Vimalakīrti Sūtra*, which has frequently appeared in commentarial traditions that promote lay Buddhism in East Asia.[40]

This elevation of the mind over conduct had important philosophical implications for Lü. Not only did it allow him to claim philosophical-cum-soteriological independence for the bodhisattva path, but it also enabled him to redefine vinaya learning as the philological bedrock of motivated social action. Let us take another look at table 5.1, which shows how he explicitly arranged the four grave offenses of both *Yoga Bodhisattva Prātimokṣa* and *Śrāvaka Prātimokṣa* in parallel and consistently stressed this dichotomy of guarding the mind vs. constraining behavior.

Two more features in table 5.1 showcase Lü's merging of spiritual purification with structural reform. First, for each offense, Lü Cheng identified a fundamental affliction (Skt: *kleśas*) to be purified, which effectively redefined all processes of acting as motivated by liberation. In both *Prātimokṣa*s, the first two precepts protect one against greed; the third precept protects one against anger; and the fourth precept protects one from ignorance.[41]

Second, once the four grave offenses had been abstracted into three root afflictions, Lü reoriented the focus of each bodhisattva grave rule toward the social and the intersubjective interconditioning and thereby portrayed bodhisattva vinaya and śrāvaka vinaya as two separate but parallel paths. The general formula also changed from the śrāvaka perspective of "what one shall not do" to the bodhisattva perspective of "what one shall not do to *others*." The first bodhisattva grave rule demands that, to protect against greed, one shall not praise oneself and slander others. In contrast with the monastic first grave offense of abstaining from sex, this bodhisattva stipulation renders "others" more visible and active partners in keeping one away from greed. The second demands that one shall not be stingy in providing wealth to others and must share Buddha Dharma broadly. Note that the second stipulation is a double negative, which then becomes an active promotion of what one shall do—selflessly provide material and spiritual support to further others' progress on the path. Similarly, the third stipulation to purge anger not only forbids one to harbor any animosity against others but also requires one to actively forgive others who have angered or irritated oneself. The fourth rule, not slandering Dharma, is concerned more with the welfare of the community: how to teach others the genuine Buddhist message. Although appearing last in the list, for Lü, the fourth bodhisattva grave rule of guarding against ignorance was considered the easiest to breach yet the most important to maintain, as Lü believed this rule alone could distinguish genuine Buddhism from Māra's heresy.[42]

Equally important, in Lü's paradigm, bodhisattva vinaya appears as guidelines to incentivize mutual commitment and collective action. These prosocial, relational rules not only institutionalize the soteriology of dismantling the self/other dichotomy but also open up one's internal psychological gaze to the intersubjective and the interdependent. When Lü criticized the śrāvaka path as overly individualistic, he did not deny the existence of altruism or compassion in early Indian Buddhism. Rather, he targeted the dualistic thinking embedded in these institutionalized practices. To remedy what he perceived as institutionalized individualism, Lü retooled the Yogācāra toolbox to support his quest for an intersubjective oneness actualized by communities guided by bodhisattva vinaya. In reviewing the rest of the forty-three minor offenses, we find an equal number of prohibition clauses and prescription clauses, which is the primary reason why Taixu also preferred the Yogācāra bodhisattva precepts over the well-established *Brahmā Net Sūtra*.[43] Both Lü and Monk Taixu valued the *Yoga Bodhisattva Prātimokṣa* for its orientation toward helping others. Nevertheless, Lü retheorized this other-orientedness into an organized practice of cultivating nirvāṇic interconditionality.

Echoing his 1920s call for establishing seed communities to actualize an aesthetic society, Lü's reinvention of bodhisattva vinaya demonstrates a keen awareness that one person alone can never revamp an unjust system and that to overcome systemic oppression, one must establish an alternative egalitarian system. As an architect of a new society, Lü theorized a joint social evolution grounded in the Buddhist principle of interdependence. Scholars must keep in mind that Lü sought to achieve two somewhat conflicting goals. On the one hand, he wanted to replace monasticism. On the other hand, he wanted to harness the prestige of monastic republicanism for a democracy in which laity and monastics would participate equally. To negotiate this tension inherent in his pursuit of Dharmic democracy, Lü turned to *Yoga Bodhisattva Prātimokṣa*, which became newly relevant precisely because it treats laity and monastics on more equal terms and thereby ensures equal conditions for liberation.

Once he had promoted Yogācāra precepts as a parallel but independent lineage, Lü was able to both harness the democratic spirit in early monasticism and replace monastics with bodhisattvas. As is well known, mainstream discourse in early Indian Buddhism stipulated that the laity be ruled under an enlightened monarchy and that monastics be governed by republicanism.[44] Once Buddhism spread to China, this stipulation was quickly integrated into the existing Chinese polity: a centralized monarchy with local communities governed under the rubric of family lineage or local elites. Therefore, it is fair to say that political theory in Chinese Buddhism remained hierarchical.[45] In the Republican era, many monastic reformers looked to Protestantism,

Catholicism, and corporations for inspiration in building new Buddhist organizational structures.[46] These social experiments contributed to the rise of the Four Mountains in Taiwanese Buddhism and imprinted a decisively nondemocratic-cum-corporate gene on modern Chinese Buddhism.[47] Embarking on a less traveled path, Lü rejected these centralized models. Instead, he merged Buddhist monastic republicanism with bodhisattva ideals to legitimize a Buddhist social democracy.[48]

Lü's theory of democracy has significant philosophical implications: he redefined democratic governance as rules of intersubjective deliberation, which reveals his commitment to building a deliberative democracy. I define "deliberative democracy" as a talk-centric process for making decisions.[49] I employ this concept to foreground Lü Cheng's proclivity toward using the nonviolent, dialogical method in building group cohesion. The concept of deliberative democracy also distinguishes Lü's project from mass democracy. Mass democracy typically requires decisions to be made by the majority and hence oppresses minorities. Lü's Buddhist democracy was modeled after early monastic republicanism, in which monastics used a predetermined set of rules to decide important matters through nonviolent means. Note that it is considered nonviolent because, at least on paper, the worst punishment for grave offenses committed by a monk or nun was excommunication, with other monks and nuns refusing to talk with the offenders anymore.

Lü's deliberative democracy is distinctively Buddhist. This is because in Lü's bodhisattva vinaya, the manner of deliberation must be not only civil but also conducive to one's purification of the consciousness: no self-aggrandizement or undermining others. The other three grave offenses work in tandem with the first to guard one's intention in deliberation and action. Lü saw the goal of deliberation not as the elimination of normativity but as the assurance that norms would emerge through a fair and civil process. The only absolute emotional norm is compassion, or speaking from the point of care and interconnectedness: in particular, helping oneself and others to purge selfish impulses and to purify the consciousness. Hence, Lü Cheng not only integrated his idealistic tendencies into Yogācāra studies but also gave his dream an institutional form by establishing a set of rules conducive for bringing forth the intersubjective potential in every participant.

To transform these rules from static words on paper to everyday lived experiences, Lü designed Yogācāra rituals to be performed. In addition to articulating the bodhisattva rules themselves, Lü Cheng included in *Essentials* a ritual text on *Yoga Bodhisattva Karman* (T.1499) mirroring the monastic biweekly assembly procedure.[50] These biweekly assemblies were confession services, when monastics confessed to their peers their personal violations of these moral codes (Skt. *karman*; Ch: *jiemo* 羯磨).[51] During a karman, a head monk would lead by reciting the monastic codes one by one, pausing after each section to ask whether anyone had committed any relevant offenses.[52] For those who violated minor rules, an open confession within the community would serve as the punishment. No further actions were needed. For those who violated the four grave offenses of sex, stealing, killing, and lying about their supernatural power, expulsion from the monastic community, or the cessation of any communication or cohabitation with peers, was required.[53] This communal ceremony, together with the monastic moral codes, served to guarantee inchoate republicanism in which vital decisions related to liberation were made by all monastics together. In the ritual text on Yogācāra communal procedures, there is no specific requirement for a biweekly assembly. Rather, the text explains in detail when and to whom to confess and repent when a violation is committed,[54] leaving the exact confession procedures open for each community to establish for itself.

As in early Indian monastic republicanism, in Lü's new bodhisattva profession, there is no centralized power. Instead, authority is granted by rigorous method of producing knowledge, epistemic openness, and the democratic deliberation process. The process of decision making, including the rules governing how one shall practice and how one shall interpret, is a process of deliberation that unfolds via questions and answers. Admittedly, in all selected textbooks in *Five Disciplines*, the Buddha has the final word, providing answers to all these questions. The role of the bodhisattva learners, then, is to keep asking questions and exhorting the Buddha to clarify matters for them. However, as I discuss in the next chapter, since the Buddha is no longer with us, Lü, inspired by Vasubandhu, abstracted the Buddha as the *dharmakāya* whose authenticity is to be extracted only by proper hermeneutics.[55] Consequently, for Lü, the saṅgha, whose members shoulder the responsibility of maintaining and spreading genuine soteriological knowledge, comes to constitute a self-governed, democratic epistemological community that maintains interpretative authority by practicing comparative hermeneutics. This reorientation of Yogācāra bodhisattva precepts lay at the core of the democratic turn in Lü's liberation Buddhology.

Bodhisattvas of Democracy in Action

This democratic turn also led to a novel interpretation of social engagement. Recall that the goal of this Buddhist democracy was to actualize one true-reality dharma realm, or nirvāṇa. Once the meaning of nirvāṇa-cum-extinguishing-suffering was reframed as establishing a new sociality, known as nirvāṇa-cum-one-true-reality-realm, the six perfections accrued a new layer of meaning as the chief means for aspiring bodhisattvas to dismantle bastions of privilege and establish alternative and just social structures. Lü's reinvention of six pāramitās did not cause them to diverge from their premodern role as skill-in-means.[56] Rather, his innovation lay crucially in reorienting the path of personal awakening into a copoietic praxis.

Lü Cheng drew inspiration from *She dacheng lun* 攝大乘論 (Skt: *Mahāyānasaṃgraha*; henceforth, *Msg*), a text considered a compass for navigating the complete Mahāyāna path. Lü Cheng located this treatise in the discipline of Yogācāra of the second phase in *Five Disciplines*. It is important to recall that the second phase is when one learns the central tenets of inner learning and that the essence of inner learning is Lü's Yogācāra doctrine of original quiescence and *āśrayaparivṛtti*. Lü marked this treatise as both the first scripture establishing the doctrine of consciousness-only and the guide for the Mahāyāna path.[57] In 1963, he elaborated further:

> *Mahāyānasaṃgraha* is a book succinctly expounding the characteristics of Mahāyāna teachings. It explicates the Mahāyāna path (i.e., the Mahāyāna path of practice) and broadly discerns its cause and effect (i.e., various causes and effects concerning insight into Dharma characteristics) as well as differentiates progressions in practice (i.e., the degrees of progress concerning the causes and effects of practice). Six pāramitās lay out the blueprint of causes and effects. Ten stages lay out the blueprint of progression in practice.
>
> 《攝大乘論》是種扼要說明大乘學說特點的書,它說大乘道 (即大乘的踐行),大分彼入因果 (有關證悟法相的各類因果) 彼修差別 (有關因果修行的次第) 兩個方面. 因果以六度為綱, 差別則以十地為綱.[58]

Both Ouyang and Lü considered *Msg* as explicating the path through two aspects: first, causes and effects, and second, progression. Though these two aspects are focused on the *hows* of this path, their theoretical foundation, or the *whys* of this path, is explained in the three sections that follow the opening section: section 2, "Ālayavijñāna"; section 3, "Three Natures"; and section 4, "Consciousness-only." Note that my English-language translation of the section titles follows Ouyang's explication of the text in the preface to *Essentials*. Ouyang's explication also echoes the internal structure of *Msg*. According to Ouyang, section 2 cites a wide range of sūtras and treatises to prove that what constitutes the mind-heart is *ālayavijñāna*—the storehouse of all mental seeds. Section 3 moves on to the explication of three natures as establishing the emptiness of all entities. For Ouyang, this section paves the way for systematizing three natures as a path of practice: the dependent nature refers to an illusory grasping of seeds in *ālayavijñāna*, the imagined nature refers to a further grasping of the illusory dependent nature as essence, and the perfected nature refers to the correct view of the dependent nature as illusory.[59] Then section 4, explicating consciousness-only, establishes the key to the path as realizing all entities as merely consciousness: a change of perspective that allows one to abandon the imagined, to see through the dependent, and to realize the perfected. For Ouyang, the distinctive feature of *Msg* was that it arranges all essential Yogācāra doctrines in the form of a path: from section 4 to section 10, *Msg* focuses on six pāramitās and their efficacy in transforming oneself and others. This pragmatist orientation in Ouyang's interpretation was expanded upon by Lü.

Two teachings from *Msg* undergird Lü's socially engaged reinterpretation of Yogācāra soteriology. The first is that six pāramitās are the means to enter the truth of consciousness-only (*vijñānamātratā*). Section 5 of this scripture describes in detail why and how a bodhisattva should practice all six perfections in order to realize the nature of consciousness-only. The second is the differentiation of the *dharmakāya* from the enjoyment body and the manifestation body. To highlight the importance of unyielding effort in revolutionizing consciousness, Lü repeatedly alluded to both the six *pāramitās* and the differentiation of *dharmakāya* doctrines in his explications of other scriptures. For example, in explicating the function of *bodhicitta* in the *Dacheng fajie wu chabie lun* 大乘法界無差別論 (*Treatise on Non-Distinction in the Great Vehicle Dharma Realm*; T.1627), Lü discussed the *bodhicitta* in terms of its efficacy in gradually purifying mental affections and in accumulating merits. He simultaneously critiqued the Huayan (華嚴; Skt: Avataṃsaka) interpretation of dependent arising grounded in the doctrine of original enlightenment. According to Lü, original enlightenment mistakes the result (*dharmakāya*) for the cause (*bodhicitta*).[60] He stressed that even though all sentient beings possess this innate original quiescence, because they have not yet realized their own spiritual potential, they must gradually accumulate merits and revolutionize their consciousness. To further justify this gradual path, Lü cited *Baoxing lun* 寶性論 (Skt: *Ratnagotravibhāga*; T.1611) and argued that the ultimate teaching of the Buddha is to awaken one's *bodhicitta* and progress through the ten stages of the path.[61] The critical term in Lü's interpretation of six perfections is "accumulation through practice" (*xiuji* 修集), which highlights the gradualness of this bodhisattva path.

This bodhisattva path is gradual because it is a path of co-liberation: when read in tandem with *Yoga Bodhisattva Prātimokṣa* and Lü's emphasis on deep learning and extensive investigation, six perfections adopt a social dimension. This is clearly seen in Lü's classification of the forty-three minor bodhisattva precepts into practices of six perfections. For example, the perfection of donation entails seven of the forty-three precepts. Among these seven precepts on donation, in addition to the well-known rules of donating time and wealth, this section demands that one share one's knowledge with others.[62]

Furthermore, all Lü's interpretations reframe the premodern teachings of *Yoga Bodhisattva Prātimokṣa* in terms of structural analysis. For example, two interpretations of the perfection of *śīla* in Lü's lecture notes on *Yoga Bodhisattva Prātimokṣa* seem to have been new. Lü's interpretation of the precept of killing allows lay bodhisattvas to kill one person to pacify the world (*sha dufu yi antianxia* 殺獨夫以安天下). Regarding stealing, Lü allowed lay bodhisattvas to seize power from corrupt officials who oppress commoners or misuse public funds and to confiscate and return unjustly gained wealth.[63] Clearly, both interpretations of the respective precepts require aspiring bodhisattvas to see through and dismantle oppressive social systems.

Another example is Lü's interpretation of the perfection of forbearance, which offers detailed instructions on how to practice organized skepticism grounded in compassion: enduring others' accusations, remaining resilient in face of difficulties, cultivating deep insights into the truth, letting go of revenge, and taking responsibility for one's mistakes.[64] Similarly, the next three perfections, according to Lü, entail different skill sets needed to engage in knowledge production and circulation. The perfection of vigor demands one learn broadly and investigate extensively to strengthen one's ability to offer soteriological knowledge to others. The perfection of *dhyāna* demands one achieve meditative absorption to gain supernatural powers to learn broadly and investigate extensively. Meanwhile, the perfection of wisdom demands one gain unobstructed wisdom to acquire unlimited ability to help others.[65]

Lü's idiosyncratic rendering of a Buddhist community cohered by motivated coactions opens up many meaningful avenues for further research. First, Lü's Yogācāra social theory raises a fundamental question about the possibility of decolonization: How can individuals build a livable world nonviolently? Lü's experiment compels us to rethink the promises of secular democracy. When the Marxists called for a violent overthrow of the existing political system, when the Chinese Nationalists and the warlords resorted to power and wealth to gain control, when some May Fourth intellectuals called for Westernization, and when mainstream Chinese culture resorted to scientism and facts as the nation's salvation, Lü Cheng, instead of succumbing to the destructive impulse to gain power or seeking refuge in the lowest common denominator—objective certainty—theorized a new model of an ideal society grounded in Yogācāra intersubjective openness.

Lü Cheng's democratic theory is radical in two senses. Rejecting destructive excitement is radical in the sense that it sets up nonviolent revolution as the norm and asks a new question: How can evil be eliminated with revolutionary nonviolence? Destructive excitement is as ancient as human civilization. As early as the third century BC the Indian epic *Mahābhārata* narrated a story of world renewal: one needs a just war to end all wars.[66] As early as the second century BC, the first emperor of China, in his Mount Zhifu inscriptions, claimed that he deployed his "punitive troops" out of "pity for the multitude" and that the punishment he meted out was "just" and his actions were "trustworthy."[67] Like the historical Buddha who refused to launch any war and watched his kin of the Shakya state be massacred by the Kosala King Viḍūḍabha, Lü swam against the torrents of violence and chose nonviolent coactions to render the destructive model obsolete.[68]

Second, Lü's socio-soteriology raises another compelling question: Can compassion serve as a substrate of ethics and as an ethos toward the thematization of religious difference and moral pluralism? Lü's revolution was neither an economic nor a political one. It could be considered a social revolution if one acknowledges its radical reimagination of what makes a nonhierarchical complex society possible: intersubjectivity and an agentless human agency sanctified by the Yogācāra theory of consciousness-only.[69] In Lü's Yogācāra paradigm, the unfolding of afflicted consciousness, *vijñāna-pārināṃa*, explains the ongoing devolution of the survival of the fittest. In his socio-soteriology, the path of emancipation is explained in terms of *āśrayaparivṛtti*, pointing toward the full manifestation of the great compassion innate to all yet accessible only through earnest scholarship and unending moral deliberation.

The appeal of this Yogācāra evolution lies in the fact that it affirms the spiritual potential of everyone yet simultaneously recognizes each person's limitations and consequently arms them with not only spiritual tools like meditation, precepts, and inspiring Jātaka stories but also guidelines for democratic coactions, reciprocal scrutiny, and nonhierarchical social engagement so as to facilitate the person's continued progress toward awakening the innate original quiescence. Its persuasive power hinges on one's willingness to take a leap of faith: one must recognize one's infinite future possibilities. However, is this leap of faith harder to accept than Deweyan natural piety, social Darwinist egoism, or the modern myth of the atomized individual?

Lü's Democratic Experiments After 1949

Studying Lü Cheng's democratic experiment underscores a thorny issue, namely, the intense intellectual demands on citizens in a social democracy. Although Lü remained optimistic about the intellectual potential of his fellow learners, history proved him wrong. After 1949, the mass democracy (*Renmin minzhu* 人民民主) in mainland China soon devolved into the mob rule of the Cultural Revolution. The Nationalist government in Taiwan abandoned martial law and turned to democracy only in 1978.[70] Equally important, the Chinese Buddhist organizations under both political systems turned away from the inchoate republicanism in the early saṅgha and instead embraced centralized control as the modus operandi. In the People's Republic of China, Zhongguo Fojiao xiehui 中国佛教协会 (the Buddhist Association of China) was an extension of the state. Under the state's aegis, the association fundamentally restructured monastic communities to suit the centralized state.[71] In Taiwan, the famous Four Mountains all adopted the corporate model, a nondemocratic hierarchy.[72]

Lü's ecology of compassion stands out among other nondemocratic forms of Buddhism. In the early years of Communist rule, Lü persistently pushed for his Dharmic social democracy. In a short 1953 essay titled "Just Awakening and Renunciation," Lü wrote,

> Because of the mutual activating and amplifying forces of shared karma, it is possible to improve upon the inferior by the force of the superior. . . . From the inception of the Buddhist teaching, [the goal] is to dismantle the unjust system [of caste]. To truly dismantle the human life of class [inequality], one must live a life grounded in what the Buddha said and form a group of people as such.

> 由共業的相互增上，可以因勝掩劣，. . .，佛家立說之始，便要打破這不平等的制度 . . . 佛家以為真能破除階級的人生，一定要依靠佛說的那樣生活，構成那一類的群眾，才做得到.[73]

"People as such," for Lü, are precisely the bodhisattvas of democracy. For Lü, these bodhisattvas would carry on the original intent of the Buddha to dismantle casteism and would continue to break down the class inequalities in this actual life. They would come from all walks of life (*you zhongzhong zhiye zhe weiqi chengyuan* 有種種職業者為其成員) and would be able overcome the limits of the renunciation lifestyle (*dapo le shamen chujia shenghuo de xianzhi* 打破了沙門出家生活的限制). They would organize a kind of social relations (*zuzhi le yilei shehui guanxi* 組織了一類社會關係) and should be the ones who are most aware of their responsibility to transform humanity (*duiyu rensheng gaige zuifu zerengan* 對於人生改革最負責任感).[74]

What remains of this short-lived experiment is a profound conviction that genuine Buddhism has always been socially engaged. In the early twentieth century, when leading intellectuals such as Cai Yuanpei proclaimed the demise of religion in public life, Lü's Yogācāra social theory offered a powerful rejoinder. Almost a century later, evolutionary psychologists of religion have started to see religion as the earliest experiment in addressing the demand for transcendence in any decent and just society that is larger than a tribe.[75] The driving force behind these studies seems not to be a desire for mere historical facts but a desire to find more harmonious ways to live together. This remarkable metamorphosis of religion from an ancient vestige to a treasure trove of techniques for social solidarity only accentuates Lü's prescience: for him, Buddhism was a valuable resource for cultivating compassionate and informed citizens of a caring global community. The aptness of Lü's socio-soteriology could not ensure its survival in a Darwinian world where Mao's aphorism "political power grows out of the barrel of guns" (*qiangganzi limian chu zhengquan* 枪杆子里面出政权) reigned supreme. However, Lü's failure is haunting: Can humanity ever escape the solipsistic trap on the one hand and the teeth and claws of evolution on the other?[76]

6
Scholarship for Salvation

In Lü's Yogācāra paradigm, it is up to humans themselves to break ground for new patterns of interconditioning to sprout; to rekindle humanness in this actual life corrupted by Darwinist competition; and to start living harmoniously, ethically, communally. However, in any communal life, conflicts are bound to arise. If one opts for nonviolent conflict resolution, it is necessary to first establish and then safeguard ethical standards. These ethical norms, in Lü's training program, must be guarded by a transformative epistemology—the third strands of Lü's tapestry of liberation Buddhology.

The term "transformative epistemology," in my use, refers to a metamethod of motivated, organized, and adaptive inquiries into alternative foundations of knowledge production, with ameliorative goals. I approach this chapter with a radical hope. Rather than position Lü's social philosophy as a "case study" to be embedded into mainstream conversations, I invite readers to see him as a partner and a collaborator so to contemplate together the theoretical generalizability of his liberation Buddhology.

What if adopting Lü's referents could bring forth a novel foundation for knowledge production? What if the new paradigm of liberation Buddhology allowed humans to build a nonelite-centered, nonhierarchical collective future? In asking these questions, I heed Leigh K. Jenco's call to study Chinese thought so to "recalibrate our expectations about what and how we learn, what counts as knowledge, and with whom and for whom we might produce it."[1] In 1985, Charles Taylor noted that social theories, unlike natural science, are "not about an independent object, but one that is partly constituted by self-understanding."[2] And part of the task of doing theory is to "extend, or criticize or even challenge" our "constitutive self-understandings." If social theory is inherently mind-dependent, then the practice of theorizing can never be objective and can only become objectified. As such, any theorizing that aspires to impartiality must acknowledge voices other than those of Greco-Euro-Americans. More than that, it must create space for minoritized voices to have their say in "structuring legitimate social theory."[3] While most scholars recognize the imperative to take on this responsibility, it is not clear how to do so in practice.

I suggest that the broader decolonial project could learn something tangible from Lü's liberation Buddhology. This is because many modern Chinese intellectuals undertook a similar project in the late nineteenth century, refashioning Buddhism as a resource for de-parochializing China and for democratic worldmaking.[4] Lü played an integral role in this project. In thinking with Lü in his struggle to globalize Buddhism and to bring forth democratic communities of compassion and interdependence, readers can learn from his rationale and gain viable strategies for producing knowledge for a just society.

More concretely, we can think with Lü on how Buddhist spiritual exercises came to be theorized as viable pathways for interconditioned unfolding of the very contexts that enable the production of nonobjectified knowledge, or social knowledge. The term "social knowledge," Helen E. Longino argues, connotes that objectivity emerges "as a function of community practices rather than an attitude of individual researchers."[5] To paraphrase Longino's theory of social knowledge in terms of Lü's epistemology—the Yogācāra three Cs, that is—"objectivity" emerges only when a community of learners (who are motivated by their quest for truth and for transforming consciousness and the world) commits to the epistemic standards of intersubjective corroboration, coherence, and causal efficacy.

Lü employed the Yogācāra epistemic standards of the three Cs to dismantle the naïve realism that underpins colonial knowledge production, the belief that there is one objective world shared by all humans and all species and the task of scholars is to see this one world as it is. This presumption of one shared world is fundamentally at odds with Yogācāra philosophy, in which every mental stream creates its own world and the larger shared cosmos consists of many karmically connected lifeworlds. Hence, the Yogācāra conception of intersubjectivity is inevitably intertwined with the problem of the incommensurability of different worlds.[6] More than a philosophical disagreement, in the eyes of Yogācāra philosophers, the single-minded ontological commitment to one shared world in Western culture came with a regrettable by-product, namely, the West's peculiar takes on objectivity and universality became institutionalized as the benchmark for scholarship and drowned out all other possible ways of philosophizing about the self and the world.[7]

But again, Lü's transformative epistemology resonates with the feminist theorizing of social epistemology. The danger of objectivity lies not in the ideas per se but in practice: once the discourse of objectivity became institutionalized, it obscured the power structure that determines what counts as valid knowledge, who gets to produce knowledge, and who gets to use knowledge to dominate others.[8] Or in Yogācāra terms, once intersubjective knowledge is objectified and universalized, this socially constructed discourse becomes naturalized as a proxy for more important social values of impartiality, fairness, and justice and thereby obscures the power dynamics that produce the discourses of objectivity. Once disappeared into the background, this invisiblized epistemic domination nudges scholars wedded to the status quo to adopt an "apolitical" posture and avoid uncomfortable yet critical reflection.

Given this widespread conflation of objectivity with impartiality, Lü's liberation Buddhology deserves to be taken seriously in structuring the contemporary reevaluation of critical theory.[9] This is because Lü's transformative epistemology, instead of hiding behind the veil of disinterestedness, made explicit its ethical norms: no-self, interdependence, and compassion. Anticipating Oreskes's recent observation that "empirical evidence alone is insufficient for understanding the basis of scientific conclusions" and Storm's call to both expose "unstated or undertheorized normative commitments [undergirding] specific subfields" and embrace a "politics of compassion and uplift,"[10] Lü theorized ethical normativity as a form of interconditioned behavioral patterns motivated by the Buddhist affect of great compassion and guided by reciprocally scrutinizing gaze of no-self and interdependence.

As a form of interconditioned normativity, Lü's revolutionary nonviolence positions itself as an ongoing, unfinished project that was started by the historical Buddha, transmitted across the world, and continues to adapt to changing circumstances. However, Lü saw the principles of adaptation to be generalizable across time and space. Therefore, unlike the intellectuals analyzed in chapter 3 who employed an inchoate notion of the three Cs to criticize the moral and ontological grounds of Western science, Lü went one step further in responding to questions of epistemology and institution building. He took concrete measures to institutionalize the three Cs into a social epistemology and organized skepticism. These institutionalized practices of the three Cs functioned to counter the institutionalized practices of objectivity and simultaneously established a model of democratic civil society whose principles and core ideas could be disseminated widely and whose form could be reproduced by and adapted to each locality correspondingly.

Furthermore, Lü inherited the well-tested Chinese strategy of grounding normativity in ritual and affect but adapted it to early twentieth-century

China.[11] Particularly, he reinterpreted the imported method of "critical thinking" (*pipan sixiang* 批判思想; or *pipan jingshen* 批判精神) as analytic rigor, which he then grounded in compassion and integrated into the supplementary readings in each phase of his *Five Disciplines*. More concretely, Lü first reinvented the "scientific method" in terms of the Yogācāra three Cs; redefined science as rigorous, intersubjective comparison; and simultaneously redefined moral inquiry as the scientific study of Buddhist teaching, seeing an opportunity to shift the conversation during the May Fourth movement, a period when many intellectuals viewed science as a promising institution and a progressive force that could save republicanism and help build a civil society.[12] With Buddhisized critical thinking, Lü refashioned the method of the day in the Buddhist terms of wisdom grounded in compassion.[13] That thinking challenges the secular discourse of "disinterested" scholarship by demonstrating the social constructedness of objectivity, the impossibility of "value neutrality," and the imperative to integrate care into all activities of knowledge production. In doing so, Lü, a century ahead of his time, problematized the positivist paradigm and philosophized scholarly standard as emergent, interconditioned social phenomena inlaid with the processes of open negotiation and intersubjective reflection.

Lü stipulated that such ongoing negotiation and intersubjective reflection must be conducted democratically, in the manner of organized skepticism, but complemented by hermeneutics of trust. Organized skepticism, a theory of scientific knowledge production first proposed by the sociologist Robert King Merton in 1942, suggests that scientists build trust based not on some so-called scientific method but on a regulated practice of cross-examining novel truth claims: (1) they examine the evidence and methods collectively and (2) they do it from a position of distrust, i.e., the burden of proof is on the person/group with a new claim.[14] The hermeneutics of trust are a well-known Gadamerian practice that requires the learner to strengthen others' arguments so that their claims might become illuminating.

In practice, Lü's transformative epistemology requires practitioners to distrust evidence and logic but trust the process of intersubjective inquiry and the possibility of mutual illumination and the fusion of horizons. This pattern of interweaving action is what I mean to suggest by defining "transformative epistemology" as a metamethod of motivated, organized, and adaptive inquiries into the foundations of scholarship and activism. Indeed, Lü envisioned knowledge production as a social practice for the purpose of democratic coliberation. Thus, Lü's liberation Buddhology is best understood as a social epistemology and a metamodel of transformative interrogation. It is transformative because it takes the foundation and values of knowledge production as an open process to be negotiated with the goal of transforming systemic oppressions into a world free from mental afflictions and social injustice.

Comparative Hermeneutics, Science, and Moral Inquiry

In 1924, in the first issue of the institute's official journal, *Neixue*, Lü published four essays. The first of these essays, "Dachengjing bijiao dufa" 大乘經比較讀法 (Comparative hermeneutics in reading Mahāyāna Sūtras; henceforth, "Comparative Hermeneutics"),[15] consists of the notes to a lecture that Lü delivered at the first research conference of the institute in July 1923. The significance of this essay should not be underestimated; indeed, it appears right after three of Ouyang's essays in the very first issue of this journal. Although praised by the contemporaneous Japanese scholar Satō Taijun 佐藤泰舜 (1890–1975) as one of only three worthy Buddhological studies in *Neixue* (all three articles praised by Satō had been written by Lü), Lü omitted this 1924 article when compiling his 1991 five-volume anthology.[16] This decision seems odd considering that Lü's other three essays published in the first issue of *Neixue* were all incorporated into *Xuanji1991*, including the one that Satō omitted. This omission also seems at odds with its centrality in Lü's transition from aesthetics to Yogācāra.

As discussed in chapter 1, in the course of refuting Bergsonian creative evolution, social Darwinism, and scientific realism, Lü theorized social reality as a subset of karmic interdependence within the broader Yogācāra causal theory of the perceptible worlds. In Lü's retooled version of Yogācāra causal theory, the scientific search for "objective" knowledge was framed in terms of intersubjective corroborations of connected, aggregated karmic processes. Although Lü's 1922 reframing lay at the heart of Lü's social epistemology, "Comparative Hermeneutics" marked Lü's first step toward replacing the benchmark of objectivity with his proposal of a systemized Yogācāra three Cs.

Philosophically speaking, once perceptible reality is equated with karmic processes, the quest of scientific truth is transformed into a quest for salvific truth—seeing reality *as is*. In practice, seeking scientific-cum-salvific truth, under this karmic paradigm, entails ridding oneself of egoistic graspings. To minimize subjective impositions, Lü designed a form of comparative hermeneutics, or a systematic procedure for setting up a robust interpretative matrix. This interpretative matrix consists of seven independent methods of cross-examination.[17] Each method has its own systemic strengths and limitations. When combined, the systemic strengths of one method promise to remedy the systemic limitations of the other methods. Lü's premise for doing so was that an unconscious, subjective imposition would be very unlikely to pass the test of all seven independent modes of comparison. At the very least, backed by this intricate matrix of cross-examination, Lü's approach maximizes the potential to lay bare both intentional manipulation and hidden prejudice, primarily through the cumulative examination of many relevant passages. Note that though Lü's seven-step interpretative matrix is innovative, each of the seven methods of cross-examination had its origins in previous Buddhist scholastic methods, Qing evidential scholarship, or European philology. When reassembled in Lü's new procedure and institutionalized as a communal practice, a particular interpretation could be transformed into well-tested, shared, salvific knowledge.

Before analyzing Lü's methodology, we must revisit Lü's philosophy of intersubjectivity. Recall that in chapter 4 I demonstrated that Lü considered original quiescence equivalent to original purity and the perfected nature in the Yogācāra doctrine of three natures. In his 1924 essay Lü set out to prove the truth of this equivalence with comparative hermeneutics. First, Lü named the Buddha's ineffable insight "the perfectly realized inner learning" (*yuanzheng zhi Neixue* 圓證之內學). He further asserted that to reach this inexpressible oneness, one must thoroughly penetrate and cohere all extant words of the Buddha.[18] As expected, under this rubric of penetrating and cohering all extant words of the Buddha, one must rely on comparative hermeneutics. To illustrate how this procedure works, Lü chose to analyze the shifting meanings of *ālayavijñāna*, which I elaborate on later. But Lü's conclusion is telling: Lü linked the early teachings of original purity (*zixing benjing* 自性本淨) with the later concepts of *Tathāgatagarbha* and *ālayavijñāna*, an intertextual link that he subsequently employed to defend his socio-soteriological project premised upon a Yogācāra intersubjective oneness.

Intersubjectivity is a given in Lü's paradigm; thus, the core question facing Lü in his project was how to eliminate egoistic obstructions to access this intersubjective oneness and to maximize and sustain intersubjective agreements. To answer this question, Lü tailored each of the seven methods of cross-examination to reflect the textual qualities and history of the objects under consideration.[19] The first step in Lü's method requires acquiring synoptic comprehension, and the next six steps entail peeling open historically sedimented interpretations layer by layer. The first through fifth steps treat texts as if they were self-enclosed, bounded entities:

(1) Cross-examination of catalogs (*duikan mulu* 對勘目錄). Here, the aim is to gain a panoramic view of the canons and their transmission history.

(2) Cross-examination of variant prints of the same sūtra (*tongjing yike zhi bijiao* 同經異刻之比較). This step entails a point-by-point examination

of printed variants. For Lü, this step mattered because it could reveal important economic and political interplays in the making of a text.

(3) Cross-examination of variant translations of the same sūtra (*tongjing yiyi zhi bijiao* 同經異譯之比較). The goal of this step is to clarify and preserve factual diversity as textual witnesses to logical, skillful, and transmission sequences. Doing so helps to identify relations between extant multilingual translations with multiple variant Indic texts and reveals the logical sequences of doctrinal interpretations.[20] To illustrate how this cross-examination works, Lü compared three translations of the *Laṅkāvatāra Sūtra*, one of which was Bodhiruci's. In his analysis, Lü clearly marked Bodhiruci's translation as a "novel" aberration. Experts in modern Chinese Buddhism will immediately recognize the significance of this comparison. As scholars have pointed out, the most heated and long-running debate in modern Chinese Buddhism is about the authenticity of *Awakening Faith*. And the most vehement critics of *Awakening Faith* were members of the institute. In their writings, the members invariably cited Lü's textual analysis to claim that the "novel" teaching of original enlightenment in *Awakening Faith* arose directly from Bodhiruci's "novel" translation.[21] Although Lü never directly participated in this particular public debate, his illustration of comparative hermeneutics was clearly used as ammunition by his colleagues.[22]

While the first three comparisons are concerned with sūtras, the next two focus on commentarial traditions:

(4) Cross-examination of variant commentaries (translated into or written in Chinese) of a sūtra accepted by different schools or commentarial traditions (*benjing shilun zhi bijiao* 本經釋論之比較). Because commentarial traditions are linked to a text's reception and transmission history, this step investigates the possibility of multiple compilations of Indic texts subsumed under the same title.

(5) Cross-examination of different commentaries on variant editions of a text (*tongjing yilun zhi bijiao* 同經異論之比較). This step entails a careful cross-verification of different commentarial interpretations, which further highlights the importance of commentaries in elucidating the historical sedimentation of a certain received text.

The final two cross-examinations invite scholars to put aside the sociohistorical constructions of the idea of an author, a translator, a text, or a school, instead philosophizing at the level of the unit of coherent meaning. In practice, these cross-examinations highlight that a coherent argument does not need to extend to a chapter, a whole book, or an entire compilation. Rather, Lü's goal in the final two cross-examinations was to treat every transmitted text as the outcome of communal and historical processes of sedimentation.

(6) Cross-examination of similar doctrines in different sūtras (*yijing tongyi zhi bijiao* 異經同義之比較). Here Lü Cheng advised researchers to disentangle some of the hermeneutical nuances resulting from parallels or feedback loops in the process of transmission so that one could achieve a fuller picture of a particular doctrine. The main texts Lü analyzed here were two Mahāyāna collection texts, *Baojijing* 寶積經 (T.310) and *Dajijing* 大集經 (T.397). However, in the last paragraph of this section, Lü mentioned both *Aṅgulimālīya Sūtra* (T.120), a Mahāyāna sūtra traditionally classified in the Tathāgatagarbha genre, and *Aṅgulimāla Sūtra* (T.118 or T.119), a text included in the Āgamas. He then made manifest the purpose of comparison: to "understand why the Mahāyāna teachings and Hīnayāna teachings differ" (*tong daxiao yishuo zhi gu* 通大小異說之故).[23] By itself, this statement seems innocent. However, when viewed in the context of Lü's manufacturing of two parallel and independent developments of the bodhisattva lineage and the śrāvaka lineage (see chapter 5), it becomes clear that Lü employed comparative hermeneutics to prove his unconventional claim: that is, that the bodhisattva lineage did not arise sequentially from the śrāvaka lineage but was in fact developed independently and in parallel.

(7) Cross-examination of similar terminology rendered in different sūtras (*yijing tongshi zhi bijiao* 異經同事之比較). Lü's use of *shi* 事 is idiosyncratic. Instead of invoking the common meaning of *shi* as "event," Lü meant *shi* to be something particular, better rendered as "terminology." *Shi* is used in contrast with *yi* 義, an abstract concept or a principle. The example Lü used to illustrate his definition of *shi* is *ālayavijñāna*, arguably the most foundational term in Yogācāra. After a lengthy cross-check,[24] Lü concluded,

> Based on the sequences in the above chart, it is clear that the teachings of *original purity* appeared first. Later, this pure mind was said to be *Tathāgatagarbha*. Next, *Tathāgatagarbha* was interpreted as the Buddha nature and *dharmakāya*. Later, *Tathāgatagarbha* became equated with pure consciousness. This pure consciousness further evolved into *ālayavijñāna* when being polluted by illusions. Then, *ālayavijñāna* became *ādānavijñāna*—the storehouse consciousness of all seeds.
>
> 依上表而次第之，蓋先有心性本淨之說．而後謂清淨心為如來藏．又次謂如來藏即佛性法身．又次後謂如來藏為淨識性有妄熏習而為阿賴耶．又次後謂阿賴耶為阿陀那為一切種子識．[25]

This passage marks the first time Lü Chen publicly presented evidence for his claim that original quiescence (*xingji* 性寂), which I term "doctrinal oneness," has its roots in original purity. The goal, for Lü, was to clarify for readers that the influential concept of original enlightenment (*xingjue* 性覺)—a doctrine that is widely recognized as the foundation of Tathāgatagarbha thought in East Asia—drastically differs from the term "Tathāgatagarbha" in "authentic" teachings such as *The Sūtra of the Lion's Roar of Queen Śrīmālā* (T.353).[26]

Original quiescence lay at the heart of Lü's social revolution. According to Lü's 1943 letters to Xiong Shili, original enlightenment leads to a look inward (philosophical solipsism), and original quiescence leads to renewal (soteriological and epistemic openness).[27] For Lü the task of scholars was socio-soteriological: to build a communism of Buddhist knowledge for renewing society. Recall that on June 22, 1922, when Wang Zhixin 王治心 visited the institute, Wang cherished Lü Cheng's epistemic openness and praised Lü's interpretation of Yogācāra as knowledge and truth that are "open for examination by everyone."[28] Written two years after Wang's impressionistic portrayal, Lü's 1924 essay on comparative hermeneutics discloses to us the concrete steps that Lü took to communalize Buddhist knowledge.

The effectiveness of Lü's reading technology is shown in his discovery of the intertextual relation between *Yogācārabhūmi*'s section on *She shi fen* 攝事分 (Skt: *Vastusaṃgrahaṇī*) (fascicle 83–98) and *Saṃyuktāgama*, which he presented in "Za'ahanjing kanding ji" (Report on collating *Saṃyuktāgama*).[29] This essay presents an important discovery that Mukai Akira rediscovered sixty years later.[30] As is well known, the Chinese translations of *Saṃyuktāgama* have long been deemed inferior and disorganized, replete with mistranslations, especially in contrast with their Pāli counterparts. This view became dominant because most Buddhologists at the time considered the Pāli Nikāyas to be the "earlier," and therefore more "original," transmission.[31] Instead of uncritically accepting this putative origin story, Lü looked into the *mātṛka* of *Yogācārabhūmi* for clues as to how to organize these ancient sūtras. Lü Cheng's discovery has since been superseded.[32] But at the time, his work revealed a critical transitional stage between early Buddhism and the rise of Yogācāra.[33] Indeed, scholarship today continues to affirm the efficacy and rigor of Lü's methods, as seen in Dan Lusthaus's recent analysis of Lü's scholarly edition of *Ālambana-parīkṣā*.[34]

However, a well-rounded understanding of Lü's scholarly achievement needs to include the soteriological drive in Lü's project. This soteriological drive was revealed in another of Lü's essays in the 1924 issue of *Neixue*, titled "*Xianyangshengjiaolun* dayi" 顯揚聖教論大意 (Main points of *Acclamation of the Holy Teaching*).[35] In the introduction, Lü repeatedly stressed the internal rhetoric of *Yogācārabhūmi*: because the text used the four Āgamas as its *mātṛka*, or the mother of its doctrines, Yogācāra was neither Mahāyāna nor Hīnayāna, neither emptiness nor existence, but the same as the four Āgamas. Taking cues from this self-conscious diffractive analysis of how *Yogācārabhūmi* had dependently arose from early teachings, Lü compared the text's *mātṛka* and set out to prove the historicity of this internal narrative. In the conclusion, Lü departed from objective scholarship. Instead, Lü celebrated this insider's view as proof of the "holy teaching" of Yogācāra.[36] Just as he had used textual gymnastics to manufacture an independent bodhisattva path, as discussed in chapter 5, here, Lü deployed analytic rigor to prove the sacredness of certain Yogācāra teachings.

As such, Lü effectively redefined the "scientific method" as an impersonal interpretative technology to identify sedimented intersubjective agreements on how to reach liberation. He weaved existing and imported hermeneutical strategies into a new tapestry and remade scientific objectivity as interconditioned rigor. In Lü's paradigm, each translation is a localized instance of the ineffable realization of the Buddha. When the Buddha's insight was materialized into words, all Buddhist texts were put on equal footing without the presumption of an urtext because the only "original" is a doctrinal whole that is beyond words. This new interpretative technology also maximized the strength of the Chinese canon. Lü saw Chinese translations as crucial in revealing the doctrinal whole precisely because of the more than two thousand years of translation enterprise that had preserved numerous Buddhist texts.[37] With this new technology at hand, the unruly Chinese canon was transformed into a gold mine teeming with snippets of salvific knowledge to be unearthed by attentive scholars.

Critical Thinking, Meditation, Wisdom, and Compassion

Lü's faith in the salvific power of Yogācāra, instead of hindering critical thinking, became the fertile ground in which to germinate a new epistemology of liberation—one grounded in the three Cs and accepted by many Buddhologists of Lü's time as their own. Lü redefined the imported notion of "critical thinking" in soteriological terms, recasting it as a trained attitude cultivated through meditation; guided by both logical analysis, or *hetuvidyā* (*yinming* 因明) and wisdom (*zhi* 智 or *hui* 慧); and grounded in great compassion.[38]

As part of Lü's project, the six supplementary texts in *Five Disciplines* function as the guidelines for transformative praxes that help learners to actualize scriptural knowledge into daily actions. Because each of the three phases has a goal, Lü supplemented each phase's scriptural learning with two texts delivering pragmatic instructions. The first phase presents two sets of meditative instructions that are intended to enable learners to focus on intellectual pursuits while remaining connected to the originally quiescent mind (*jiyin zuoyi* 寂因作意). This selection reveals the soteriological motivation behind Lü's scholarship: Yuanxue (the Institute's Learning) must be grounded in the realization of the originally quiescent mind-heart (*zixing benji zhi xin* 自性本寂之心)—the generative cause of achieving buddhahood (*zuofo zhi yin* 作佛之因). Lü supplemented the second phase with texts about analytic methods in *hetuvidyā* and the cultivation of compassion as a self-care strategy that he believed would keep learners energized during the long and arduous path of co-liberation through learning (*yi zi tiaofu fangyu wushang puti xinqiu wuyan ye* 以自調伏方與無上菩提欣求無厭也). To the last phase Lü added instructions on how to engage in analysis and how to select what to learn, with the goal of enabling learners to actualize the empathetic interdependence and togetherness of sentient beings and buddhas (*shengfo jiaogan* 生佛交感). Thus, Lü designed the path of co-transformation from learners' initial entry into the originally quiescent mind, to the maintenance of energy and effort despite worldly suffering, and, ultimately, to interpenetration into what the Buddha preached (*yu fo suoshuo wubu tongda* 與佛所說無不通達) and the actualization of the profound nirvāṇic interconditioned equality (*niepan pingdeng shenshen liqu* 涅槃平等甚深理趣).[39]

In the first phase, Lü married intellectual pursuits with Yogācāra meditation. Lü believed that the focus of the first phase should be realizing the essence of the nature of the mind (*xinxing zhi yaoyi* 心性之要義) as the foundation of Buddhist learning (*foxue zhi yiju* 佛學之依據). He stated, "Because this [originally quiescent] mind-heart exists, therefore this [Institute's Learning] exists" (*xincun ze xuecun* 心存則學存). For him, learning was only a means to access, manifest, and sustain this originally quiescent mind-heart. Both supplementary texts of the first phase thus provide instructions on various meditative methods: *Jietuodao lun* 解脫道論 (*The Path of Liberation*, T.1648) and *Liumen jiaoshou xiding lun* 六門教授習定論 (*Six Doors of Teaching Dhyāna*, T.1607; henceforth, *Six Doors*). Lü saw the first as representing the "Southern" transmission of Yogācāra (better known as Theravāda Buddhism), referring to the fifth-century Theravāda philosopher Buddhaghoṣa, and the second as representing the "Northern" transmission (to which the Chinese lineage belongs) of Yogācāra, stressing again that both the bodhisattva vehicle and the śrāvaka vehicle developed directly from the historical Buddha's teachings.[40]

These two texts are the only two of the six supplemental texts that Lü had a chance to lecture on. According to Lü's notes, he valued the first text, *The Path of Liberation*, because he saw it as instructions for meditation from the sect of

Mahīśāsaka (Ch: *Huadi bu* 化地部). Lü considered this sect to be the historical foundation of the Yogācāra school of thought, mainly because Asaṅga had been ordained in the Mahīśāsaka lineage. Interestingly, Lü surmised that because *The Path of Liberation* and Buddhaghoṣa's *The Path of Purification* were based on the same matrix (Ch: *benmu* 本母; Skt: *mātṛkā*) Buddhaghoṣa's text might be what Xuanzang had referred to as the "Southern" Yogācāra.[41]

Lü valued the second text, *Six Doors*, for two reasons. First, *Six Doors* instructs learners on how to engage in intellectual analysis (*zuoyi* 作意) while relying upon the causes and conditions (*yin* 因) that lead to the relinquishment of afflictions (Ch: *jimie* 寂滅; Skt: *nirodha*). Second, *Six Doors* is attributed to Asaṅga and was commented on by Vasubandhu, both of whom are widely recognized as the founders of Yogācāra. Lü valued it as the only existent Yogācāra instructions for meditation. While an in-depth analysis of Lü's theory of meditation must wait for another occasion, here, it suffices to highlight that Lü saw Mahīśāsaka's *The Path of Liberation* as the foundation of all meditative practices and considered Yogācāra's *Six Doors* as training learners to maintain and apply the mind-heart corresponding to the characteristics of nirvāṇa without interruption (*baoren yu niepan xiangying zhi xin xiangxu bujue* 保任與涅槃相應之心相續不絕).[42] Thus, Lü grounded all intellectual activities of the first phase in Yogācāra meditative insight.

In the second phase, Lü refashioned critical thinking as logic grounded in compassion. Lü considered the second phase to be the orthodox (*zhengzong* 正宗) of all five disciplines, with a focus on revolutionizing consciousness. Lü supplied two texts so as to hasten and sustain (*zengshang xiangzi* 增上相資) this revolution. Revolutionizing consciousness, in Lü's vision, entailed the thorough application of the mind-heart (*jin xin zhi yong* 盡心之用). Lü deemed *hetuvidyā* and the cultivation of a compassionate mind-heart (*xiu cixin* 修慈心) as the two sets of conducive conditions for thoroughly applying this originally quiescent mind-heart. These intellectual and affective abilities could be trained by learning two texts, *Yinming ruzhengli lun* 因明入正理論 (*Introduction to Logic*; Skt: *Nyāyapraveśa*, T.1630) and *Dafangguangfo huayan jing—xiucifen* 大方廣佛華嚴經·修慈分 ("The Chapter on Cultivating Compassion" from *Flower Ornament Sūtra*, T.306; henceforth, "Cultivating Compassion"). According to Lü, *hetuvidyā*, a term typically rendered as "logic," was the foundation of analytical thinking (*siwei* 思維) and philosophical discussion (*lunyi* 論義). Lü argued that the efficacy of *hetuvidyā* lies in its ability to accelerate the enlightenment process of both the self and others by halving the effort while doubling the impact (*shiban gongbei* 事半功倍).[43]

Lest readers mistake Lü's choice of a chapter from *Flower Ornament Sūtra* as a deviation from his Yogācāra commitment, it is important to note that Lü valued "Cultivating Compassion" precisely because this chapter documents the questions of the future Buddha Maitreya—the mythical founder of Yogācāra whose Chinese name Cishi 慈氏 means "the compassionate one." Lü further likened compassion to the root of all virtuous dharmas: Confucian humaneness (*ren* 仁), the Buddha nature, and the mind-heart of the Buddha (*foxin* 佛心). Lü thought that the value of compassion lies in its efficacy to assist learners to maintain *bodhicitta* even when facing adversity, obstacles, and difficulties.[44] Departing from the commonsense interpretation of compassion as a motivation to help others, here, Lü characterized compassion as a self-help stratgy for learners embarking on the difficult path.

For the third phase, during which learners bring forth one true-reality dharma realm by reaching the ultimate of each discipline (*qiongji geke zhi jiu jing* 窮極各科之究竟) and by actualizing the empathetic interdependence and togetherness of sentient beings and buddhas, Lü prescribed two texts on the methods and formats of democratic deliberation. The first is *Selected Passages from Compendium of Validities*.[45]This was a key text attributed to the renowned Buddhist logician Dignāga (Chenna 陳那; c. 480–540 CE), which lays out what Lü deemed the most important method for mastering and interpenetrating all Buddhist teachings—*apoha* (*zhequan* 遮詮) or double negation (*ruyun jia, yiyun fei yi* 如云甲, 意云非乙). Lü imbued *apoha* with a new social function: to discern other (inauthentic) teachings (*jianbie yufa* 簡別餘法) during deliberation so that intersubjective agreement on authentic teachings would become possible without presuming an absolute, mind-independent truth.[46]

In broad terms, *apoha* is a Yogācāra analytic method of explaining how intersubjective agreement can be reached without presuming the existence of (1) a universal substance (e.g., a treeness shared by all trees), (2) one objective world, and (3) any external, mind-independent objects such as trees. Instead, *apoha* theorists argue that what unites seemingly objective trees is their very difference in perception from that of all non-trees.[47] In Lü's words, when we seek out perception A, we are in reality selecting a perception that is not non-A. Thus, Lü argued, when learners follow the *apoha* mode of analysis, it is easy to see that all Buddhist teachings—from the Prajñāpāramitā teaching of emptiness, to the Yogācāra teaching of *vijñaptimātra*, to the Nirvāṇa teaching of Buddha nature—are different ways to discern inauthentic teachings, thereby ensuring that scholarship can lead one into the one true-reality dharma realm where sentient beings and buddhas are empathetically connected.[48]

The second text, "The Section on Deciding and Selecting" from *Daji xukong-zang suowen jing—juezefen* 大集虛空藏所問經·抉擇分 (Sūtra of the Questions of Bodhisattva Ākāśagarbha; Skt: *Mahāsaṃnipata-Ākāśagarbha-paripṛcchā-nirvedhabhāgīya*; T.404), further describes what Lü deemed the proper format of democratic deliberation. Democratic deliberation, according to Lü, entailed a general assembly (*zhonghui* 眾會) where bodhisattvas from ten directions could freely ask questions and obtain answers and whose ultimate goal was to arrive at equality (*pingdeng wei gui* 平等為歸) and to realize the profound meaning of equality (*pingdeng liqu* 平等理趣) in all Buddhist teachings and all Buddhist practices (*liudu wanxing* 六度萬行). In Lü's reading, this text argues that democratic deliberation must be grounded in supreme wisdom (*shengzhi* 勝智) and be guided through the gradual revolution of consciousness (*fenfen zhuanyi* 分分轉依). This gradual revolution of consciousness is in turn grounded in meditative insight into original quiescence/nirvāṇa/nonaction (*zheng zemie wuwei zhi yi* 證擇滅無為之意).[49] Lü ended his outline of the Institute's Learning with this text and considered its instructions the ultimate means of deciding and selecting. At this point, we have come full circle in Lü's project of scholarship for salvation:

> Why must *Five Disciplines* be studied in three phases? On the one hand, [we must] rely on analytical deductions of philosophy and principle. On the other hand, [we must] rely on the historical unfolding. Only by combining both philosophical principles and historical facts can [we] perfect this learning. Thus by merging horizontal and vertical [perspectives], [we] see the wholeness.

> 五科講習之必歷三週者, 一方依義理推闡, 一方依歷史開展, 理事兼至, 乃得盡其學. 故一經一緯, 合之乃見其全.[50]

These six supplementary texts in three phases capture the critical methods that Lü hoped to impart to his students: that is, that rigorous engagement with scholarship must be motivated by collaborative liberation, grounded in meditative insight into original quiescence, sustained by both analytic methods and compassionate self-care, regulated by egalitarian mutual scrutiny, and guided by methods for reaching intersubjective agreement.

Informed by thus-far presented evidence, a reasonable reader would agree that Lü's project was hardly about producing objective scholarship. And yet the mischaracterization of him as a pure scholar persists in existing studies. The continuing sway of this distorted image reflects the much broader epistemic myopia of the modern era. In fact, the distorted image was projected onto Lü from the very beginning of his Yogācāra project of revolutionizing consciousness. For example, in 1922, Wang Zhixin, a Chinese Christian who intended to learn Buddhism to effectively convert the Chinese people, favorably appraised Lü's teaching of *hetuvidyā* as "Buddhist science" (*foxue zhong de kexue* 佛學中的科

學) and "the most sophisticated rhetoric" (*zui jingmi de xiucixue* 最精密的修辭學). At the same time, he criticized the Buddhist community in general and the China Inner Learning Institute in particular for their perceived lack of social engagement and their penchant for internal purification and quiet contemplation.[51] Four decades later, the renowned scholar of Chinese Buddhism Holmes Welch translated the name of the institute, Neixueyuan (which I translate as "the Inner Learning Institute") as "The Metaphysical Institute," pigeonholing Lü's project as mere musing in the Greco-European substance metaphysical tradition. Welch further lamented that "religious cultivation, in fact, was banned" by the institute, "though residents . . . observed certain ascetic principles," and dismissed Lü's *Five Disciplines* as "sterile philosophizing and academic studies in libraries and museums."[52] It is little wonder why the scholarly consensus to this day is that Lü's lifetime goal was to reestablish genuine Buddhism.

To a certain extent, Lü's post-1949 self-presentation fixed his reputation as a pedantic scholar. However, a careful reading of his 1959 autobiography reveals that he started to see himself as a scholar of Buddhism only when his hometown Danyang was "liberated" and when he started to read Mao Zedong's writings and "deepened" his understanding of "revolution."[53] A careful examination of his publications after 1949 reveals that, until 1954 (two years after the China Inner Learning Institute was officially dissolved), he publicly identified Buddhist learning as a powerful means to transform this unsatisfactory world.[54] In these essays, Lü continued to portray Buddhism, especially Yogācāra causal theory (e.g., *siyuan* 四緣 and *sanxing* 三性) and the soteriology of renouncing the world by transforming it (*zhuanshi er chushi* 轉世而出世), as a means to purify and uplift the human life (*shi weizhe rensheng de jinghua, xiangshang* 是為著人生的淨化向上).[55] The only noticeable change is that he no longer used "revolution" (*geming* 革命) to interpret *āśrayaparivṛtti* and instead repackaged it as *gexin* 革新 (renewal), *gaige* 改革 (reform), *biange* 變革 (fundamental change), *zhuanbian* 轉變 (transform), or *zhuanhua* 轉化 (repattern). Equally important, he never publicly renounced his dream of reforming this world through Yogācāra scholarship. Rather, he silently channeled his energy into more acceptable forms of scholarship: teaching and textual analysis.

For Lü and his colleagues who employed experience-informed-cum-action-oriented moral reasoning, inner change and social change were neither separate nor opposed. Rather, both belonged to the same meshwork of an inextricably linked mycelium of actions that are constantly shaping and being shaped by every living creature, a karmascape. Indeed, by redefining the social as intersubjective oneness, Lü integrated mental purification, scholarship, and social activism into one interconditioning karmascape.

Institutionalized Bodhicitta and Organized Skepticism

Combining Lü's comparative hermeneutics and Buddhisized critical thinking with his bodhisattva precepts that were intended to serve as communal rules for deliberative democracy (analyzed in chapter 5) yields what I term "institutionalized *bodhicitta*." In institutionalized *bodhicitta*, individual learners practice comparative hermeneutics and Buddhisized critical thinking as a group. By engaging in the collaborative practice of making skeptical inquiries into truth claims, the learners establish interpretative authority, gain the trust of the public, and produce knowledge for co-liberation. This structural feature of "organized skepticism" marks a new ideal type of *bodhicitta*, in contrast to all its premodern varieties.[56]

Merton, the U.S. sociologist who coined the term "organized skepticism" in 1942, argued that normative structures such as organized skepticism represent a distinctly new way for groups to establish public trust. In his analysis, Merton diverged from the dominant discourses—empiricism's promotion of experiments and critical rationalism's advancement of falsifiability, to name a couple—that see trustworthiness as grounded in scientific methods. Instead, Merton argued that what makes scientific enterprise trustworthy is the normative structures. He identified four institutional features of a scientific enterprise in his time: a quest for universalism, a communism of knowledge, disinterestedness, and organized skepticism.[57] For Merton, organized skepticism represented an essential self-correction mechanism that promises to eliminate false claims over time. Departing from the prevailing view of science as a methodological enterprise, Merton argued that it is group dynamics that establish authority in their collective truth claims and thereby deserve public trust.

In significant ways, Lü's framing of Yuanxue resembles Mertonian normative structures of science.[58] Once critical thinking, empathy, and skepticism are organized by bodhisattva precepts into coactions, then the shared wisdom produced and sedimented under these motivated, reciprocal inquiries gains maximal freedom from subjective projections and personal limitations. Institutionalized *bodhicitta* entails a critical attitude similar to Mertonian disinterestedness. Challenging the mainstream understanding of disinterestedness as an attitude of detachment, or a pure intellectual pursuit of knowledge production, Merton defined it as "a distinctive pattern of institutional control of a wide range of motives which characterizes the behavior of scientists." In other words, for Merton, disinterestedness was neither an individual trait nor an ontological claim. Rather, it was an institutional structure that requires individuals to conform to collective behavior norms and subject themselves to institutional control. Meanwhile, Merton saw organized skepticism as "both a methodological and an institutional mandate" that requires the "temporary suspension of judgment and the detached scrutiny of beliefs in terms of empirical and logical criteria."[59] That is, what makes an inquiry scientific is an organizational principle: scientists correct each other by mutually interrogating their evidence, methods, and logic.

Seven decades later, Naomi Oreskes elaborated on this social process that makes science trustworthy and impartial, describing it as a process of "transformative interrogation." For Oreskes, transformative interrogation takes place in a diverse community and entails an institutionalized pattern of behavior that allows individual subjective elements to be openly and freely challenged. In the long run, this pattern of behavior produces knowledge more trustworthy than that produced by any individual researcher.[60]

The key philosophical insight that uncouples science from an unnecessary commitment to philosophical realism or materialism lies in the fact that "objectivity" is not a natural property of a mind-independent world or some essential substance outside human consciousness but is instead the outcome of an ongoing collective historical process of open interrogation whereby diverse communities gradually eliminate arbitrary, partial, unfair impositions. In contrast to previous philosophizing that equated science with realism and empiricism and conflated objectivity with impartiality, the current understanding of what makes scientific knowledge "objective" and "impartial" is grounded in the structural features of epistemic openness, democratic deliberation, and intersubjective cross-examination.[61]

Informed by Western academia's public recognition of science as a product of social processes, readers will appreciate Lü's sharp insight: he reframed the Yogācāra three Cs into organized skepticism and thereby redefined "objective" knowledge as the result of the historical sedimentation of intersubjective scrutiny. In Lü's project, institutionalized *bodhicitta* is the cultivated attitude one takes when evaluating truth claims with comparative hermeneutics, conducting textual analysis with Buddhisized critical thinking, and engaging in discussions following bodhisattva precepts. Consequently, Yuanxue inaugurated a nonviolent means of ushering in social equality by practicing an épistémè of compassion.

However, unlike contemporary scholars who avoid philosophical speculations about the ontological grounding of "social knowledge," Lü did not have the luxury of such equivocation. Beleaguered by the epistemic domination of scientific realism, empiricism, historical materialism, and theological idealism of his time, Lü offered a robust alternative philosophy to explain what makes social knowledge real enough. This alternative philosophy is Yogācāra processual social philosophy. Under the Yogācāra processual framework, Lü justified his transformative epistemology and his theorization of community as motivated, collective actions as real enough based on intersubjective corroboration, coherence, and causal efficacy. Jettisoning both realism and the static view of social facts or natural kinds, Lü's Yogācāra socio-soteriology opens up another path for scholars to move away from objective humanities and toward reflexive humanities.[62]

Two soteriological tools were central to Lü's philosophical justification of his transformative epistemology. The first is Lü's reframing of *prasiddha* (intersubjective agreement; Ch: *jicheng* 極成) as an epistemological outcome that arises only after sustained, rational, mutual engagement. And the second is Yogācāra causal theory's role as the philosophical foundation for the social epistemology (*renshi de shehuixing* 認識的社會性) of organized skepticism.

Prasiddha is the primary tool Lü used for demonstrating how intersubjective corroboration could be formed when there was no objective world out there. *Prasiddha* is best known as a term of Buddhist logic (Skt: *hetuvidyā*), describing a theorem or axiom to be accepted by both parties in a debate. The Tibetan Buddhist scholar Sakya Paṇḍita (1182–1251) skillfully employed this term to solve the problem of the meaning of language in the Yogācāra system. As is well known, in linguistic realism, the meaning of a word is tied to its objectively existing referent, independent from subjective experiences. The word "tree," for example, is meaningful because trees exist outside consciousness. However, when there are no trees out there, how do people agree on the meaning of "tree"? As incisively argued by Jonathan C. Gold, Sakya Paṇḍita's answer was elegant: the relations of words and their nonexisting referents are maintained solely by linguistic conventions. However, these linguistic conventions are not arbitrary; preferably, they are maintained by a group of scholars. Therefore, a word only becomes *prasiddha* through devoted scholars' concerted and intentional maintenance of linguistic conventions.[63] As such, in Sakya Paṇḍita's paradigm, *prasiddha* justifies the necessity of an elite interpretative community whose task is to guard linguistic conventions and thereby guarantee the purity of Buddha's teaching. Despite its elitist orientation, this Tibetan interpretative tradition reveals the essential role of *prasiddha* in establishing intersubjective accord without resorting to the idea of objectivity.

To understand Lü's use of this term, scholars must distinguish between the dual functions of *prasiddha*: its philosophical function in establishing the possibility of intersubjectivity and its social function in determining how and by whom intersubjective agreements are maintained. Lü shared with Sakya Paṇḍita the philosophical conviction that *prasiddha* could be used to establish intersubjectivity without presuming some mind-independence. However, instead of seeing *prasiddha* as precarious linguistic conventions to be carefully guarded by specialists, Lü took the existence of *prasiddha* to be self-evident. Furthermore, Lü considered *prasiddha* to be indisputable proof of the possibility of collective perceptual experiences, evidencing the "fact" that shared karmic seeds generate intersubjective agreements. Thus, Lü considered the social function of *prasiddha* to be enabling collective and democratic processes of moral inquiry.

Lü's naturalistic take on *prasiddha* stemmed from his need to justify a different kind of social arrangement: a democratically organized interpretative community built from the ground up. In Lü's view, once *prasiddha* became a "natural" condition, the validity of these well-known conventions would be maintained by scientific inquiries alone. The divergences in conventions were to be understood in terms of common or uncommon characteristics specific to a local group of persons bound together by their shared karmic seeds. This democratic potential was further guaranteed by the affirmation of all human beings' innate intellectual potential: namely, their potential to expand their own intellectual horizons by discussing their views with others while following rigorous procedures of engaging in intellectual pursuit. Ideally, as everyone expanded their own horizon, the shared pure karmic seeds would grow and intersubjective discord would diminish.

To see how Lü retooled this Yogācāra doctrine into a social theory, a detour is needed. In *Yogācārabhūmi*, *prasiddha* has a broader connotation, often referring to things generally accepted as true. *Prasiddha* has two senses: a generally acknowledged truth (Ch: *shijian Jicheng* 世間極成; Skt: *lokaprasiddha*; Tib: *grags pa*) and a universal truth established by reason (Ch: *daoli jicheng* 道理極成; Skt: *yuktiprasiddha*; Tib: *rigs pas grags pa*).[64] In Xuanzang's *CWSL*, this term takes on an additional connotation as the rational foundation of intersubjective resonance. For example, in the subcommentary defending the existence of *ālayavijñāna*, where Xuanzang argued that Mahāyāna teachings are the words of the Buddha, Xuanzang repeatedly used *prasiddha* and *yuktiprasiddha* to convey the sense of intersubjective consensus.[65]

To fully appreciate this social turn of *prasiddha*, readers must closely read the commentary under verse 17 of *Triṃśikā*, a line that establishes the truth of consciousness-only:

As table 6.1 shows, there is a critical difference between Xuanzang's interpretation and the Sanskrit and Tibetan interpretations, i.e. the interpretation of *vikalpa*.[66] Admittedly, in verse 17, Xuanzang's interpretation can be reconciled with the Sanskrit and Tibetan interpretations. This is because the Sanskrit verb *vikalpyate* is a passive construction of *vi-√kḷp*. The corresponding

TABLE 6.1. Verse 17 of *Triṃśikā*

Xuanzang	*Sanskrit*	*Tibetan*
是諸識轉變	*vijñānapariṇāmo ’yaṃ*	*rnam par shes par gyur pa ‘di*
These transformations of consciousness,	That transformation of consciousness	This transformation of consciousness
分別所分別	*vikalpo yad vikalpyate*	*rnam rtog yin te de yis gang*
are mental discriminations and the mentally discriminated.	is a conceptual discrimination. That which is conceptually constructed,	is a mental discrimination. And because of that, that which
由此彼皆無	*tena tan nāsti tenedaṃ*	*rnam brtags de med des na ‘di*
Because of this, both of those do not exist,	thus, does not exist. Therefore,	is mentally imputed does not exist. Hence, this
故一切唯識	*sarvaṃ vijñaptimātrakam*	*thams cad rnam par rig pa tsam*
therefore, everything is consciousness-only.	all this is mere mental representation.	all is mere mental representation.

Tibetan term *rnam brtags* also conveys a passive sense. Both terms can be legitimately reconciled with the Chinese translation (*suo fenbie* 所分別), which functions as a noun denoting "that which is the discriminated."

Though its meaning is similar across translations, the term's grammatical function depends on the particular translation. In Xuanzang's translation, this second line, if translated back into Sanskrit literally, is *vikalpa* (Ch: *fenbie* 分別; an action noun from *vi-√kḷp*) and *vikalpita* (Ch: *suo fenbie* 所分別; the past participle of *vi-√kḷp*) in apposition, serving as the predicate of the first line that is the subject of this sentence—the transformations of various consciousnesses.[67] In contrast, in both the Sanskrit and Tibetan editions, *vikalpo* (Tib: *rnam rtog*) alone serves as the predicate of the first line. The second half, *yad vikalpyate* (Tib: *gang rnam brtags*), serves as the subordinate clause of the following line. This new paraphrase does not change the overall meaning of the verse: because all are mere mental discriminations, therefore, everything is consciousness-only.

However, Xuanzang's paraphrase significantly changes the scheme of interpretation concerning why everything is mental discrimination. In both Xuanzang's main prose and Kuiji's commentary on this passage, it is clear that both *fenbie* and *suo fenbie* are glossed as two independent nouns in apposition. The basis for their interpretation follows Dharmapāla's distinction between the seeing part (Ch: *jianfen* 見分; Skt: *darśana-bhāga*) and the seen part (Ch: *xiangfen* 相分; Skt: *nimitta-bhāga*).[68] More important, while Kuiji attributed this two-part interpretation of consciousness to Sthiramati, Lü, in the footnotes of his scholarly edition of this text in *Essentials*, pointed out that this distinction between the seeing and seen parts does not exist in the Sanskrit edition of Sthiramati's commentary and thereby should be seen as Xuanzang's own position.[69] Through careful comparative studies, Lü accentuated Xuanzang's retelling of the Yogācāra causal story: highlighting the Chineseness of the doctrinal innovation of the seeing and seen parts.

This distinction has been identified by some scholars as Xuanzang's mistranslation.[70] In contrast, Dan Lusthaus singles out this passage and persuasively argues that Xuanzang's equation of *vijñāna mātra* with *vijñapti mātra* only indicates Xuanzang's Yogācāra is closer to phenomenology than metaphysical idealism.[71] Lusthaus's argument is worthy of rehearsing here. First, he lays out Xuanzang's alternative model of consciousness in terms of the seeing and seen parts. He then analyzes how Xuanzang's model of consciousness resembles Husserlian phenomenology in that they both "reject the notion of a univocal referent independent of sense." Lusthaus argues that there is an implied plurality in the referent: (1) there are many different streams (Skt: *sāntana*) of consciousness, and (2) one stream of consciousness can perceive entities engendered by other consciousnesses. Lusthaus argues that, if a theory admits other minds and the existence of perceptual objects that are independent from one's own perceptual field, then it cannot be characterized as metaphysical idealism.[72] Lusthaus's prescient argument has only recently been corroborated by scholars interested in the problem of intersubjectivity in Buddhist traditions.[73]

Lü enlisted *prasiddha* as evidence for the ontological primacy of intersubjectivity over the dualistic view of subjectivity/objectivity. Lü was keenly aware of the historical and philosophical significance of translating *vijñapti* as consciousness. Indeed, he showcased his accurate understanding of the term's different shades of meaning in his analysis of various translations of *vijñapti* in Xuanzang's treatise. Lü meticulously noted all instances in which Xuanzang deviated from the term's original meaning; he also pointed out other Chinese characters that could be mistaken for a translation of *vijñapti*.[74] Given Lü's acumen in identifying the polysemic nature of this term, it is difficult to read his silence on Xuanzang's "mistranslation" as a scholarly slip.

A more generous reading of Lü's silence is that Lü was confident in the truth of Xuanzang's causal theory. The core of Xuanzang's theory is the concept of karmic seeds as agentive potentials stored in *ālayavijñāna*. We observed Lü's emphasis on this causal story in his 1922 refutation of Bergsonian *élan vital*.

However, in 1922, Lü employed the concept of agentive potential only to push against the argument that nature or the objective world has any transformative agency. In his early experiments with Western aesthetics, beyond making a vague reference to Lippsian *Einfühlung*, Lü never explained how sentient beings, without an objective world out there, could reach agreement and cohere as a society. Decades later, when editing *Essentials*, Lü fleshed out a defensible social ontology in terms of the Yogācāra theory of consciousness. Lü moored his early conceptualization of intersubjective agreement onto *prasiddha*. In the conclusion to the prose explication of verse 17, Xuanzang commented and Kuiji elaborated as follows:

> XUANZANG: Therefore, in everything, there is mere consciousness because there are intersubjective agreements in erroneous discriminations.[75]
>
> 是故一切皆唯有識,虛妄分別有極成故 (T.1585. 39a1–2).
>
> KUIJI: I explain [as follows]: All dharmas, such as the conditioned, the unconditioned, the true, and the false, in all [of these dharmas], there is mere consciousness. This is because [the consciousness] can turn into erroneous discriminations.
>
> 述曰:有為、無為,實、假等法,皆唯有識,以能轉變虛妄分別 (T.1830.487c24–25).

Xuanzang understood intersubjective agreement as the proof of consciousness-only, and so did Lü. Kuiji took Xuanzang's argument one step further by identifying consciousness as the agentive force that can engender erroneous discriminations that manifest *as if* they are entities outside consciousness. Kuiji saw the shared causal story as what makes intersubjective consensus possible.[76] Note that for both Xuanzang and Kuiji, *prasiddha*, when used to justify consciousness-only doctrines, meant "intersubjective agreement."[77] In contrast to realist thinkers who take it to be self-evident that intersubjective agreement is a natural manifestation of the truth of one objective world, Xuanzang adopted a different philosophical attitude, taking intersubjective agreement as a manifestation of consciousness-only.

Once again Lü Cheng employed comparative hermeneutics to accentuate the intersubjective aspects of Xuanzang's causal theory. First he summarized Sthiramati's main points in explicating this verse, underscoring the differences between Xuanzang's interpretation (especially in terms of the use of *prasiddha*) and Sthiramati's. Second, in analyzing Xuanzang's subsequent subcommentary, Lü played up Xuanzang's intention to prove consciousness-only by noting the absence of Sthiramati's voice in another of the editor's footnote.[78] The opening of this subcommentary is vital because it declares,

> It is not that once other positions are repudiated, one's own position shall be established. One must explain and ascertain this teaching [of consciousness-only].
>
> 非破他義己義便成; 應更[勘]確陳, 成此教理.[79]

For readers familiar with the historical debates between the Madhyamaka and Yogācāra schools, this statement calls to mind the Yogācāra critique of the deconstructive method traditionally ascribed to Nāgārjuna.[80] This proclamation also reveals to us the intent of this subcommentary: to defend the truth of consciousness-only by establishing a coherent, defensible theory in addition to dismantling all alternatives.

To further shore up the legitimacy of Xuanzang's translation of *vijñaptimātra* as consciousness-only, in editing Xuanzang's subsequent proof of consciousness-only doctrine, Lü duly alerted the reader to where Xuanzang in his *CWSL* combined Vasubandhu's *Viṃśika* to refute the existence of entities outside consciousness. Experts in Yogācāra philosophy can recall that Vasubandhu, in the opening of *Viṃśika*, defines *citta*, *manas*, *vijñāna*, and *vijñapti* as different names for the concept that is consciousness-only. Naturally, in Lü's edition of *CWSL*, he underscored this doctrinal point with an interlinear note, substantiating Xuanzang's translation of *vijñaptimātra* with multilingual cross-examinations.[81]

Following Xuanzang's causal theory, Lü promoted *prasiddha* as evidence of a reliable causal explanation of the perceptual world. In his lecture notes on the discipline of Yogācāra in 1943, Lü on multiple occasions insisted that real intersubjective agreements are not established by worldly conventions but by reason.[82] This reliance on reason calls to mind Lü's early propensity for assuming a universal beauty achievable by engaging in a thorough comparative study of all aesthetic trends. Rather than presuming an objective world outside consciousness, Lü presumed a mycelial meshwork of interconditioning conscious processes only understandable through Xuanzang's Yogācāra causal enframing. Unsurprisingly, in the late 1920s, after he transitioned into Yogācāra studies, Lü began to produce multilingual comparative studies of Buddhist logic.[83] Though Buddhist logic is a central branch of Yogācāra philosophy, Lü's intention in engaging with it was initially unknown. By 1943, however, Buddhist logic had become key to Lü's establishment of institutionalized *bodhicitta*.

According to Lü, unenlightened beings who desire liberation need to work together through rigorous textual analysis and self-cultivation to rediscover the most essential *prasiddha*—the truth of consciousness-only. In chapter 4 I argued that Lü redefined nirvāṇa as one true-reality dharma realm, an intersubjective buddhahood connected through karmic processes and processes of purification. Here I highlight Lü's description of the causal processes that can lead learners to this intersubjective oneness. Lü emphasized that society is a collection of individual streams of *ālayavijñāna* who are bound together in saṃsāra through mutual support of four kinds of nutriment (*sishi* 四食). Because of this irreducible interdependence, a person (understood as aggregated karmic processes) can choose to work with others to revolutionize consciousness. These individual mental streams, or beings with deluded selves, can be released from their unsatisfactory existences by hearing and internalizing the continual flow of the same-true teachings in the dharma realm (*fajie dengliu zhengfa* 法界等流正法).[84]

While this idea appeared frequently in Lü's earlier notes and essays, Lü crystallized it in a short talk on November 13, 1945, just two months after Japan had officially surrendered to the Allied forces and the Soviet Union. This talk coincided with the end of his lecture series on *Five Disciplines*, where the four kinds of nutriment metamorphosized into a Yogācāra social philosophy:

> People of Hīnayāna do not know that the entirety of worldly relations are sustained collectively by all sentient beings. Therefore, they unrealistically wish to become liberated alone and think of themselves as transcendent. How could this be possible? . . . The twelve links of dependent arising only explain the continual [process of] life and death. If one understands that sentient beings exist because of nutriments, then if one needs nutriments, naturally, one needs to hope for and to acquire support. Thereby, life can unfold. The desire to become virtuous also becomes manifest. Nutriments include four kinds: physical food, sensory contact, mental nutriment, and sustenance of consciousness [all grounded in *ālayavijñāna*].[85] First, one needs basic sustenance. Next, one seeks peace and ease. Further, one hopes for and obtains [a sense of] fulfillment. All of these are nutriments. All sentient beings, relying on these four kinds of nutriment, can expand their lives and move upward. Based on this [teaching of four nutriments], Buddha Dharma grounds its provisional teachings and strategies in the reality of sentient existence. Because living beings rely on nutriments and therefore have the desire for permanence, joy, [genuine] ego, and purity, they further demand emancipation. All sentient beings' desire in life is to become virtuous.

小乘人不知世間關係全體有情共相維繫, 漫欲獨自擺脫, 以為超出, 安有此事? . . . 十二有支只解得生死相續, 如知有情依食而住, 食即有所資取希求, 则生活可有開展, 向善之義乃顯著矣. 食分段觸思流四類, 先有資長, 次求安逸, 進而希望, 而把握充實, 莫非食也. 一切有情依此四食而役生活可有開展向上, 佛法施設根據於有情生存事實云者, 即

> 着眼於此. 因眾生由食住, 進而有常樂我净之要求, 更進而有自在解脱之要求, 此即有情生存之向善意欲也.[86]

Three points are important for understanding Lü's project. First, Lü expressed dissatisfaction with the individualistic understanding of twelve-link dependent arising that confines the twelve links to the life, death, and rebirth of one sentient being. Then he employed the notion of nutriment to demonstrate the social dimension of dependent arising and redefined worldly existence as the intersubjective coactions of all sentient beings. Indeed, in Pāli literature, *Sammāditthi Sutta*, the notion of four kinds of nutriment, is understood through the lens of the Four Noble Truths, a means of modeling causal relations of lived experiences.[87] In this early teaching, the four kinds of nutriment are seen as part of the worldly suffering that arises from craving and should be abandoned.[88] Lü flipped this Pāli interpretation and instead posited the notion of nutriment for establishing social reality.[89]

Second, by making *xiangshan yiyu* (the desire to become virtuous) inherent to all sentient beings and by making this desire the foundation of all worldly interconditioning, Lü opened up the possibility for understanding society as maintained by horizontal actions and equal relations. Third, echoing his 1944 talk that is quoted at the end of chapter 4, Lü was not afraid of talking about a genuine self that is the intersubjective oneness precisely because for him the karmascape of suffering sustained by structural violence and systems of domination was real enough and had to be transformed through joint effort. Together with Lü's investment in the continual flow of the same-true teachings, this talk makes evident that, in Lü's vision, all sentient beings have equal access to the true teachings that ensure equal support for life and liberation.

Lü saw the task of knowledge producers as safeguarding that equal access to the knowledge of liberation. This is why Lü appended a note to this essay. In the note, he professed his volition to help the commoners (*renqun* 人群):

> What kind of world is today's world so that [some] could vainly talk about nature and life without benefiting the commoners? This teacher [referring to himself] still has some remnant conscience. Therefore, even though [I am] plucking an ancient tune without anyone else's echo, [I] cannot bear to distort [Buddha Dharma] even a little and use Buddha Dharma to court favor. [I] hope the audience will understand.
>
> 今世何世, 豈更容空談性命, 無補人群? 講者良心未死, 雖古調獨彈, 無人隨和, 亦不忍絲毫曲解, 而以佛法為人情也. 聞者諒之.[90]

In Lü's socio-soteriology knowledge is never objective, but it can become impartial. The process of achieving impartiality relies on the collective karmic unfolding of establishing *prasiddha*. Even after 1949, when historical materialism became the master narrative, Lü continued to insist that *prasiddha* must be a skillful means established through recursive and complex (*yizaifanfu er xiangdangfuza* 一再反覆而相當複雜) processes of transforming consciousness and reducing ego. Lü termed this process of learning and knowledge production "the sociality of epistemology" (*renshi de shehuixing* 認識的社會性), or social epistemology, grounded in Yogācāra causal theory that he referred to as *fenbie zixing yuanqi* 分別自性緣起 ([the mode of analysis] that diffracts the dependent arising of *svabhāva*).[91]

Lü saw Yogācāra causal theory as an ever-expanding process of interconditioned transformation resulting in the continuity of former and latter instances of knowing and the agreement between self and others.[92] To be sure, all the elements of Lü's social epistemology were present even before 1949: from the comparative hermeneutics and Buddhisized critical thinking discussed in this chapter to the bodhisattva precepts as rules for democratic deliberation discussed in chapter 5, every piece of evidence points to the gradual development of his transformative epistemology. It was only in 1953 and 1954 that Lü explicitly identified his method as such.

In 1954 Lü announced that this transformative social epistemology must be practiced with others as organized skepticism and grounded in *Yoga Bodhisattva Prātimokṣa*, whose first main stipulation forbids praising oneself and undercutting others (*zizan huita* 自讚毀他):

> It is absolutely impossible to access complete insight into the true knowledge and penetrating view of human experience based a few persons' insight. Rather, [reaching complete insight] must rely on the accumulation of the masses. Therefore, it is only possible to reach the stage of completeness by humbly learning from others' experiences and by gradually expanding and deepening [insight].
>
> 人們對於人生實踐的真知灼見,決非由少數人的悟解便能獲得完全,而必須依賴大眾的積累,所以虛心地向他人吸取經驗,逐漸擴充,逐漸深厚,才會到達完全的地步.[93]

Because knowledge production must rely on collaborative deliberation, Lü repeated that the evil habit (*exi* 惡習) of praising oneself and undercutting others must be eliminated before producing knowledge. Lü considered social epistemology part of the bodhisattva practice and the only way to gradually resolve social issues and open up a new path of *zhuanyi*—revolutionizing consciousness.[94]

Beyond the Empire of Religion

I will rejoice if this exercise of recovering Lü's transformative epistemology serves as a mirror to reflect upon the task of knowledge production today: as scholars ensnared in the imperialist history of comparative religions, how can we take responsibility for this problematic past and assume responsibility for moving beyond this Orientalist legacy? David Chidester styles this question as to how to "be in the empire of religion but not of it."[95] As I have argued throughout this chapter, Lü's lifetime quest was to discover how to be in this unsatisfactory world without being of it. Although Lü started his exploration with Western aesthetics and Buddhology, he eventually discovered in Yogācāra soteriology the essential tools to achieve his goal: namely, weaving a bodhisattva path for aspiring learners to abide in this world while transforming it into an ideal society through concerted, repeated, and motivated coactions. In reading Chidester and Lü side by side, I hope to show how their critical reflections not only illuminate each other but also spark new insights in our search for a way beyond the empire of religion.

Joining Chidester's search for a meaningful alternative way of doing humanities, I have examined Lü's hermeneutic maneuvers to illustrate the political implications of philology and its democratic potential. Far from serving as a benchmark of impartiality, "the realist claims of objectivity" is nothing more than a pure idea of "the view from nowhere."[96] As a conjured-up idea, it has conveniently shielded European Buddhologists from the comparative gaze. By offering an interconditioning ontology as the basis of both social arrangements and scholarly pursuits, Lü indirectly problematized the positivist agenda inherent in philological and Buddhological studies. I hope that my analysis of these forgotten encounters will facilitate future research on how the "non-Western" traditions might structure actional sociopolitical theory and thereby expand discussions of alternative futures.

Unlike his teacher Ouyang, who thrived in polemical debates, Lü disliked full-frontal confrontation. Lü preferred to illustrate the right path with the naïve trust that, once the right path was illuminated, all other mistaken paths would naturally fall out of view. His lifelong effort to carve a right path brought forth both a new professionalization of Buddhist knowledge and a new social theory: Buddhist knowledge was mined for its power as a social critique of modern depravities, its soteriological potential to revert Darwinist devolution, and its efficacy in building an egalitarian, complex sociality grounded in compassion and the wisdom of emptiness.

Here also lies Lü's implicit answer to Chidester's question about the social function of scholarship: like a lotus absorbing nutrients from the mud that then blooms above its muddy roots, a scholar absorbs soteriological knowledge from this unsatisfactory and often violent world and then establishes a new world above the muddy water through the vigorous pursuit of beauty and truth.[97] Rather than feign an objective aloofness, Lü firmly embedded his own knowledge production in the karmic web that is society: he saw scholarship as a vital force in revolutionizing consciousness and in bringing forth social transformation through nonviolence and knowledge.[98] To rephrase Lü's answer in the style of Sheldon Pollock: You transcend *worldly sufferings* by mastering and overmastering those discourses through study and critique.... You cannot simply go around *this world* to overcome it ... you must go through it.[99] In short, like the second-century Madhyamaka philosopher Nāgārjuna, Lü Cheng conjured up an imaginary being—an intersubjective oneness—to negate the "deluded" views of society stemming from scientific realism and social Darwinism.[100]

Equally important, Lü's retelling of Yogācāra causal theory inaugurated a new perspective. In contrast to the traditional scriptural stance, in which the sūtra ventriloquizes an enlightened being instructing commoners as to why and how they shall embark on the bodhisattva path, in Lü's new bodhisattva profession, comparative hermeneutics transforms the one-way instructive gaze into mutual illumination and becomes a tool of organized skepticism for establishing intersubjective accord. In this paradigm Yogācāra doctrines such as indirectly perceived objects and intersubjective agreement become the cornerstones of a communism of knowledge. In this new public court of soteriological knowledge, everyone is assumed to have equal spiritual potential. Everyone is expected to practice comparative hermeneutics and to engage in debates through moral inquiry and a nuanced understanding of texts. And everyone is expected to nurture their resolve to save all sentient beings through learning and teaching.

It is in this sense that I characterize Lü's project as deliberative democracy. Lü took the intense intellectual demand on citizens of a democracy seriously, sanctified everyone's intellectual potential with Yogācāra doctrines, and designed a path for all to develop their intellectual potential fully. Lü did not imagine the ideal citizens of this deliberative democracy to be mere rational thinkers. On the contrary, Lü considered compassion to be a crucial characteristic of the new citizens. This compassion combined with the wisdom of emptiness-cum-interdependence is Lü's understanding of *bodhicitta*. Rationality serves only to harness the affective power of compassion. In the mainstream Buddhist worldview, emotion and rationality are always mutually constitutive. As convincingly demonstrated by Bhikkhu Anālayo, the historical Buddha (as presented by the Pāli texts) treated deluded views by analyzing their affective underpinnings, mainly because the rationalization of a particular view is often a materialization and reification of petty selfish desire and attachment.[101] Lü Cheng's social project picked up these premodern characteristics and integrated both rationality and emotional education into a new path of co-liberation.

Not a Coda

Bending the Arc Together

> Because that arc [of the moral universe] doesn't bend on its own. It takes effort. It takes action. It takes speech after speech and march after march. It takes public pressure and public demonstration. It takes time and it takes energy. It takes a firm commitment by multitudes. The arc doesn't passively bend on its own. It must be bent. We all must bend it together.
>
> —Chris Weigant

I struggle to conclude this book because, halfway through the writing process, I realized that Lü Cheng's vision of liberation Buddhology might not include people like me. What if he meant this "open" bodhisattva path only for able-bodied, heterosexual, cisgender men? This is not a hypothetical question. In my previous work, I have analyzed the gendered soteriology of Lü's teacher Ouyang Jingwu and its social implications, paying particular attention to the following questions: Why did Ouyang consider it necessary to tell his able-bodied, heterosexual, cisgender male students horrid stories about a woman cutting off her breasts and turning herself into an able-bodied, heterosexual, cisgender man? Why did neither Ouyang nor his male students, all of whom were self-proclaimed revolutionaries and aspiring bodhisattvas, ever openly question the Mahāyāna discourse that a woman must turn herself into a man before she can embark on the bodhisattva journey?[1] I remember meticulously and repeatedly searching through all of Lü's manuscripts, private notes, and published works, each from the main text to the footnotes, for an answer. Maddeningly, the archives remained silent.

I reached a turning point when I realized that the silence of the archives that was stonewalling my inquiries into the past reflected the epistemic blindness in my own inquiry: Lü's personal attitude is beside the point. The central goal of practicing transformative epistemology is to produce knowledge democratically and collectively so that the arc of the moral universe can be bent toward justice; accordingly, effective inquiries must include at least three levels: the personal, the collective, and the reflexive. The first entails carefully examining the personal attitudes of historical actors. The second requires discerning the legacy of these historical actors' actions. And the third involves reflecting on how humans today can do better given what we now know about these historical actors' past actions and how these past actions have shaped both the material conditions and ideological formations of the present.

In this forward-looking conclusion, I first comment on the legacy of Lü's socio-soteriology and reflect upon the importance of better collective practices for producing socially responsible knowledge. Then I highlight some innovations of contemporary liberation Buddhologists who have bent the arc of Buddhist social philosophy and practices further toward justice. I have chosen to analyze the socio-soteriologies of two scholars-cum-activists whose work is influenced by the father of engaged Buddhism, the Vietnamese monk-activist Thich Nhat Hanh: bell hooks and Larry Ward. Finally, I reflect on how academics can learn from these liberation Buddhologists about the social responsibility of knowledge production.

Complexity Is the Refuge of the Powerful

> Most social problems are complicated, of course, but a retreat into complexity is often a reflection of our social standing than evidence of critical intelligence. Hungry people want bread. The rich convene a panel of experts. Complexity is the refuge of the powerful.[2]

I take to heart Matthew Desmond's critique of a common academic practice: retreating to complex analysis as a means of avoiding the more challenging process of reflection. Indeed, in many cases, the rhetoric of complexity reveals less about intellectual maturity than it does about one's own implication in systems of domination, especially epistemic domination. Practicing reflexive humanities requires scholars to emerge from behind the veil of complexity and ask an honest question: How can we produce knowledge without reproducing the unfair systems that we ourselves are often part of?

With regard to the gender trouble in Buddhism, thus far the most eye-opening perspective can be found in Vanessa Sasson's historical fiction on the founding of the Buddhist nuns' order: rather than lament that the historical Buddha refused his nurse mother and his aunt Mahāpajāpati's request to be fully ordained three times and that the nuns' order was institutionally subordinated to the monks' order, Sasson emphasizes that "those first Buddhist women did not take no for an answer."[3] By asking why these first Buddhist women refused to take no for an answer, Sasson turns the attention to the concerns and social actions of these women and helps readers arrive at a new answer: thanks to their actions and persistence, the Buddhist traditions have a nuns' order, which could arguably be the first all-female network of support outside the sexual politics of patriarchy.[4]

Turning back to Lü's liberation Buddhology and his silence on gender issues, as a scholar unwilling to participate in reproducing the patriarchal domination looming behind Lü's vision, I wonder about the legacy of Lü's gender-neutral stance in light of Ouyang's overt sexism. I also wonder what would have happened if the Inner Learning Institute's members had heeded the challenges put forth by radical nuns of the Republican era like Hengbao 恆寶. As Yuan Yuan points out, Hengbao challenged traditional androcentric presumptions about women's social roles by paraphrasing an passage from *Ekottara Āgama* (*Zenyi ahanjing* 增一阿含經; T125) to redraw the boundary between masculinity and femininity based on one's spiritual progress: "One has to see the Buddha nature to be a man; otherwise, one is a woman."[5] Rather than yoke gender to perceived biological differences, such as the presence or absence of breasts, Hengbao defined masculinity as the spiritual achievement of seeing the Buddha nature and femininity as an unenlightened state of being. In hindsight, there are many weaknesses in Hengbao's gender theory. What is undeniable, however, is that Hengbao severed the sociopolitical construction of gender from its purportedly biological ties, exposed the male gaze that has naturalized social inequality based on physiology, and demanded a new social reality built upon the ideal of spiritual equality.

Hengbao was not the first Buddhist woman who challenged this patriarchal domination. The earliest recorded challenge can be found two thousand years before Hengbao in Soma's verse in *Therīgāthā*, the poems of the first Buddhist women. When Māra, the evil one, questions Soma on her ability to achieve nirvāṇa because she is a woman (Pāli: *itthi*) with "only two fingers' worth of wisdom," Soma retorts, "What does the femaleness (Pāli: *itthibhāva*) have to do with it? When the mind-heart (Pāli: *citta*) is collected and when wisdom (Pāli: *ñāṇa*) arises, one clearly sees dhamma."[6] Note that *bhāva* (becoming), when standing alone, signifies the physical nature of sex; when used as one of the twelve links of dependent arising, it indicates physical formation. Like

Hengbao, Soma prioritized the spiritual quality of *citta* and *ñāṇa* over the corporeality of *bhāva* and refused to let any bodily features limit her spiritual potential.

This intense quest for spiritual equality was also manifested as a rallying call for women's social equality in modern China. As powerfully argued by Zhang Ruzhao 張汝釗 (1900–1969) in her essay "The Meaning of Buddhist Teaching for Women" (Fojiao guanyu nüxing de yiyi 佛教關於女性的意義),

> Women can not only govern the country and administer the family as well as engage in all worldly enterprises of farming, manufacturing, and business but also can achieve buddhahood, become an ancestor [i.e., the founder of a lineage], realize Chan enlightenment, and thoroughly understand the teaching and thereby accomplish all sorts of otherworldly achievements.
>
> 女子非但能做就治國齊家和世間上一切農工商等事業，並且能夠成佛作祖悟禪通教而成辦種種出世間功行.[7]

In contrast to Ouyang's dismissal of women's ability to become bodhisattvas and Lü's silence, Zhang Ruzhao not only affirmed women's spiritual equality but also went one step further than Hengbao and Soma by employing spiritual equality as the very foundation upon which to demand social equality. At the end of this short essay Zhang calls on all women to become heroes themselves so to create their own tide of the time (*yingxiong zao shishi* 英雄造時勢) and to take on the responsibility of Buddhisizing the world (*fuqi hongyang fohua de danzi* 負起宏揚佛化的擔子).[8]

Nor were there only women who challenged this patriarchal domination. There had always been men as allies in women's struggle for equality. When Mahāpajāpati and her group repeatedly asked to be ordained, it was Ānanda who pleaded on their behalf and challenged the Buddha to reevaluate his refusal. If scholars look outside the established institutions in Republican China, they will see that male allies were present. As has been mentioned in passing, in a popular modern theatrical restaging of Buddhist love lore between Ānanda and an outcaste girl, the playwright Qingyi Jushi reverts the patriarchal gaze and makes Ānanda's skeleton tools to facilitate the outcaste girl's spiritual awakening.[9] This retelling is in stark contrast with the canonical narratives where the foulness of the body is commonly portrayed through the corporal decay of women's bodies for the edification of monks.

In light of these known critiques of patriarchal biopolitics, the silent archives brim with meaning. Individuals with more power were better positioned to propagate cultural concepts such as gender and shape their associative meanings. Groundbreaking ideas often were sidelined: Hengbao's, Zhang Ruzhao's, and Soma's critiques of Buddhist biopolitics remained obscure even during their lifetimes, while male practitioners' visions of gendered soteriology and the Buddhisized family structure were repeated and reproduced.[10] The Inner Learning Institute occupied a position of power. In addition to being the center of the Chinese Yogācāra revival, it functioned for decades as a Buddhist educational institute. Irrespective of the thinkers' personal beliefs, Ouyang's overt sexism and Lü's silence fueled patriarchal domination. Through their scholarship, the two thinkers granted spiritual equality to women in some future life but refused to allow this promise to challenge contemporaneous and concrete structural inequalities.

While Lü and his students at the Inner Learning Institute failed to challenge patriarchy, Lü's approach merits further investigation: Do Lü's liberation Buddhology and the ideas of Buddhability-cum-humanity, bodhisattvas of democracy, and transformative epistemology have the capacity to be taken up and improved upon by others? I am pessimistic about the liberative potential of Lü and his contemporaries' socio-soteriology. After all, despite their different philosophical commitments, Ouyang, Lü, Taixu, and others who had associations with the institute were seemingly oblivious to how their own actions contributed to the reproduction of patriarchy.

And yet, to my surprise, when I look elsewhere for others who are inspired by their ideas, I find better practices. The reason, I surmise, lies more in institutional features than philosophical sophistications: all of the socio-soteriologies analyzed in this monograph envisioned a social movement without centralized control. Lü and Ouyang saw their institute as one among many seed communities of change. Taixu envisioned civil society organizations bounded by shared karma, joint action, and common goals. As such, their projects serve as an open invitation for future generations to bend the arc together.

In the next section, I briefly analyze the socio-soteriologies proposed by two contemporary thinkers: bell hooks and Larry Ward. These socio-soteriologies were partially inspired by Thich Nhat Hanh's engaged Buddhism, a school of thought that itself was partially influenced by Taixu's Humanistic Buddhism.[11] The goal of this analysis is not to trace a Buddhist lineage but to highlight the strength of transformative epistemology. As a form of decentralized social epistemology with the goal of co-liberation, this practice of knowledge co-production functions as an open-ended call to join the ameliorative project of making a better future. In the hands of this new generation of scholar-activists, liberation Buddhology has gained a new afterlife that actualizes its suppressed potential for post-patriarchal and postracial worldmaking.

Spreading Ideas, Not Institutions

This new generation of liberation Buddhologists deploys the Buddhist message of spiritual equality to fight for true democracy and equality in a nonviolent manner and with the power of knowledge. First, for them, spirituality grows from embodied experiences. Second, scholarship must serve the larger purpose of dismantling unjust systems. Finally, structural change must start from a revolution of the heart. And this revolution of the heart entails liberation from not only individual mental afflictions of ignorance, hatred, and greed but also the institutionalized afflictions of epistemological ignorance, mutual repulsion, and moral egoism.

I begin my analysis with bell hooks's two works describing her philosophy of education, *Teaching to Transgress: Education as the Practice of Freedom* (1994) and *Teaching Critical Thinking: Practical Wisdom* (2010). Let us focus on her pedagogy for co-liberation, a tapestry that she weaved together through her readings of her teachers Thich Nhat Hanh (1926–2022) and Paulo Freire (1921–1997), both of whom she described as touching her "deeply with their work."[12] Like Thich Nhat Hanh, Paulo Freire combined spirituality and social justice into one project. Paulo Freire was a Brazilian educator and philosopher whose critical pedagogy in the 1940s shaped the rise of liberation theology in 1970s Latin America.[13]

hooks's pedagogy for co-liberation focuses on the wholeness of embodied processes. hooks takes from Thich Nhat Hanh the Buddhism-influenced pedagogical approach of "teacher as a healer," which is based on the idea of "a union of mind, body, and spirit" and the Buddhist goal of liberation that necessitates the commitment of the teacher to "a process of self-actualization that promotes their own wellbeing."[14] A classroom, in hooks's engaged pedagogy, is a space "where the teacher and students can share their 'inner light'" so that "we have a way to glimpse who we are and how we might learn together." Co-liberation as practiced in the process of learning together must be rooted in compassion, which hooks describes as a "mental formation" that "intensifies awareness and makes connection possible."[15]

hooks also weaves her tapestry of pedagogy for co-liberation using threads of Paulo Freire's pedagogy for the oppressed, especially Freire's focus on the privilege of the poor and refusal to participate in any forms of domination. To be sure, when hooks found Freire, she was already questioning the politics of domination. Freire's pedagogy for the oppressed made her feel seen, understood, and included as an equal subject in a collective effort to question and dismantle systems of domination. hooks writes, "I heard him state emphatically that 'we cannot enter the struggle as objects in order later to become subjects.' This statement resonated with my being. It affirmed for me the importance of finding and having a voice."[16] Entering into the struggle as subjects, for her, means calling on "students to be active participants, to link awareness with practice." To better elucidate the empowerment found in Freire's affirmation of the subject position of the most disenfranchised and those "who suffer the gravest forces of oppression," hooks's quotation of Freire's passage is worthy of reproducing here: "Authentic help means that all who are involved help each other mutually, growing together in the common effort to understand the reality which they seek to transform. Only through such praxis—in which those who help and those who are being helped help each other simultaneously—*can the act of helping become free from the distortion in which the helper dominates the helped.*"[17]

To paraphrase Freire's insights using Lü's terminology, these actions of help are the six perfections of the bodhisattvas of democracy: the act of helping must be free from any relations of domination and must be mutually liberating.

I find bell hooks's constructive critique of Freire's sexism useful in my own struggle to come to terms with the explicit and implicit sexism in the work of the Inner Learning Institute's members. hooks is painfully aware of Freire's blind spot: "For me this is always a source of anguish for it represents a blind spot in the vision of men who have profound insight. And yet, I never wish to see a critique of this blind spot overshadow anyone's (and feminists' in particular) capacity to learn from the insights. . . . Freire's own model of critical pedagogy invites a critical interrogation of this flaw in the work. But *critical interrogation is not the same as dismissal.*"[18]

For bell hooks, constructive critique requires first recognizing all that is valuable and respected in a given work, an approach that calls to mind Lü's Buddhisized critical thinking grounded in compassion. Just as Freire's critical pedagogy invites critical interrogation of its own flaws, Lü's transformative epistemology calls on others to participate in transformative interrogation with the goal of co-liberation. hooks embraces these contradictions in Freire's critical pedagogy "as part of the learning process, part of what one struggles to change," that is, part of a "protracted" struggle.[19]

To better appreciate the wide range of innovations and philosophical sophistication of the contemporary liberation Buddhologists, it is fruitful to read their writings in conjunction with Larry Ward's *America's Racial Karma* (2020), which combines meditative instruction with a self-conscious philosophizing project that throws into relief the implicit social theory of many similar social justice movements informed by Buddhist processual thought. Like hooks, Ward is deeply influenced by Thich Nhat Hanh. Yet unlike hooks, Ward choses to accentuate Thich Nhat Hanh's retheorization of Mahāyāna Buddhism, especially Yogācāra karmic theory.[20]

Ward is the first to employ the ancient Yogācāra philosophical toolbox to bring into focus a new paradigm for understanding how racial karma works and how to disrupt its anchoring schemas, as seen in the following two passages:

> Within us are infinite variety of *seeds*: *seeds* of suffering, happiness, hatred, delusion, jealousy, joy, kindness, justice, greed, forgetfulness, and enlightenment. The *seeds* of racialized consciousness are also present in our internalized trauma, racial perceptions and names, and our social habits. The *seeds* of racialized consciousness and its karmic effects are part of the very fabric of American life, so much so that many don't know how to breathe outside the climate of white supremacy. How sad a retribution that is.
>
> These *seeds* or potentials manifest themselves as a living presence in *the individual and collective* thinking, speech, and behaviors fueling the turning of America's karmic wheel. These *seeds* are all stored in our deepest consciousness. Some *seeds* are innate; others are handed down by our evolutionary and immediate biological ancestors. Some were sown while we were still in the womb, others were sown when we were children. Very importantly, whether transmitted by family, friends, society, or education, all our *seeds* are, by nature, *both individual and collective*. These *seeds* or possibilities are in what is called "*store consciousness*," the reservoir, the warehouse, or museum of our *individual and collective consciousness*. The quality of our lives *individually and collectively* depends on the quality of the *seeds* that lie deep in our consciousness.[21]

The Yogācāra roots of Ward's sociopolitical philosophy show up in his use of individual and collective karmic seeds and the concept of storehouse consciousness, that is, *ālayavijñāna*. Deploying the Yogācāra karmic paradigm, Ward identifies the anchoring schemas that propel the reproduction of America's racial karma. According to Ward, "the turning of America's karmic wheel" is fueled by the seeds of racialized consciousness, internalized trauma, and social habits in both individual and collective thinking, speech, and behaviors. In his own words, "The issues we have in the world today are about hearts and minds trapped in *patterns* that are no longer adequate. *Our systems come out of these patterns*. So we have to do the inner work at the same time as outer work. Otherwise we're just rearranging furniture on the deck of the Titanic."[22]

Whereas Lü Cheng and Monk Taixu employed Yogācāra's shared karma to envision coactions that could lead to a new world of nonviolence, equality, and democracy, hooks and Ward, each deploying a unique set of Buddhist doctrines, reveal to us the behavior patterns of actions and coactions that fuel the slow burn of systemic injustices such as racism and sexism. Precisely because the anchoring schemas are the result of human actions, these thinkers show us how the world can be made otherwise through new patterns of coactions.

For a Brighter Tomorrow

The world can be otherwise only if we work together to bend the arc of the moral universe. Humans have inherited a world of suffering with deeply ingrained systems of domination. In this actual world, no one is free from the inherited racialized and gendered terms, concepts, and material conditions that condition everyday affairs. No one is immune because, seen from the Buddhist processual worldview, individuals and groups are mere aggregated karmic processes: as long as the anchoring schemas continue to turn, the wheels of systemic domination will continue to churn.

Translating these Buddhist insights using philosopher Sally Haslanger's terminology, racism is not merely an ideology but also an *ideological formation*: a racist ideology is "a cultural technē—the web of meanings, symbols, scripts, and such—that functions to create or stabilize unjust social practices," and a racist ideological formation entails "the unjust practices, institutions, behavior, and other artifacts that are guided or formed by a racist ideology."[23] Racism reproduces itself through "the looping effects that connect agents, meanings, and material conditions."[24] Or, in Buddhist terms, racism reproduces itself through cycles of actions fueled by epistemological ignorance, mutual repulsion, and moral egoism.

Subscribing to the binaries of racists and antiracists, nonfeminists and feminists, white persons and persons of color, will only deepen the problem. Such binaristic thinking lets individuals off the hook too easily: it allows people to stay safely on the side of good "us" against the evil "them." This habit of thinking then abets individuals in acting defensively by "*otherizing* racist actions and systems" and "by looking away and wishing to have nothing to do with it."[25]

This defensive posture also fails to disrupt the unjust ideological formation. As Sally Haslanger powerfully argues, broad social change requires revolutionary nonviolent actions on multiple levels: personal, cultural, structural, legal and political, and material. Disrupting the very terms and concepts that frame everyday experiences requires "queering our language, playing with meanings, and monkey-wrenching or otherwise shifting the material conditions that support our tutored dispositions."[26]

Haslanger ends her 2017 analysis of racist ideological formation by quoting Chris Weigant's call to bend the arc together. I started this forward-looking conclusion with the same quotation: the path of revolutionary nonviolence laid out by Lü, Ouyang, Hengbao, Zhang Ruzhao, bell hooks, Ward, and Haslanger can bring forth a new world only if we work together. In many ways, these scholars, past and present, have shown us repeatedly that the power to form new social realities lies in each one of us. The question now is whether and how we plan to use this power of nonviolence. I offer the analysis in this monograph as a springboard for deeper and more challenging transformative interrogations of how scholarship can assist in the work of bringing forth a brighter tomorrow.

Notes

Abbreviations

CWSL Xuanzang 玄奘, *Cheng weishi lun* 成唯識論. T.1585

Essentials Ouyang Jingwu 歐陽竟無, ed., *Zangyao* 藏要 (Essentials of a new Buddhist canon), 10 vols. (Nanjing: Zhina neixueyuan, 1929–43; rpt., Nanjing: Jinling Sūtra Press, 2002)

OJNWX Ouyang Jingwu 歐陽竟無, *Ouyang Jingwu xiansheng neiwai xue* 歐陽競無先生內外學 (The inner and outer learnings of Mr. Ouyang Jingwu), 30 vols. Chongqing: Zhina neixueyuan shuyuan, 1943 (Reprint. Nanjing: Jinling Sūtra Press, 2008)

QGBKSY Quanguo baokan suoyin 全國報刊索引, https://www.cnbksy.com

T. Takakusu Junjirō 高楠順次郎, Watanabe Kaikyoku 渡辺海旭, Ono Genmyō 小野玄妙, and Taishō Issaikyō Kankōkai 大正一切経刊行会, eds., *Taishō shinshū dai zōkyō* 大正新脩大藏經 (Tokyo: Taishō Issaikyō Kankōkai, 1924–32)

X. Maeda Eun 前田慧雲 and Nakano Tatsue 中野達慧 eds., *Shinsan Dainippon zoku zōkyō* 新纂大日本續藏經 (Tokyo: Kokusho Kankokai 國書刊行會, 1905–12)

Xuanji1991 Lü Cheng, *Lü Cheng foxue lunzhu xuanji* 呂澂佛學論著選集 (Selected writings on Buddhist studies by Lü Cheng), ed. Li An 李安 (Jinan: Qilu shushe, 1991)

Introduction

1. Lü Cheng 呂澂, "Meishu geming" 美術革命, *Xin qingnian* 新青年 6, no. 1 (January 1919): 84–86. Chen Duxiu added the title to the letter, "Meishu geming." In the letter, Lü Cheng himself used *geming* 革命, *gexin* 革新, and *gaige* 改革 interchangeably. Throughout his life, Lü developed an idiosyncratic rhetoric of *geming* "revolution" from its basic sense of fundamental transformation, or literally "change of fate/destiny/life," to his later adoption of the Buddhist soteriological term *āśrayaparivṛtti* (Ch: *zhuanyi* 轉依), which literally means

"transformation of basis" or "fundamental transformation," which I here translate as "revolutionizing consciousness." I use "fine arts" and "aesthetics" interchangeably in translating *meishu* 美術 and *meixue* 美學. This is because (1) fine arts have played a key role in the emergence of academic studies of aesthetics, and (2) Lü Cheng was well versed in the historical relation between fine arts and aesthetics and used the two senses of *mei* interchangeably.

2. The monographs include the following: Lü Cheng, *Xiyang meishu shi* 西洋美術史 (Shanghai: Commercial Press, 1922); Lü Cheng, *Meixue qianshuo* 美學淺說 (Shanghai: Commercial Press, 1923); Lü Cheng, *Meixue gailun* 美學概論 (Shanghai: Commercial Press, 1923); Lü Cheng, *Wanjin meixue sichao* 晚近美學思潮 (Shanghai: Commercial Press, July 1924); Lü Cheng, *Secaixue gangyao* 色彩學綱要 (Shanghai: Commercial Press, 1926); and Lü Cheng, *Guohua jiaocai gailun* 國畫教材概論 (Shanghai: Zhonghua [Chunghwa] shuju, 1927); Lü Cheng, *Xiandai meixue sichao* 現代美學思潮 (Shanghai: Commercial Press, 1934). Because of space limitations, I do not list Lü's essays in newspapers or periodicals. However, in these monographs and essays Lü introduced a wide range of Western aesthetic movements to Chinese students. Below is a partial list of important works that Lü introduced to Chinese readers: George Santayana's 1896 *The Sense of Beauty*; Bernard Bosangquet's 1915 *Three Lectures on Aesthetics*; Kaarle Laurila's 1909 *Zur Theorie der ästhetischen Gefühle*; Theodor Lipps's 1903 *Aesthetik*; Inagaki Suematsu's (稲垣末松) 1921 *Bigaku hanron* 美學汎論; Richard Hamann's 1915 *Zur Begründung der Ästhetik*; Benedetto Croce's 1902 *Esthetica*; Oskar Bie's 1895 *Zwischen den Künsten*; Hermann Cohen's *Ästhetik des reinen Gefühls*; Conrad Fiedler's 1887 *Der Ursprung der künstlerischen Thätigkeit*; Max Dessoir's 1906 *Zeitschrift für Ästhetik und allgemeine Kunstwissenschaft*; Karl Groos's 1892 *Einleitung in die Aesthetik*; Georg Wilhelm Friedrich Hegel's 1826 *Philosophie der Kunst oder Ästhetik*; Immanuel Kant's 1790 *Kritik der Urteilskraft*; Edward von Hartmann's 1887 *Philosophie des Schönen*; Konrad von Lange's 1902 *Das Wesen der Kunst*; Henry Marshall's 1895 *Aesthetic Principles*; Ethel Puffer Howes's 1905 *The Psychology of Beauty*; Johannes Immanuel Volkelt's 1895 *Ästhetische Zeitfragen*; Wilhelm Wundt's 1900 *Völkerpsychologie*; Jean-Marie Guyau's 1887 *L'art au point de vue sociologique*; Yrjö Hirn's 1901 *The Origins of Art*; Ernst Grosse's 1894 *Die Anfänge der Kunst*; Paul Gaultier's 1911 *Le sens de l'art*; Jonas Cohn's 1901 *Allgemeine Ästhetik*; and Eleonore Kühn's 1908 *Das Problem der ästhetischen Autonomie*.
3. The laudatory titles awarded him since the 1930s include "guru of Buddhist learning" (foxue dashi 佛學大師), "maestro of Buddhist learning" (foxue taidou 佛學泰斗), and "expert of Buddhist learning" (foxue jia 佛學家).
4. For two essays praising the quality of Lü's scholarship, see Chen-kuo Lin, "The Uncompromising Quest for Genuine Buddhism: Lü Cheng's Critique of Original Enlightenment," in *Transforming Consciousness: Yogācāra Thought in Modern China*, ed. John Makeham (New York: Oxford University, 2014), 346–52; and Dan Lusthaus, "Lü Cheng, Epistemology, Genuine Buddhism," in the same book, 318–45.
5. Ouyang Jingwu 歐陽竟無, ed., *Zangyao* 藏要 (Nanjing: Jinling Sūtra Press, 2002). Lü Cheng is not listed as the editor, but he did most of the comparative studies.
6. "Épistémè" follows Michel Foucault's theorization in *The Order of Things: An Archaeology of the Human Sciences* (New York: Vintage Books, 1970). For Foucault, "épistémè" refers to the historical construction of an a priori that grounds knowledge and its discourses for a culture or an epoch. But I use it in a concrete sense: the condition of their possibility in a particular epistemological community. For a thorough philosophical examination of the core issues regarding how to reconcile the modern scientific view of one objective world (a view from

nowhere) and the individual subjective view of the same world, see Thomas Nagel, *The View from Nowhere* (New York: Oxford University Press, 1986).

7. For an incisive analysis of Yogācāra nonduality and its rejection of the subject–object structure, see William Waldron, *Making Sense of Mind Only: Why Yogācāra Buddhism Matters* (Somerville: Wisdom Publications, 2023), 147–308.
8. For both quotations from Zhuangzi, see "The Floods of Autumn," in *Zhuangzi—Outer Chapters*, Chinese Text Project, https://ctext.org/dictionary.pl?if=en&id=2828#s10041701. The Chinese idiom of a "frog in a well" (*jingdi zhiwa* 井底之蛙) also finds cross-cultural resonances in Sanskrit and Bengali folklore of "kūpamaṇḍuka." See Amartya Sen, *The Argumentative Indian: Writings on Indian History, Culture, and Identity* (New York: Picador, 2006), 93–94.
9. The earliest articulation of a research paradigm and its related parts can be found in Egon G. Guba, "The Alternative Paradigm Dialog," in *The Paradigm Dialog*, ed. Egon G. Guba (Newbury Park, CA: Sage Publications, 1990), 17–30. The outline of the four incommensurable yet competing research paradigms in Euro-American academia, including their divergent ontologies, epistemologies, methodologies, and axiologies, can be found in Egon G. Guba and Yvonna S. Lincoln, "Competing Paradigms in Qualitative Research," in *Handbook of Qualitative Research*, ed. Norman K. Denzin and Yvonna S. Lincoln (Thousand Oaks: Sage Publications, 1994), 105–17.
10. François Jullien, *De l'être au vivre: Lexique euro-chinois de la pensée* (Paris: Gallimard, 2015), 9, 251, 275, 313.
11. Many scholars since the 1980s have incisively pointed out the limitations of postpositivism and its concomitant secular rationality model in producing knowledge about Buddhism. It is indisputable that postpositivism is the dominant research paradigm in sinology, philology, and Buddhist studies. Students of Buddhist studies typically read Jan Willem de Jong's classic historiography of Buddhist studies, focusing on the study of Indian Buddhism while touching upon Southeast Asian, Chinese, and Tibetan Buddhist traditions. See Jan Willem de Jong, *A Brief History of Buddhist Studies in Europe and America* (Delhi: Sri Satguru Publications, 1987). Students of East Asian Buddhism typically read Akira Hiragawa's introduction to methodology. See Hiragawa Akira 平川彰, *Bukkyō kenkyū nyūmon* 仏教研究入門 (Tokyo: Daisō syuppan, 1984). Students of Chinese Buddhism typically read another seminal work on methodology; see Okabe Kazuo 岡部和雄 and Tanaka Ryōsyō 田中良昭, eds., *Chūgoku Bukkyō kenkyū nyūmon* 中国仏教研究入門 (Tokyo: Daisō syuppan, 2006). There are other similar monographs on methodologies of Buddhist studies, but these three are enough to demonstrate the default research paradigm in Buddhist studies. The study of Buddhist philosophy follows a different track, where methodological secularism remains the standard. Andrew P. Tuck frames this secular paradigm in this way: "Traditional hermeneutics insists that there is one true meaning that is the goal of any interpretation, and that this meaning is effectively identical with the author's intention. The interpreter's job is to set aside his own cultural, historical, and personal biases and to retrieve this objective meaning by entering the world of the author." See Andrew P. Tuck, *Comparative Philosophy, and the Philosophy of Scholarship: On the Western Interpretation of Nāgārjuna* (New York: Oxford University Press, 1990), 9. This methodological commitment to Western naturalism (often bifurcated into objective naturalism and subjective naturalism), according to Peter Harrison's incisive analysis, is more like "an ersatz theology," "a paradoxical amalgam of two contradictory impulses, a theistically grounded assumption . . . combined with the denial of the supernatural," and "a totalizing crypto-theology" that was given legitimacy through "an appeal to narratives of progress,"

which is itself informed by "providential or eschatological notions of historical directionality." See Peter Harrison, *Some New World: Myths of Supernatural Belief in a Secular Age* (Cambridge: Cambridge University Press, 2024), 367, 10. The training of Buddhist philosophy still follows the terms and conditions dictated by philosophical naturalism. Take, for example, the anthology of influential Buddhist texts introduced by a group of leading experts: Jay L. Garfield and William Edelglass, eds., *Buddhist Philosophy: Essential Readings* (New York: Oxford University Press, 2009). While each individual text has been carefully contextualized historically within Buddhist traditions, the organization as a whole follows the professionalized philosophy that has redefined "authentic" branches of philosophical studies as the ones grew out of the Greek naturalist origins, namely, ontology, hermeneutics, epistemology, philosophy of mind, and ethics. While the anthology enriches the Western canon by including Buddhist texts, these texts are included not on their own terms and not appreciated as theoretical resources to reimagine how to produce knowledge differently. Rafal Stepien's recent monograph offers a powerful and systematic critique of the entrenched Christian and Western assumptions in the academic studies of non-Western philosophies, using scholarship on Nāgārjuna's philosophy as a probe to lay out three main modes of misreading, "philological-not-religious," "the rationality model of interpretation," and "universal sovereignty." See Rafal K. Stepien, *Buddhism Between Religion and Philosophy: Nāgārjuna and the Ethics of Emptiness* (New York: Oxford University Press, 2024), 61–91.

12. Charles Hallisey has shared this idea on multiple occasions. In a 2022 public talk Hallisey reiterated this idea and credited it to Kenneth Morgan, who was instrumental in establishing the disciplinary studies of world religions. See Charles Hallisey, "Expanding the Ways We Read the Expanding Biographies of the Buddha," Evans-Wentz Lecture, Ho Center for Buddhist Studies, Stanford University, April 11, 2022, https://youtu.be/7GzyW6MNm9w?si=p6e7i3Poq_UorWv5. The clip about "learn about" and "learn from" appears at 4′30″–5′30″.
13. Leigh K. Jenco, *Changing Referents: Learning across Space and Time in China and the West* (New York: Oxford University Press, 2015), 17–24.
14. The rise of postcolonial studies is typically pegged to the publication of Edward Said's *Orientalism* (New York: Pantheon, 1978). The field has since then blossomed into many subfields. I myself follow more closely the seminal work by Dipesh Chakrabarty, which I see Jenco's project as belonging to. See Dipesh Chakrabarty, *Provincializing Europe: Postcolonial Thought and Historical Difference* (Princeton, NJ: Princeton University Press, 2000). Like Jenco's monograph, her edited volume showcases the collective effort to decenter European modes of knowing and to diversify paradigms of knowledge production. See Leigh K. Jenco, ed., *Chinese Thought as Global Theory: Diversifying Knowledge Production in the Social Sciences and Humanities* (Albany: State University of New York Press, 2016). This systematic reflection on how to learn from the other is also seen in many other works. See, for example, John Makeham, ed., *Learning from the Other: Australian and Chinese Perspectives on Philosophy* (Canberra: Australian Academy of the Humanities, 2016).
15. Norman K. Denzin and Yvonna S. Lincoln, "Paradigms and Perspectives in Contention," in *Handbook of Qualitative Research*, ed. Norman K. Denzin and Yvonna S. Lincoln, 5th ed. (Thousand Oaks, CA: Sage Publications, 2018), 97.
16. Tao Jiang, *Origins of Moral-Political Philosophy in Early China: Contestation of Humaneness, Justice, and Personal Freedom* (Oxford: Oxford University Press, 2021), 21–25.
17. Critiques of positivism coemerged with the formation of this paradigm but became more systematized only in the 1970s. For an incisive analysis of early social science's double

indebtedness to Christian theological models, see Harrison, *Some New World*, 306–19. Notable alternative paradigms are American pragmatism in the late nineteenth century and critical theory of the Frankfort school in the 1930s.

18. In table I.1 I have combined two tables from Guba and Lincoln's 1994 article. See Guba and Lincoln, "Competing Paradigms in Qualitative Research," 109, 112. The last column is my new analysis. To be sure, the competing paradigms have only multiplied. Readers interested in other competing paradigms can consult the most recent edition of the handbook. See Yvonna S. Lincoln, Susan A. Lynham, and Egon G. Guba, "Paradigmatic Controversies, Contradictions, and Emerging Confluences, Revisited," in Denzin and Lincoln, *Handbook of Qualitative Research*, 108–50.
19. I am referring to the "participatory paradigm" in table 5.4 of Lincoln et al., "Paradigmatic Controversies," 112–31.
20. I borrow this idea of "anchoring schema" or "anchoring process" from Jason Ānanda Josephson Storm. According to Storm, when social kinds and social facts are seen as emerging from causally linked processes, then the natural next step of analysis is to consider what kinds of repeated processes give rise to seemingly stable properties of social kinds and social facts. See Jason Ānanda Josephson Storm, *Metamodernism: The Future of Theory* (Chicago: University of Chicago Press, 2021), 113–14, 126–29.
21. Denzin and Guba, "Paradigms and Perspectives in Contention," 106.
22. Denzin and Guba, "Paradigms and Perspectives in Contention," 106, 100.
23. Denzin and Guba, "Paradigms and Perspectives in Contention," 106.
24. Katherine Jenkins, *Ontology and Oppression: Race, Gender, and Social Reality* (New York: Oxford University Press, 2023), 3, original emphasis.
25. Jenkins, *Ontology and Oppression*, 5, 9, 239.
26. The existing research is too vast to summarize in an endnote. Interested readers can consult the two following monographs on premodern Yogācāra systems in India and in China, respectively: Sonam Kachru, *Other Lives: Mind and World in Indian Buddhism* (New York: Columbia University Press, 2021), and Dan Lusthaus, *Buddhist Phenomenology: A Philosophical Investigation of Yogācāra Buddhism and the Ch'eng Wei-shih Lun* (New York: Routledge Curzon, 2002).
27. Note that I present only those Yogācāra arguments that were adopted and further developed by modern Chinese Yogācārins. Readers interested in the premodern Yogācāra system should read Kachru, *Other Lives*, and Lusthaus, *Buddhist Phenomenology*, and review the references therein. In fact, this epistemic challenge to objectivity, might be more pan-Buddhist in the karmic tales; see Francisca Cho, "Buddhism, Science, and the Truth about Karma," *Religion Compass* 8, no. 4 (2014): 125.
28. There are many verses challenging the notions of object and objectivity. For a more in-depth analysis of this argument, see the section headed "Replacing Objectivity."
29. Willard van Orman Quine, "Main Trends in Recent Philosophy: Two Dogmas of Empiricism," *Philosophical Review* 60, no. 1 (1951): 41. Quine was critiquing the Kantian notion of an a priori standard for determining truth, which Kant termed "analytic" truth, and which is independent of fact and stood in contrast to the empiricist projects in the sciences. Kant termed this "synthetic" truth grounded in fact. See also Willard van Orman Quine, "Two Dogmas in Retrospect," *Canadian Journal of Philosophy* 21, no. 3 (1991): 266–71.
30. Kachru, *Other Lives*, 111.
31. Kachru, *Other Lives*, 85.

32. Kachru, *Other Lives*, 96–99, 118.
33. Kachru, *Other Lives*, 111.
34. Ed Yong, *An Immense World: How Animal Senses Reveal the Hidden Realms Around Us* (New York: Random House, 2022), 10–11.
35. Yong, *An Immense World*, 11.
36. In fact, the contestations about what can be known and how to know, or the "knowledge-generating processes called *pramāṇa*" are not limited to the Buddhist or even Yogācāra tradition. For a lucid review of *pramāṇa* theories and debates in classical Indian philosophy, see Stephen Phillips, "Epistemology in Classical Indian Philosophy," in *The Stanford Encyclopedia of Philosophy* (Winter 2021 Edition), ed. Edward N Zalta, https://plato.stanford.edu/archives/win2021/entries/epistemology-india.
37. For a lucid translation-interpretation of these points, see Kachru, *Other Lives*, 208–10.
38. For a translation and analysis of these verses, see Kachru, *Other Lives*, 213–16. The common translation of *jiwei* is "atom." Kachru translates the term as "minimal part." I translate it as "elemental event" to highlight the sense of momentariness implied by the term.
39. Kachru likens Vasubandhu's use of the dream metaphor to a "virtual space" created by the human tendency to affirm that the content of one's experience occurs "in a spatiotemporal framework that is not, however, commensurable with a spatiotemporal frame of physical things." See Kachru, *Other Lives*, 71.
40. Kachru, *Other Lives*, 209–11.
41. For a seminal study of Yogācāra as phenomenology and its theorization of intersubjectivity, see Lusthaus, *Buddhist Phenomenology*. For recent journal articles on this topic, see Roy Tzohar, "Imagine Being a *Preta*: Early Indian Yogācāra Approaches to Intersubjectivity," *Sophia* 56, no. 2 (2016): 337–54; Catherine Prueitt, "Karmic Imprints, Exclusion, and the Creation of the Worlds of Conventional Experience in Dharmakīrti's Thought," *Sophia* 57, no. 2 (2018): 313–35; Ching Keng, "How Do We Understand the Meaning of a Sentence under the Yogācāra Model of the Mind? On Disputes among East Asian Yogācāra Thinkers of the Seventh Century," *Journal of Indian Philosophy* 46 (2018): 475–504; Sonam Kachru, "Ratnakīrti and the Extent of Inner Space: An Essay on Yogācāra and the Threat of Genuine Solipsism," *Sophia* 58, no. 1 (2019): 61–83; Roy Tzohar, "The Buddhist Philosophical Conception of Intersubjectivity: An Introduction," *Sophia* 58, no. 1 (2019): 57–60; Jay Garfield, "'I Take Refuge in the Sangha. But How?': The Puzzle of Intersubjectivity in Buddhist Philosophy Comments on Tzohar, Prueitt, and Kachru," *Sophia* 58, no. 1 (2019): 85–89; and Jingjing Li, "Through the Mirror: The Account of Other Minds in Chinese Yogācāra Buddhism," *Dao: A Journal of Comparative Philosophy* 18, no. 3 (2019): 435–51.
42. I have highlighted this intersecting problem of incommensurable worlds and intersubjectivity and analyzed two ways of resolving it in "*Adhipati*, Yogācāra Intersubjectivity, and Soteriology in Kuiji's Commentaries," *Sophia*, June 5, 2024. https://link.springer.com/article/10.1007/s11841-024-01019-9; and Jessica Zu, "Karma, *Adhipati*, and Weapons of Mass Destruction: Wang Enyang's (1897–1964) Yogācāra Theory of Intersubjective Responsibility," *Journal of Buddhist Philosophy* 6, no. 1 (2025).
43. Jenny Wiley Legath suggested the term "socio-soteriology" to me in 2019. Duncan Williams suggested the term "liberation Buddhology" to me in 2021.
44. Stepien, *Buddhism between Religion and Philosophy*, 89. In the quote, I replaced "Nāgārjuna" with "modern Yogācārins" and changed the pronouns when necessary.

45. For diffractive analysis, see Donna Haraway, "The Promise of Monsters: A Regenerative Politics for Inappropriate/d Others," in *Cultural Studies*, ed. Lawrence Grossberg, Cary Nelson, and Paula A. Treichler (New York: Routledge, 1992), 299–300. For "ameliorative" philosophy, see Sally Haslanger, "What Good Are Our Intuitions? Philosophical Analysis and Social Kinds," *Proceedings of the Aristotelian Society*, Sup. 80, no. 1 (2006): 89–118.
46. For an insightful review of process philosophy in Greco-European thought, see Johanna Seibt, "Process Philosophy," in *The Stanford Encyclopedia of Philosophy* (Summer 2023 Edition), ed. Edward N. Zalta and Uri Nodelman, https://plato.stanford.edu/entries/process-philosophy/. To the best of my knowledge, there is no comparable review article on process philosophy in non-Western traditions.
47. Peter D. Hershock, *Consciousness Mattering: A Buddhist Synthesis* (London; New York: Bloomsbury, 2023), 33–34.
48. For a thoughtful study of Whiteheadian process ontology and its relation with Darwinism and processual thoughts in William James, John Dewey, and Henri Bergson, see Isabelle Stengers, *Thinking with Whitehead: A Free and Wild Creation of Concepts*, trans. Michael Chase (Cambridge, MA: Harvard University Press, 2011).
49. See Seibt, "Process Philosophy," and the bibliography therein.
50. Vincent Eltschinger, *"Caste" et philosophie bouddhique: Continuité de quelques arguments bouddhiques contre le traitement réaliste des dénominations sociales* (Vienna: Universität Wien, 2000), 14, 161.
51. For works arguing for the lack of a sociopolitical philosophy in premodern Buddhist traditions, see for example, Eltschinger, *Caste*, 157–58. In addition, according to Johannes Bronkhorst, after Ashoka's time, Vedic Brahmanism gradually developed a strong sociopolitical philosophy and practice and all subsequent Buddhist traditions across Asia adapted to this new social order in two main ways. The first was to withdraw into soteriology and to adapt its institutional existence to this Brahmanical social order. See Johannes Bronkhorst, *Buddhism in the Shadow of Brahmanism* 2, *South Asia*, vol. 24 (Leiden: Brill, 2011), 99–113. The second path was to adopt the Brahmanical social order together with tantric rites and magical rituals in its own doctrinal systems so as to make Buddhist masters function as protectors of the court and the state. See Bronkhorst, *Buddhism in the Shadow*, 238–46. Either way, for Bronkhorst, Buddhism in premodern era had not developed any sociopolitical philosophy of its own. I disagree with this approach because, following Adam S. Green's insight, I think they all presume hierarchy and political elite as the foundation of a complex political theory and thereby exclude sociopolitical theories of egalitarian complex society. See Adam S. Green, "Killing the Priest-King: Addressing Egalitarianism in the Indus Civilization," *Journal of Archaeological Research* 29 (2021): 153–202.
52. For an incisive review of how this epistemic blindness has hindered studies of sociopolitical complexities of ancient egalitarian societies, see Green, "Killing the Priest-King."
53. In works arguing for the presence of a sociopolitical message of equality and a coherent social vision, the consensus seems to be as follows. The Buddhist tradition prefers a tripartite sociopolitical structure in which a Dharmic king is held responsible for social and political well-being, the householder or *ganapati* offers the saṅgha economic support, and the task of the saṅgha is to offer spiritual care. Complete eradication of social inequalities does not seem to be the chief goal of premodern Buddhist teaching. See, for example, Uma Chakravarti, *The Social Dimension of Early Buddhism* (Delhi: Oxford University Press, 1987), 180–81. For her more forceful argument for a Buddhist social philosophy, see Uma

Chakravarti, *On the Social Philosophy of Buddhism: Four Essays* (Shimla: Indian Institute for Advanced Study, 2015). See also Trevor Ling, *Buddhist Revival in India: Aspects of the Sociology of Buddhism* (London: Macmillan, 1980), 19–23. Xinru Liu recently made a similar argument; see Xinru Liu, *Early Buddhist Society: The World of Gautama Buddha* (Albany: State University of New York Press, 2022). In addition to historical studies, in recent decades, philosophers also acknowledged and expanded the Buddhist social ethics. For an incisive critical reconstruction of Buddhist social ethics as seen in early canonical sources, see Hsiao-Lan Hu, *This-Worldly Nibbāna: A Buddhist-Feminist Social Ethics for Peacemaking in the Global Community* (Albany: State University of New York Press, 2011), 31–61. For an in-depth investigation into the philosophical underpinnings of engaged Buddhism and their deep historical roots in Buddhist thought, see Sallie King, *Being Benevolence: The Social Ethics of Engaged Buddhism* (Honolulu: University of Hawai'i Press, 2009). While I agree with both Hu and King regarding the details of their analysis, I think their framing of Buddhist social philosophy as social "ethics" could use an update. A decade after their scholarship, today's conditions are ripe to challenge the parochial division of philosophy into metaphysics, epistemology, and ethics, a division premised upon Aristotelian and later Platonic substance metaphysics. It is about time to name them what they are—social philosophy.

54. Seibt, "Process Philosophy."
55. Jullien, *De l'être au vivre*, 289
56. Eltschinger, *Caste*, 161.
57. Storm, *Metamodernism*, 117–28.
58. Mercedes Valmisa, *Adapting: A Chinese Philosophy of Action* (New York: Oxford University Press, 2021), 1, 7.
59. Wendi L. Adamek, *Practicescapes and the Buddhists of Baoshan* (Bochum: Hamburg University Press, 2021), 124.
60. Cho, "Buddhism, Science, and the Truth about Karma," 120–21. For another argument for karmic tales as enabling "mutual empathy," see Reiko Ohnuma, "When Animals Speak: Animal Ethics from the Mouths of Buddhist Animals," unpublished.
61. David B. Wong, *Moral Relativism and Pluralism* (Cambridge: Cambridge University Press, 2023), 3–17.
62. This section is based on Lü's autobiography and his colleague Li An's memoir, cross-checked and complemented by my archival findings. See Lü Cheng, "Wo de jingli yu Neixuyuan fazhan licheng" 我的经历与内学院发展历程, ed. Gao Shanshan 高山杉, *Shijie zhexue* 3 (2007): 77–79, 86. Li An 李安, *Li An foxue lunzhu xuanji* 李安佛學論著選集 (Nanjing: Jinling kejing chu, 2003), 145–73.
63. Lü Cheng, *Lü Cheng foxue lunzhu xuanji* 呂澂佛學論著選集, ed. Li An 李安 (Jinan: Qilu shushe, 1991).
64. Lü Cheng, *LC Lü Cheng foxue zhuzuoji* LC 呂澂佛學著作集, http://cbeta.buddhism.org.hk/catalog/LC%20呂澂佛學著作集.
65. The metaphor of the birdcage was first deployed by the renowned feminist philosopher Marilyn Frye in 1983 to highlight systemic oppression. The thrust of her argument is that systemic oppression works like a birdcage. If we focus on only one wire, then we cannot see other wires. Consequently, no matter how carefully and how extensively we study this wire, we cannot comprehend why the caged bird cannot fly around freely and go elsewhere. See Marilyn Frye, *The Politics of Reality: Essays in Feminist Theory* (Freedom, CA: Crossing Press, 1983), 2–7. In my understanding, this metaphor has equal illustrative power in

capturing the birdcage of substance metaphysics and its associated categories and concepts that underpin colonial epistemic domination and its obscuring other ways of doing philosophy.

1. Lü Cheng and the Birth of Yogācāra Social Philosophy

This chapter is a shortened version of Jessica Zu, "A Spiritual Evolutionism: Lü Cheng, Aesthetic Revolution, and the Rise of a Buddhism-Inflected Social Ontology in Modern China," *Journal of Global Buddhism* 22, no. 1 (2021): 49–75.

1. Lü Cheng, "Wanjin de meixueshuo he meide yuanli, wu zhi qi" 晚近的美學說和美的原理, 五之七, *Jiaoyu zazhi* 14, no. 3 (March 1922): 3.
2. For historical analysis of the formations of these binaries, see Vincent Goossaert and David A. Palmer, *The Religious Question in Modern China* (Chicago: University of Chicago Press, 2011); Paul R. Katz and Vincent Goossaert, *The Fifty Years That Changed Chinese Religion, 1898–1948* (Ann Arbor, MI: Association for Asian Studies, 2021).
3. Amartya Sen, "Secularism and Its Discontents," in *The Argumentative Indian: Writings on Indian History, Culture, and Identity* (New York: Picador, 2006), 288.
4. Lü Cheng, "Meishu geming" 美術革命, *Xin qingnian* 6, no. 1 (January 1919): 85.
5. For a pervasiveness of this sense of upwardness and its eventual politicization, see Wang Fansen 王汎森, *Zhongguo jindai sixiang yu xueshu de xipu* 中國近代思想與學術的系譜, expanded edition (Shanghai: Shanghai sanlian chubanshe, 2018), 14, 161, 181–202.
6. Lü Cheng, "Wo de jingli yu Neixuyuan fazhan licheng" 我的经历与内学院发展历程, ed. Gao Shanshan 高山杉, *Shijie zhexue* 3 (2007): 77–78.
7. Sascha Bru, Luca Somigli, and Bart van den Bossche, eds., *Futurism: A Microhistory* (Cambridge: Legenda, 2017), 1–12. It is well known that futurism played a key role in the rise of Italian fascism, but in 1920s China few thinkers foresaw its troublesome implications.
8. Lü, "Meishu geming," 85.
9. Lü, "Meishu geming," 85.
10. Lü, "Meishu geming," 85.
11. Lü, "Wo de jingli," 78.
12. Lü, "Meishu geming," 85.
13. Lü, "Wo de jingli," 78.
14. For an overview of social ontology in the European intellectual traditions, especially with regard to Gabriel Tarde's individualism vs. Émile Durkheim's holism, see Brian Epstein, "Social Ontology," in *The Stanford Encyclopedia of Philosophy* (Summer 2018 Edition), ed. Edward N. Zalta, https://plato.stanford.edu/archives/sum2018/entries/social-ontology/.
15. Erik Hammerstrom, *The Science of Chinese Buddhism: Early Twentieth-Century Engagements* (New York: Columbia University Press, 2015), 128–49.
16. Lü Cheng [Chengshu 澄叔], "Liboshi meixue dayao" 栗泊士美學大要, *Dongfang zazhi* 17, no. 5 (1920): 69–75.
17. Lü Cheng, "Meishu fazhan de tujing" 美術發展的途徑, *Meishu* 3, no. 2 (May 1922): 29. This essay was last edited on December 9, 1921.
18. This argument is made in multiple essays. See Lü Cheng, "Wanjin de meixueshuo he meide yuanli, wu zhi qi," 晚近的美學說和美的原理, 五之七, *Jiaoyu zazhi* 14, no. 3 (March 1922): 6–7. The essay itself was dated January 1922. See also Lü Cheng, "Meishu fazhan de tujing," 31–34;

"Meishu chengxing zhi jingguo" 美術成形之經過, *Shanxisheng jiaoyuhui zazhi* 9, no. 1 (January 1923): 50–58.

19. Lü, "Meishu fazhan de tujing," 28–30.
20. Judith Butler, *The Force of Nonviolence: An Ethico-Political Bind* (London: Verso, 2021), 129, 36.
21. Lü, "Wanjin de meixueshuo he meide yuanli, wu zhi qi," 1. In this essay, Lü cited Jean-Marie Guyau to substantiate his claim. Guyau argued that the purpose of art is not pleasure but the creation of sympathy among members of a society. See Keith Ansell-Pearson, "Beyond Obligation? Jean-Marie Guyau on Life and Ethics," *Royal Institute of Philosophy Supplement* 77 (2015): 215–17.
22. Lü used the phrase "an aesthetic life" in many of his essays. See, for example, Lü, "Meishu fazhan de tujing," 20, 27–28, 32–35. See also Lü, "Yishu he meiyu" 藝術和美育, *Jiaoyu zazhi* 14, no. 10 (October 1922): 1–2.
23. Michael C. Behrent, "Le débat Guyau-Durkheim sur la théorie sociologique de la religion: Une nouvelle querelle des universaux?" *Archives de sciences sociales des religions* 53, no. 142 (2008): 9–26. See also Frank James William Harding, *Jean-Marie Guyau, 1854–1888, Aesthetician and Sociologist: A Study of His Aesthetic Theory and Critical Practice* (Geneva: Droz, 1973), 112–13.
24. Michael C. Behrent, "The Mystical Body of Society: Religion and Association in Nineteenth-Century French Political Thought," *Journal of the History of Ideas* 69, no. 2 (2008): 219–43. See also Jacques Donzelot, *L'invention du social: Essai sur le déclin des passions politiques* (Paris: Fayard, 1984), 74–86.
25. Viren Murthy, *The Political Philosophy of Zhang Taiyan: The Resistance of Consciousness* (Leiden: Brill, 2011), 54–55.
26. Ying-shih Yü, "The Radicalization of China in the Twentieth Century," in *China in Transformation*, ed. Wei-ming Tu (Cambridge, MA: Harvard University Press, 1994), 134.
27. Lü, *Meixue qianshuo* (Shanghai: Commercial Press, 1923), appendix. In note 6 "on the relation between art and society," Lü referenced Ōnishi Yoshinori's Japanese translation together with the French original, as well as another of Guyau's works. See Ōnishi Yoshinori 大西克礼 and Ogata Tsunemasa 小方庸正, trans., *Shakaigaku jō yori mitaru geijutsu: Gyuiyō* 社会学上より見たる芸術: ギユイヨー (Tokyo: Iwanami Bunko, 1914); Jean-Marie Guyau, *Les problèmes de l'esthétique contemporaine*, 6th ed. (Paris: F. Alcan, 1904). The Japanese translation seems to be based on an 1889 edition, Jean-Marie Guyau, *L'art au point de vue sociologique* (Paris: Félix Alcan Éditeur, 1889).
28. Guyau, *L'art au point de vue sociologique*, vi–xii, xxix–xxxvi, 1–15. See also Harding, *Jean-Marie Guyau*, 126–27.
29. For a comprehensive evaluation of Lippisan empathy and its impact, see Karsten Stueber, "Empathy," in *The Stanford Encyclopedia of Philosophy* (Fall 2019 Edition), ed. Edward N. Zalta, https://plato.stanford.edu/archives/spr2018/entries/empathy.

    Theodor Lipps not only inspired the Freudian theorization of the unconscious but also played a key role in the rise of Husserlian phenomenology. This accidental influence occurred because a group of his students in Munich rebelled against Lippsian psychologism and championed Edmund Husserl's *Logische Untersuchungen* as their philosophical bible. Both schools of Western thought have been employed academically as interpretative lenses through which to analyze various strands of Yogācāra philosophy. For a nuanced analysis of Lipps, Husserl, and their cultural circles, see Alessandro Salice, "The Phenomenology of the Munich and Göttingen Circles," in *The Stanford Encyclopedia of Philosophy* (Winter 2020

Edition), ed. Edward N. Zalta, https://plato.stanford.edu/archives/win2020/entries/phenomenology-mg/.

30. Teiichi Hijikata, "On the *Aesthetics* of Abe Jirō," in *A History of Modern Japanese Aesthetics*, ed. Michael F. Marra (Honolulu: University of Hawai'i Press, 2001), 197–203. See also Ōishi Masayoshi 大石昌史, "Abe Jirō to kanjō inyū bigaku" 阿部次郎と感情移入美学, *Tetsugaku* 113, no. 3 (2005): 93–130.
31. Harding also noted the resonances between Lippsian empathy and Guyau's socio-emotional function of aesthetics; see Harding, *Jean-Marie Guyau*, 57–76, 114.
32. Lü, "Wanjin de meixueshuo he meide yuanli, yi zhi si" 晚近的美學說和美的原理, 一之四, *Jiaoyu zazhi* 14, no. 2 (February 1922): 2–7.
33. Lü, "Meishu chengxing zhi jingguo," 55. Hermann von Helmholtz is known for his argument that aesthetic induction is a mode of knowing that is unique to human sciences and nonreducible but complementary to methods in natural sciences—logical induction. Helmholtz advocates a particular way of artists' portraying the surroundings of objects in paintings: "The artist cannot transcribe nature; he must translate her; yet this translation may give us an impression in the highest degree distinct and forcible." See Hermann Helmholtz, "On the Relation of Optics to Painting," *Humboldt Library of Popular Science Literature* 1, no. 24 (1881): 9. Lü Cheng took this out of context because Helmholtz employed translation to naturalize the subject-object duality while Lü used translation to create an intersubjective oneness.
34. Lü Cheng 呂澂 and Tang Zhean 唐哲安, "Guanyu 'yishu piping he chuangzuo' wenti taolun de jifengxin" 關於"藝術批評和創作"問題討論的幾封信, *Meishu* 3, no. 2 (May 1922): 154–56, 162. These publications include two letters from Tang and two replies from Lü.
35. Lü Cheng, "Yishu piping de genju" 藝術批評的根據, *Meishu* 2, no. 4 (March 1921): 2. Walter Pater, *The Renaissance: Studies in Art and Poetry*, 6th ed. (London: Macmillan, 1901 [1873]).
36. Pater, *The Renaissance*, preface. See also Lionel Lambourne, *The Aesthetic Movement* (London: Phaidon, 1996), 12.
37. Lü and Tang, "Guanyu 'yishu piping he chuangzuo,'" 154, 162.
38. Lü, "Yishu piping de genju," 3.
39. For Cai's role in modern education, see William Duiker, *Ts'ai Yüan-P'ei: Educator of Modern China* (University Park: Pennsylvania State University Press, 1977). For Cai's view of religion in general, see Douglas Gildow, "Cai Yuanpei (1868–1940), Religion, and His Plan to Save China Through Buddhism," *Asia Major* 31, no. 2 (2018): 107–48. For Cai's aesthetic education, see Ning Luo, "Cai Yuanpei's Vision of Aesthetic Education and His Legacy in Modern China," *Nordic Journal of Comparative and International Education* 5, no. 2 (2021): 51–64.
40. Lü, "Yishu he meiyu," 7; Lü Cheng, "Shicen wuxiong zuoyou" 石岑吾兄左右, *Jiaoyu zazhi* 14, no. 1 (January 1922): 1. The letter was dated November 20, 1921.
41. Olúfẹ́mi O. Táíwò, *Elite Capture: How the Powerful Took Over Identity Politics (And Everything Else)* (Chicago: Haymarket Books, 2022), 23–24.
42. All of Lü's quotations in this paragraph come from "Yishu he meiyu," 5–8.
43. Lü, "Yishu he meiyu," 7.
44. See also Lü, "Meishu fazhan de tujing," 28–29.
45. Butler, *Force of Nonviolence*, 16–7, 24.
46. See, for example, Táíwò, *Elite Capture*, 114–21.
47. Lü, "Yishu he meiyu," 8, 7.
48. Lü, "Shicen wuxiong zuoyou," 2.

49. Hammerstrom, *Science of Chinese Buddhism*, 135–37. See also Viren Murthy, "Transfiguring Modern Temporality: Zhang Taiyan's Yogācāra Critique of Evolutionary History," *Modern China* 38, no. 5 (2012): 505–6.
50. For Bergson in China, see Joseph Ciaudo, "Introduction à la métaphysique bergsonienne en Chine: Échos philosophiques et moralization de l'intuition," *Noesis* 21 (2013): 293–328. See also Joseph Ciaudo, "Bergson's 'Intuition' in China and Its Confucian Fate (1915–1923): Some Remarks on Zhijue in Modern Chinese Philosophy," *Problemos* (2016): 35–50.
51. Alex Owen, *The Place of Enchantment: British Occultism and the Culture of the Modern* (Chicago: University of Chicago Press, 2004), 114–47.
52. For the rise of New Confucianism and its syncretism, see Ku-ming Chang, "'Ceaseless Generation': Republican China's Rediscovery and Expansion of Domestic Vitalism," *Asia Major* 30, no. 2 (2017): 101–31. For the popularization of consciousness-only ideas, see Erik Hammerstrom, "The Expression 'The Myriad Dharmas Are Only Consciousness' in Early 20th Century Chinese Buddhism," *Chung-Hwa Buddhist Journal* 23 (2010): 71–92.
53. For an incisive analysis of the broader debate of subjectivity and the problems of solipsism (*duwo lun* 獨我論) and dogmatism (*duduan lun* 獨斷論), see Lin Chen-kuo 林鎮國, "*Qixinlun* yu xiandai Dongya zhutixing zhexue—yi Neixueyuan yu Xinrujia de zhenglun wei zhongxin de kaocha"《起信論》與現代東亞主體性哲學—以內學院與新儒家的爭論為中心的考察, *Hanyu foxue pinglun* 6 (2018): 12–16.
54. Gal Gvili, "In Search of the National Soul: Writing Life in Chinese Literature, 1918–1937" (PhD diss., Columbia University, 2015), 39–48.
55. Hammerstrom, *Science of Chinese Buddhism*, 128–29.
56. For the European bourgeois fascination with animal occultism, see William Barnard, *Living Consciousness: The Metaphysical Vision of Henri Bergson* (Albany: State University of New York Press, 2011), 249–56. For the European fascination with supra consciousness and life as a whole, see Owen, *Place of Enchantment*, 135–38.
57. Ciaudo, "Bergson's 'Intuition' in China," 44–46.
58. Li Shicen 李石岑, "Xiandai zhexue zaiping—Duwei yu Luosu, Luosu yu Bogesen, Bogesen yu Wokeng" 現代哲學再評—杜威與羅素, 羅素與柏格森, 柏格森與倭鏗, *Minduo* 2, no. 4 (1921): 2.
59. Lü Cheng, "Bogesen zhexue yu weishi" 柏格森哲學與唯識, *Minduo* 3, no. 1 (December 1921): 1–6. See also Yao Binbin 姚彬彬, "1921–1922 nian Zhang Taiyan, Lü Cheng, Li Jinxi lunxue shujian kaoshi" 1921–1922 年章太炎, 呂澂, 黎錦熙論學書簡考釋, *Foxue yanjiu* 23 (2014): 326–39. Other cultural luminaries who contributed to this special issue include Li Shicen, Zhang Dongsun, Cai Yuanpei, Liang Shuming, Li Jinxi, and Feng Youlan.
60. Liang Shuming's position is more complicated. While he considered Yogācāra and Bergsonism incompatible, he saw the moral potential of Bergsonian *zhijue* in building his version of New Confucianism. Over the years, Liang changed his view of Bergsonism. See Ciaudo, "Bergson's 'Intuition' in China," 42–43. See also Yangming An, "Liang Shuming and Henri Bergson on Intuition: Cultural Context and the Evolution of Term," *Philosophy East and West* 47, no. 3 (1997): 337–62. For an analysis of Liang's views of Bergson in Chinese, see Wu Xianwu 吳先伍, *Xiandaixing de zhuiqiu yu piping—Bogesen yu zhongguo jindai zhexue* 现代性的追求与批评—柏格森与中国近代哲学 (Hefei: Anhui renmin chubanshe, 2005), 63–73.
61. Zhang Taiyan is known for having studied many Chinese translations of Yogācāra treatises from the sixth month of 1903 till the seventh month of 1907. A full evaluation of his Yogācāra scholarship is beyond the scope of this study. It suffices to know that Zhang Taiyuan's

interpretation of Yogācāra was shaped by Chinese Chan, the Huayan school, and *Awakening Faith* (*Qixin lun* 起信論; T.1666); see Lin, "*Qixinlun* yu xiandai Dongya zhutixing zhexue," 8–9. As for Li Jinxi 黎錦熙, his dabbling with Yogācāra was even more superficial. Li was a self-trained philologist who played a key role in the making of modern Chinese; for details see Janet Y. Chen, *The Sounds of Mandarin: Learning to Speak a National Language in China and Taiwan, 1913–1960* (New York: Columbia University Press, 2023), 118–62. The essay for the December 1921 issue of *People's Bell* consisted of Li Jinxi's notes from Taixu's lecture on *Vimalakīrti Sūtra* in 1919, combined with his reading of the Chinese translation of Bergson's *Creative Evolution*. See Li Jinxi 黎錦熙, "Weimojie jing jiwen ba" 維摩詰經紀聞跋, *Minduo* 3, no. 1 (1921): 1–6.

62. Huei-Yun Lai, "Les études sur Henri Bergson en Chine, 1913–1941" (PhD thesis, École des Hautes Études en Sciences Sociales, 1993), 49–50.
63. Yao, "1921–1922," 327–28.
64. Zhang Taiyan interprets *lixiang* 理想 as *minxiang zhenli* 冥想真理, literally, "meditating on true principles"; see Yao, "1921–1922," 328. This is Zhang's unique terminology. The common meaning of *lixiang* is "ideal" or "aspiration."
65. Tom Tillemans, "Dharmakīrti," in *The Stanford Encyclopedia of Philosophy* (Spring 2021 Edition), ed. Edward N. Zalta, https://plato.stanford.edu/archives/spr2017/entries/dharmakiirti/.
66. Shino Yoshinobu 志野好伸, "Testugaku no kyōkai kakutei: Kindai Chūgoku ni okeru Berukuson juyō no ichi rei" 哲学の境界画定—近代中国におけるベルクソン受容の一例, *Chūgoku testugaku kenkyū* 24 (2009): 146–62.
67. Jimena Canales, *The Physicist and the Philosopher: Einstein, Bergson, and the Debate That Changed Our Understanding of Time* (Princeton, NJ: Princeton University Press, 2015). See also Gilles Deleuze, *Bergsonism*, trans. Hugh Tomlinson and Barbara Habberjam (New York: Zone Books, 1988), 115–18.
68. Lü, "Bogesen zhexue yu weishi."
69. Yogācāra causal enframing is also called *laiye yuanqi* 賴耶緣起. This term stems from a later Huayan school characterization of Xuanzang and Kuiji's main teachings. For details see Charles Muller, "賴耶緣起," *Digital Dictionary of Buddhism*, http://www.buddhism-dict.net/cgi-bin/xpr-ddb.pl?q=賴耶緣起. Both Lü and his teacher Ouyang Jingwu used these labels to characterize their own doctrinal positions.
70. Yao, "1921–1922," 331.
71. All other essayists and translators in this issue relied on German, English, Japanese, and Chinese translations of Bergson. This includes Cai Yuanpei, who, despite his proficiency in French, only chose to translate selected passages from a German translation; see Ciaudo, "Introduction à la métaphysique bergsonienne en Chine," 306n34.
72. Ciaudo, "Bergson's 'Intuition' in China," 43.
73. In this letter, Lü not only substantiated his own interpretation with canonical texts but also pointed out where Zhang's misreading of Yogācāra could have come from, namely, the controversial text *Awakening Faith*, adumbrating the controversy of *Awakening Faith* between the China Inner Learning Institute and Taixu's disciples in late 1922—a debate that lasted well into the 1930s. At this time, Lü only used Chinese-language sources. He was still learning Sanskrit and classical Tibetan on his own. He became proficient in both classical languages around 1925.
74. Yao, "1921–1922," 330–31.
75. Lü, "Bogesen yu weishi," 4.

76. Yao, "1921–1922," 328.
77. Lü, "Bogesen yu weishi," 1.
78. Yao, "1921–1922," 327, 328, 330.
79. Verse 16 of *Thirty Verses* says "manovijñānasaṃbhūtiḥ sarvadāsaṃjñikād ṛte/ samāpattidvayān middhān mūrchanād apy acittakāt" (manovijñāna—the sixth consciousness—functions at all times, except for those who are in the state of no-thought, during the two kinds of concentrations, that is, nonconceptual and total cessation, as well as deep sleep and fainting). Xuanzang translates this verse as "意識常現起/除生無想天/及無心二定/睡眠與悶絕." This verse points out that, other than when individuals are in deep concentration or have lost consciousness (similar to drug-induced general anesthesia), the sixth consciousness always arises and functions. This is in direct contradiction to Zhang's understanding of the Yogācāra theory of consciousness. For an online edition of Vasubandhu's *Thirty Verses* in Sanskrit and the main Chinese and Tibetan translations, see Vasubandhu, *Triṃśikāvijñapti*, https://www2.hf.uio.no/polyglotta/index.php.
80. Yao, "1921–1922," 328.
81. Lü, "Bogesen yu weishi," 3.
82. Lawlor and Moulard-Leonard, "Henri Bergson," in *The Stanford Encyclopedia of Philosophy* (Winter 2022 Edition), ed. Edward N. Zalta and Uri Nodelman. https://plato.stanford.edu/entries/bergson/.

2. Karma, Evolutionism, and Buddhist Social Consciousness

1. Hui Wang, *China from Empire to Nation-State*, trans. Michael Gibbs Hill (Cambridge, MA: Harvard University Press, 2014), 63–64.
2. The Christian missionaries were the earliest to introduce racism and racial ontology into nineteenth-century China. But their influence was limited. For a pre-Yan Fu history of race and racism in China, see Daniel Barth, "The Propagation of Racial Thought in Nineteenth-Century China," in *Race and Racism in Modern East Asia*, vol. 2, *Interactions, Nationalism, Gender and Lineage*, ed. Rotem Kowner and Walter Demel (Leiden: Brill, 2015), 123–50.
3. This essay was first published in 1903 in *Subao* 蘇報 and is now digitized. See Zou Rong 鄒容, *Gemingjun* 革命軍, https://ctext.org/wiki.pl?if=gb&chapter=838418.
4. Viren Murthy, *Political Philosophy of Zhang Taiyan: The Resistance of Consciousness* (Leiden: Brill, 2011), and "Transfiguring Modern Temporality: Zhang Taiyan's Yogācāra Critique of Evolutionary History," *Modern China* 38, no. 5 (2012): 483–522. For the Chinese and Japanese language scholarship on this topic, please see Murthy's bibliography.
5. This reproduction of society occurs via processes that create collective effervescence or a form of collective consciousness and collective representation. See Émile Durkheim, *The Elementary Forms of the Religious Life* (Mineola, NY: Dover Publications, 2012).
6. Benjamin Schwartz, *In Search of Power and Wealth: Yen Fu and the West* (Cambridge, MA: Belknap Press, 1964), 25.
7. For Yan Fu's key role in introducing Western revolutionary ideas and in creating a new vocabulary of modern Chinese, see, for example, Schwartz, *In Search of Wealth and Power.* See also James Reeve Pusey, *China and Charles Darwin* (Cambridge, MA: Harvard University Asia Center, 1983).

8. See Huang Ko-wu 黃克武, "Minguo chunian Shanghai de lingxue yanjiu: Yi Shanghai lingxuehui weili" 民國初年上海的靈學研究: 以上海靈學會為例, *Bulletin of the Institute of Modern History, Academia Sinica* 55 (2007): 116, 126–30.
9. Jason Ānanda Josephson Storm, *The Myth of Disenchantment: Magic, Modernity, and the Birth of the Human Sciences* (Chicago: University of Chicago Press, 2017), 4–11.
10. See, for example, Max Ko-wu Huang, *The Meaning of Freedom: Yan Fu and the Origins of Chinese Liberalism* (Hong Kong: Chinese University of Hong Kong Press, 2008), 104.
11. For an incisive analysis of the broader implications of this encounter of karma and evolutionism in the Chinese experience of becoming modern, see Lei Ying, "Huxley's Karma and Lu Xun's Ghosts: Rethinking the Secularist Assumption and Chinese Modernity," *Journal of Asian Studies* 83, no. 3 (August 2024): 533–52.
12. Barth, "The Propagation of Racial Thought in Nineteenth-Century China," 149–50. I am aware of Frank Dikötter's work; see Frank Dikötter, *The Discourse of Race in Modern China* (New York: Oxford University Press, 1992), 34–60. I disagree with his main thesis that the development of a racial consciousness during nineteenth-century China "was due largely to internal development" (34). This claim has been discredited by Barth and many other scholars. See also Sufen Sophia Lai, "Racial Discourse and Utopian Visions in Nineteenth-Century China," in *Race and Racism in Modern East Asia: Western and Eastern Constructions*, ed. Rotem Kowner and Walter Demel (Leiden: Brill, 2013), 327–50. For an incisive and systematic analysis of Dikötter's philosophical and philological errors in treating premodern Chinese concepts, see Shuchen Xiang, "Decolonizing Sinology: On Sinology's Weaponization of the Discourse of Race," *Social Dynamics: A Journal of African Studies* 49, no. 2 (2023): 280–98.
13. Eric Voegelin, "The Growth of the Race Idea," *Review of Politics* 2, no. 3 (1940): 283–84.
14. See, for example, Ronald W. Neufeldt, ed., *Karma and Rebirth: Post Classical Developments* (Albany: State University of New York Press, 1986). See also Charles F. Keyes and E. Valentine Daniel, eds., *Karma: An Anthropological Inquiry* (Berkeley: University of California Press, 1983).
15. Jonathan S. Walters, "Communal Karma and Karmic Community in Theravāda Buddhist History," in *Constituting Communities: Theravāda Buddhism and the Religious Cultures of South and Southeast Asia*, ed. John Holt, Jacob N. Kinnard, and Jonathan S. Walters (Albany: State University of New York Press, 2003), 9–40.
16. Hsiao-Lan Hu, *This-Worldly Nibbāna: A Buddhist-Feminist Social Ethics for Peacemaking in the Global Community* (Albany: State University of New York Press, 2011), 91–125.
17. The first is a symposium, "Lived Karma: Situating Interbeing in Society," Buddhist Door Global, October 28, 2022, https://www.buddhistdoor.net/news/lived-karma-situating-interbeing-in-society-conference-held-at-dartmouth-college/. A set of critical notes resulting from this symposium is published in *Journal of Global Buddhism*. For an introduction to this set of research notes, see Susanne Kerekes and Jessica Zu, "Introduction: Critical Notes on the Lived Karma Conference," *Journal of Global Buddhism* 24, no. 2 (2023): 83–87. The second ongoing collaboration is the newly launched five-year seminar, "Collective Karma and Karmic Collectives: Conversations without Borders," American Academy of Religion, https://papers.aarweb.org/pu/collective-karma-and-karmic-collectives-conversations-without-borders-seminar.
18. Both points are made in Jessica Zu, "Collective-Karma-Cluster-Concepts in Chinese Canonical Sources: A Note," *Journal of Global Buddhism* 24, no. 2 (2023): 88–94.
19. Gareth Fisher, "Universal Karma," *Journal of Global Buddhism* 24, no. 2 (2023): 100–103; Susanne Kerekes, "Sociokarma and Kindred Spirits: An Acknowledgement," *Journal of Global*

Buddhism 24, no. 2 (2023): 104–8; Justin Ritzinger, "Interpersonal Karma: A Note," *Journal of Global Buddhism* 24, no. 2 (2023): 109–13; Joey Yan, "Karma as a Means of Wartime Political Mobilization: A Reading of Chinese Buddhists' Response to the Second Sino-Japanese War, 1937–1945," *Journal of Global Buddhism* 24, no. 2 (2023): 95–99.

20. I use "Orientalist" to describe what Amartya Sen identified as the "magisterial" approaches to studying Indian and other cultures for readability. As incisively argued by Sen, "Orientalism" is an umbrella term that can be broken down into at least three recognizable subcategories: the "exoticist" approaches, the "magisterial" approaches, and the "curatorial" approaches. See Sen, *The Argumentative Indian: Writings on Indian History, Culture, and Identity* (New York: Picador, 2006), 147–48. According to Sen, all three approaches can be found in the historical accounts of Indian culture penned by non-Indians. The exoticists, from the Greek historian and diplomat Megasthenes, who wrote *Indika* (ca. third century BCE), to modern romantic figures such as the Schlegel brothers, Karl Wilhelm and August Wilhelm, and Friedrich Wilhelm Joseph Schelling, were primarily stimulated by the observation of exotic ideas and views there (156–59). Those who adopted "magisterial" approaches were primarily burdened by the need to rule a foreign country, and scholars and writers such as the well-known novelist Rudyard Kipling and the influential historian James Mill, who penned the notorious Orientalist text *The History of British India* in 1817, produced popular narratives and scholarship to cultivate and sustain a sense of superiority and guardianship needed by the imperial powers for their effective governance of a new territory (152–56). In contrast to those who adopted the previous two approaches, those who took "curatorial" approaches were mostly motivated by intellectual curiosity and a quest for knowledge. Their portrayal of India was largely respectful and responsible, although their scholarship was sometimes appropriated by the exorcists and the magisterialists (148–52). The current monograph does not engage with the exoticists. I instead mark the "curatorial" approaches in scholarship as secular and call out scholarship that reproduces the "magisterial" gaze by marking it as "Orientalist." I situate Thomas H. Huxley's scholarship within this magisterial approach, as he engaged in "curatorial" Buddhologist scholarship in service of the colonial powers.

21. Thomas H. Huxley, "Evolution and Ethics: The Romanes Lecture" (1894), in *Collected Essays*, vol. 9, *Evolution & Ethics and Other Essays* (London, 1893–94), 46–116. T. W. Rhys David's and H. Oldenburg's interpretations of karma were constricted by the Western antinomy of the individual against the collective. For an in-depth overview of Western academia's entrenched propensity to read karma as individualist, see Walters, "Communal Karma and Karmic Community." Indeed, eminent scholars such as James P. McDermott have mistakenly portrayed group karma as a twentieth-century invention and by no means operative in canonical sources; see, for example, James P. McDermott, "Is There Group Karma in Theravāda Buddhism?" *Numen* 23, fasc. 1 (1976): 67–80. That said, the understanding of karma as energy or magnetism has Theosophical resonances, although their precise relations remain unclear. See, for example, for example, Helena Petrovna Blavatsky, *The Key to Theosophy: A Clear Exposition in the Form of Question and Answer of the Ethics, Science, and Philosophy for the Study of Which the Theosophical Society Has Been Founded* (London: Theosophical Publishing Company, 1889), 222. Annie Besant further developed the theory of karma as energy or magnetic link in *Karma* (Chennai: Theosophical Publishing House, 1895).

22. For a careful examination of Huxley's comparison of Buddhist ethics with other ancient thought systems such as stoicism in his *Evolution and Ethics*, Huxley's ambivalence about Buddhist soteriology, and the implications of this attempt, see Vijitha Rajapakse,

"Buddhism in Huxley's 'Evolution and Ethics': A Note on Victorian Evaluation and Its 'Comparativist Dimension,'" *Philosophy East and West* 35, no. 3 (1985): 295–304.

23. For a more recent encyclopedia entry that repeats McDermott's mistaken claims, see Wilhelm Halbfass, "Karma and Rebirth, Indian Conceptions of," in *Routledge Encyclopedia of Philosophy* (Milton Park, UK: Taylor and Francis, 1998), https://www.rep.routledge.com/articles/thematic/karma-and-rebirth-indian-conceptions-of/v-1.
24. See, for example, Blavatsky, *Key to Theosophy*, 202–5, 245. Note that Annie Besant also amply theorized notions like "family karma," "national karma," and "collective karma" within the same raciological discourses. See Besant, *Karma*.
25. For the impact and substance metaphysical underpinnings of the Great Chain of Being in the Western thought, see Shuchen Xiang, *Chinese Cosmopolitanism: The History and Philosophy of an Idea* (Princeton, NJ: Princeton University Press, 2023), 113–27.
26. See Mackenzie C. Brown, *Hindu Perspectives on Evolution: Darwin, Dharma, and Design* (New York: Routledge, 2012). See also Robert N. Minor, "In Defense of Karma and Rebirth: Evolutionary Karma," in Neufeldt, ed., *Karma and Rebirth*, 15–40.
27. For example, Philips Thompson (1843–1933), a devoted political activist, writer, labor reformer, and Theosophist, not only believed in collective, national, and social karma but also trusted that "only the law of karma could explain existing social inequalities and point to a more just future." See Ramsay Cook, *The Regenerators: Social Criticism in Late Victorian Canada* (Toronto: University of Toronto Press, 1985), 168.
28. Halbfass, "Karma and Rebirth." At the end of this essay, Halbfass claims, "6. The notions of 'collective karma,' 'group karma' or even 'national karma,' *which have no place in traditional thought*, but seem to be taken for granted in Theosophy, emerge in Neo-Hindu thought and discourse, although their uses are somewhat elusive and in some cases merely rhetorical" (my emphasis). Halbfass seems to have based his argument on McDermott's scholarship, whose work is cited in Halbfass's references. However, Jonathan S. Walters traces this scholarly bias earlier to Winston L. King and Max Weber. See Walters, "Communal Karma and Karmic Community," 31n21.
29. Richard Hayes, "Is There Such a Thing as Collective Karma?," https://www.unm.edu/~rhayes/Lecture10.pdf.
30. Gong Jun 龔雋, "Jindai foxue cong jingshi dao xueshu de mingyun zouxiang" 近代佛學從經世到學術的命運走向, *Zhexue yanjiu* 5 (1997): 39–47.
31. There exist many drafts/manuscripts of Yan Fu's translation of Huxley, all collected in *The Complete Works of Yan Fu*. See Yan Fu 嚴復, *Yan Fu Quanji* 嚴復全集, ed. Wang Zhenglu 汪征魯, Fang Baochuan 方寶川, and Ma Yong 馬勇, 11 vols. (Fuzhou: Fujian jiaoyu chubanshe, 2014). I have cross-checked all versions of the translation and have confirmed that Yan Fu's use of *zhongye* is consistent.
32. Different manuscripts of Yan's translation have slightly different wordings, but the general sense remains consistent; see Yan Fu, *Yan Fu Quanji*, 1:46, 130, 195, 241, 311.
33. Once again, different versions of Yan's translation contextualize this concept of "liberating oneself" differently. However, the term *zidu* appears in all versions and is used to indicate an individual effort.
34. For a scholarly edition and translation of *Śālistambasūtra* as well as its Chinese and Tibetan parallels, see N. Ross Reat, *The Śālistamba Sūtra* (New Delhi: Motilal Banarsidass, 1998). Here *zhongzi* and *yeshi* are deployed to explain the nondual, processual teaching of dependent arising.

35. See Yan Fu, *Yan Fu Quanji*, 1:195. Indeed, in different drafts, this term appears frequently in the set phrase *yezhong ziran* 業種自然, which otherwise seems to appear only in the *Śūraṅgama Sūtra* and its commentarial traditions, including Chan commentaries such as *Zongjing lu* 宗鏡錄 (T.2016), *Lidai fabao ji* 歷代法寶記 (T.2075), and *Wanshan tonggui ji* 萬善同歸集 (T.2017). Nevertheless, as an indigenous text, the *Śūraṅgama Sūtra* appropriated quite a few Yogācāra concepts, *yezhong* being but one of them. Therefore, it is not farfetched to consider this indigenous sūtra and its appropriated concept of *yezhong* as part of the extended Yogācāra tradition in East Asia.
36. See, for example, "Do not terminate the [untainted] enterprise of the Buddha family" 不斷佛種業 (T.1522.26.140c10–12). Here I translate *ye* 業 as "enterprise" because, generally speaking, karma means the actions that bind one in saṃsāra, yet buddhas and bodhisattvas' actions lead to liberation of all; hence, "enterprise" better captures this positive connotation of *ye* as a soteriological project.
37. See, for example, Yan Fu, *Yan Fu Quanji*, 1:46. Note that the editors of Yan Fu's manuscripts of *Theory of Heavenly Process* uncritically glossed this term following Yan Fu's translation, 1:46n3.
38. For example, in *Yogācārabhūmi*, *zhongxing* is defined as the realm of the karmic seeds (T.1579.30.395c26–27 and T.1579.30.396a10). However, rather than use karmic seeds to explain social groups, earlier Abhidharma texts seem to use the realm of karmic seeds (*zhongzi jie* 種子界) to explain the seemingly objective, natural world or the desire realm where humans and animals live more generally (T.354.12.225b27–c3; T.1546.28.318b2–3). A more in-depth study of how the uses and meanings of *zhongye* and *yezhong* evolved and became entangled must wait for another occasion.
39. For the Yogācāra critique of caste in the sixth and seventh centuries CE and their opponents' arguments, see Eltschinger, *"Caste" et philosophie bouddhique: Continuité de quelques arguments bouddhiques contre le traitement réaliste des dénominations sociales* (Vienna: Universität Wien, 2000), 94–155; for a Yogācārin critique of the naturalization of caste grounded in *gotra* (lineage), see 146–53.
40. The core issue of this debate on *gotra* and Buddha-nature is soteriological: it centers on who can achieve buddhahood. Medieval Yogācārins proposed many different classifications of *gotra* but tended to retain their belief in a special group of people called *icchantikas* who would never be able to achieve buddhahood. The literature on the debates and historical developments of *gotra*, Buddha-nature, and *icchantika* is vast. For a brief outline, see Makoto Yoshimura, "The Wéishì School and the Buddha-Nature Debate in Early Táng Dynasty," in *The Foundation for Yoga Practitioners: The Buddhist Yogācārabhūmi Treatise and Its Adaptation in India, East Asia, and Tibet*, ed. Ulrich Timme Kragh (Cambridge, MA: Harvard University Press, 2013), 1234–53.
41. Yan Fu, *Yan Fu Quanji*, 3: 70. This translation, like all Yan Fu's translations, has a complicated publication history. I use the scholarly edition of this text, which uses the 1931 edition as the base text. I have also consulted the 1903, 1981, and 1998 editions; see Yan Fu, *Yan Fu Quanji*, 3:4. For Spencer's text, see Herbert Spencer, *The Study of Sociology* (London: Henry S. King & Co., 1873).
42. Herbert Spencer, *Social Statics, or, the Conditions Essential to Human Happiness Specified, and the First of Them Developed* (London: John Chapman, 1851).
43. For an in-depth analysis of Spencer's sociological principles and a historiographical analysis of how Spencerian Darwinism was used to justify unbridled capitalism, see David

Weinstein, "Herbert Spencer," in *The Stanford Encyclopedia of Philosophy* (Fall 2019 Edition), ed. Edward N. Zalta, https://plato.stanford.edu/archives/fall2019/entries/spencer/. For Yan's translation of Spencer's understanding of Auguste Comte's positivism seen in *Social Physics*, see Yan Fu, *Yan Fu Quanji*, 3:79, 201, 266.

44. Yan Fu, *Yan Fu Quanji*, 3:17; 3:76, 210, 234; 3:228.
45. Ying, "Huxley's Karma and Lu Xun's Ghosts," 542.
46. Readers well versed in Yogācāra will note important differences among these terms. On the one hand, both *gongye* and *tongye* often convey a sense of karmic confluence: that is, that a social group is formed by the members' similar karmic actions in the past. On the other hand, they sometimes convey a sense of joint karma: that is, shared experiences (through teaching, abetting of bad actions, or support of good actions) create shared karmic results. This sense of shared intersubjective experiences, in the Yogācāra model of the mind, is further developed using new terms and vocabulary such as indirect *ālambana* and *adhipati* to explain the karmic interactions between different mental continuums. See Jingjing Li, "Through the Mirror: The Account of Other Minds in Chinese Yogācāra Buddhism," *Dao: A Journal of Comparative Philosophy* 18, no. 3 (2019): 435–51; Jessica Zu, "*Adhipati*, Yogācāra Intersubjectivity, and Soteriology in Kuiji's Commentaries," *Sophia*, June 5, 2024, https://link.springer.com/article/10.1007/s11841-024-01019-9; Jessica Zu, "Karma, *Adhipati*, and Weapons of Mass Destruction: Wang Enyang's (1897–1964) Yogācāra Theory of Intersubjective Responsibility," *Journal of Buddhist Philosophy* 6, no. 1 (2025).
47. Personally, I find this caste-inspired view of human soteriological future to bear a remarkable resemblance to Immanuel Kant's teleological view of human perfection, in which Kant surmises that among the four races, only whites "possess all the driving forces, talents, and so on that are needed for the most advanced culture. They alone can continue to progress in perfecting themselves." See Huaping Lu-Adler, *Kant, Race, and Racism: Views from Somewhere* (New York: Oxford University Press, 2023), 227–28. There are noticeable differences: the *icchantikas* are doomed to transmigrate in saṃsāra (a processual view of how a select group cannot achieve buddhahood), whereas the nonwhite races in Kantian raciology are doomed to become extinct (a teleological evolutionary story of how a select group can survive). However, the resemblance is also undeniable: both conjure up unbridgeable paths of perfection between different families/races and human perfection is denied to certain group/races. I often wonder if this train of Buddhist thought gave rise to Aryan or so-called alt-right Buddhism today.
48. For a seminal study of modern Chinese Buddhism, see Holmes Welch, *The Buddhist Revival in China* (Cambridge, MA: Harvard University Press, 1968). For the Yogācāra revival, see John Makeham, ed., *Transforming Consciousness: Yogācāra Thought in Modern China* (New York: Oxford University Press, 2014), and Eyal Aviv, *Differentiating the Pearl from the Fish-Eye: Ouyang Jingwu and the Revival of Scholastic Buddhism* (Leiden: Brill, 2020).
49. For an incisive analysis of economics in early Indian Buddhism, see Gregory Schopen, *Buddhist Monks and Business Matters: Still More Papers on Monastic Buddhism in India* (Honolulu: University of Hawai'i Press, 2004). For a related study of monasticism and economy in medieval China, see Michael J. Walsh, *Sacred Economies: Buddhist Monasticism and Territoriality in Medieval China* (New York: Columbia University Press, 2009). A recent and impressive edited volume that explores Buddhism and politics in East Asia is Stephanie S. Balkwill and James A. Benn's *Buddhist Statecraft in East Asia* (Leiden: Brill, 2022). For an important study of Yogācāra political theory in modern China, see Murthy, *Political Philosophy of Zhang Taiyan*.

50. Gong, "Jindai foxue," 43.
51. For the rise of sociology in Republican China's nation-building project, see Tong Lam, *A Passion for Facts: Social Surveys and the Construction of the Chinese Nation State, 1900–1949* (Berkeley: University of California Press, 2011).
52. For a more in-depth analysis of Wang's take on Buddhism and science, see Erik Hammerstrom, "A Buddhist Critique of Scientism," *Journal of Chinese Buddhist Studies* 27 (2014): 35–57.
53. Wang Jitong 王季同, "Fofa yu kexue zhi bijiao" 佛法與科學之比較, https://book.bfnn.org/books2/1275.htm#a03, para. 13.
54. Wang's reply to Guan indicates that Guan was Wang's nephew and was raised by Wang after Guan's parents passed away unexpectedly.
55. Wang, "Fofa yu kexue," https://book.bfnn.org/books2/1275.htm#a002.
56. Wang Jitong, *Makesi zhuyi pipan ji fulu—foxue licheng* 馬克思主義批判及附錄—佛學立場 (Suzhou: Suzhou jueshe 蘇州覺社, 1936). This booklet is self-published and is housed in Cheena Bhavana at Viśva-Bhārati University.
57. Wang, "Fofa yu kexue," https://book.bfnn.org/books2/1275.htm#a05.
58. Jessica Zu, "Three Plays and a Shared Socio-Spiritual Horizon in the Modern Buddhist Revivals in India and China," *International Journal of Asian Studies* 19, no. 2 (2022): 215–38.
59. On the broad social impact of Yinguang, including his message during Republican China's prison reform, see Jan Kiely, *The Compelling Ideal: Thought Reform and the Prison in China, 1901–1956* (New Haven, CT: Yale University Press, 2014), 123–60.
60. Jessica Zu, "War, Public Letters, and Piety: the Making of a New Pure Land Patriarch," *History of Religions* 63, no. 1 (2023): 75–119.
61. Gong, "Jindai foxue," 40–46. Note that *jingxue* 經學 (the study of classics), *zixue* 子學 (the study of important thinkers), and *shixue* 史學 (the study of history) are traditional Chinese categories of knowledge. In very broad terms, *jingxue* means hermeneutics or commentaries on classical texts. Gong also used the categories *jingxue* and *shixue* to measure the success and failure of Ouyang's and Lü's scholarship, equated *jingxue* with "exegesis," identified their institute as the "Chinese Metaphysical Institute," and deemed their work "an unfinished modernization project" (*meiyou wancheng de xiandaixing jihua* 沒有完成的現代性計畫), see Gong Jun, "Jindai Zhongguo Fojiao jingxue yanju: yi Neixueyuan yu Wuchang Foxueyuan wei li" 近代中國佛教經學研究：以內學院與武昌佛學院為例, *Xuanzang foxue yanju* 24 (2015): 85, 114.
62. For an incisive historiographical analysis of extant English scholarship on modern Chinese Buddhism, especially the success and limitations of the push models and the need for a pull model that takes seriously the attractions of modernity and Asian historical actors' role in constructing their own modernity, see Justin Ritzinger, *Anarchy in the Pure Land: Reinventing the Cult of Maitreya in Modern China* (Oxford: Oxford University Press, 2018), 3–11.
63. In the Chinese-language scholarship, there is a consensus that modern Buddhism was often revolutionary in spirit. However, most scholars, like Gong Jun, have attributed this "newness" to the late Qing literati's projection of their own revolutionary fervor. Consequently, they fail to investigate how the sociopolitical message in ancient Buddhism, as has long been identified by scholars like Uma Chakravarti, was repackaged by modern Buddhists to challenge Western ideas about being human and being social. By contrast, the English-language scholarship of socially engaged Buddhism, by and large, widely explores Southeast, South Asian, and Japanese Buddhists' efforts since the nineteenth century to translate spiritual inclusiveness into a better, more just society. See Uma Chakravarti, *The Social*

Dimension of Early Buddhism (Delhi: Oxford University Press, 1987) and *On the Social Philosophy of Buddhism: Four Essays* (Shimla: Indian Institute for Advanced Study, 2015). See also Christopher S. Queen, Charles S. Prebish, and Damien Keown, eds., *Action Dharma: New Studies in Engaged Buddhism* (New York: Routledge Curzon, 2003).

64. Gajendran Ayyathurai, "Foundations of Anticaste Consciousness: Pandit Iyothee Thass, Tamil Buddhism, and the Marginalized in South India" (PhD diss., Columbia University, 2011).
65. Dharmanand Kosambi, *Dharmanand Kosambi: The Essential Writings*, trans. Meera Kosambi (Ranikhet: Permanent Black, 2017). For a scholarly analysis of Kosambi's Buddhism and Marxism, see Douglas Ober, "Socialism, Russia and India's Revolutionary Dharma," in *Buddhism in the Global Eye: Beyond East and West*, ed. John S. Harding, Victor Sōgen Hori, and Alexander Soucy (London: Bloomsbury Academic, 2020), 71–86. See also Douglas Ober, "'Like Embers Hidden in Ashes, or Jewels Encrusted in Stone': Rahul Sankrityayan, Dharmanand Kosambi and Buddhist Activity in Colonial India," *Contemporary Buddhism: An Interdisciplinary Journal* 14, no. 1 (2013): 134–48.
66. To the best of my knowledge, Sankrityayan, like Lü Cheng, was also a great admirer of the sixth-century Indian Yogācāra philosopher Dharmakīrti. There is much more to be investigated about Yogācāra and revolution around the world. For scholarly studies of this intriguing figure, see Maya Joshi, "Rahul Sankrityayan and Ambedkar as Contrapuntal Contemporaries: Unpacking Their 'Metaphysics and Politics,'" in *India and Civilizational Futures*, ed. Vinay Lal (New Delhi: Oxford University Press, 2019), 182–214; Maya Joshi, "Rahula Sankrityayan and Buddhism: A Complex Engagement," in *On the Trail of Buddhism in Asia: Reflections on Tradition and Practice*, ed. Suchandana Chatterjee and Sushmita Bhattacharya (Kolkata: Maulana Abul Kalam Azad Institute of Asian Studies/Pentagon Press, 2016), 76–87.
67. Two book-length studies dive deep into the history of modern Indian Buddhism and the salient revolutionary spirit; see Ober, *Dust on the Throne: The Search for Buddhism in Modern India* (New Delhi: Navayana Press, 2023) and Gitanjali Surendran, "'The Indian Discovery of Buddhism': Buddhist Revival in India, c. 1890–1956" (PhD diss., Harvard University, 2013). See also Timothy Loftus, "Ambedkar and the Buddha's Saṃgha: A Ground for Buddhist Ethics," *CASTE: A Global Journal on Social Exclusion* 2, no. 2 (2021): 265–80.
68. Miller V. Tikhonov, *Selected Writings of Han Yongun: From Social Darwinism to "Socialism with a Buddhist Face"* (Leiden: Brill, 2008). For Paek Sŏnguk's philosophy and social theory see Jin Y. Park, "Philosophizing and Power: East-West Encounter in the Formation of Modern East Asian Buddhist Philosophy," *Philosophy East and West* 61, no. 3 (2017): 802–9.
69. James M. Shields, "Blueprint for Buddhist Revolution: The Radical Buddhism of Seno'o Girō (1889–1961) and the Youth League for Revitalizing Buddhism," *Japanese Journal of Religious Studies* 39, no. 2 (2012): 333–51.
70. Bikkhu Buddhadāsa, *Dhammic Socialism*, trans. Donald K. Swearer, with a preface by Prawase Wasi, 2nd ed. (Bangkok: Thai Inter-Religious Commission for Development, 1993); Alicia Marie Turner, Laurence Cox, and Brian Bocking, *The Irish Buddhist: The Forgotten Monk Who Faced Down the British Empire* (Oxford: Oxford University Press, 2020).
71. Trevor Ling, *Buddha, Marx and God: Some Aspects of Religion in the Modern World* (Ann Arbor: University of Michigan Press, 1979).
72. Prasenjit Duara, *Culture, Power, and the State: Rural North China, 1900–1942* (Redwood City, CA: Stanford University Press, 1988), 15–16, 118–57.
73. A shared horizon does not mean shared strategies. An important division is the role of the nation-state. Although many saw the state and politics as part of their toolbox to effect

social change, like Ouyang and Taixu, there were many others who strived to maintain their independence from the military-industrial complex.

74. See, for example, Shi Shengkai 釋聖凱, *Fojiao xiandai hua yu hua xiandai* 佛教現代化與化現代 (Beijing: Jincheng chubanshe, 2014). See also, Kiely, *The Compelling Ideal*, 123–60.
75. Chakravarti, *Social Dimension of Early Buddhism*, 180; Xinru Liu, *Early Buddhist Society: The World of Gautama Buddha* (Albany: State University of New York Press, 2022), 115.

3. Karma, Science, and a Just Society

1. Wang Xiaoxu is also known as Wang Jitong. See Wang "Fofa yu kexue," https://book.bfnn.org/books2/1275.htm#a003, 1275.htm#a004.
2. Many scholars have adopted similarly broad definitions of philosophy and have successfully decentered Europe in their works. For example, Bryan Van Norden suggests that scholars reconceptualize philosophy as dialogues about "important unresolved problems." See Van Norden, *Taking Back Philosophy: A Multicultural Manifesto* (New York: Columbia University Press, 2017), 142. Jay L. Garfield also directly cites Wilfrid Sellars's reconceptualization of philosophy; see, for example, Garfield, *Engaging Buddhism: Why It Matters to Philosophy* (New York: Oxford University Press, 2015), 90. For Wilfrid Sellars's seminal work on broadening the study of philosophy, see Wilfrid Sellars, *Science, Perception and Reality* (New York: Routledge and Kegan Paul, 1963).
3. Jason Ānanda Josephson Storm, *Metamodernism: The Future of Theory* (Chicago: University of Chicago Press, 2021), 85–104.
4. Note that although Alfred North Whitehead (1861–1947) is widely recognized for his pioneering approach to process philosophy, his influence in twentieth-century China was limited. Instead, as I have shown in chapter 1, it was early processual thoughts of John Dewey and Henri Bergson with which the modern Yogācārins conversed and argued. To fully spell out the historical encounters and philosophical crosscurrents of Yogācāra casual theories, quantum physics, and Western processual philosophies would require an independent book-length study. Here, I refer to Wilfrid Sellars's process ontology when discussing the parallels between Western and Buddhist process philosophies. Sellars spelled out his process philosophy during three Carus Lectures from 1977 to 1978; see Wilfrid Sellars, "Foundations for a Metaphysics of Pure Process," *Monist* 64, no. 1 (1981): 3–90. For a collection of insightful essays on the shared inquiries of antifoundationalism between Sellarsian and Buddhist process philosophy, see Jay L. Garfield, ed., *Wilfrid Sellars and Buddhist Philosophy: Freedom from Foundations* (New York: Routledge, 2019).
5. Katherine Jenkins, *Ontology and Oppression: Race, Gender, and Social Reality* (New York: Oxford University Press, 2023), 200–40.
6. The expansion of secularism as a requirement of "symmetric treatment" of all religious traditions and communities and individual rights comes from Amartya Sen's theorization. See Amartya Sen, *The Argumentative Indian: Writings on Indian History, Culture, and Identity* (New York: Picador, 2006), 288–90.
7. To be sure, these Chinese thinkers conflated a wide range of Western philosophical traditions, including realism, empiricism, materialism, mechanism, atomism, and physicalism, under the umbrella term of "materialism." I choose not to engage with questions such as how and why these different traditions became conflated or why the Chinese thinkers

failed to engage with issues deemed "important yet unresolved" by Western philosophy proper. I consider it a self-evident truth that important and resolved questions are specific to different hermeneutic communities. Here I analyze what the Chinese intellectuals considered important yet unresolved questions and how their resolutions addressed the issues that mattered to them.

8. These Chinese thinkers similarly conflated a wide range of Western philosophical traditions, including idealism, antirealism, essentialism, absolutism, and psychologism, under the umbrella term of "idealism."
9. Readers well versed in Buddhist philosophy will note that this critique of external and internal worlds is a simplification. However, for the purposes of this chapter, this simplified version is sufficient to highlight the central tension and core concerns of the historical figures under investigation. Historically, the Yogācāra critique of the dualistic worldview has taken many forms (e.g., grasped/grasper, object/subject, and self/other), but none of them maps neatly onto the Cartesian idea of mind/matter duality. In fact, how to resituate Yogācāra in view of imported philosophical categories has engendered many vehement debates in twentieth-century China. The literature on Yogācāra nonduality is similarly vast. I recommend interested readers consult the review by William Waldron, *Making Sense of Mind Only: Why Yogācāra Buddhism Matters* (Somerville, MA: Wisdom Publications, 2023), and the bibliography therein. For an in-depth analysis of the untenability of the external and internal worlds written for a Western audience, see Jan Westerhoff, *The Non-Existence of the Real World* (Oxford: Oxford University Press, 2020), 1–151.
10. Broadly, moral egoism is a common feature of Western ethics that assumes self-interest as a rational, natural starting point of moral reflection. For a review of the different forms of moral egoism, their central claims, and relevant debates, see Robert Shaver, "Egoism," in *The Stanford Encyclopedia of Philosophy* (Winter 2021 Edition), ed. Edward N. Zalta, https://plato.stanford.edu/archives/win2021/entries/egoism. For a critique of moral egoism from the Buddhist perspective, see Garfield, *Engaging Buddhism*, 310–12. See also Jay L. Garfield, *Losing Ourselves: Learning to Live without a Self* (Princeton, NJ: Princeton University Press, 2022). For a similar argument based on the ancient Chinese philosophy of co-action, see Mercedes Valmisa, "We Are Interwoven Beings," *Aeon*, November 25, 2022, https://aeon.co/essays/in-classical-chinese-philosophy-all-actions-are-collective.
11. For the Christian influence on the modern notion of self, see the seminal work by Charles Taylor, *Sources of the Self* (Cambridge, MA: Harvard University Press, 1989). Taylor sees Descartes playing an important role in the rise of modern self, 143–209. For a philosophical analysis of this Great Chain of Being, see Shuchen Xiang, *Chinese Cosmopolitanism: The History and Philosophy of an Idea* (Princeton, NJ: Princeton University Press, 2023), 113–27. For a longue durée study of the misalignments of modern methodological naturalism and science as well as the deep influence of Christian models of knowledge production, see Peter Harrison, *Some New World: Myths of Supernatural Belief in a Secular Age* (Cambridge: Cambridge University Press, 2024).
12. Hsiao-Lan Hu, *This-Worldly Nibbāna: A Buddhist-Feminist Social Ethics for Peacemaking in the Global Community* (Albany: State University of New York Press, 2011), 63–90.
13. None of these Chinese thinkers read Durkheim in depth. Their knowledge of Durkheimian sociology was mediated by their indirect engagement with either post-Durkheimian social theories or sociologists who were trained in European systems of knowledge and gained governmental or academic posts.

14. There are many Yogācāra critiques of this common conflation of ontology with causality. For a concise analysis of the renowned Yogācāra logician Dharmakīrti's (fl. ca. sixth- or seventh-century) argument on this issue, see Catherine Prueitt, "Is There an Ideal Scientific Image? Sellars and Dharmakīrti on Levels of Reality," in Garfield, ed., *Wilfrid Sellars and Buddhist Philosophy*, 48–66.
15. I am using the senses of "correct" and "true" first proposed by Jan Westerhoff. In his interpretation of the Madhyamaka two-truth doctrine, "truth" refers to statements and things in the fundamental metaphysical sense, while "correctness" conveys the "in-a-manner-of-speaking" sense that is useful for daily interactions yet devoid of ontological claims. See Westerhoff, *The Non-Existence of the Real World*, 146–47. This distinction is useful because the Chinese thinkers studied in this chapter rarely attempted to engage deeply with Western ontological debates. Rather, they devoted their analytic energy to examining how to theorize the self, others, and the world so to establish a just society and world peace. To put it differently, they focused on offering a "correct" instead of a "true" social ontology, which calls to mind Quine's positioning of physical objects and gods on the same epistemological footing in terms of efficacious cultural posits; see Willard van Orman Quine, "Main Trends in Recent Philosophy: Two Dogmas of Empiricism," *The Philosophical Review* 60, no. 1 (1951): 41.
16. For the emergence of the individual/society antinomy in the Euroatlantic intellectual landscape and the concomitant need to distinguish human and social sciences from natural sciences, see, for example, Joly Marc, "L'antinomie individu/société dans les sciences humaines et sociales: Genèse(s) et usages," *Cahiers Vilfredo Pareto* 52, no. 1 (2014): 193–223.
17. Note that all of the thinkers read widely about Western science, philosophy, and social theory in Chinese translation. A few of them, including Lü Cheng and Wang Enyang, were well versed in these traditions and engaged with them in their own ways.
18. The term "karmic confluence" was coined by Jonathan S. Walters as one of the seven types of "sociokarma"; see Walters, "Communal Karma and Karmic Community in Theravāda Buddhist History," in *Constituting Communities: Theravāda Buddhism and the Religious Cultures of South and Southeast Asia*, ed. John Holt, Jacob N. Kinnard, and Jonathan S. Walters (Albany: State University of New York Press, 2003), 20–21. Because each historical actor used similar Chinese terms to denote a variety of types of sociokarma, in this chapter my claims hold true only for each passage analyzed. A more well-rounded picture of each historical actor's philosophical position on sociokarma remains necessary.
19. I use Jay L. Garfield's insight of "parallel play or karmic coincidence" to characterize karmic confluence and highlight how karmic confluence differs from genuine intersubjective interactions that require mutual recognition of each other's subjectivity. See Garfield, " 'I Take Refuge in the Sangha. But How?': The Puzzle of Intersubjectivity in Buddhist Philosophy Comments on Tzohar, Prueitt, and Kachru," *Sophia* 58, no. 1 (2019): 85–89.
20. That said, war requires a high degree of interpersonal collaboration. The narrators of these stories of collective karma rarely mentioned the karmic retributions of those persons and organizations who had initiated the war. But had they used collective karma to describe the future sufferings of the warmongers, then this use of collective karma would have implied genuine intersubjective karmic influence.
21. This is an understudied area in the history of modern China. For a study of how Buddhists employed collective karma to address the wartime crisis in Sichuan, see Joey Yiqiao Yan, "Buddhist Monks, Lay Buddhist Local Elites, and Wartime Relief Activism in Chengdu and Chongqing, 1938–1945" (MA thesis, Chinese University of Hong Kong, 2020), 59–80.

22. Taixu 太虛, "Zenyang lai jianshe renjian Fojiao" 怎樣來建設人間佛教, in *Taixu dashi quanshu* 太虛大師全書, https://www.zhonghuadiancang.com/foxuebaodian/taixudashiquanshu/136573.html.
23. Yinguang 印光, "Yinguang dashi huguo xiza fayu" 印光大師護國息災法語, http://book.bfnn.org/books/0356.htm#a04.
24. Jessica Zu, "War, Piety, and Public Letters: The Making of a New Pure Land Patriarch in Modern China," *History of Religions* 63, no. 1 (2023): 75–119.
25. Walters, "Communal Karma and Karmic Community," 25.
26. Yinguang, "Yinguang dashi huguo xiza fayu." Yinguang mentions his distinction between *zhengbao* and *yubao* in day three.
27. Yuanying 圓瑛, "Tichang sushi jucan hui" 提倡素食聚餐會, http://book.bfnn.org/books2/1601.htm#a17. Here Yuanying uses *gongye* and *bieye* to highlight the different kinds of karmic responsibilities of individual vs. collective actions.
28. Taixu, "You zhizhi de zhongzhong guojizuzhi zaochang renshi heleguo" 由職志的種種國際組織造成人世和樂國, in *Taixu dashi quanshu*, https://www.zhonghuadiancang.com/foxuebaodian/taixudashiquanshu/136533.html.
29. For Taixu's deeper engagement with Yogācāra and his effort to Buddhisize the world with Maitreya's earthly paradise, see Justin Ritzinger, *Anarchy in the Pure Land: Reinventing the Cult of Maitreya in Modern China* (New York: Oxford University Press, 2018), 171–210.
30. Taixu, "You zhizhi de zhongzhong guojizuzhi zaochang renshi heleguo."
31. Note that Taixu's politics are very complicated. His positions on society and the nation-state also varied throughout the years. Thus, the socio-soteriology in this chapter represents his thinking only in this particular essay.
32. Mercedes Valmisa, *Adapting: A Chinese Philosophy of Action* (New York: Oxford University Press, 2021), 31–32. For details on how this *ganying* paradigm became a mainstream political idea for establishing social harmony during the Han dynasty, see Erica Brindley, *Music, Cosmology, and the Politics of Harmony in Early China* (Albany: State University of New York Press, 2012), 192n83.
33. For the mainstream relational and processual philosophies in early China, see, for example, François Jullien, *De l'être au vivre: Lexique euro-chinois de la pensée* (Paris: Gallimard, 2015); Valmisa, *Adapting*; and Xiang, *Chinese Cosmopolitanism*.
34. Tim Ingold, "When ANT Meets SPIDER: Social Theory for Anthropods," in *Material Agency: Towards a Non-Anthropocentric Approach*, ed. Carl Knappett and Lambros Malafouris (New York: Springer, 2008), 209–15.
35. Valmisa, *Adapting*, 41, 63–64. For a discussion of how this *ganying* paradigm works in the miracle tales of Guanyin, the goddess of half Asia, see, for example, Marcus Bingenheimer, *Island of Guanyin: Mount Putuo and Its Gazetteers* (New York: Oxford University Press, 2016), 78–79.
36. For in-depth analyses of shared karmic seeds as intersubjective agreements, see, for example, Catherine Prueitt, "Karmic Imprints, Exclusion, and the Creation of the Worlds of Conventional Experience in Dharmakīrti's Thought," *Sophia* 57, no. 2 (2018): 313–35; Tzohar Roy, "Imagine Being a *Preta*: Early Indian Yogācāra Approaches to Intersubjectivity," *Sophia* 56, no. 2 (2016): 337–54.
37. For objectivity as an outcome of social practice and science as social knowledge, see, for example, Helen E. Longino, *Science as Social Knowledge: Values and Objectivity in Scientific Inquiry* (Princeton, NJ: Princeton University Press, 1990). As powerfully argued by Isabelle Stengers, "No unifying body of knowledge will ever demonstrate that the neutrino of physics can coexist with the multiple worlds mobilized by ethnopsychiatry. Nonetheless, such

coexistence has a meaning . . . such beings can be collectively affirmed in a 'cosmopolitical' space where the hopes and doubts and fears and dreams they engender collide and cause them to exist." See Isabelle Stengers, *Cosmopolitics I*, trans. Robert Bononno (Minneapolis: University of Minnesota Press, 2010), vii–viii.

38. For representationalism, see Westerhoff, *The Non-Existence of the Real World*, 52–53. For a philosophically sound defense of irrealism, see 1–80.
39. Jessica Zu, "Ouyang Jingwu's *Must-Read Buddhist Classics for Laity*: Body Politics and Gendered Soteriology," *Journal of Chinese Religions* 47, no. 1 (2019): 65.
40. For modern and contemporary forms of "secular" Confucianism that are in line with Amartya Sen's vision of "secular symmetry," see Philip J. Ivanhoe and Sungmoon Kim, *Confucianism, a Habit of the Heart: Bellah, Civil Religion, and East Asia* (Albany: State University of New York Press, 2016), 2, 213, 219.
41. Sen, *The Argumentative Indian*, 306–7.
42. This essay was coauthored by Ouyang Jingwu and Wang Enyang. See Ouyang, "Fofa fei zongjiao fei zhexue" 佛法非宗教非哲學, http://www.guoxue123.com/new/0002/bfehyx/001.htm, para. 32.
43. Wang Enyang 王恩洋, "Fofa wei jinshi suo bixu" 佛法為今時所必需, *Guoxue daohang* 國學導航, http://www.guoxue123.com/new/0002/bfehyx/002.htm, para. 7.
44. Judith Butler, *The Force of Nonviolence: An Ethico-Political Bind* (London: Verso, 2021), 33.
45. Wang Enyang, "Chengli weishi yi" 成立唯識義, *Neixue* 1 (1924): 147–68.
46. Wang used Kuiji's commentary on *Twenty Verses*. Unlike Lü, he did not have access to Sanskrit or Tibetan texts. For an important analysis of how Xuanzang employed indirect *ālambana* to provide a satisfactory solution to the problem of other minds, see Jingjing Li, "Through the Mirror: The Account of Other Minds in Chinese Yogācāra Buddhism," *Dao: A Journal of Comparative Philosophy* 18, no. 3 (2019): 435–51.
47. For Xuanzang's and Kuiji's uses of *adhipati* for establishing the soteriological efficacy of teaching through scholarship, see Jessica Zu, "*Adhipati*, Yogācāra Intersubjectivity, and Soteriology in Kuiji's Commentaries," *Sophia*, June 5, 2024, https://link.springer.com/article/10.1007/s11841-024-01019-9.
48. "Species" is the term that most closely reflects Wang's distinctions among different kinds of sentient beings. The examples Wang gave are that fish see a river as a palace, humans see a river as filled with water, and hungry ghosts see a river as filled with pus and blood. See Wang, "Chengli weishi yi," 165–66.
49. Wang, "Chengli weishi yi," 165.
50. Wang Enyang, "You fofa laikan guannian lun" 由佛法來看觀念論", in *Wang Enyang xiansheng lunzhuji*, ed. Tang Zhongrong 唐仲容 (Chengdu: Sichuan renmin chubanshe, 1999), 2:411–18.
51. Wang Enyang, "Xinjing tongshi" 心經通釋, in *Wang Enyang xiansheng lunzhuji*, ed. Ed. Tang Zhongrong 唐仲容 (Chengdu: Sichuan renmin chubanshe, 1999), 3:585–635. These lecture notes were first published in 1946. But according to the text's own narrative, the lectures were delivered in winter 1941 in Chongqing, 3:634.
52. Wang, "Xinjing tongshi," 3:590.
53. Wang, "Xinjing tongshi," 3:608.
54. On the problem of the disappearing agent, see Markus Schlosser, "Agency," in *The Stanford Encyclopedia of Philosophy* (Winter 2019 Edition), ed. Edward N. Zalta, https://plato.stanford.edu/archives/win2019/entries/agency.

55. Erik Hammerstrom, "A Buddhist Critique of Scientism," *Journal of Chinese Buddhist Studies* 27 (2014): 35–57.
56. This is an online collection of a series of Wang's writings from 1931 to 1947. Because my goal is to map out a type of socio-soteriological response, the particular timeline is not relevant to my argument. See Wang, "Fofa yu kexue," https://book.bfnn.org/books2/1275.htm#a01.
57. Wang, "Fofa yu kexue," https://book.bfnn.org/books2/1275.htm#a05.
58. Wang, "Fofa yu kexue," para. 11.
59. Wang, "Fofa yu kexue," para. 19.
60. Both quotations are from Yinsun 印順, "Xuefo sanyao" 學佛三要, http://www.mahabodhi.org/files/yinshun/19/yinshun19-01.html, para. 9, para. 10.
61. It is not surprising that these Yogācāra thinkers had similar social visions, as Wang Xiaoxu, Han, Zhu, and Zhou formed the Yogācāra group most active in Beijing and northern China, in contrast to China Inner Learning Institute that was most active in Nanjing and southern China.
62. See verses 2c–d to 4a–b of Vasubandhu's *Thirty Verses* and Xuanzang's *CWSL*, T.1585.7c15–19.
63. T.1666_.32.0576b09–10. For an in-depth analysis of the debate on *Awakening Faith* during Republican China, see Eyal Aviv, *Differentiating the Pearl from the Fish-Eye: Ouyang Jingwu and the Revival of Buddhist Scholasticism* (Leiden: Brill, 2020), 69–106.
64. Yao Binbin 姚彬彬, "1921–1922 nian Zhang Taiyan, Lü Cheng, Li Jinxi lunxue shujian kaoshi" 1921–1922 年章太炎, 呂澂, 黎錦熙論學書簡考釋, *Foxue yanjiu* 23 (2014): 328.
65. Joseph Ciaudo, "Bergson's 'Intuition' in China and Its Confucian Fate (1915–1923): Some Remarks on *Zhijue* in Modern Chinese Philosophy," *Problemos* (2016): 35–50.
66. Yao, "1921–1922," 329–30.
67. Wang, "Fofa yu kexue," preface by Cai Yuanpei.
68. Douglas Gildow, "Cai Yuanpei (1868–1940), Religion, and His Plan to Save China through Buddhism," *Asia Major* 31, no. 2 (2018): 117–18.
69. Sally Haslanger, "What Good Are Our Intuitions?: Philosophical Analysis and Social Kinds," *Proceedings of the Aristotelian Society*, Sup. 80, no. 1 (2006): 89–118.
70. Russell Goodman, "William James," in *The Stanford Encyclopedia of Philosophy* (Winter 2021 Edition), ed. Edward N. Zalta, https://plato.stanford.edu/archives/win2021/entries/james.
71. David Hildebrand, "John Dewey," in *The Stanford Encyclopedia of Philosophy* (Winter 2021 Edition), ed. Edward N. Zalta, https://plato.stanford.edu/archives/win2021/entries/dewey.
72. David Scott, "William James and Buddhism: American Pragmatism and the Orient," *Religion* 30, no. 4 (2000): 333–52. For an in-depth analysis of John Dewey's activities in China and their implications for the making of modern China, see Jessica Ching-Sze Wang, *John Dewey in China: To Teach and to Learn* (Albany: State University of New York Press, 2007).

4. Buddhability as Humanity

The first epigraph is from Lü, "Dabanniepanjing zhengfafen jiangyao" 大般涅槃經正法分講要, *Xuanji1991*, 2:1170. The second is from *Xuanji1991*, 2:1163. This refrain appears quite frequently in Lü's lecture on the saṅgha jewel in this text; see *Xuanji1991*, 2:1163–76. The third can be found in Lü, "Shengman Furen shizihuojing jiangyao" 勝鬘夫人獅子吼經講要, *Xuanji1991*, 2:930.

1. François Jullien, *De l'être au vivre: Lexique euro-chinois de la pensée* (Paris: Gallimard, 2015), 9–18.

2. For a similar argument about action-oriented ethics and its relation to a moral imagination grounded in "karmic embeddedness," see Jessica Zu, "Self-Driving Cars and an Age-Old Buddhist Moral Dilemma," *Buddhist Door Global*, November 22, 2019, https://www.buddhistdoor.net/features/self-driving-cars-and-an-age-old-buddhist-moral-dilemma/. This view also resonates with Cho's characterization of karma as speech act; see Francisca Cho, "Buddhism, Science, and the Truth about Karma," *Religion Compass* 8, no. 4 (2014): 117–27. For how karma functions to orient actions, see Peter D. Hershock, *Consciousness Mattering: A Buddhist Synthesis* (London; New York: Bloomsbury, 2023), 26–30. As for "interconditioning," it is inspired by two contemporary terms to capture Lü's rendering of humanity in terms of *pratītyasamutpāda* (commonly translated as dependent co-arising), which illustrates the pan-Buddhist processual view that personhood always arises and changes depending on conditions and causes. The first is Thich Nhat Hanh's interbeing, see Thich Nhat Hanh, *Interbeing: Fourteen Guidelines for Engaged Buddhism* (Berkeley: Parallax Press, 1993). The second is Hsiao-Lan Hu's interconditionality, see Hsiao-Lan Hu, *This-Worldly Nibbāna: A Buddhist-Feminist Social Ethics for Peacemaking in the Global Community* (Albany: State University of New York Press, 2011), 5, 108. Interconditioning, for me, best illustrates the processual underpinnings of Lü's social theory.
3. The neologism "Buddhability" should be credited to Soka Gakkai International's youth program, https://buddhability.org. Although I could not find any direct relationship between Lü's revolution of consciousness and the human revolution promoted by Soka Gakkai (founded in 1930), the striking parallels between the two movements warrant this cross-reference. For an analysis of Soka Gakkai's history, vision, and global impact, see Levi McLaughlin, *Soka Gakkai's Human Revolution: The Rise of a Mimetic Nation in Modern Japan* (Honolulu: University of Hawai'i Press, 2020).
4. Charles Taylor, *Sources of the Self* (Cambridge, MA: Harvard University Press, 1989), 3.
5. The scholarship is vast. Most relevant to this chapter is a historical analysis of the rise of many visions regarding "new people" and the new social order prompted by the introduction of social Darwinism in modern China; see, for example, Jilin Xu, "Social Darwinism in Modern China," *Journal of Modern Chinese History* 6, no. 2 (2012): 182–97. For a broader history of how visions of new humanity undergirded the Communist social orders in the Soviet Union and China, see Yinghong Cheng, *Creating the New Man: From Enlightenment Ideals to Socialist Realities* (Honolulu: University of Hawai'i Press, 2009).
6. Well-trained scholars of Buddhist studies will immediately recognize that Lü narrated a fictional transmission lineage that sounded convincing to those familiar with Chinese Buddhism. The reality is always messier. For example, at the time that Xuanzang and Yijing traveled to India, Tantric Buddhism was already well developed in all of South and Southeast Asia. In fact, many of the Yogācāra masters traveled frequently to seek esoteric teaching not only at established monasteries in India (such as Nālandā) but also in kingdoms dotting the Maritime Silk Routes. These kingdoms are known today as Sri Lanka, Sumatra, and Java, as well as the Malay Peninsula and the Cam and Khmer domains. See Andrea Acri, "Introduction: Esoteric Buddhist Networks along the Maritime Silk Routes, 7th–13th Century AD," in *Esoteric Buddhism in Medieval Maritime Asia: Networks of Masters, Texts, Icons*, ed. Andrea Acri (Singapore: ISEAS Yusof Ishak Institute, 2016), 1–28.
7. Lü Cheng, "Neixueyuan foxue wuke jiangxi gangyao" 內學院佛學五科講習綱要, *Xuanji1991*, 2:605. See also Lü, "Zang Jing liangshi suochuan de wuke foxue" 奘淨兩師所傳的五科佛學, *Xuanji1991*, 3:1381–91. Note that the first time that Lü described his teaching as the

Institute's Learning (Yuanxue) was much earlier, on June 2, 1943, about one hundred days after Ouyang had passed away. See Lü, "Tan yuanxue" 談院學, *Xuanji1991*, 1:435–39.

8. *Xuanji1991*, 2:608.
9. *Xuanji1991*, 2:585.
10. In this chapter I give only the English-language translations of the titles of the texts in Lü's curriculum. Readers interested in the corresponding Chinese, Tibetan, Sanskrit, and Pāli titles can consult Jessica Zu, "Theorizing Social Consciousness: Lü Cheng (1896–1989) and the Rise of a New Buddhist Idealism in Modern China" (PhD diss., Princeton University, 2020), appendix 3, 343–47.
11. See, for example, *Xuanji1991*, 2:604. Though Lü repeatedly made this point in his lectures on *Five Disciplines*, three essays stand out with regard to his soteriological intent: "Tan yuanxue" 談院學, *Xuanji1991*, 2:435–39; "Neiyuan foxue wuke jiangxi gangyao" 內院佛學五科講習綱要, *Xuanji1991*, 2:585–604; and "Neiyuan foxuewuke jiangxi gangyao jiangji" 內院佛學五科講習綱要講記, *Xuanji1991*, 2:605–42.
12. See, for example, Su Yuanlei 蘇淵雷, "Zhina Neixue zhi fazhan: Lü Qiuyi jushi xueshuo juyao" 支那內學之發展: 呂秋一居士學說舉要, *Juexun* 覺訊 3, no. 8 (July 1949): 3.
13. *Xuanji1991*, 2:606–7. The work he was referring to is Lü Cheng, *Yindu fojiao shi luo* 印度佛教史略 (Shanghai: Commercial Press, 1925). This work is also included in *Xuanji1991*, vol. 4. Lü repeated this theme in multiple variations, see for example *Xuangji1991*, 2:1214–15, 3:1389.
14. Note that I use capitalized letters to indicate the names of the disciplines in both Nālandā's and Lü's curricula and lowercase letters to indicate either a concept itself or the body of texts. For example, I distinguish Nirvāṇa the discipline from nirvāṇa the doctrine.
15. *Xuanji1991*, 3:1381–91.
16. Ouyang, "Neixueyuan yuanxun · shijiao · shuojiao san" 內學院院訓·釋教訓·說教三, *Neixueyuan yuanxun* in OJNWX 1:1, 76, 85. This text has been digitized; see http://www.guoxue123.com/new/0002/bfehyx/017.htm.
17. *Xuanji1991*, 2:679–80.
18. Lü elaborated on the nature of one dharma realm with *dharmakāya* and nirvāṇa in the essay "Explicating 'Dharma-Realm'" (*Fajie shiyi* 法界釋義), *Xuanji1991*, 1:415–18. This essay is undated but is most likely based on a lecture given in 1944–45. Lü further explained that the meaning of "Dharma-realm" should follow the interpretation of the *Treatise on the Buddha-stage Sūtra* (*Fodi jinglun* 佛地經論; T.1530). T.1530 is included in the third stage of the discipline of Nirvāṇa. Lü valued T.1530 for its illustration of one true-reality dharma realm and the fruition of the originally quiescent *ālayavijñāna*. See *Xuanji1991*, 2:638–39.
19. *Xuanji1991*, 2:767.
20. *Xuanji1991*, 2:1094. He started his abridged lecture of the second phase with the chapter on skill-in-means (*fangbian pin* 方便品) from the *Lotus Sūtra*. He pointed out that while the first phase explicates that the root of the Institute's Learning is original quiescence, the second phase teaches that one must activate this original quiescence and then apply exhaustively the potential and function of original quiescence. He further commented that to become a Buddha, a saint, or a virtuous man, one need only to activate the function of this original quiescence that is innate in all sentient beings.
21. *Xuanji1991*, 1:417.
22. I struggle to make sense of this one true-reality dharma realm, which, according to Lü, encompasses all karmically connected cosmoses engendered by all mental streams. It cannot be the same as the multiverse in string theory or in science fiction because, for both

Ouyang and Lü, each mental stream generates its own cosmos. By contrast, a multiverse consisting of multiple parallel, nonintersecting, hypothetical universes. Within each universe, all persons share the same space-time. But a person X^a in universe A would not know the existence of another version of this person X^b in Universe B. The best metaphor for the Yogācāra multiple lifeworlds I can come up with is the mycelial network that connects all plants (all mental streams) in the ecosystem (connected multi-lifeworlds) of a forest. This is where the distinction between the countable and uncountable breaks down. That said, the path of *āśrayaparivṛtti*, that is, the path from human interconditioning to nirvāṇic interconditioning is more consistent with East Asian Madhyamaka rhetoric of the nonduality of saṃsāra and nirvāṇa, but here is presented as the two sides of a Möbius strip, locally seen as dualistic but globally seen as one.

23. There is no consensus regarding whether these were two autonomous Indian doctrinal schools or whether such doctrinal animosity was projected back to India due to the medieval Chinese debates. All we know is that the traditional Chinese narrative is unreliable. The traditional narrative posits that the two well-formed opposing schools were transplanted into sixth-century China and caused a conflict for over two centuries. Paramārtha was said to have integrated these two transplanted schools. Radich's article offers the strongest evidence against the traditional narrative and Paramārtha's role in "combining" the two. See Michael Radich, "The Doctrine of **Amalavijñāna* in Paramārtha (499–569) and Later Authors to Approximately 800 C.E.," *ZINBUN* 41 (2008): 45–174.
24. Ching Keng argues that Vasubandhu himself incorporated a weak reading, i.e., *Tathāgatagarbha* contains the unconditioned Thusness-cum-dharma-body, into Yogācāra; see Ching Keng, *Toward a New Image of Paramārtha: Yogācāra and Tathāgatagarbha Buddhism Revisited* (London: Bloomsbury, 2023), 186–92.
25. *Xuanji1991*, 2:638–39.
26. Lü, "Miaofa lianhua jing fangbianpin jiangyao" 妙法蓮華經方便品講要, *Xuanji1991*, 2:1094.
27. I use the term "revolutionary nonviolence" to highlight the striking parallels between Lü's project and many other postcolonial struggles around the world, particularly the shared worldview that rejects the mainstream discourse of inevitable violent revolution and that sees inner change and social change as interconditioned. The literature on the history and theory of nonviolence is rich. For a good starting point, see Imraan Coovadia, *Revolution and Nonviolence in Tolstoy, Gandhi, and Mandela* (New York: Oxford University Press, 2020).
28. Note that Lü also packaged this path into an institutional format, with three phases hinting toward the Yogācāra doctrine of three natures (Ch: *sanxing* 三性; Skt: *trisvabhāva*). For a detailed study of how the three phases map onto the *trisvabhāva*, see Zu, "Theorizing Social Consciousness," 288–96. For a systematic study of *āśrayaparivṛtti* in the Indian Yogācāra tradition, see Ronald Mark Davidson, "Buddhist Systems of Transformation: Āśraya-parivṛtti/-parāvṛtti Among the Yogācāra (India)" (PhD diss., University of California, Berkeley, 1985). See particularly Davidson's part II of chapter 5, "Psycho-Ontological Transformation" (228–46), which explicitly addresses the merging of transformation of basis and three natures. Note that Davidson chose to translate *āśrayaparivṛtti* as "fundamental transformation" in order to maintain the multivalence inherent in the Sanskrit *tatpuruṣa* compound.
29. To be sure, Lü's soteriology courses firmly within the bounds of Xuanzang and Kuiji's path of interconditioned awakening as elegantly laid out in Jingjing Li's monograph. See Jingjing Li, *Comparing Husserl's Phenomenology and Chinese Yogācāra in a Multicultural World: A Journey*

Beyond Orientalism (London; New York: Bloomsbury, 2022), 183–93. Lü's innovation becomes manifest only when we contextualize his Yogācāra within the broader twentieth-century discourse of how to establish a just society through nonviolent strategies.

30 In an undated essay collected in *Xuanji1991*, most likely published after 1949, Lü explicitly linked *zhuanyi* to social reform. He claimed that late Mahāyāna teachings like *zhuanyi* were closer to the commoners' worldview because it argued against the Gupta Empire's official ideology of Brahman supremacy. He further claimed that concepts such as *zhuanyi* implied a quest to transform this actual society (*yinhanzhe yaoqiu biange xianshi shehui de yiwei* 隱含着要求變革現實社會的意味). See *Xuanji1991*, 3:1416. In another 1953 essay, "Zhengjue yu chuli," Lü concluded it by redefining renunciation as 轉世 (reform this world), which he defined as a quest for a fundamental transformation of this world (*shijian benzhishang de biange* 世間本質上的變革) instead of escaping from worldly life (*tuoli shijian shenghuo* 脫離世間生活). See *Xuanji1991*, 3:1341.

31 *Xuanji1991*, 1336–37.

32. *Xuanji1991*, 2:585. Note that I translate *xin* 心 as "originally quiescent consciousness" because Lü linked this term with *xin xiangxu* 心相續 that will eventually transform into one true-reality realm, see *Xuanji1991*, 1:417.

33. For Ouyang's interpretations, see Eyal Aviv, *Differentiating the Pearl from the Fish-Eye: Ouyang Jingwu and the Revival of Buddhist Scholasticism* (Leiden: Brill, 2020), 102–5. For Lü's position and relevant debates on original quiescence, see Chen-Kuo Lin, "The Uncompromising Quest for Genuine Buddhism: Lü Cheng's Critique of Original Enlightenment," in *Transforming Consciousness: Yogācāra Thought in Modern China*, ed. John Makeham (New York: Oxford University Press, 2014), 346–52.

34. *Xuanji1991*, 2:609. Note that *kechen* is traditionally translated as "adventitious dust." I do not use this translation because "adventitious" calls to mind the Cartesian ontological distinction of innate, adventitious, and factitious ideas, an ontological paradigm that is at odds with Yogācāra. I maintain the literal sense of *ke* as "guest," which leaves the door open to interpret this sentence through a relational lens of visitor-host, foreign-indigenous, or secondary-primary.

35. Sally Haslanger, "What Good Are Our Intuitions?: Philosophical Analysis and Social Kinds," *Proceedings of the Aristotelian Society*, Sup. 80, no. 1 (2006): 89–118.

36. All relevant statements are paraphrased from Lü in *Xuanji1991*, 2:610.

37. For a detailed analysis of the translation and compilation of the *Forty-Two Sections Sūtra*, see Okabe Kazuo 岡部和雄, "Shijūnishōkyō' no seiritsu to tenkai: Kenkyūshiteki oboegaki" 四十二章經の成立と展開—研究史的覚え書き, *Komazawa daigaku bukkyōgakubu kenkyū kiyō* 25 (1967): 103–18. However, it is worth mentioning that in the 1940s Lü Cheng already knew about the complicated translation-compilation history and further commented on it in his 1950s lectures on the history of Chinese Buddhism, see Lü Cheng, *Zhongguo foxue yuanliu luejiang* 中國佛學源流略講, *Xuanji1991*, 5:2463–82.

38. *Dhammapada* was included in the Pāli canon's Khuddaka Nikaya (Minor Collection), the fifth division of the Pāli Sutta Piṭaka that is known to be the repository for materials that were left out of the four Āgamas/Nikayas. Lü was aware of *Dhammapada*'s ambiguous canonical status; see *Xuanji1991*, 2:643–44, 5:2466–70.

39. See also *Xuanji1991*, 2:644–45, on Lü's evaluation of three Chinese translations of this scripture.

40. For the intertwined history of this scripture and the European quest for an ur-tradition, see Urs App, *The Birth of Orientalism* (Philadelphia: University of Pennsylvania Press, 2010), 223–31.
41. *Xuanji1991*, 2:643–46. Lü's conviction in an urtext of *Dhammapada* formed during the Buddha's lifetime is not defensible. As carefully analyzed by Richard Salomon, the bewildering variations among multiple versions of this widely circulated scripture in Gāndhārī and other languages attest to multiple instances of oral transmission before this scripture was written down. Therefore, using textual-critical methods to reconstruct an ur-text would be futile. For details, see Richard Salomon, *The Buddhist Literature of Ancient Gandhāra: An Introduction with Selected Translations* (Somerville, MA: Wisdom Publications, 2018), 183–92. Also note that Lü's claim is much more modest: he admits the existence of multiple versions of this scripture (mainly three types: short, middle, and long, with variations) but insists that the message is consistent. See *Xuanji1991*, 2:643–44.
42. *Xuanji1991*, 2:662.
43. *Xuanji1991*, 2:662–64. Lü's interpretation of perfuming is consistent with Xuanzang's position, in that perfuming only functions as an indirect cause of activation.
44. The passage Lü cited is T.1600.0466b13.
45. *Xuanji1991*, 2:861. For readers familiar with Yogācāra studies, it is crucial to note that, unlike thinkers like Zhang Taiyuan and Cai Yuanpei who mistook *ālayavijñāna* as a universal consciousness, Lü grounded universal oneness in the perfected nature after the deluded consciousness qua *ālayavijñāna* was fundamentally revolutionized. For an in-depth analysis of the different interpretations of perfuming through hearing in medieval Chinese Yogācāra and in the later Huayan school of thought, see Yoshimura Makoto 吉村誠, "Chūgoku yuishiki ni okeru mon kunjū ni tsuite" 中国唯識における聞熏習説について", *Journal of Indian and Buddhist Studies* 58, no. 1 (2010): 246–51.
46. Lü, "Dachengjing bijiao dufa" 大乘經比較讀法, *Neixue* 1 (1924): 40.
47. *Xuanji1991*, 2:585.
48. *Xuanji1991*, 2:589.
49. *Xuanji1991*, 2:610. Note that Lü's program by and large inherited the attentiveness to the Abhidharmic distinction between conditioned dharmas and the unconditioned (nirvāṇa, the perfected nature, original quiescence). His soteriology is premised upon this distinction and aims to eliminate conditioned afflictions through perfuming.
50. *Xuanji1991*, 2:610. For an incisive analysis of the relational agency of things in the Chinese philosophy of coaction, see Mercedes Valmisa, *Adapting: A Chinese Philosophy of Action* (New York: Oxford University Press, 2021), 32, 35–42.
51. *Xuanji1991*, 2:585. See also *Xuanji1991*, 2:596, 610.
52. This interpretation of perfected nature is from the three kinds of absence of nature (*san wuxing* 三無性) in Xuanzang's *CWSL*, T.1585.09.0048a03.
53. Lü, "Meishu fazhan de tujing," 29.
54. For the history and sociopolitical implications of the *ganying* paradigm in early China, see Erica Brindley, *Music, Cosmology, and the Politics of Harmony in Early China* (Albany: State University of New York Press, 2012), 192n83.
55. Wendi L. Adamek, *Practicescapes and the Buddhists of Baoshan* (Bochum: Hamburg University Press, 2021), 124.
56. *Xuanji1991*, 2:604.
57. *Xuanji1991*, 2:631.

58. *Xuanji1991*, 2:1169.

59. Ouyang, "Neixueyuan yuanxun· shijiao · shuojiao san," OJNWX 1:73. See also the digitized version, http://www.guoxue123.com/new/0002/bfehyx/019.htm.

60. Jessica Zu, "Ouyang Jingwu's *Must-Read Buddhist Classics for Laity*: Body Politics and Gendered Soteriology," *Journal of Chinese Religions* 47, no. 1 (2019): 61–86.

61. See, for example, Yuanzhao's commentary on the *Four-Part Vinaya* (*Sifenlü* 四分律), T.1805.40.0161b01–06. See also Daoxuan's treatise, T.1896.45.0860b22–23. See Huiyuan's commentary on the *Nirvāṇa Sūtra*, T.1764.37.0686c18–20. In his commentary on Mahāyāna teachings, Huiyuan devotes a whole section to explaining the meaning of four kinds of people as the support for this world, T.1851.44.0676c26–0678c27. He also compares and then reconciles this concept with the earlier doctrine of four reliances, T.1851.44.0680b03–06. See also Jizang's commentary on Mahāyāna teachings, T.1853.45.0064b18–22. Note that, these commentaries use the term *rensiyi* 人四依, which can have a different connotation as "four kinds of reliable people" and are thereby less controversial than Ouyang and Lü's claim.

62. T.2122.53.1013b01–03.

63. *Xuanji1991*, 2:1163.

64. T.374.12.0399b29; T0375.12.0640a12.

65. For a reliable translation of T.374, see Mark L. Blum, trans., *Nirvana Sutra (Mahāparinirvāna-sūtra): Translated from the Chinese* (Berkeley: BDK America Inc., 2013). I am following Blum's translation of 世間依 as "support for this world."

66. *Xuanji1991*, 2:1163. This refrain appears frequently; see, for example, *Xuanji1991*, 2:1167, 1170–71.

67. Blum, *Nirvana Sutra*, 169.

68. Note that to harmonize with the traditional understanding of Dharma as worldly support, Lü used hierarchical inclusion, subordinating Dharma as worldly support as a teaching for people at lower levels while considering Dharmic humans as worldly support as the ultimate teaching; see, for example, *Xuanji1991*, 2:1172–73. Here Lü argues that the preaching of the four kinds of people as the support for this world constitutes the teachings for people who have opened their wisdom eyes (Skt: *prajñācakṣus*; Ch: *huiyan* 慧眼), and the earlier teachings of the four kinds of reliance of Dharma are the teachings for people with only fleshy eyes (Skt: *māṃsacakṣus*; Ch: *rouyan* 肉眼).

69. *Xuanji1991*, 2:1170.

70. Aimé Césaire, *Discours sur le colonialism*, 4th ed. (Paris: Présence Africaine, 1955), 22. "Structural violence" is a term coined in 1969 to refer to the ways that structures and institutions that keep people from meeting basic needs. See Johan Galtung, "Violence, Peace, and Peace Research," *Journal of Peace Research* 6, no. 3 (1969): 167–91.

71. *Xuanji1991*, 2:1164.

72. Adamek, *Practicescapes and the Buddhists of Baoshan*, 150–56.

73. *Xuanji1991*, 2:929–30.

74. During Lü's lifetime this processual view of the subjectivities of humans as products of aggregated processes may have sounded unconventional. However, it hews closely to traditional Buddhist philosophy of no-self and works well with feminist understanding of performativity. See for example Hsiao-Lan Hu, *This-Worldly Nibbāna*, 63–90. In addition, many contemporary studies in sociology and neuroscience have echoed what Lü claimed in the 1940s. For a sociological study on the making of individualism, see Peter L. Callero, *The Myth of Individualism: How Social Forces Shape our Lives* (Lanham, MD: Rowman & Littlefield, 2017).

For a neuroscientific study of the same issue, see Thomas Metzinger, *The Ego Tunnel: The Science of the Mind and the Myth of the Self* (Boulder, CO: Basic Books, 2019). See also Michael S. A. Graziano, *Consciousness and the Social Brain* (Oxford; New York: Oxford University Press, 2013).

75. *Xuanji1991*, 2:1170.
76. Lü stressed this point of *zengshang* 增上 (being activated and enhanced) by learning the Buddhist teachings on multiple occasions; see, for example, *Xuanji1991*, 2:960, 1030, 1038, 1144, 1166, 1193, 1203–4.
77. Blum, *Nirvana Sutra*, 169.
78. T.1805.40.0161b01; T.2248.62.0267b03; T.1851.44.0677a03.
79. *Xuanji1991*, 2:1164.
80. *Xuanji1991*, 2:1168.
81. *Xuanji1991*, 2:1171.
82. Alternatively termed *pusachanti* 菩薩闡提, this term is well known in Chinese traditions, e.g. T. 672.16.597c18–22, T.1828.42.521a4–7, T.2297.70.188c7–8. But the Chinese commentaries all cite the *Laṅkāvatāra Sūtra* (T. 672 or T.670) as the sources. Lü's interpretation of *icchantika* is consistent with the position of the *Laṅkāvatāra Sūtra*, which was the last text about which Lü lectured (*Xuanji1991*, 2:1214–1280). This sūtra claims that due to the power of Tathāgata, good roots can still arise from the *icchantikas*; see T.670:16.487b29-c3. See also *Xuanji1991*, 1:432. In this sense, Lü followed the *Laṅkāvatāra Sūtra* and rejected the existence of *icchantika* as an ontological reality.
83. For an analysis of these historical debates on the *icchantika*, see Whalen Lai, "Sinitic Speculations on Buddha-nature: The Nirvāṇa School (420–589)," *Philosophy East and West* 32, no. 2 (1982): 135–49. See also Ming-Wood Liu, "The Problem of the Icchantika in the *Mahāyāna Mahāparinirvāṇa Sūtra*," *Journal of the International Association of Buddhist Studies* 7, no. 21 (1984): 57–81. For an analysis of the term "icchantika" in early Buddhism, see Seishi Karashima, "Who Were the Icchantikas?," *Annual Report of the International Research Institute for Advanced Buddhology at Soka University* 10 (2007): 61–80.
84. For a defense of this reading of *icchantika* in medieval China, see Keng, *Toward a New Image of Paramārtha*, 205–6.
85. *Xuanji1991*, 2:626, 1194–98, 1256.
86. *Xuanji1991*, 2:1207.
87. *Xuanji1991*, 2:1256. The scripture that Lü included in his *Five Disciplines* is Tang translation T.672, a later version than the one translated then included in *Essentials*, T.670. For his justification for using this translation, see *Xuanji1991*, 1216–17. However, in collating T.670, Lü referred to all three translations of the *Laṅkāvatāra Sūtra* as well as the Tibetan and Sanskrit editions; for Lü's collating notes, see *Essentials*, 1:881–2. An additional reason that Lü ended his shortened lecture series with this text is that Lü deemed the *Laṅkāvatāra Sūtra* the end of Indian Buddhism (*yindufojiao zhizhong* 印度佛教之終) and the beginning of Chinese practice gate (*kai Zhongguo zongmen zhi shi* 開中國宗門之始). See *Xuangji1991*, 2:1214–15.
88. According to Lü's memoir, in academic year 1923–24 he had three teaching jobs. The main one was to lecture for the Inner Learning Institute's advanced studies program and to edit the institute's journal, *Neixue*. The other two were to teach at Nanjing Academy of Art and to teach philosophy at a high school in Nanjing; see Lü, "Wo de jingli," 78.
89. Little is known about Huang Jusu. However, there were several newspaper articles published in 1931 mocking Huang's mixing of politics and Buddhism, his connections with the Inner Learning Institute, and his friendship with Chen Mingshu—another Buddhist

politician and military leader with close ties to the Inner Learning Institute. See Yun Yun 雲雲, "Huang Jusu bie zhuan" 黄居素別傳, *Shehui ribao* 社会日报, March 14, 1931, 1, and He Manzi 河满子, "Huang Jusu bie zhuan bu" 黄居素別傳補, *Shehui ribao*, March 16, 1931, 1. A keyword search in QGBKSY with "黄居素" yields many entries detailing Huang's political appointments in the 1920s and 1930s.

90. Lü Cheng and Chen Zhenru, "Zhenru zuo shusuoyuanyuan yi" 真如作疏所緣緣義, *Neixue* 1 (1924): 279–86.
91. This is an established term in early Yogācāra teachings; its full expression is *pṛṣṭha-labdha-śuddha-laukika-jñāna*, which translates to subsequent mundane pure awareness. It specifically refers to one's way of seeing after realizing the nonconceptual and ineffable perfected nature that nonetheless allows the enlightened being to function in saṃsāra by seeing dependently arising things as essenceless.
92. Lü and Chen, "Zhenru zuo shusuoyuanyuan yi," 283.
93. His other name is Chen Mingshu. For his political and military career, see QGBKSY, search word "陳銘樞."
94. Lü and Chen, "Zhenru zuo shusuoyuanyuan yi," 281, 283. Note that Wang Enyang's position was more extreme. For him, even for bodhisattvas who obtain subsequent awareness, the Thusness that they perceive is still an indirectly perceived objective support, i.e., merely a shadow of Thusness.
95. The main scriptural sources cited in this debate came from Xuanzang and Kuiji; however, Asaṅga's and Vasubandhu's works such as *Mahāyānasaṃgraha* and *Mahāyānasaṃgrahabhāṣya* had long established subsequent awareness as the norm of the bodhisattva's salvific career to enable her to function in the mundane world while dwelling in the realm of the ineffable. See Roy Tzohar, *A Yogācāra Theory of Metaphor* (New York: Oxford University Press, 2018), 183–88.
96. Lü Cheng, "Guan suoyuan shilun huiyi" 觀所緣釋論會譯, *Neixue* 4 (1927): 1–33.
97. For the lemmas accentuated, see *Essentials*, 7:308–9. The central theme of this treatise is that *ālambana* is a manifestation of consciousness as if they are objects outside consciousness. Lü's new edition accentuated this point through page design and interlinear notes. In addition, in his note on p. 309 explaining "shi you bixiang gu deng" 識有彼相故等, he cited another version of the lemma "yishi shiti gu. Youshi bi yinyuan gu" 以是識體故，又是彼因緣故." Both passages express the same meaning: the body of [the seemingly substantial object] is consciousness, and consciousness is its causes and conditions. This note further accentuates the meaning of "[appearing *as if* things outside] whose body is consciousness, i.e., its causes and conditions."
98. Recall that those who objected to Lü's position insisted that indirectly perceived objects are substances and directly perceived objects are substanceless. This dualistic position was popular among institute alumni such as Xiong Shili and Liang Shuming. Both Wang Enyang and Lü rejected this reading.
99. Hui Wang, *China's Twentieth Century: Revolution, Retreat, and the Road to Equality* (New York: Verso, 2016), 48, 109.
100. Hui Wang, *China from Empire to Nation-State*, trans. Michael Gibbs Hill (Cambridge, MA: Harvard University Press, 2014), 66.
101. *Xuanji1991*, 1:453.
102. Joseph Walser, "When Did Buddhism Become Anti-Brahmanical? The Case of the Missing Soul," *Journal of the American Academy of Religion* 86, no. 1 (2018): 94–125.

5. Bodhisattva of Democracy

1. For republicanism or egalitarian philosophy and practices in early saṅgha, see Uma Chakravarti, *On the Social Philosophy of Buddhism: Four Essays* (Shimla: Indian Institute for Advanced Study, 2015), 21–24; Chakravarti, *Social Dimensions of Early Buddhism* (Delhi: Oxford University Press, 1987), 108–9; Rekha Daswani, *Buddhist Monasteries and Monastic Life in Ancient India: From the Third Century BC to the Seventh Century AD* (New Delhi: Aditya Prakashan, 2006), 100; Vincent Eltschinger, *"Caste" et philosophie bouddhique: Continuité de quelques arguments bouddhiques contre le traitement réaliste des dénominations sociales* (Vienna: Universität Wien, 2000), 164–66; Xinru Liu, *Early Buddhist Society: The World of Gautama Buddha* (Albany: State University of New York Press, 2022), 51, 180; Gail Omvedt, *Buddhism in India: Challenging Brahmanism and Caste* (New Delhi: Sage Publications, 2003), 66–68, 96; and J. P. Sharma, *Republics in Ancient India* (Leiden: Brill, 1968), 12, 114. For an overview of the topic, see Matthew J. Moore, "Buddhism and Politics," in *Oxford Bibliographies Online*, https://www.oxfordbibliographies.com/display/document/obo-9780195393521/obo-9780195393521-0251.xml.
2. *Homeostasis* is a term borrowed from biology. In social philosophy or the theory of social systems, homeostasis has been used to describe mechanisms that self-correct and self-regulate to stabilize certain properties of the system; for the first use of the term in this regard, see Richard Boyd, "Homeostasis, Species, and Higher Taxa," in *Species: New Interdisciplinary Essays*, ed. Robert A Wilson (Cambridge, MA: MIT Press, 1999), 141–85. For a helpful outline of the key characteristics of a processual social philosophy, see Jason Ānanda Josephson Storm, *Metamodernism: The Future of Theory* (Chicago: University of Chicago Press, 2021), 85–104. For Storm's further refinement of different social kinds such as homeostatic property-cluster kinds and a process-cluster account of social kinds, see Storm, *Metamodernism*, 108–29. While Storm's proposal aims to offer a means of accommodating all known social kinds, my purpose in this chapter is more modest: I investigate how Lü reinvented Yogācāra philosophy to theorize the possibility and functionality of a Buddhist civil society in initiating a worldwide nonviolent democratic revolution.
3. Lü, "Zhengjue yu chuli" 正覺與出離, *Xuanji1991*, 3:1337–41. All three lectures focus on *zhuanyi* as a processual social revolution. The first lecture, "Zhengjue yu chuli," dispels the misreading of Buddhism as mere a search for inner peace and further links inner peace and social justice on a Möbius strip. See *Xuangji 1991*, 3:1330–1342. The second lecture, "Yuanqi yu shixiang" 緣起與實相 (part I and part II), explicates in detail how different premodern teachings of dependent co-arising evolved and how and which kind of causal theory could be retooled for building a just society. See *Xuanji1991*, 3:1343–1368. The third lecture, "Guanxing yu zhuanyi" 觀行與轉依, lays out actionable items that scholars and practitioners could take on to actualize the project of revolutionizing consciousness. See *Xuanji1991*, 3:1369–80.
4. *Xuanji1991*, 2:606–7, 1214–15. Lü was not alone. Monk Yinshun, in his 1942 monograph *Buddhism in Indian* (*Yindu zhi fojiao* 印度之佛教), made a similar point. However, Yinshun defined "primitiveness" by likening the history of Buddhism in India to a human life: early Indian Buddhism was akin to childhood, early Mahāyāna Buddhism represented the period of youth, and Tantric Buddhism constituted the senile period. See Yinshun, *Yindu zhi fojiao* 印度之佛教, Yinshun wenjiao jijinhui, http://www.mahabodhi.org/files/yinshun/35/yinshun35-02.html.

5. *Prātimokṣa* literally means "toward liberation." It is the shortest part of a vinaya text. Each tradition organizes its vinaya differently. Some mix each code in *prātimokṣa* with exegesis and commentary. In the Pāli tradition, for example, these comments are called *vibhaṅga*. Many others separate *prātimokṣa* from *vibhaṅga*. The *prātimokṣa* part of the vinaya is highly consistent across different traditions. See Lü Cheng, Shi Cunhou 釋存厚, Feng Zhuo 馮卓, and Liu Dingquan 劉定權, "Zhujia jieben tong long" 諸家戒本通論, *Neixue* 3 (1926): 47–87, with an appendix on the sectarian history of Indian Buddhism, 87–101.
6. Lü et al., "Zhujia jieben," 86. Lü's critique of Taixu was very harsh. He accused Taixu of flowing with the tides and engaging in empty chatter about a grand plan.
7. Lü et al., "Zhujia jieben," 86–87.
8. For a lucid historiographical review of early Buddhist studies methods, see Jonathan S. Walters, "Suttas as History: Four Approaches to the Sermon on the Noble Quest (Ariyapariyesanasutta)," *History of Religions* 38, no. 3 (1999): 247–84.
9. Wendi L. Adamek, *Practicescapes and the Buddhists of Baoshan* (Bochum: Hamburg University Press, 2021), 24.
10. Lü Cheng, "Yishu he meiyu" 藝術和美育, *Jiaoyu zazhi* 14, no. 10 (October 1922): 8.
11. For a representative study of an earlier effort to reestablish the "original" saṅgha and the trenchant critique of the monastic community, see Daniel Boucher, *Bodhisattvas of the Forest and the Formation of the Mahāyāna: A Study and Translation of the Rāṣṭrapālaparipṛcchā-sūtra* (Honolulu: University of Hawai'i Press, 2008), 64–84.
12. *Xuanji1991*, 3:1331–32. Lü based this claim on a quote from *Mahāyānasūtrālaṃkāra* (T.1604.591a13–14); see *Xuanji1991*, 3:1344n3.
13. T.1489.24.1077c01–1078a24.
14. *Xuanji1991*, 2:988–90.
15. *Essentials*, 9:636n1. Careful examination of Lü's editorial notes in *Essentials* and in his 1943 explication of this point (*Xuanji1991*, 2:588) reveals that he only reached this conclusion much later in his process of editing *Essentials*. In his collation of *Mahāyānasaṃgraha* in the first collection of *Essentials* published in 1929, Lü provided no notation to indicate how T.1594 is linked with *Extensive Pure Vinaya* (T.1489); see *Essentials*, 3:115–16. But at this time he is already keen to accentuate the idea that bodhisattva precepts are just like (*xiangsi* 相似) śrāvaka precepts. See *Essentials*, 3:115n5. He only linked T.1594 with T.1489 later in the edition of T.1489 in the third collection of *Essentials*, which had to have been published after 1940.
16. *Xuanji1991*, 2:616, 979–1004. In his lecture on this vinaya text, Lü provided an extensive list of where and how the so-called *Vinaya Ghoṣa Extensive Sūtra* is cited in the bodhisattva vinaya chapters of various treatises and commentaries in multilingual translations by Asaṅga and Vasubandhu.
17. *Xuanji1991*, 2:988–89, 998–1000.
18. As Pei-ying Lin points out, this sūtra, compiled between 440 and 480 CE, reflects the relation between the Buddhist order and the state. Its subsequent adaptations reflected other power differentials between ordained clergy and laity; see Pei-ying Lin, "The Doctrinal Evolution of Formless Precepts: The Theory of Mind Purification in the *Laṅkāvatāra Sūtra* and the *Brahmā Net Sūtra*," in *Rules of Engagement: Medieval Traditions of Buddhist Monastic Regulation*, ed. Susan Andrews, Jinhua Chen, and Cuilan Liu (Bochum: Projekt Verlag, 2017), 198–201. That said, Lü only made this critique of Buddhist complicity with the court and the state explicitly after 1949, see *Xuanji1991*, 1416. In the early 1940s, Lü's critique is still focused on the hierarchies between the monastics and laity.

19. For an insightful analysis of the existential anxiety and reproductive desire reflected in the narrative strategies common to all Mahāyāna scriptures, see Charlotte Eubanks, *Miracles of Book and Body: Buddhist Textual Culture and Medieval Japan* (Berkeley: University of California Press, 2011).
20. Lü et al., "Zhujia jieben," 86.
21. *Essentials*, 2:709n2. In this footnote, Lü pointed out that, according to the Tibetan translation by Guṇaprabha (Tib: *yon tan 'od*; Ch: *Deguang* 德光), the text is a commentary on vinaya (*Byang chub sems dpa'i tshul khrims kyi le'u'i bshad pa*), and these four pārājikas (grave offenses) are just like the four pārājikas in the śrāvaka precepts. Lü suspected that Xuanzang had mistranslated this passage by omitting the phrase "resembling" (*xiangsi* 相似). See also *Essentials*, 2:714n4. In this footnote, Lü provided a Chinese translation of the Tibetan translation, which stressed that the bodhisattva's practice is just like the śrāvaka's.
22. For Lü's explication and comparisons of these four grave offenses in śrāvaka and bodhisattva precepts, see *Xuanji1991*, 2:1011–17.
23. *Xuanji1991*, 2:1007. In another essay Lü not only repeated this narrative but also matter-of-factly claimed that Yogācāra should be the *zhengzong* 正宗 (authentic lineage) of Mahāyāna vinaya. See *Xuanji1991*, 3:1386.
24. T.1501.24.1115c18–21.
25. The weak link in this new lineage is Bodhisattva Maitreya, a mythical figure whose authorship of *Yogācārabhūmi* has been analyzed by many scholars. While Xuanzang attributed it to Maitreya, the extant Tibetan version attributes it to Asaṅga. The core issue might be what counts as an "author" in different traditions.
26. Hidenori S. Sakuma, "Remarks on the Lineage of Indian Masters of the Yogācāra School: Maitreya, Asaṅga, and Vasubandhu," in *The Foundation for Yoga Practitioners: The Buddhist Yogācārabhūmi Treatise and Its Adaptation in India, East Asia, and Tibet*, ed. Ulrich Timme Kragh (Cambridge, MA: Harvard University Press, 2013), 330–66. This kind of intertextual authorship is not unique to Lü or Sakuma. As pointed out by Matthew T. Kapstein, Bhikkhu Ñāṇamoli (Osbert Moore) dismissed the modern Western construction of authorship based on individualism and rather saw Buddhaghoṣa as a committee. See Matthew T. Kapstein, review of *The Foundation of Yoga Practitioners: The Buddhist Yogācārabhūmi Treatise and Its Adaptations in India, East Asia, and Tibet*, by Ulrich Timme Kragh, *Indo-Iranian Journal* 60, no. 3 (2017): 295.
27. *Xuanji1991*, 2:1007.
28. *Xuanji1991*, 2:1007. Lü words this as 且此綜集亦非漫無所據率而成篇，實際本於菩薩藏之《十六門教授》(《寶積迦葉品》). The *Yoga Bodhisattva Precepts* is included in the Vinaya discipline in the first phase. As for the sixteen doors of teaching (*shiliumen jiaoshou* 十六門教授) in *Heap of Jewels Sūtra—Mahākāśyapa Chapter* (*Baoji jiayepin* 寶積迦葉品), Lü was referring to his own edition of two Chinese texts, T.351 *Foshuo moheyan baoyanjing* 佛說摩訶衍寶嚴經 and T.310 *Dabaojiying · Pumingpusahui di sishisan* 大寶積經·普明菩薩會第四十三 (T.310.11.631c15–638c04), included in the third collection of *Essentials*, 8:1063–91, and which he had appended with two excerpts. The second appendix was selected from the *Yogācārabhūmi* chapter "Yujia shidi lun pusadi jueze shi" 瑜伽師地論菩薩地抉擇釋. Lü pointed out several other parallel versions: T.350 and T.352, a Tibetan translation, and a scholarly edited Sanskrit text. He dismissed the Sanskrit text because it was a later scholarly edition by Alexander von Staël-Holstein (1877–1937), and he deemed the Sanskrit base text inauthentic because the Chinese

translation is dated earlier, and the Sanskrit text does not conform to the commentaries from *Yogācārabhūmi*. See *Xuanji1991*, 2:819–20.

29. *Xuanji1991*, 2:819–20.
30. *Xuanji1991*, 2:839. The Chinese original reads 乃自內精勤，觀察自心，不賴他緣，而有異於聲聞之依佛聲而得解脫. The bodhisattva vinaya is further identified as the training in higher disciplines (*zenghang jiexue* 增上戒学; *Xuanji1991*, 2:846) and the ultimate and true vinaya (*shengyi lüyi* 勝義律儀, *zhenshi lüyi* 真實律儀; *Xuanji1991*, 2:852). Both are common terms in the *Yogācārabhūmi*.
31. *Xuanji1991*, 2:846.
32. T. W. Rhys Davids, *Buddhist India* (New York: G. P. Putnam's Sons, 1903), 17–23.
33. The starting point of my philosophical analysis is that most of us theorize about the nature of social reality and social kinds, but only a handful of us have been trained to articulate such theoretical intuitions in academic terminology. As the first step in mapping out how lay people philosophize social reality and social dynamics in telling karmic tales, in 2021 I organized with Susanne Kerekes and Sara Swenson a conference titled "Lived Karma: Situating Interbeing in Society." Readers can find analyses of some of the conference themes in a series of critical notes in *Journal of Global Buddhism*. For an introduction of these critical notes, see Susanne Kerekes and Jessica Zu, "Introduction: Critical Notes on the Lived Karma Conference," *Journal of Global Buddhism* 24, no. 2 (2023): 83–87.
34. My contention is that these processual philosophies of democracy fundamentally change the terms of debate, especially regarding the dynamics of collective action for public good. The Western classics on this topic, such as Mancur Olson Jr.'s seminal work *The Logic of Collective Action: Public Goods and the Theory of Groups* (Cambridge, MA: Harvard University Press, 1965), start with the unexamined axioms that society is the sum of its individual members and collective action is the outcome of the actions of all active agents. Anyone familiar with basic Buddhist teachings will immediately see how such unexamined axioms mistake the Christianity-informed view of a human being (i.e., a unitary agent endowed with free will) as the universal standard and, moreover, how such a parochial view of humanity excludes many Buddhist discussions of democracy, collectivity, and public good grounded in no-self, interdependence, and compassion. Moreover, the founding of philosophy as an academic discipline has institutionalized an unwarranted raciology by defining philosophy an exclusively Greco-European intellectual enterprise and by denigrating other peoples as incapable of engaging with abstract concepts, thinking universally, and reasoning. See Peter K. Park, *Africa, Asia, and the History of Philosophy: Racism in the Formation of the Philosophical Canon, 1780–1830* (Albany: State University of New York Press, 2013). For how Kant's raciology is still shaping the curriculum and canon of philosophy, see Huaping Lu-Adler, *Kant, Race, and Racism: Views from Somewhere* (New York: Oxford University Press, 2023), 329–35. Due to this Orientalist legacy, scholars of Asian philosophy today routinely label nonwhite thinkers as "Buddhist" philosophers, "Confucian" philosophers, "Jain" philosophers, and so on to mark that these thinkers draw from religious traditions. However, thinkers in the Western philosophical canon such as Immanuel Kant, Georg Wilhelm Friedrich Hegel, Martin Heidegger, and many others who draw extensively from Christian traditions in their theorizing are never labeled "Christian" philosophers. To continue to label Lü as a "Buddhist" philosopher is to reproduce this Orientalist bias.
35. Storm, *Metamodernism*, 117–28.

36. Tim Ingold, "Taking Taskscape to Task," in *Forms of Dwelling: 20 Years of Taskscapes in Archeology*, ed. Ulla Rajala and Philip Millis (Oxford: Oxbow Books, 2017), 23.
37. *Xuanji1991*, 2:979.
38. *Xuanji1991*, 2:979.
39. Note that this emphasis on the mental aspect of precepts is quite common in Mahāyāna literature. For the importance of the originally pure mind-heart in Chinese vinaya transmission, see Pei-Ying Lin, "The Doctrinal Evolution of Formless Precepts in the Early Chan Tradition." Equally important is the emphasis on the originally pure consciousness, which appears frequently in Lü's scriptural explications; see, for example, his comments on Dhammapada, *Xuanji1991*, 2:662.
40. *Xuanji1991*, 2:980. For a classic analysis of the popularity of the *Vimalakīrti Sūtra* in East Asia, see Richard B. Mather, "Vimalakīrti and Gentry Buddhism," *History of Religions* 8, no. 1 (1968): 60–73.
41. These represent Lü's own reading; see *Xuanji1991*, 2:1011–13. However, scholars of religious studies should not take these embedded discourses at face value. There have been many studies illustrating the social function of precepts that seem to be merely about individual behavior. For example, Janet Gyatso analyzes vinaya narratives around the rule of celibacy and concludes that, contrary to the explicit explications in vinaya commentary, the unsaid attitude about no-sex has less to do with individual purification and more to do with communal identity. See Janet Gyatso, "Sex," in *Critical Terms for the Study of Buddhism*, ed. Donald S. Lopez (Chicago: University of Chicago Press, 2005), 271–90.
42. *Xuanji1991*, 2:1172–73.
43. Justin Ritzinger, *Anarchy in the Pure Land: Reinventing the Cult of Maitreya in Modern China* (New York: Oxford University Press, 2018), 182–87.
44. Matthew J. Moore, *Buddhism and Political Theory* (New York: Oxford University Press, 2016), 15–30.
45. Vinaya in medieval China is an understudied area. A valuable resource is a recent edited volume; see Andrews, Chen, and Liu, *Rules of Engagement*. The three articles in the fourth section of this book, "Exploring Communities of Vinaya-Related Practice," provide a glimpse into monastic-lay-local communal dynamics. For Buddhist political theory in East Asia, see Stephanie Balkwill and James A. Benn, *Buddhist Statecraft in East Asia* (Leiden: Brill, 2022).
46. For an in-depth study of the emergence of Buddhism civic engagement in Shanghai lay communities and its use of a corporate business model, see, for example, James Brooks Jessup, "The Householder Elite: Buddhist Activism in Shanghai, 1920–1956" (PhD diss., University of California, Berkeley, 2010), 49–59. For an overview of the complicated interactions among Buddhism, Christianity, and Islam, see, for example, Goossaert and Palmer, *The Religious Question in Modern China* (Chicago: University of Chicago Press, 2011), 67–90.
47. For an analysis of the history and corporate structure of the Four Mountains in Taiwan, see Richard Madsen, *Democracy's Dharma: Religious Renaissance and Political Development in Taiwan* (Berkeley: University of California Press, 2007).
48. It is not clear whether Lü was influenced by the colonial Buddhological knowledge that the historical Buddha most likely grew up in a republican state. For a review of the scholarship on the historical Buddha, the time he lived, and the debate about tribal democracy in ancient India, see Oskar von Hinüber, "The Buddha as a Historical Person," *Journal of the International Association of Buddhist Studies* 42 (2019): 231–64. For an interesting hypothesis

that links the birth of the myth of Buddha as a prince with Aśvaghoṣa (c. 80–150 CE), see Walters, "Suttas as History," 275. It is clear that Lü noticed the republican rules in the monastic vinaya and tried to expend them to build his own theory of civil society.

49. For a general definition of deliberative democracy, see Stephen Elstub and Peter McLaverty, "Introduction: Issues and Cases in Deliberative Democracy," in *Deliberative Democracy: Issues and Cases*, ed. Stephen Elstub and Peter McLaverty (Edinburgh: Edinburgh University Press, 2014), 1–16.
50. *Essentials*, 2:733–39.
51. See *Digital Dictionary of Buddhism* (DDB), ed. Charles A. Muller, http://buddhism-dict.net/ddb, search words "羯磨" and "羯磨法."
52. This is an idealized representation of a karman. Little is known about how these ceremonies were actually implemented in premodern era. For a discussion on ceremony and format in Theravāda communities, see Oskar von Hinüber, "Buddhist Law According to the Theravāda-Vinaya: A Survey of Theory and Practice," *Journal of the International Association of Buddhist Studies* 18, no. 1 (1995): 7–45.
53. This is a very idealized version of how a monastic community should function. In reality, there were often unresolvable disputes that required interventions of worldly power (e.g., kings, ministers). For details on the development of monastic legal thought and legal codes, see von Hinüber, "Buddhist Law According to the Theravāda-Vinaya." For our purposes here, it is enough to note that such a seed of republicanism existed and functioned in the earliest monastic codes and has since become the kernel of truth for the modern invention of Dharmic democracy.
54. *Essentials*, 2:739. T.1499.24.1106b16. However, Lü omitted the specific procedures and claimed confession as similar to what a *bhikṣu* does in communal repentance.
55. For Vasubandhu's hermeneutic theory, see, for example, Sonam Kachru, "Minds and Worlds: A Philosophical Commentary on the 'Twenty Verses' of Vasubandhu" (PhD diss., University of Chicago, 2015), 10–12, 22–25.
56. A representative and still influential text on this topic is Śāntideva's *Bodhicaryāvatāra* (A Guide to the Bodhisattva's Way of Life; Ch: *Ru pusaxing lun* 入菩薩行論) written around 700 CE. While social good and common well-being are central in this text, the orientation is about the psychological transformation. Śāntideva's text is in contrast to Lü's theory that links psychological training with the clear guidelines for social actions to dismantle bastions of privilege and to establish justice and equality. See Śāntideva, *The Bodhicaryāvatāra*, trans. Kate Crosby and Andrew Skilton (Oxford: Oxford University Press, 1998).
57. Ouyang and Lü agree on this point. For Ouyang's view, see *Essentials*, 3:61–64. For Lü's view, see *Xuanji1991*, 2:593, 624–25.
58. Lü, *Xinbian hanwen dazangjing* 新编汉文大藏経目录, *Xuanji1991*, 3:1626.
59. *Essentials*, 3:61–63. Note that while both Ouyang and Lü followed *Msg* traditional sectioning, they added their own interpretation of how these eleven sections function and connect to one another.
60. *Xuanji1991*, 2:956–58, 962–63, 966–67. For Lü's critique of original enlightenment, see also *Xuanji1991*, 2:1143–44.
61. *Xuanji1991*, 2:957–58; 2:975–77.
62. *Xuanji1991*, 2:1018–20.
63. *Xuanji1991*, 2:1022.

64. I discuss Lü's "organized skepticism" in chapter 6. For now, it suffices to say it is a collaborative practice wherein (1) participants examine the evidence and methods collectively and (2) they do it from a position of distrust (i.e., the burden of proof is on the person/group with a new claim).
65. *Xuanji1991*, 2:1025; 2:1026–30.
66. For just-war theories in India, see, for example, Matthew Kosuta, "Ethics of War and Ritual: The Bhagavad-Gita and Mahabharata as Test Cases," *Journal of Military Ethics* 19, no. 3 (2020): 186–200.
67. Martin Kern, trans., "Imperial Tours and Mountain Inscriptions," in *The First Emperor: China's Terracotta Army*, ed. Jane Portal (Cambridge, MA: Harvard University Press, 2007), 110.
68. This story itself appeared rather late but has been widely circulated. For details, see Rhys Davids, *Buddhist India*, 10–12.
69. Lü's proposal for a nonhierarchical complex society was merely one of many throughout history. For a powerful argument for the Indus Valley egalitarianism, see Adam S. Green, "Killing the Priest-King: Addressing Egalitarianism in the Indus Civilization," *Journal of Archaeological Research* 29 (2021): 153–202. For an extensive study of the Amerindian egalitarianism from the 1000s to today, see Kathleen Duval, *Native Nations: A Millennium of North America* (New York: Random House, 2024).
70. However, the nationalist monopolization of the meaning of revolution occurred much earlier in the Nanjing Decade; see, for example, Brian Tsui, *China's Conservative Revolution: The Quest for a New Order, 1927–1949* (Cambridge: Cambridge University Press, 2018), 26–67.
71. Zhe Ji, "Secularization as Religious Restructuring: Statist Institutionalization of Chinese Buddhism and Its Paradoxes," in *Chinese Religiosities: Afflictions of Modernity and State Formation*, ed. Mayfair Mei-hui Yang (Berkeley: University of California Press, 2008), 233–60.
72. For an overview of how the political environment made the corporation the preferred model of Buddhist organizations in Taiwan, see Charles B. Jones, *Buddhism in Taiwan: Religion and the State, 1660–1990* (Honolulu: University of Hawai'i Press, 1999), 189–98.
73. *Xuanji1991*, 3:1334.
74. *Xuanji1991*, 3:1338.
75. See, for example, Alcorta R. Sosis, "Signaling, Solidarity, and the Sacred: The Evolution of Religious Behavior," *Evolutionary Anthropology* 12, no. 6 (2003): 264–74. See also Tamás Dávid-Barrett and James Carney, "The Deification of Historical Figures and the Emergence of Priesthoods as a Solution to a Network Coordination Problem," *Religion, Brain & Behavior* 6, no. 4 (2016): 307–17.
76. This violent logic still reproduces itself in many anti-oppression movements as well as states' responses to them. For a case study in contemporary India and the haunting question Shah raised, "Is it not often the case that the power flowing from the barrel of your gun will reproduce the very systems that you are trying to extinguish," see Alpa Shah, *Nightmarch: Among India's Revolutionary Guerrillas* (Chicago: University of Chicago Press, 2019), 36, 105. At the same time, efforts to revive the early Buddhist spiritual republicanism also continue. For a more recent articulation on why good friends are seen as the "entire holy life" and evidence for egalitarian social arrangements in both early Buddhism and contemporary engaged Buddhists, see Hsiao-Lan Hu, *This-Worldly Nibbāna: A Buddhist-Feminist Social Ethics for Peacemaking in the Global Community* (Albany: State University of New York Press, 2011), 42–61.

6. Scholarship for Salvation

1. Leigh K. Jenco, "Introduction: On the Possibility of Chinese Thought as Global Theory," in *Chinese Thought as Global Theory: Diversifying Knowledge Production in the Social Sciences and Humanities*, ed. Leigh K. Jenco (Albany: State University of New York Press, 2017), 1.
2. Charles Taylor, "Social Theory as Practice," in *Philosophical Papers*, vol. 2, *Philosophy and the Human Sciences* (Cambridge: Cambridge University Press, 2012), 98, 94.
3. Jenco, "Introduction," 1.
4. For an in-depth analysis of a small selection of these de-parochializing strategies and theories, see Leigh K. Jenco, *Changing Referents: Learning Across Space and Time in China and the West* (New York: Oxford University Press, 2015). Lü's path crossed with those of many of the figures in Jenco's study.
5. Helen E. Longino, *Science as Social Knowledge: Values and Objectivity in Scientific Inquiry* (Princeton, NJ: Princeton University Press, 1990), 216.
6. Jessica Zu, "*Adhipati*, Yogācāra Intersubjectivity, and Soteriology in Kuiji's Commentaries," *Sophia*, June 5, 2024. https://link.springer.com/article/10.1007/s11841-024-01019-9.
7. For how literature can be a way of doing philosophy, see Rafal K. Stepien, ed., *Buddhist Literature as Philosophy, Buddhist Philosophy as Literature* (Albany: State University of New York Press, 2020). For nontextual ways, such as performance, movement, art, and architecture, of doing philosophy, see, for example, Alexus McLeod, *An Introduction to Mesoamerican Philosophy* (Cambridge: Cambridge University Press, 2023), 40–45.
8. Many feminist philosophers have incisively argued for this obscuring effect of the idea of objectivity and its harmful implications. For a recent analysis of how universality functioned in Kant's racism and the insurmountable social implications brought by Kant's philosophizing from a location of power, see Huaping Lu-Adler, *Kant, Race, and Racism: Views from Somewhere* (New York: Oxford University Press, 2023), 238–40.
9. Jason Ānanda Josephson Storm, *Metamodernism: The Future of Theory* (Chicago: University of Chicago Press, 2021), 209–75.
10. Naomi Oreskes, *Why Trust Science* (Princeton, NJ: Princeton University Press, 2019), 57; Storm, *Metamodernism*, 273–74.
11. Takahiro Nakajima, "Grounding Normativity in Ritual," in Jenco, ed., *Chinese Thought as Global Theory*, 55–74.
12. For an analysis of how science was used as a means for social transformation by some civil society organizations in modern China, see Zuoyue Wang, "Saving China Through Science: The Science Society of China, Scientific Nationalism, and Civil Society in Republican China," *Osiris* 17, no. 1 (2002): 291–322.
13. For a succinct evaluation of reason and logic in early Indian Buddhism, see Richard F. Gombrich, *What the Buddha Thought* (London: Equinox, 2009), 161–79. For the soteriological import of logic and reason in the Mahāyāna path, see, for example, Śāntideva, *The Bodhicaryāvatāra*, trans. Kate Crosby and Andrew Skilton (Oxford: Oxford University Press, 1998), xx–xxvi.
14. Robert K. Merton, "The Normative Structure of Science," in *The Sociology of Science: Theoretical and Empirical Investigations*, ed. Norman W. Storer (Chicago: University of Chicago Press, 1973), 267-78; Naomi Oreskes, "Why We Should Trust Scientists," June 25, 2014, https://youtu.be/RxyQNEVOElU.
15. Lü, "Dachengjing bijiao dufa" 大乘經比較讀法, *Neixue* 1 (1924): 13–42.

16. Satō Taijun 佐藤泰舜, "Gendai Shina no bukkyō kenkyū ippan—Nankin nai gakuin hakkō no 'naigaku' ni tsuite" 現代支那の仏教研究一斑—南京内学院発行の「内学」に就て, *Shukyō kenkyū* 宗教研究 3, no. 6 (1926): 149–56. The three articles that Satō praised were all written by Lü: "Dachengjing bijiao dufa," "Report on Collating Saṃyuktāgama" 雜阿含經刊定記, and "On *Mahāyānasūtrālamkārakārikā* and the Old School of Yogācāra" 論莊嚴經論與唯識古學. According to the editor of the anthology, Li An 李安, Lü himself arranged the table of contents and decided what was to be included. See *Xuanji1991*, preface.
17. Lü, "Dachengjing bijiao dufa," 13.
18. Lü, "Dachengjing bijiao dufa," 13.
19. Note that Lü used a single phrase, *bijiao* 比較, to describe six out of the seven steps of cross-examination.
20. Lü, "Dachengjing bijiao dufa," 23–26.
21. Many scholars have examined this influential debate. For a well-organized summary of this issue and Lü's role in it, see, for example, Eyal Aviv, *Differentiating the Pearl from the Fish-Eye: Ouyang Jingwu and the Revival of Buddhist Scholasticism* (Leiden: Brill, 2020), 101–4. See also Chen-kuo Lin, "The Uncompromising Quest for Genuine Buddhism: Lü Cheng's Critique of Original Enlightenment," in *Transforming Consciousness: Yogācāra Thought in Modern China*, ed. John Makeham (New York: Oxford University Press, 2014), 359.
22. Lü did not publish anything directly related to this debate in the 1920s. All his essays on *Awakening Faith* were published in the 1950s or later.
23. Lü, "Dachengjing bijiao dufa," 35.
24. Lü, "Dachengjing bijiao dufa," 36–40. The first is the aforementioned *Aṅgulimālīya Sūtra* (T.120), which Lü used to prove the parallel development of Mahāyāna and Theravāda teachings. The other six are well-known Yogācāra and Tathāgatagarbha texts: *The Lion's Roar of Queen Śrīmālā* (T.353), *Tathāgatagarbha Sūtra* (T.666), *Laṅkāvatāra Sūtra* (T.672), *Mahāyānaghanavyūha Sūtra* (T.681), *Saṃdhi-nirmocana-sūtra* (T.676), and *Prajñāpāramitā-naya-śatapañcaśatikā* (T.261).
25. Lü, "Dachengjing bijiao dufa," 40. This line of argument and this way of doing philology are unacceptable in contemporary academia. As clearly explained by Lambert Schmithausen, given the plethora of close synonyms with "storehouse consciousness" and the problem of dating, it is impractical to conduct an exhaustive study (as Lü attempted to do in this short essay) that links this term—as both a distinctive label and an independent kind of consciousness (from six consciousnesses)—with its Śrāvakayānist and Mahāyānist precursors. Schmithausen settled on a much more modest pursuit of mapping out the contexts and possible causes of the birth of storehouse consciousness as a particular type of consciousness. See Lambert Schmithausen, *Ālayavijñāna: On the Origin and the Early Development of a Central Concept of Yogācāra Philosophy* (Tokyo: International Institute for Buddhist Studies, 1987), 9–10. Note, however, most Yogācāra texts identify *ādānavijñāna* (which is also translated as *zhishou shi* 執受識 and *zhichi shi* 執持識, both meaning "maintaining consciousness") with *ālayavijñāna*.
26. The topic is too broad to summarize here. For a well-organized literature review on the emergence of original enlightenment in the Chinese context, see Jacqueline I. Stone, *Original Enlightenment and the Transformation of Medieval Japanese Buddhism* (Honolulu: University of Hawai'i Press, 1999), 3–10. In 1943, when Lü directly criticized Xiong Shili's 熊十力 (1885–1968) "new" Yogācāra, he recycled and defended his 1924 findings. Note that there is no evidence for Lü's direct involvement in the debate about Xiong Shili's *Xin weishi lun* 新唯

識論 (A new treatise on consciousness-only) when it was first published in 1932. However, after Ouyang passed away in February 1943, Lü was angered by Xiong's disrespect of Ouyang and wrote a few private letters to Xiong. Lü's earliest publication on this topic was a May 1949 article in a journal sponsored by an institute established by Liang Shuming; see Lü Cheng, "*Qixin* yu *Lengqie*"《起信》與《楞伽》, *Mianren wenxueyuan yuankan* 1 (1949): 1–5.

27. For an English translation of the letters between Lü Cheng and Xiong Shili on original quiescence and original enlightenment, see Lin, "Lü Cheng's Uncompromising Quest for Genuine Buddhism," 360–74.
28. Wang Zhixin, *Jidujiao zhi Foxue yanjiu* 基督教之佛學研究 (Shanghai: Shanghai guangxuehui, 1924), 53.
29. Lü Cheng, "Za'ahanjing kanding ji" 雜阿含經刊定記, *Neixue* 1 (1924): 223–42.
30. Mukai Akira 向井亮, "Yugashichiron no setsukotobun to Zatsuagongyō" 『瑜伽師地論』の摂事分と『雜阿含経』, *Hokkaidō Daigaku bungakubu kiyō* 北海道大學文學部紀要 33, no. 2 (1985): 1–41.
31. See, for example, Masaharu Anesaki, "The Four Buddhist Āgamas in Chinese: A Concordance of Their Parts and of the Corresponding Counterparts in the Pāli Nikāyas," *Transaction of the Asiatic Society of Japan* 35, no. 3 (1908): 1–148. Anesaki published a series of preliminary studies on similar topics before this article, trying to reorganize Chinese Āgamas according to Pāli Nikāyas.
32. Regarding contemporary scholarship on this topic, one methodological issue was the circular logic of using *Yogācārabhūmi* to organize Āgama and then using the two concepts' relation to prove the authenticity of Yogācāra; see Bhikkhu Anālayo, *A Comparative Study of the Majjhima-nikāya* (Taipei: Dharma Drum, 2011), 2:697n69. Here Anālayo cites Monk Yinshun's work on Āgamas, but Yinshun based his research on Lü Cheng's findings. It is important to point out that Lü only argued for a historical continuity, that is, *Yogācārabhūmi* derived its doctrines from one transmission of Āgamas, which he later identified as Mahīśāsaka.
33. For a summary of the philosophical conversation on how Yogācāra addressed early Buddhist (including Abhidharmic and early Mahāyānist) concerns, see William Waldron, *Making Sense of Mind Only: Why Yogācāra Buddhism Matters* (Somerville, MA: Wisdom Publications, 2023), 309–13.
34. Dan Lusthaus, "Lü Cheng, Epistemology, and Genuine Buddhism," in Makeham, ed., *Transforming Consciousness*, 317–42.
35. Lü Cheng, "Xianyang shengjiao lun dayi" 顯揚聖教論大意, *Neixue* 1 (1924): 87–105. For the still-contested relation between this text and *Yogācārabhūmi*, see Schmithausen, *Ālayavijñāna*, 261n99.
36. Lü, "Xianyang shengjiao lun dayi," 104–5.
37. Lü saw all words as mere translations; see Lü, *Fodian fanlun* 佛典汎論 (Shanghai: Commercial Press, 1925), fols. 5–9. In these pages Lü analyzes the possible language spoken by the Buddha, the languages that his disciples used to recite sūtras and vinayas, and the languages that might have been used in the first and second *Saṅgītī* (assembly) when the Buddha's teachings became standardized. For Lü's praise of the quality of Chinese translations, see Lü, *Fodian fanlun*, fol. 17. Note that this is qualified praise; he offers it only after pointing out the myriad complications in Chinese translational practices; see Lü, *Fodian fanlun*, fols. 12–17. Lü makes similar comments in his 1926 booklet; see Lü Cheng, *Fojiao yanjiu fa* 佛教研究法 (Shanghai: Commercial Press, 1926), fol. 4. These evaluations of the Chinese translations are taken directly from Fukaura Seibun's work, which was first published as various

journal articles in the early 1920s and later collected into a monograph; see Fukaura Seibun 深浦正文, *Bukkyō kenkyhō* 佛教研究法 (Tokyo: Seishin shobō, 1963), 36–37.

38. Lü's uses of *li* 理, *zhi* 智, and *hui* 慧 are complex, but they all convey a sense of nondualistic knowing. There are many Sanskrit terms that were translated as either *zhi* 智 or *hui* 慧 or a combination of these two terms with many other qualifiers in different doctrinal systems. This complicated translation history is compounded by different processes of indigenization in Chinese commentaries that extend the Sanskrit senses of *prajñā*, *jñāna*, and *vidyā* to a Chinese system of wisdom and knowledge. Furthermore, Lü extended the Chinese terms by imbuing them with Western senses of rationality, intelligence, judgment, and reason. It is beyond the scope of this chapter to disentangle all these layers of meanings. I only highlight the general pattern and main strategy in *Five Disciplines*, where Lü interfaced these Buddhist terms with a modern sense of criticism.
39. *Xuanji1991*, 2:617–18; 2:628; 2:640; 2:641–42.
40. *Xuanji1991*, 2:617–18; 2:1042–43.
41. *Xuanji1991*, 2:617; 2:1043. There are Pāli sources that portray Buddhaghoṣa as Bodhisattva Maitreya. Maitreya is seen as the founder of Yogācāra in Chinese transmission. See Henry Clarke Warren and Dharmananda Kosambi, ed. *Visuddhimagga of Buddhaghosāchariya* (Cambridge, MA: Harvard University Press, 1950), xii–xiii.
42. *Xuanji1991*, 2:617–18.
43. *Xuanji1991*, 2:618; 2:628.
44. *Xuanji1991*, 2:628.
45. Lü, "Jilianglun jieben" 集量論釋節本, *Xuanji1991*, 1:176–243. This text has been digitized and can be accessed at http://tripitaka.cbeta.org/zh-cn/B09n0037_001. *Compendium of Validities* (Skt: *Pramāṇasamuccaya*) is a key text on Buddhist logic whose Chinese translation and Sanskrit original have been lost. In 1937, Lü selectively translated some passages from a version preserved in the Tibetan Narthang Canon housed in Beijing Library; see *Xuanji1991*, 1:178.
46. *Xuanji1991*, 2:641.
47. *Apoha* is a well-studied subject. See, for example, Mark Siderits, Tom Tillemans, and Arindam Chakrabarti, eds., *Apoha: Buddhist Nominalism and Human Cognition* (New York: Columbia University Press, 2011).
48. *Xuanji1991*, 2:641. Lü never had the opportunity to lecture on these texts; therefore, I can comment only on how he hoped *apoha* and democratic deliberation to work.
49. *Xuanji1991*, 2:641–42.
50. *Xuanji1991*, 2:642. This lecture was dated to October 1, 1943, seven months after Ouyang passed away.
51. Wang, *Jidujiao zhi Foxue yanjiu*, 89–90, 95, 53, 57, 73.
52. Holmes Welch, *The Buddhist Revival in China* (Cambridge, MA: Harvard University Press, 1968), 117–20, 268.
53. Lü, "Wo de jingli yu Neixuyuan fazhan licheng" 我的经历与内学院发展历程, ed. Gao Shanshan 高山杉, *Shijie zhexue* 3 (2007): 85.
54. These thoughts appeared as a series of lecture notes in 1953–54; see Lü, *Xuanji1991*, 3:1330–79.
55. *Xuanji1991*, 3:1347, 1333–40; *Xuanji1991*, 3:1370.
56. Dorji Wangchuk, "A Typology of Bodhicitta," in *The Resolve to Become a Buddha* (Tokyo: International Institute for Buddhist Studies, 2007), 195–234. Wangchuk maps out five ideal types of *bodhicitta*: ethico-spiritual, gnoseological, ontological, psycho-physical, and semiological.
57. Merton, "Normative Structure of Science," 267–78.

58. Note that Merton's and Lü's views of "universalism" differ. The resemblances are limited to the structures or the processes of institutionalization of collective behavioral patterns.
59. Merton, "Normative Structure of Science," 267–78; Merton, "Science and the Social Order," in *Sociology of Science*, 264–66.
60. Oreskes, *Why Trust Science*, 51–54.
61. Oreskes, *Why Trust Science*, 263n91.
62. Jessica Zu, "Objective Humanities, Reflexive Humanities," *Religious Studies Review* 48, no. 4 (2022): 501–4.
63. Jonathan C. Gold, *The Dharma's Gatekeepers: Sakya Paṇḍita on Buddhist Scholarship in Tibet* (Albany: State University of New York Press, 2007), 64, 76–89.
64. T.1579.30.486b13; T.1579.30.486b13. For a brief introduction to these terms, see DDB, search terms "世間極成" and "道理極成."
65. T.1585.14c25–15a17.
66. For Sthiramati's understanding of intersubjectivity, see Roy Tzohar, *A Yogācāra Theory of Metaphor* (New York: Oxford University Press, 2018), 178–208.
67. The Chinese language rarely distinguishes singular from plural nouns; however, in this particular line, the character *zhu* 諸 makes it clear that what follows is a plural noun. My translation follows the interpretation of Xuanzang's subcommentary, T.1585.38c19–21, and Kuiji's commentary, T.1830.487a17–26.
68. T.1585.38c19–21. Dharmapāla's theorization of consciousness is a bit more complicated. It is a four-part system. For a brief introduction to this doctrine, see DDB, search term "四分." For a brief explanation of the soteriological significance of the two parts related to self-consciousness, see Jingjing Li, "From Self-Attaching to Self-Emptying: An Investigation of Xuanzang's Account of Self-Consciousness," *Open Theology* 3, no. 1 (2017): 184–97.
69. *Essentials*, 4:704n3. Lü also duly noted the key doctrinal interpretation in the verses; see *Essentials*, 4:703n2.
70. Methodologically speaking, I find it more fruitful to investigate why and how a term or a passage or a concept has been translated differently. This is because the unsaid premise of the question of accuracy is that it is possible to find a uniform standard in translation, which will inevitably obscure other relevant questions such as who decides what counts as right or wrong and why and how that standard becomes accepted as such. In his writing Lü himself is very attentive to all variants of translations and refrains from simply marking some translations as right and others as wrong. For example, Lü points out that Xuanzang's translation represented a later development stemming from Dharmapāla's interpretation of Yogācāra (晚起變本之說); see *Xuanji1991*, 1:57. On the different terms for consciousness-only, Lü is quite careful in laying out the historical changes in the interpretation of these terms. In an earlier interlinear note, Lü clearly points out the historical evolution from vijñapti- to vijñāna-mātra. See *Essentials*, 4:589n5. The original Chinese reads 唯識原名唯了別者意當於此 (*Vijñāna-mātra* is originally named *vijñapti-mātra*, whose meaning should be as such).
71. For Yogācāra as idealism, see Dharmapāla, Xuanzang, and Louis de la Vallée Poussin, *Vijñaptimātratāsiddhi: La Siddhi de Hiuan-Tsang* (Paris: P. Geuthner, 1928–29).
72. Dan Lusthaus, *Buddhist Phenomenology: A Philosophical Investigation of Yogācāra Buddhism and the Ch'eng Wei-Shih Lun* (New York: Routledge Curzon, 2002), 434–37, 442, 487–91.
73. Roy Tzohar, "The Buddhist Philosophical Conception of Intersubjectivity: An Introduction," *Sophia* 58, no. 1 (2019): 57–60. For a robust defense of Yogācāra as phenomenology and cognitive constructivism, see Waldron, *Making Sense of Mind Only*.

74. See, for example, *Essentials*, 4:565n10, 589n5. In addition, Lü thoroughly documented all instances in which the Chinese translation of *vijñapti* (*liaobie* 了別) could be confused with translations of completely different terms such as *upalabdhi* (*liaojing* 了境; Tib: *rig par byed pa* or *yul rnam par rig pa*) due to similarity in form and in doctrinal context; see *Essentials*, 4:658n2.
75. Lusthaus translates this sentence as "Therefore everything is 'only existent in consciousness' "; see Lusthaus, *Buddhist Phenomenology*, 439. I see the verb *you* 有 in Chinese function in a different way. *You*'s grammatical function resembles the Tibetan verb *yod*, in that the phrase "A 有 B" resembles "A *la* B *yod*." Both are translated as "There is B in A." Lusthaus's translation equates *you* 有 with "to be," a linking verb in English, and unnecessarily accentuates the ontological implications of this phrase.
76. Lusthaus translates *jicheng* 極成 as "ultimately established"; see Lusthaus, *Buddhist Phenomenology*, 439. I prefer "intersubjective agreement." In my reading, throughout *CWSL*, Xuanzang consistently uses *prasiddha* to indicate consensus by either worldly convention or reason. To be sure, when referring to the use of this term by the twenty Nikāya schools, *prasiddha* indeed means "ultimately established" because this is the Nikāya schools' consensus. When Xuanzang quotes the Nikāya schools, he follows this convention. However, one cannot uncritically apply this sense of *prasiddha* to Xuanzang's own system. The central tenet of Yogācāra philosophy is that what has been grasped as "ultimately established" by the Nikāya schools and Abhidharma literature merely appears so because of an underlying causal framework grounded in *ālayavijñāna*.
77. My point is substantiated by Kuiji's commentary immediately following the quotation from Xuanzang's treatise. In his commentary on this passage, Kuiji raises an objection to the doctrinal position of the twenty Nikāya schools, which says that because there exist ultimately established [things], the Yogācāra doctrines are not tenable. Kuiji offers his own refutation of this objection, which clarifies that *vijñaptimātra* (*weiyan* 唯言) only refutes the existence of things outside consciousness and because suchness and mental functions are not separate from consciousness, they all have a body (*gu ti jieyou* 故體皆有). This interpretation suggests that the extant body (i.e., consciousness) is what has been mistaken for the ultimately existing body of things outside consciousness.
78. *Essentials*, 4:705nn1–2.
79. T.1585.39a5–6. *Essentials*, 4:705.
80. For a recent study on this topic, see Jay L. Garfield and Jan Westerhoff, eds., *Madhyamaka and Yogācāra: Allies or Rivals?* (New York: Oxford University Press, 2015). On how this debate played out in Xuanzang's lineage, see Mitsukawa Toyoki 光川豊芸, "*Daijō shōchin ron* kanken: Chūgan, Yuishiki kōshō ni okeru ichishiten toshite" 「大乘掌珍論」管見一中觀・瑜伽交涉における一視點として, *Indogaku bukkyōgaku kenkyū* 13, no. 2 (1965): 613–18.
81. *Essentials*, 4:707n3. T.1585.39b27–c9; 4:495n3. *Viṃśika*: cittaṃ mano vijñānaṃ vijñaptiś ceti paryāyāḥ; Xuanzang's translation reads "xin yi shi liao, ming zhi chabie" 心意識了名之差別, suggesting that *citta*, *manas*, *vijñāna*, and *vijñapti* are different names for the same phenomenon.
82. See, for example, *Xuanji1991*, 2:889–90, 1234. Note that on these occasions, Lü consistently links *yuktiprasiddha* with *zhenshi* 真實 (truth/reality).
83. These include three essays on Buddhist logic published in *Neixue* and later collected into his anthology of Buddhist studies; see *Xuanji1991*, 1:151–243.
84. *Xuanji1991*, 2:598, 626, 881, 920–921, 935, 975.

85. Lü cited *Yogācārabhūmi* T.1579.30.288b28 to support his interpretation of *sishi* (Skt. *āhāra-catuṣka* or *catvāra āhārāḥ*).
86. Lü, "Fofa yu shijian" 佛法與世間, *Xuanji1991*, 1:443–44. He drew on many more scriptures to prove his interpretation of Xuanzang's Yogācāra causal theory (e.g., T.1599.31.0452c16 and T.1599.31.0453a21). In *Five Disciplines* Lü constantly refers to this retelling of Yogācāra causal enframing to justify the relation between scholarship and activism.
87. Waldron identifies Four Noble Truths as a way of modeling causal relations. See Waldron, *Making Sense of Mind Only*, 22–25.
88. MN 9, PTS I 46–55. For an English translation of this text, see Bhikkhu Bodhi, "Majjhima Nikāya, 9. Right View," https://suttacentral.net/mn9/en/bodhi.
89. There is an intermediate step. In sixth-century China, nirvāṇa, the soteriological goal, was reinterpreted as permanence, joy, (genuine) ego, and purity. See Wendi L. Adamek, "Nirvāṇa as Permanence, Joy, Self and Purity in a Medieval Chinese Buddhist Context," unpublished manuscript. Lü combined the early ways of modeling worldly causal relations with the Chinese refashioning of nirvāṇa and reinterpreted four nutrients as social reality.
90. *Xuanji1991*, 1:447.
91. All quotations in this paragraph are from Lü, "Yuanqi yu shixiang" 緣起與實相, *Xuanji1991*, 3:1363.
92. *Xuanji1991*, 3:1363–64.
93. Lü, "Guanxing yu zhuanyi" 觀行與轉依, *Xuanji1991*, 3:1374–75.
94. *Xuanji1991*, 3:1379.
95. David Chidester, *Empire of Religion: Imperialism and Comparative Religion* (Chicago: University of Chicago Press, 2014), xviii.
96. Thomas Nagel, *The View from Nowhere* (New York: Oxford University Press, 1986), 70–71. *Xuanji1991*, 1:435.
97. *Xuanji1991*, 1:442–43.
98. Lü emphasized the social function of inner learning on multiple occasions in 1943-46; see, for example, *Xuanji1991*, 1:414, 438–39, 443, 448–53.
99. Sheldon Pollock, "Crisis in the Classics," *Social Research: An International Quarterly* 78, no. 1 (2011): 39.
100. One central Madhyamaka argument against realism is that everything is illusory. Even Nāgārjuna's famous statement that "everything is emptiness" is also empty, that is, the truth of the statement itself is void of substantial existence or is interconditioned upon other illusions. Texts attributed to Nāgārjuna often explain this self-referential paradox in terms of its heuristic efficacy; see Jan Westerhoff, *The Dispeller of Disputes: Nāgārjuna's Vigrahavyāvartanī* (Oxford: Oxford University Press, 2010), 27–29.
101. Anālayo, *Satipaṭṭhāna: The Direct Path to Realization* (Cambridge: Windhorse Publications, 2004), 163.

Not a Coda

1. Jessica Zu, "Ouyang Jingwu's *Must-Read Buddhist Classics for Laity*: Body Politics and Gendered Soteriology," *Journal of Chinese Religions* 47, no. 1 (2019): 62–63, 73, 78.
2. Matthew Desmond, *Poverty, by America* (New York: Crown, 2023), 44.

3. Vanessa R. Sasson, "When Women Showed Up," *Tricycle*, May 26, 2023, https://tricycle.org/article/first-female-buddhist/.
4. I am borrowing Stephanie Balkwill's wording here. Her argument focuses on the all-female networks of support that Buddhist monasticism afforded to women in sixth-century China. I personally think it is a worthy scholarly project to investigate what opportunities such an all-female network of court might have opened up for women ensnared in the sexual politics of different Buddhist countries throughout history. See Stephanie Balkwill, *The Women Who Ruled China: Buddhism, Multiculturalism, and Governance in the Sixth Century* (Berkeley: University of California Press, 2024), 105–6.
5. Yuan Yuan, "Chinese Buddhist Nuns in the Twentieth Century: A Case Study in Wuhan," *Journal of Global Buddhism* 10 (2009): 388–89.
6. Soma, "Somātherīgāthā," *Therīgāthā* 3.8, SuttaCentral, https://suttacentral.net/thig3.8/pli/ms.
7. Fang Zuyou 方祖猷 and Wang Jietang 王介堂, eds., *Zhang Ruzhao jushi ji* 張汝釗居士集 (Beijing: Zongjiao wenhua chubanshe, 2017), 92.
8. Fang and Wang, *Zhang Ruzhao jushi ji*, 94.
9. Jessica Zu, "Three Plays and a Shared Socio-Spiritual Horizon in the Modern Buddhist Revivals in India and China," *International Journal of Asian Studies* 19, no. 2 (2022): 233.
10. Feminist scholarship on the gender issue in premodern East Asian Buddhism is rich. For a recent reflexive study of the subfield and how feminist scholarship can shed new light on ancient texts, see Stephanie Balkwill, "Disappearing and Disappeared Daughters in Medieval Chinese Buddhism: Sūtras on Sex Transformation and an Intervention into Their Transmission History," *History of Religions* 60, no. 4 (2021): 255–86. For studies of the mainstream Buddhist view of gender and family in modern China, see, for example, Zu, "Ouyang Jingwu's *Must-Read Buddhist Classics for Laity*." See also Paul Katz, "Chen Hailiang's Vision of Buddhist Family Life: A Preliminary Study," *Journal of Chinese Religions* 47, no. 1 (2019): 33–60. For an excellent review of existing scholarship on religion and gender in modern China, see Xiaofei Kang, "Women, Gender, and Religion in Modern China: 1900s–1950s: An Introduction," *Nan Nü* 19 (2017): 1–27.
11. Elise A. DeVido, "The Influence of Chinese Master Taixu on Buddhism in Vietnam," *Journal of Global Buddhism* 10 (2015): 413–58.
12. bell hooks, *Teaching to Transgress: Education as the Practice of Freedom* (New York: Routledge, 2014), 14.
13. James D. Kirylo, "Chapter Seven: Liberation Theology and Paulo Freire," *Counterpoints* 385 (2011): 167–93.
14. hooks, *Teaching to Transgress*, 14–15.
15. hooks, *Teaching Critical Thinking: Practical Wisdom* (New York: Routledge, 2012), 20, 186.
16. hooks, *Teaching Critical Thinking*, 45. She reiterates this point in *Teaching to Transgress*, 46, 148–49.
17. hooks, *Teaching to Transgress*, 14, 53–54. My emphasis.
18. hooks, *Teaching to Transgress*, 49. My emphasis.
19. hooks, *Teaching to Transgress*, 56.
20. For consciousness-only thought in Thich Nhat Hanh, see Trent Walker, "Cognition's Embrace: Yogācāra Themes in the Writings of Thích Nhất Hạnh," *Berkeley Student Journal of Asian Studies* 6 (2016): 109–37. For Thich Nhat Hanh's theory of karma, see Alexander Soucy,

"Individual and Collective Karma in the Works of Thích Nhất Hanh," *Journal of Vietnamese Studies* 19, no. 1 (2024): 77–108.

21. Larry Ward, *America's Racial Karma: An Invitation to Heal* (Berkeley: Parallax Press, 2020), 88. My emphasis. For a contextualized analysis of Ward's Yogācāra in American Buddhism, see Jessica Zu, "Liberation Buddhology for Postracial Worldmaking," *Religious Studies Review* 50, no. 1 (2024): 119–29.
22. Larry Ward and Julie Flynn Badal, "*America's Racial Karma*: Buddhist Teacher Larry Ward's New Book Invites Us to Heal from the Karma of Racism," *Tricycle*, September 22, 2020, https://tricycle.org/article/larry-ward-racial-karma/. My emphasis.
23. Sally Haslanger, "Racism, Ideology, and Social Movements," *Res Philosophica* 94, no. 1 (2017): 16.
24. Haslanger, "Racism, Ideology, and Social Movements," 17.
25. Huaping Lu-Adler, *Kant, Race, and Racism: Views from Somewhere* (New York: Oxford University Press, 2023), 321.
26. Haslanger, "Racism, Ideology, and Social Movements," 15–16, 10.

Bibliography

Primary Sources

Anesaki, Masaharu. "The Four Buddhist Āgamas in Chinese: A Concordance of Their Parts and of the Corresponding Counterparts in the Pāli Nikāyas." *Transaction of the Asiatic Society of Japan* 35, no. 3 (1908): 1-148.

Besant, Annie. *Karma*. Chennai: Theosophical Publishing House, 1895.

Blavatsky, Helena Petrovna. *The Key to Theosophy: A Clear Exposition in the Form of Question and Answer of the Ethics, Science, and Philosophy for the Study of Which the Theosophical Society Has Been Founded*. London: Theosophical Publishing Company, 1889.

Buddhadāsa, Bikkhu. *Dhammic Socialism*, trans. Donald K. Swearer, with a preface by Prawase Wasi. 2nd ed. Bangkok: Thai Inter-Religious Commission for Development, 1993.

Césaire, Aimé. *Discours sur le colonialism*. 4th ed. Paris: Présence Africaine, 1955.

Cheena Bhavana Library Collection, Viśva-Bhārati University.

Fang Zuyou 方祖猷 and Wang Jietang 王介堂, eds. *Zhang Ruzhao jushi ji* 張汝釗居士集 (Anthology of lay practitioner Zhang Ruzhao). Beijing: Zongjiao wenhua chubanshe, 2017.

Fukaura Seibun 深浦正文. *Bukkyō kenkyūhō* 佛教研究法 (Methodologies in studying Buddhism). Tokyo: Seishin shobō, 1963.

Guyau, Jean-Marie. *L'art au point de vue sociologique*. Paris: Félix Alcan Éditeur, 1889.

——. *Les problèmes de l'esthétique contemporaine*. 6th ed. Paris: F. Alcan, 1904.

He Manzi 河滿子. "Huang Jusu bie zhuan bu" 黃居素別傳補 (Additions to a supplementary biography of Huang Jusu). *Shehui ribao*, March 16, 1931, 1.

Helmholtz, Herman. "On the Relation of Optics to Painting." *Humboldt Library of Popular Science Literature* 1, no. 24 (1881): 1–9.

Huxley, Thomas H. "Evolution and Ethics: The Romanes Lecture" (1894). In *Collected Essays*, vol. 9, *Evolution & Ethics and Other Essays*, 46–116. London, 1893–94.

Li Jinxi 黎錦熙. "Weimojie jing jiwen ba" 維摩詰經紀聞跋 (Notes on hearing the lectures of *Vimalakīrti Sūtra*). *Minduo* 民鐸 3, no. 1 (1921): 1–6.

Li Shicen 李石岑. "Xiandai zhexue zaiping—Duwei yu Luosu, Luosu yu Bogesen, Bogesen yu Wokeng" 現代哲學再評—杜威與羅素, 羅素與柏格森, 柏格森與倭鏗 (Miscellaneous comments on modern philosophy—Dewey and Russell, Russell and Bergson, Bergson and Eucken). *Minduo* 民鐸 2, no. 4 (1921): 1–4.

Lü Cheng 呂澂. "Bogesen zhexue yu weishi" 柏格森哲學與唯識 (Bergsonian philosophy and Yogācāra). *Minduo* 民鐸3, no. 1 (December 1921): 1–6.

——. [Chengshu 澄叔]. "Liboshi meixue dayao" 栗泊士美學大要 (Essentials of Lippsian aesthetics). *Dongfang zazhi* 東方雜誌17, no. 5 (1920): 69–75.

——. "Dachengjing bijiao dufa" 大乘經比較讀法 (Comparative hermeneutics in reading Mahāyāna Sūtras), *Neixue* 內學1 (1924): 13–42.

——. *Fodian fanlun* 佛典汎論 (A summary of Buddhist scriptures). Shanghai: Commercial Press, 1925.

——. *Fojiao yanjiu fa* 佛教研究法 (Methodologies in studying Buddhism). Shanghai: Commercial Press, 1926.

——. "Guan suoyuan shilun huiyi" 觀所緣釋論會譯 (A comparative exposition of the [Chinese and Tibetan] translations of the *Ālambana-parīkṣa*). *Neixue* 內學4 (1927): 1–33.

——. *Guohua jiaocai gailun* 國畫教材概論 (A summary of textbooks of Chinese painting). Shanghai: Zhonghua [Chunghwa] shuju, 1927.

——. *LC: Lü Cheng foxue zhuzuoji* LC 呂澂佛學著作集 (LC: A collection of Lü Cheng's Buddhist studies essays), http://cbeta.buddhism.org.hk/catalog/LC%20呂澂佛學著作集.

——. "Lun 'Zhuangyan jinlun' yu weishi guxue" 論《莊嚴經論》與唯識古學 (On *Mahāyānasūtrālamkārakārikā* and the old school of Yogācāra), *Neixue* 內學1 (1924): 203–22.

——. "Meishu chengxing zhi jingguo" 美術成形之經過 (Processes of the formation of art). *Shanxisheng jiaoyuhui zazhi* 山西省教育會雜誌9, no. 1 (January 1923): 50–58.

——. "Meishu fazhan de tujing" 美術發展的途徑 (Paths of aesthetic development). *Meishu* 美術3, no. 2 (May 1922): 15–35.

——. "Meishu geming" 美術革命 (Aesthetic revolution). *Xin qingnian* 新青年 6, no. 1 (January 1919): 84–86.

——. *Meixue gailun* 美學概論 (A summary of aesthetics). Shanghai: Commercial Press, 1923.

——. *Meixue qianshuo* 美學淺說 (An elementary introduction of aesthetics). Shanghai: Commercial Press, 1923.

——. "*Qixin* yu *Lengqie*"《起信》與《楞伽》(*Awakening Faith* and *Laṅkāvatāra Sūtra*). *Mianren wenxuyuan yuankan* 勉仁文學院院刊1 (1949): 1–5.

——. *Secaixue gangyao* 色彩學綱要 (An outline of the theory of colors). Shanghai: Commercial Press, 1926.

——. "Shicen wuxiong zuoyou" 石岑吾兄左右 (To my elder brother Shicen). *Jiaoyu zazhi* 教育雜誌14, no. 1 (January 1922): 1–4.

——. "Wanjin de meixueshuo he meide yuanli, wu zhi qi" 晚近的美學說和美的原理, 五之七 (Recent aesthetic theories and aesthetic principles, five to seven). *Jiaoyu zazhi* 教育雜誌14, no. 3 (March 1922): 1–11.

——. "Wanjin de meixueshuo he meide yuanli, yi zhi si" 晚近的美學說和美的原理，一之四 (Recent aesthetic theories and aesthetic principles, one to four). *Jiaoyu zazhi* 教育雜誌14, no. 2 (February 1922): 1–12.

——. *Wanjin meixue sichao* 晚近美學思潮 (Recent trends in aesthetics). Shanghai: Commercial Press, 1924.

——. "Wo de jingli yu Neixuyuan fazhan licheng" 我的经历与内学院发展历程 (My autobiography and the development of the Inner Learning Institute). Ed. Gao Shanshan 高山杉. *Shijie zhexue* 世界哲學3 (2007): 77–79, 86.

——. *Xiandai meixue sichao* 現代美學思潮 (Modern trends in aesthetics). Shanghai: Commercial Press, 1934.

——. "Xianyang shengjiao lun dayi" 顯揚聖教論大意 (Main points of *Acclamation of the Holy Teaching*). *Neixue* 內學1 (1924): 87–105.

——. *Xinbian hanwen dazangjing mulu* 新编汉文大藏経目录 (A new catalog of the Chinese Buddhist canon). Jinan: Qilu shushe, 1980.

——. *Xiyang meishu shi* 西洋美術史 (The history of Western arts). Shanghai: Commercial Press, 1922.

——. *Yindu fojiao shi luo* 印度佛教史略 (A brief history of Indian Buddhism). Shanghai: Commercial Press, 1925.

——. "Yishu he meiyu" 藝術和美育 (Art and aesthetic education). *Jiaoyu zazhi* 教育雜誌14, no. 10 (October 1922): 1–8.

——. "Yishu piping de genju" 藝術批評的根據 (Standards of art critique). *Meishu* 美術2, no. 4 (March 1921): 1–3.

——. "Za'ahanjing kanding ji" 雜阿含經刊定記 (Report on collating *Saṃyuktāgama*). *Neixue* 內學1 (1924): 223–42.

——. *Zhongguo foxue yuanliu luejiang* 中國佛學源流略講 (A brief lecture on the origin and development of Chinese Buddhist studies). Beijing: Zhonghua shuju, 1979.

Lü Cheng 呂澂 and Chen Zhenru 陳真如. "Zhenru zuo shusuoyuanyuan yi" 真如作疏所緣緣義 (The meaning of Thusness as the indirectly perceived object). *Neixue* 內學1 (1924): 279–86.

Lü Cheng 呂澂, Shi Cunhou 釋存厚, Feng Zhuo 馮卓, and Liu Dingquan 劉定權. "Zhujia jieben tong long" 諸家戒本通論 (A comprehensive study of *prātimokṣa* in various sects). *Neixue* 內學3 (1926): 47–101.

Lü Cheng 呂澂 and Zhean Tang 唐哲安. "Guanyu 'yishu piping he chuangzuo' wenti taolun de jifengxin" 關於"藝術批評和創作"問題討論的幾封信 (Several letters on art critique and artistic creation). *Meishu* 美術3, no. 2 (May 1922): 153–63.

Ōnishi Yoshinori 大西克礼 and Ogata Tsunemasa 小方庸正, trans. *Shakaigaku jō yori mitaru geijutsu: Gyuiyō* 社会学上より見たる芸術: ギュイヨー (Art seen from a sociological point of view by Guyau). Tokyo: Iwanami Bunko, 1914.

Ouyang Jingwu 歐陽竟無. "Fofa fei zongjiao fei zhexue" 佛法非宗教非哲學 (Buddha Dharma is neither religion nor philosophy). *Guoxue daohang* 國學導航. http://www.guoxue123.com/new/0002/bfehyx/001.htm.

Pater, Walter. *The Renaissance: Studies in Art and Poetry*. 6th ed. London: Macmillan, 1901 [1873].

Satō Taijun 佐藤泰舜. "Gendai Shina no bukkyō kenkyū ippan — Nankin nai gakuin hakkō no 'naigaku' ni tsuite" 現代支那の仏教研究一斑—南京内学院発行の「内学」に就て (One bright spot of modern Chinese Buddhist research: With regard to *Inner Learning* published by Nanjing Inner Learning Institute). *Shukyō kenkyū* 宗教研究3, no. 6 (1926): 149–56.

Soma. "Somātherīgāthā." *Therīgāthā* 3.8. SuttaCentral. https://suttacentral.net/thig3.8/pli/ms.

Spencer, Herbert. *The Principles of Biology*, vol. 1. Rev. ed. New York: D. Appleton and Company, 1910 [1864].

——. *Social Statics, or, the Conditions Essential to Human Happiness Specified, and the First of Them Developed*. London: John Chapman, 1851.

——. *The Study of Sociology*. London: Henry S. King & Co., 1873.

Su Yuanlei 蘇淵雷. "Zhina Neixue zhi fazhan: Lü Qiuyi jushi xueshuo juyao" 支那內學之發展：呂秋一居士學說舉要 (The development of Chinese inner learning: A summary of Layman Lü Qiuyi's studies and theories). *Juexun* 覺訊 3, no. 8 (July 1949): 3.

Taixu 太虛. *Taixu dashi quanshu* 太虛大師全書 (Complete works of Master Taixu). *Zhonghua dianzang* 中華典藏. https://www.zhonghuadiancang.com/foxuebaodian/taixudashiquanshu/.

Vasubandhu. *Triṃśikāvijñapti*. https://www2.hf.uio.no/polyglotta/index.php.

Wang Enyang 王恩洋. "Chengli weishi yi" 成立唯識義 (Establishing the doctrine of consciousness-only). *Neixue* 內學 1 (1924): 147–68.

——. "Fofa wei jinshi suo bixu" 佛法為今時所必需 (Buddha Dharma is what the world needs now). *Guoxue daohang* 國學導航. http://www.guoxue123.com/new/0002/bfehyx/002.htm.

——. *Wang Enyang xiansheng lunzhuji* 王恩洋先生論著集 (Collected essays of Wang Enyang). Ed. Tang Zhongrong 唐仲容. 10 vols. Chengdu: Sichuan renmin chubanshe, 1999.

Wang Jitong 王季同. "Fofa yu kexue zhi bijiao" 佛法與科學之比較 (A comparative study of Buddhism and science). https://book.bfnn.org/books2/1275.htm.

——. *Makesi zhuyi pipan ji fulu—foxue licheng* 馬克思主義批判及附錄—佛學立場 (A critique of Marxism and appendixes: The Buddhist perspective). Suzhou: Suzhou jueshe 蘇州覺社, 1936.

Wang Zhixin 王治心. *Jidujiao zhi Foxue yanjiu* 基督教之佛學研究 (A Christian study of Buddhist learning). Shanghai: Shanghai guangxuehui, 1924.

Warren, Henry Clarke, and Dharmananda Kosambi, eds. *Visuddhimagga of Buddhaghosāchariya*. Cambridge, MA: Harvard University Press, 1950.

Yan Fu 嚴復. *Yan Fu Quanji* 嚴復全集 (Complete works of Yan Fu). Ed. Wang Zhenglu 汪征魯, Fang Baochuan 方寶川, and Ma Yong 馬勇. 11 vols. Fuzhou: Fujian jiaoyu chubanshe, 2014.

Yao Binbin 姚彬彬. "1921–1922 nian Zhang Taiyan, Lü Cheng, Li Jinxi lunxue shujian kaoshi" 1921–1922 年章太炎，呂澂，黎錦熙論學書簡考釋 (A textual analysis of the letters on scholarly issues between Zhang Taiyan, Lü Cheng, and Li Jinxi in 1921–1922). *Foxue yanjiu* 佛學研究 23 (2014): 326–39.

Yinguang 印光. "Yinguang dashi huguo xiza fayu" 印光大師護國息災法語 (Master Yinguang's Dharma talks on protecting the nation and preventing disaster). https://book.bfnn.org/books/0356.htm.

Yinsun 印順. "Xuefo sanyao" 學佛三要 (Three principles of learning Buddhism). http://www.mahabodhi.org/files/yinshun/19/yinshun19-01.html.

——. *Yindu zhi fojiao* 印度之佛教 (Indian Buddhism). http://www.mahabodhi.org/files/yinshun/35/yinshun35-02.html1942.

——. *Yinshun fashi foxue zhuzuoji* 印順法師佛學著作集 (Collected writings of Dharma Master Yinshun on Buddhist studies). http://www.mahabodhi.org/files/yinshun/index.html.

Yuanying 圓瑛. "Tichang sushi jucan hui" 提倡素食聚餐會 (Encouraging vegetarian dinner parties). http://book.bfnn.org/books2/1601.htm.

Yun Yun 雲雲. "Huang Jusu bie zhuan" 黃居素別傳 (A supplementary biography of Huang Jusu). *Shehui ribao* 社會日報 (March 14, 1931): 1–2.

Zou Rong 鄒容. *Gemingjun* 革命軍 (The revolutionary army). https://ctext.org/wiki.pl.

Secondary Materials

Acri, Andrea, ed. *Esoteric Buddhism in Medieval Maritime Asia: Networks of Masters, Texts, Icons*. Singapore: ISEAS Yusof Ishak Institute, 2016.

Adamek, Wendi L. "Nirvāṇa as Permanence, Joy, Self and Purity in a Medieval Chinese Buddhist Context." Unpublished manuscript.

——. *Practicescapes and the Buddhists of Baoshan*. Bochum: Hamburg University Press, 2021.

An, Yangming. "Liang Shuming and Henri Bergson on Intuition: Cultural Context and the Evolution of Term." *Philosophy East and West* 47, no. 3 (1997): 337–62.

Anālayo. *A Comparative Study of the Majjhima-nikāya*. 2 vols. Taipei: Dharma Drum, 2011.

——. *Satipaṭṭhāna: The Direct Path to Realization*. Cambridge: Windhorse Publications, 2004.

Andrews, Susan, Jinhua Chen, and Cuilan Liu, eds. *Rules of Engagement: Medieval Traditions of Buddhist Monastic Regulation*. Bochum: Projekt Verlag, 2017.

Ansell-Pearson, Keith. "Beyond Obligation? Jean-Marie Guyau on Life and Ethics." *Royal Institute of Philosophy Supplement* 77 (2015): 207–25.

App, Urs. *The Birth of Orientalism*. Philadelphia: University of Pennsylvania Press, 2010.

Aviv, Eyal. *Differentiating the Pearl from the Fish-Eye: Ouyang Jingwu and the Revival of Buddhist Scholasticism*. Leiden: Brill, 2020.

Ayyathurai, Gajendran. "Foundations of Anticaste Consciousness: Pandit Iyothee Thass, Tamil Buddhism, and the Marginalized in South India." PhD diss., Columbia University, 2011.

Balkwill, Stephanie. "Disappearing and Disappeared Daughters in Medieval Chinese Buddhism: Sūtras on Sex Transformation and an Intervention into Their Transmission History." *History of Religions* 60, no. 4 (2021): 255–86.

——. *The Women Who Ruled China: Buddhism, Multiculturalism, and Governance in the Sixth Century*. Berkeley: University of California Press, 2024.

Balkwill, Stephanie and James A. Benn, eds. *Buddhist Statecraft in East Asia*. Leiden: Brill, 2022.

Barnard, William. *Living Consciousness: The Metaphysical Vision of Henri Bergson*. Albany: State University of New York Press, 2011.

Barth, Daniel. "The Propagation of Racial Thought in Nineteenth-Century China." In *Race and Racism in Modern East Asia*, vol. 2, *Interactions, Nationalism, Gender and Lineage*, ed. Rotem Kowner and Walter Demel, 123–50. Leiden: Brill, 2015.

Behrent, Michael C. "Le débat Guyau-Durkheim sur la théorie sociologique de la religion: Une nouvelle querelle des universaux?" *Archives de sciences sociales des religions* 53, no. 142 (2008): 9–26.

——. "The Mystical Body of Society: Religion and Association in Nineteenth-Century French Political Thought." *Journal of the History of Ideas* 69, no. 2 (2008): 219–43.

Bingenheimer, Marcus. *Island of Guanyin: Mount Putuo and Its Gazetteers*. New York: Oxford University Press, 2016.

Blum, Mark L., trans. *Nirvana Sutra (Mahāparinirvāna-sūtra): Translated from the Chinese*. Berkeley: BDK America Inc., 2013.

Boucher, Daniel. *Bodhisattvas of the Forest and the Formation of the Mahāyāna: A Study and Translation of the Rāṣṭrapālaparipṛcchā-sūtra*. Honolulu: University of Hawai'i Press, 2008.

Bourdieu, Pierre, and Loïc Wacquant. *An Invitation to Reflexive Sociology*. Chicago: University of Chicago Press, 1992.

Boyd, Richard. "Homeostasis, Species, and Higher Taxa." In *Species: New Interdisciplinary Essays*, ed. Robert A Wilson, 141–85. Cambridge: MIT Press, 1999.

Brindley, Erica. *Music, Cosmology, and the Politics of Harmony in Early China*. Albany: State University of New York Press, 2012.

Bronkhorst, Johannes. *Buddhism in the Shadow of Brahmanism*. Leiden: Brill, 2011.

Brown, Mackenzie C., ed. *Asian Religious Responses to Darwinism: Evolutionary Theories in Middle Eastern, South Asian, and East Asian Cultural Contexts*. Cham, Switzerland: Springer International, 2020.

——. *Hindu Perspectives on Evolution: Darwin, Dharma, and Design*. New York: Routledge, 2012.

Bru, Sascha, Luca Somigli, and Bart van den Bossche, eds. *Futurism: A Microhistory*. Cambridge: Legenda, 2017.

Butler, Judith. *The Force of Nonviolence: An Ethico-Political Bind*. London: Verso, 2021.

Callero, Peter L. *The Myth of Individualism: How Social Forces Shape Our Lives*. Lanham, MD: Rowman & Littlefield, 2017.

Canales, Jimena. *The Physicist and the Philosopher: Einstein, Bergson, and the Debate That Changed Our Understanding of Time*. Princeton, NJ: Princeton University Press, 2015.

Chakrabarty, Dipesh. *Provincializing Europe: Postcolonial Thought and Historical Difference*. Princeton, NJ: Princeton University Press, 2000.

Chakravarti, Uma. *On the Social Philosophy of Buddhism: Four Essays*. Shimla: Indian Institute for Advanced Study, 2015.

——. *The Social Dimension of Early Buddhism*. Delhi: Oxford University Press, 1987.

Chang, Ku-ming. "'Ceaseless Generation': Republican China's Rediscovery and Expansion of Domestic Vitalism." *Asia Major* 30, no. 2 (2017): 101–31.

Chen, Janet Y. *The Sounds of Mandarin: Learning to Speak a National Language in China and Taiwan, 1913–1960*. New York: Columbia University Press, 2023.

Cheng, Yinghong. *Creating the New Man: From Enlightenment Ideals to Socialist Realities*. Honolulu: University of Hawai'i Press, 2009.

Chidester, David. *Empire of Religion: Imperialism and Comparative Religion*. Chicago: University of Chicago Press, 2014.

Cho, Francisca. "Buddhism, Science, and the Truth About Karma." *Religion Compass* 8, no. 4 (2014): 117–27.

Ciaudo, Joseph. "Bergson's 'Intuition' in China and Its Confucian Fate (1915–1923): Some Remarks on *Zhijue* in Modern Chinese Philosophy." *Problemos* (2016): 35–50.

——. "Introduction à la métaphysique bergsonienne en Chine: Échos philosophiques et moralization de l'intuition." *Noesis* 21 (2013): 293–328.

Cook, Ramsay. *The Regenerators: Social Criticism in Late Victorian Canada*. Toronto: University of Toronto Press, 1985.

Coovadia, Imraan. *Revolution and Nonviolence in Tolstoy, Gandhi, and Mandela*. New York: Oxford University Press, 2020.

Daswani, Rekha. *Buddhist Monasteries and Monastic Life in Ancient India: From the Third Century BC to the Seventh Century AD*. New Delhi: Aditya Prakashan, 2006.

Dávid-Barrett, Tamás, and James Carney. "The Deification of Historical Figures and the Emergence of Priesthoods as a Solution to a Network Coordination Problem." *Religion, Brain & Behavior* 6, no. 4 (2016): 307–17.

Davidson, Ronald Mark. "Buddhist Systems of Transformation: Āśraya-parivṛtti/-parāvṛtti Among the Yogācāra (India)." PhD diss., University of California, Berkeley, 1985.

De Jong, Jan Willem. *A Brief History of Buddhist Studies in Europe and America*. Delhi: Sri Satguru Publications, 1987 [1976].

Deleuze, Gilles. *Bergsonism*. Trans. Hugh Tomlinson and Barbara Habberjam. New York: Zone Books, 1988.

Denzin, Norman K., and Yvonna S. Lincoln, eds. *Handbook of Qualitative Research*. Thousand Oaks, CA: Sage Publications, 1994; 5th ed., 2018.

Desmond, Matthew. *Poverty, by America*. New York: Crown, 2023.

DeVido, Elise A. "The Influence of Chinese Master Taixu on Buddhism in Vietnam." *Journal of Global Buddhism* 10 (2015): 413–58.

Dharmapāla, Xuanzang, and Louis de la Vallée Poussin. *Vijñapatimātratāsiddhi: La Siddhi De Hiuan-Tsang*. Paris: P. Geuthner, 1928–29.

Dikötter, Frank. *The Discourse of Race in Modern China*. New York: Oxford University Press, 1992.

Donzelot, Jacques. *L'invention du social: Essai sur le déclin des passions politiques*. Paris: Fayard, 1984.

Duara, Prasenjit. *Culture, Power, and the State: Rural North China, 1900–1942*. Redwood City, CA: Stanford University Press, 1988.

Duiker, William. *Ts'ai Yüan-P'ei: Educator of Modern China*. University Park: Pennsylvania State University Press, 1977.

Durkheim, Émile. *The Elementary Forms of the Religious Life*. Mineola, NY: Dover Publications, 2012 [1912].

Duval, Kathleen. *Native Nations: A Millennium of North America*. New York: Random House, 2024.

Elstub, Stephen, and Peter McLaverty. "Introduction: Issues and Cases in Deliberative Democracy." In *Deliberative Democracy: Issues and Cases*, ed. Stephen Elstub and Peter McLaverty, 1–16. Edinburgh: Edinburgh University Press, 2014.

Eltschinger, Vincent. *"Caste" et philosophie bouddhique: Continuité de quelques arguments bouddhiques contre le traitement réaliste des dénominations sociales*. Vienna: Universität Wien, 2000.

Epstein, Brian. "Social Ontology." In *The Stanford Encyclopedia of Philosophy* (Summer 2018 Edition), ed. Edward N. Zalta. Stanford University, 1977–. https://plato.stanford.edu/archives/sum2018/entries/social-ontology/.

Eubanks, Charlotte. *Miracles of Book and Body: Buddhist Textual Culture and Medieval Japan*. Berkeley: University of California Press, 2011.

Fisher, Gareth. "Universal Karma." *Journal of Global Buddhism* 24, no. 2 (2023): 100–103.

Foucault, Michel. *The Order of Things: An Archaeology of the Human Sciences*. New York: Vintage Books, 1970.

Frye, Marilyn. *The Politics of Reality: Essays in Feminist Theory*. Freedom, CA: Crossing Press, 1983.

Galtung, Johan. "Violence, Peace, and Peace Research." *Journal of Peace Research* 6, no. 3 (1969): 167–91.

Garfield, Jay L. *Engaging Buddhism: Why It Matters to Philosophy*. New York: Oxford University Press, 2015.

——. "'I Take Refuge in the Sangha. But How?' The Puzzle of Intersubjectivity in Buddhist Philosophy Comments on Tzohar, Prueitt, and Kachru." *Sophia* 58, no. 1 (2019): 85–89.

——. *Losing Ourselves: Learning to Live without a Self*. Princeton: Princeton University Press, 2022.

Garfield, Jay L., ed. *Wilfrid Sellars and Buddhist Philosophy: Freedom from Foundations*. New York: Routledge, 2019

Garfield, Jay L., and William Edelglass, eds. *Buddhist Philosophy: Essential Readings*. New York: Oxford University Press, 2009.

Garfield, Jay L., and Jan Westerhoff, eds. *Madhyamaka and Yogācāra: Allies or Rivals?* New York: Oxford University Press, 2015.

Gildow, Douglas. "Cai Yuanpei (1868–1940), Religion, and His Plan to Save China through Buddhism." *Asia Major* 31, no. 2 (2018): 107–48.

Gold, Johnathan C. *The Dharma's Gatekeepers: Sakya Paṇḍita on Buddhist Scholarship in Tibet*. Albany: State University of New York Press, 2007.

Gombrich, Richard F. *What the Buddha Thought*. London: Equinox, 2009.

Gong, Jun 龔儁. "Jindai foxue cong jingshi dao xueshu de mingyun zouxiang" 近代佛學從經世到學術的命運走向 (The teleological trajectory of modern Buddhism from administering the world to scholarship). *Zhexue yanjiu* 5 (1997): 39–47.

——. "Jindai Zhongguo Fojiao jingxue yanju: yi Neixueyuan yu Wuchang Foxueyuan wei li" 近代中國佛教經學研究: 以內學院與武昌佛學院為例 (Exegesis in Buddhist studies of modern China: taking examples of the Chinese Metaphysical Institute and the Wuchang Buddhist Academy). *Xuanzang foxue yanju* 玄奘佛學研究 24 (2015): 85–116.

Goodman, Russell. "William James." In *The Stanford Encyclopedia of Philosophy* (Winter 2021 Edition), ed. Edward N. Zalta. https://plato.stanford.edu/archives/win2021/entries/james.

Goossaert, Vincent, and David A. Palmer. *The Religious Question in Modern China*. Chicago: University of Chicago Press, 2011.

Graziano, Michael S. A. *Consciousness and the Social Brain*. Oxford; New York: Oxford University Press, 2013.

Green, Adam S. "Killing the Priest-King: Addressing Egalitarianism in the Indus Civilization." *Journal of Archaeological Research* 29 (2021): 153–202.

Guba, Egon G. "The Alternative Paradigm Dialog." In *The Paradigm Dialog*, ed. Egon G. Guba, 17–30. Newbury Park, CA: Sage Publications, 1990.

Guba, Egon G., and Yvonna S. Lincoln. "Competing Paradigms in Qualitative Research." In Denzin and Lincoln, *Handbook of Qualitative Research*, 1st ed., 105–17.

Gvili, Gal. "In Search of the National Soul: Writing Life in Chinese Literature, 1918–1937." PhD diss., Columbia University, 2015.

Gyatso, Janet. "Sex." In *Critical Terms for the Study of Buddhism*, ed. Donald S. Lopez, 271–90. Chicago: University of Chicago Press, 2005.

Halbfass, Wilhelm. "Karma and Rebirth, Indian Conceptions of." In *Routledge Encyclopedia of Philosophy*. Milton Park, UK: Taylor and Francis, 1998.

Hammerstrom, Erik. "A Buddhist Critique of Scientism." *Journal of Chinese Buddhist Studies* 27 (2014): 35–57.

——. "The Expression 'The Myriad Dharmas Are Only Consciousness' in Early 20th Century Chinese Buddhism." *Chung-Hwa Buddhist Journal* 23 (2010): 71–92.

——. *The Science of Chinese Buddhism: Early Twentieth-Century Engagements*. New York: Columbia University Press, 2015.

Haraway, Donna. "The Promise of Monsters: A Regenerative Politics for Inappropriate/d Others." In *Cultural Studies*, ed. Lawrence Grossberg, Cary Nelson, and Paula A. Treichler, 295–337. New York: Routledge, 1992.

Harding, Frank James William. *Jean-Marie Guyau, 1854–1888, Aesthetician and Sociologist: A Study of His Aesthetic Theory and Critical Practice*. Geneva: Droz, 1973.

Harrison, Peter. *Some New World: Myths of Supernatural Belief in a Secular Age*. Cambridge: Cambridge University Press, 2024.

Haslanger, Sally. "Gender and Race: (What) Are They? (What) Do We Want Them to Be?" *Nous* 34, no. 1 (2000): 31–55.

——. "Racism, Ideology, and Social Movements." *Res Philosophica* 94, no. 1 (2017): 1–22.

——. "What Good Are Our Intuitions? Philosophical Analysis and Social Kinds." *Proceedings of the Aristotelian Society*, Sup. Vol. 80, no. 1 (2006): 89–118.

Hayes, Richard. "Is There Such a Thing as Collective Karma?" https://www.unm.edu/~rhayes / Lecture10.pdf.

Hershock, Peter D. *Consciousness Mattering: A Buddhist Synthesis*. London; New York: Bloomsbury, 2023.

Hijikata, Teiichi. "On the *Aesthetics* of Abe Jirō." In *A History of Modern Japanese Aesthetics*, ed. Michael F. Marra, 197–203. Honolulu: University of Hawai'i Press, 2001.

Hildebrand, David. "John Dewey." In *The Stanford Encyclopedia of Philosophy* (Winter 2021 Edition), ed. Edward N. Zalta. https://plato.stanford.edu/archives/win2021/entries/dewey.

Hiragawa Akira 平川彰. *Bukkyō kenkyū nyūmon* 仏教研究入門 (Introduction to Buddhist Studies). Tokyo: Daisō syuppan, 1984.

hooks, bell. *Teaching Critical Thinking: Practical Wisdom*. New York: Routledge, 2012.

——. *Teaching to Transgress: Education as the Practice of Freedom*. New York: Routledge, 2014 [1994].

Hu, Hsiao-Lan. *This-Worldly Nibbāna: A Buddhist-Feminist Social Ethics for Peacemaking in the Global Community*. Albany: State University of New York Press, 2011.

Huang, Max Ko-wu. *The Meaning of Freedom: Yan Fu and the Origins of Chinese Liberalism*. Hong Kong: Chinese University of Hong Kong Press, 2008.

—— 黄克武. "Minguo chunian Shanghai de lingxue yanjiu: Yi Shanghai lingxuehui weili" 民國初年上海的靈學研究: 以上海靈學會為例 (Studies of spiritualism in early Republican Shanghai: The case of the Shanghai Spiritualism Society). *Bulletin of the Institute of Modern History, Academia Sinica* 55 (2007): 99–136.

Ingold, Tim. "Taking Taskscape to Task." In *Forms of Dwelling: 20 Years of Taskscapes in Archeology*, ed. Ulla Rajala and Philip Millis, 16–27. Oxford: Oxbow Books, 2017.

——. "When ANT Meets SPIDER: Social Theory for Anthropods." In *Material Agency: Towards a Non-Anthropocentric Approach*, ed. Carl Knappett and Lambros Malafouris, 209–15. New York: Springer, 2008.

Ivanhoe, Philip J., and Sungmoon Kim. *Confucianism, a Habit of the Heart: Bellah, Civil Religion, and East Asia*. Albany: State University of New York Press, 2016.

Jenco, Leigh K. *Changing Referents: Learning Across Space and Time in China and the West*. New York: Oxford University Press, 2015.

Jenco, Leigh K., ed. *Chinese Thought as Global Theory: Diversifying Knowledge Production in the Social Sciences and Humanities*. Albany: State University of New York Press, 2017.

Jenkins, Katherine. *Ontology and Oppression: Race, Gender, and Social Reality*. New York: Oxford University Press, 2023.

Jessup, James Brooks. "The Householder Elite: Buddhist Activism in Shanghai, 1920–1956." PhD diss., University of California, Berkeley, 2010.

Ji, Zhe. "Secularization as Religious Restructuring: Statist Institutionalization of Chinese Buddhism and Its Paradoxes." In *Chinese Religiosities: Afflictions of Modernity and State Formation*, ed. Mayfair Mei-hui Yang, 223–60. Berkeley: University of California Press, 2008.

Jiang, Tao. *Origins of Moral-Political Philosophy in Early China: Contestation of Humaneness, Justice, and Personal Freedom*. New York: Oxford University Press, 2021.

Jones, Charles B. *Buddhism in Taiwan: Religion and the State, 1660–1990*. Honolulu: University of Hawai'i Press, 1999.

Joshi, Maya. "Rahul Sankrityayan and Ambedkar as Contrapuntal Contemporaries: Unpacking Their 'Metaphysics and Politics.'" In *India and Civilizational Futures*, ed. Vinay Lal, 182–214. New Delhi: Oxford University Press, 2019.

——. "Rahula Sankrityayan and Buddhism: A Complex Engagement." In *On the Trail of Buddhism in Asia: Reflections on Tradition and Practice*, ed. Suchandana Chatterjee and Sushmita Bhattacharya, 76–86. Kolkata: Maulana Abul Kalam Azad Institute of Asian Studies/Pentagon Press, 2016.

Jullien, François. *De l'être au vivre: Lexique euro-chinois de la pensée*. Paris: Gallimard, 2015.

Kachru, Sonam. "Minds and Worlds: A Philosophical Commentary on the 'Twenty Verses' of Vasubandhu." PhD diss., University of Chicago, 2015.

——. *Other Lives: Mind and World in Indian Buddhism*. New York: Columbia University Press, 2021.

——. "Ratnakīrti and the Extent of Inner Space: An Essay on Yogācāra and the Threat of Genuine Solipsism." *Sophia* 58, no. 1 (2019): 61–83.

Kang, Xiaofei. "Women, Gender, and Religion in Modern China: 1900s–1950s: An Introduction." *Nan Nü* 19 (2017): 1–27.

Kapstein, Matthew T. Review of *The Foundation of Yoga Practitioners: The Buddhist Yogācārabhūmi Treatise and Its Adaptations in India, East Asia, and Tibet*, by Ulrich Timme Kragh. *Indo-Iranian Journal* 60, no. 3 (2017): 292–301.

Karashima, Seishi. "Who Were the Icchantikas?" *Annual Report of the International Research Institute for Advanced Buddhology at Soka University* 10 (2007): 61–80.

Katz, Paul R. "Chen Hailiang's Vision of Buddhist Family Life: A Preliminary Study." *Journal of Chinese Religions* 47, no. 1 (2019): 33–60.

Katz, Paul R., and Vincent Goossaert. *The Fifty Years That Changed Chinese Religion, 1898–1948*. Ann Arbor, MI: Association for Asian Studies, 2021.

Keng, Ching. "How Do We Understand the Meaning of a Sentence Under the Yogācāra Model of the Mind? On Disputes Among East Asian Yogācāra Thinkers of the Seventh Century." *Journal of Indian Philosophy* 46 (2018): 475–504.

——. *Toward a New Image of Paramārtha: Yogācāra and Tathāgatagarbha Buddhism Revisited*. London: Bloomsbury, 2023.

Kerekes, Susanne. "Sociokarma and Kindred Spirits: An Acknowledgement." *Journal of Global Buddhism* 24, no. 2 (2023): 104–8.

Kerekes, Susanne, and Jessica Zu. "Introduction: Critical Notes on the Lived Karma Conference." *Journal of Global Buddhism* 24, no. 2 (2023): 83–87.

Kern, Martin, trans. "Imperial Tours and Mountain Inscriptions." In *The First Emperor: China's Terracotta Army*, ed. Jane Portal, 104–13. Cambridge, MA: Harvard University Press, 2007.

Keyes, Charles F., and E. Valentine Daniel, eds. *Karma: An Anthropological Inquiry*. Berkeley: University of California Press, 1983.

Kiely, Jan. *The Compelling Ideal: Thought Reform and the Prison in China, 1901–1956*. New Haven, CT: Yale University Press, 2014.

King, Sallie B. *Being Benevolence: The Social Ethics of Engaged Buddhism*. Honolulu: University of Hawai'i Press, 2009.

Kirylo, James D. "Chapter Seven: Liberation Theology and Paulo Freire." *Counterpoints* 385 (2011): 167–93.

Kosambi, Dharmanand. *Dharmanand Kosambi: The Essential Writings*. Trans. Meera Kosambi. Ranikhet: Permanent Black, 2017.

Kosuta, Matthew. "Ethics of War and Ritual: The Bhagavad-Gita and Mahabharata as Test Cases." *Journal of Military Ethics* 19, no. 3 (2020): 186–200.

Kowner, Rotem, and Walter Demel, eds. *Race and Racism in Modern East Asia: Western and Eastern Constructions*. Leiden: Brill, 2013.

——. *Race and Racism in Modern East Asia*. Vol. 2, *Interactions, Nationalism, Gender and Lineage*. Leiden: Brill, 2015.

Kragh, Ulrich Timme, ed. *The Foundation for Yoga Practitioners: The Buddhist Yogācārabhūmi Treatise and Its Adaptation in India, East Asia, and Tibet*. Cambridge, MA: Harvard University Press, 2013.

Lai, Huei-Yun. "Les études sur Henri Bergson en Chine, 1913–1941." PhD thesis, École des Hautes Études en Sciences Sociales, 1993.

Lai, Sufen Sophia. "Racial Discourse and Utopian Visions in Nineteenth-Century China." In Kowner and Demel, eds., *Race and Racism in Modern East Asia: Western and Eastern Constructions*, 327–50.

Lai, Whalen. "Sinitic Speculations on Buddha-nature: The Nirvāṇa School (420–589)." *Philosophy East and West* 32, no. 2 (1982): 135–49.

Lam, Tong. *A Passion for Facts: Social Surveys and the Construction of the Chinese Nation State, 1900–1949.* Berkeley: University of California Press, 2011.

Lambourne, Lionel. *The Aesthetic Movement*. London: Phaidon, 1996.

Lawlor, Leonard, and Valentine Moulard-Leonard. "Henri Bergson." In *The Stanford Encyclopedia of Philosophy* (Winter 2022 Edition), ed. Edward N. Zalta and Uri Nodelman. https://plato.stanford.edu/entries/bergson/.

Li, An 李安. *Li An foxue lunzhu xuanji* 李安佛學論著選集 (Selected writings on Buddhist studies by Li An). Nanjing: Jinling kejing chu, 2003.

Li, Jingjing. *Comparing Husserl's Phenomenology and Chinese Yogācāra in a Multicultural World: A Journey Beyond Orientalism*. London; New York: Bloomsbury, 2022.

——. "From Self-Attaching to Self-Emptying: An Investigation of Xuanzang's Account of Self-Consciousness." *Open Theology* 3, no. 1 (2017): 184–97.

——. "Through the Mirror: The Account of Other Minds in Chinese Yogācāra Buddhism." *Dao: A Journal of Comparative Philosophy* 18, no. 3 (2019): 435–51.

Lin, Chen-kuo. 林鎮國. "*Qixinlun* yu xiandai Dongya zhutixing zhexue—yi Neixueyuan yu Xinrujia de zhenglun wei zhongxin de kaocha" 《起信論》與現代東亞主體性哲學—以內學院與新儒家的爭論為中心的考察 (On *Awakening Faith* and modern East Asian philosophy of subjectivity: An investigation of the debates between the China Inner Learning Institute and New Confucianism). *Hanyu foxue pinglun* 漢語佛學評論 6 (2018): 3–24.

——. "The Uncompromising Quest for Genuine Buddhism: Lü Cheng's Critique of Original Enlightenment." In Makeham, *Transforming Consciousness: Yogācāra Thought in Modern China*, 346–52.

Lin, Pei-ying. "The Doctrinal Evolution of Formless Precepts: The Theory of Mind Purification in the *Laṅkāvatāra Sūtra* and the *Brahmā Net Sūtra*." In *Rules of Engagement: Medieval Traditions of Buddhist Monastic Regulation*, ed. Susan Andrews, Jinhua Chen, and Cuilan Liu, 197–222. Bochum: Projekt Verlag, 2017.

Lincoln, Yvonna S., Susan A. Lynham, and Egon G. Guba. "Paradigmatic Controversies, Contradictions, and Emerging Confluences, Revisited." In Denzin and Lincoln, *Handbook of Qualitative Research*, 5th ed., 108–50.

Ling, Trevor. *Buddha, Marx and God: Some Aspects of Religion in the Modern World*. Ann Arbor: University of Michigan Press, 1979.

——. *Buddhist Revival in India: Aspects of the Sociology of Buddhism*. London: Macmillan Press, 1980.

Liu, Ming-Wood. "The Problem of the Icchantika in the *Mahāyāna Mahāparinirvāṇa Sūtra*." *Journal of the International Association of Buddhist Studies* 7, no. 21 (1984): 57–81.

Liu, Xinru. *Early Buddhist Society: The World of Gautama Buddha*. Albany: State University of New York Press, 2022.

Loftus, Timothy. "Ambedkar and the Buddha's Saṃgha: A Ground for Buddhist Ethics." *CASTE: A Global Journal on Social Exclusion* 2, no. 2 (2021): 265–80.

Longino, Helen E. *Science as Social Knowledge: Values and Objectivity in Scientific Inquiry*. Princeton, NJ: Princeton University Press, 1990.

Lu-Adler, Huaping. *Kant, Race, and Racism: Views from Somewhere*. New York: Oxford University Press, 2023.

Luo, Ning. "Cai Yuanpei's Vision of Aesthetic Education and His Legacy in Modern China." *Nordic Journal of Comparative and International Education* 5, no. 2 (2021): 51–64.

Lusthaus, Dan. *Buddhist Phenomenology: A Philosophical Investigation of Yogācāra Buddhism and the Ch'eng Wei-Shih Lun*. New York: RoutledgeCurzon, 2002.

——. "Lü Cheng, Epistemology, Genuine Buddhism." In Makeham, *Transforming Consciousness: Yogācāra Thought in Modern China*, 318–45.

Madsen, Richard. *Democracy's Dharma: Religious Renaissance and Political Development in Taiwan*. Berkeley: University of California Press, 2007.

Makeham, John, ed. *Learning from the Other: Australian and Chinese Perspectives on Philosophy*. Canberra: Australian Academy of the Humanities, 2016.

——. *Transforming Consciousness: Yogācāra Thought in Modern China*. New York: Oxford University Press, 2014.

Marc, Joly. "L'antinomie individu/société dans les sciences humaines et sociales: Genèse(s) et usages." *Cahiers Vilfredo Pareto* 52, no. 1 (2014): 193–223.

Mather, Richard B. "Vimalakīrti and Gentry Buddhism." *History of Religions* 8, no. 1 (1968): 60–73.

McDermott, James P. "Is There Group Karma in Theravāda Buddhism?" *Numen* 23, fasc. 1 (1976): 67–80.

McLaughlin, Levi. *Soka Gakkai's Human Revolution: The Rise of a Mimetic Nation in Modern Japan*. Honolulu: University of Hawai'i Press, 2020.

McLeod, Alexus. *An Introduction to Mesoamerican Philosophy*. Cambridge: Cambridge University Press, 2023.

Merton, Robert K. *The Sociology of Science: Theoretical and Empirical Investigations*. Ed. Norman W. Storer. Chicago: University of Chicago Press, 1973.

Metzinger, Thomas. *The Ego Tunnel: The Science of the Mind and the Myth of the Self*. Boulder, CO: Basic Books, 2019.

Minor, Robert N. "In Defense of Karma and Rebirth: Evolutionary Karma." In Neufeldt, *Karma and Rebirth*, 15–40.

Mitsukawa, Toyoki 光川豊芸. "*Daijō shōchin ron* kanken: Chūgan, Yuishiki kōshō ni okeru ichishiten toshite" 「大乗掌珍論」管見—中観・瑜伽交渉における一視點として (A perspective on the *Daijō shōchin ron*: An aspect of the exchanges between Madhyamaka and Yogācāra). *Indogaku bukkyōgaku kenkyū* 13, no. 2 (1965): 613–18.

Moore, Matthew J. *Buddhism and Political Theory*. New York: Oxford University Press, 2016.

——. "Buddhism and Politics." In *Oxford Bibliographies Online*. https://www.oxfordbibliographies.com/display/document/obo-9780195393521/obo-9780195393521-0251.xml.

Mukai, Akira 向井亮. "Yugashichiron no setsukotobun to Zatsuagongyō" 『瑜伽師地論』の摂事分と『雑阿含経』(The *Vastusaṁgrahaṇī* of the *Yogācārabhūmi* and the *Saṁyuktāgama*). *Hokkaidō Daigaku bungakubu kiyō* 33, no. 2 (1985): 1–41.

Murthy, Viren. *The Political Philosophy of Zhang Taiyan: The Resistance of Consciousness*. Leiden: Brill, 2011.

——. "Transfiguring Modern Temporality: Zhang Taiyan's Yogācāra Critique of Evolutionary History." *Modern China* 38, no. 5 (2012): 483–522.

Nagel, Thomas. *The View from Nowhere*. New York: Oxford University Press, 1986.

Nakajima, Takahiro. "Grounding Normativity in Ritual." In Jenco, *Chinese Thought as Global Theory*, 55–74.

Neufeldt, Ronald W., ed. *Karma and Rebirth: Post Classical Developments*. Albany: State University of New York Press, 1986.

Nhat Hanh, Thich. *Interbeing: Fourteen Guidelines for Engaged Buddhism*. Berkeley: Parallax Press, 1993.

Ober, Douglas. *Dust on the Throne: The Search for Buddhism in Modern India*. New Delhi: Navayana Press, 2023.

——. "'Like Embers Hidden in Ashes, or Jewels Encrusted in Stone': Rahul Sankrityayan, Dharmanand Kosambi and Buddhist Activity in Colonial India." *Contemporary Buddhism: An Interdisciplinary Journal* 14, no. 1 (2013): 134–48.

——. "Socialism, Russia and India's Revolutionary Dharma." In *Buddhism in the Global Eye: Beyond East and West*, ed. John S. Harding, Victor Sōgen Hori, and Alexander Soucy, 71–86. London: Bloomsbury Academic, 2020.

Ohnuma, Reiko. "When Animals Speak: Animal Ethics from the Mouths of Buddhist Animals." Unpublished manuscript.

Ōishi, Masayoshi 大石昌史. "Abe Jirō to kanjō inyū bigaku" 阿部次郎と感情移入美学 (Abe Jirō and the aesthetics of emotional transfer). *Tetsugaku* 113, no. 3 (2005): 93–130.

Okabe, Kazuo 岡部和雄. "Shijūnishōkyō' no seiritsu to tenkai: Kenkyūshiteki oboegaki" 四十二章經の成立と展開—研究史的覚え書き (On the formation and development of the *Forty-Two Sections Sūtra*: A memorandum of historiography). *Komazawa daigaku bukkyōgakubu kenkyū kiyō* 駒澤大學佛教學部研究紀要25 (1967): 103–18.

Okabe, Kazuo 岡部和雄, and Tanaka Ryōsyō 田中良昭, eds. *Chūgoku Bukkyō kenkyū nyūmon* 中国仏教研究入門 (Introduction to the study of Chinese Buddhism). Tokyo: Daisō syuppan, 2006.

Olson Jr., Mancur. *The Logic of Collective Action: Public Goods and the Theory of Groups*. Cambridge, MA: Harvard University Press, 1965.

Omvedt, Gail. *Buddhism in India: Challenging Brahmanism and Caste*. New Delhi: Sage Publications, 2003.

Oreskes, Naomi. *Why Trust Science*. Princeton, NJ: Princeton University Press, 2019.

——. "Why We Should Trust Scientists." June 25, 2014. https://youtu.be/RxyQNEVOElU.

Owen, Alex. *The Place of Enchantment: British Occultism and the Culture of the Modern*. Chicago: University of Chicago Press, 2004.

Park, Jin Y. "Philosophizing and Power: East-West Encounter in the Formation of Modern East Asian Buddhist Philosophy." *Philosophy East and West* 61, no. 3 (2017): 801–24.

Park, Peter K. *Africa, Asia, and the History of Philosophy: Racism in the Formation of the Philosophical Canon, 1780–1830*. Albany: State University of New York Press, 2013.

Phillips, Stephen. "Epistemology in Classical Indian Philosophy." In *The Stanford Encyclopedia of Philosophy* (Winter 2021 Edition), ed. Edward N Zalta, https://plato.stanford.edu/archives/win2021/entries/epistemology-india.

Pollock, Sheldon. "Crisis in the Classics." *Social Research: An International Quarterly* 78, no. 1 (2011): 21–48.

Prueitt, Catherine. "Is There an Ideal Scientific Image? Sellars and Dharmakīrti on Levels of Reality." In *Wilfrid Sellars and Buddhist Philosophy*, ed. Jay Garfield, 48–66. New York: Routledge, 2019.

——. "Karmic Imprints, Exclusion, and the Creation of the Worlds of Conventional Experience in Dharmakīrti's Thought." *Sophia* 57, no. 2 (2018): 313–35.

Pusey, James Reeve. *China and Charles Darwin*. Cambridge, MA: Harvard University Asia Center, 1983.

Queen, Christopher S., Charles S. Prebish, and Damien Keown, eds. *Action Dharma: New Studies in Engaged Buddhism*. New York: Routledge Curzon, 2003.

Quine, Willard van Orman. "Main Trends in Recent Philosophy: Two Dogmas of Empiricism." *Philosophical Review* 60, no. 1 (1951): 20–43.

——. "Two Dogmas in Retrospect." *Canadian Journal of Philosophy* 21, no. 3 (1991): 265–74.

Radich, Michael. "The Doctrine of **Amalavijñāna* in Paramārtha (499–569) and Later Authors to Approximately 800 C.E." *ZINBUN* 41 (2008): 45–174.

Rajapakse, Vijitha. "Buddhism in Huxley's 'Evolution and Ethics': A Note on Victorian Evaluation and Its 'Comparativist Dimension.'" *Philosophy East and West* 35, no. 3 (1985): 295–304.

Reat, N. Ross *The Śālistamba Sūtra*. New Delhi: Motilal Banarsidass, 1998.

Rhys Davids, T. W. *Buddhist India*. New York: G. P. Putnam's Sons, 1903.

Ritzinger, Justin. *Anarchy in the Pure Land: Reinventing the Cult of Maitreya in Modern China*. New York: Oxford University Press, 2018.

——. "Interpersonal Karma: A Note." *Journal of Global Buddhism* 24, no. 2 (2023): 109–13.

Said, Edward. *Culture and Imperialism*. New York: Knopf, 1993.

——. *Orientalism*. New York: Pantheon, 1978.

Sakuma, Hidenori S. "Remarks on the Lineage of Indian Masters of the Yogācāra School: Maitreya, Asaṅga, and Vasubandhu." In Kragh, *Foundation for Yoga Practitioners*, 330–66.

Salice, Alessandro. "The Phenomenology of the Munich and Göttingen Circles." In *The Stanford Encyclopedia of Philosophy* (Winter 2020 Edition), ed. Edward N. Zalta. https://plato.stanford.edu/archives/win2020/entries/phenomenology-mg/.

Salomon, Richard. *The Buddhist Literature of Ancient Gandhāra: An Introduction with Selected Translations*. Somerville, MA: Wisdom Publications, 2018.

Śāntideva. *The Bodhicaryāvatāra*. Trans. Kate Crosby and Andrew Skilton. Oxford: Oxford University Press, 1998.

Sasson, Vanessa R. "When Women Showed Up." *Tricycle*, May 26, 2023. https://tricycle.org/article/first-female-buddhist/.

Schlosser, Markus. "Agency." In *The Stanford Encyclopedia of Philosophy* (Winter 2019 Edition), ed. Edward N. Zalta. https://plato.stanford.edu/archives/win2019/entries/agency.

Schmithausen, Lambert. *Ālayavijñāna: On the Origin and the Early Development of a Central Concept of Yogācāra Philosophy*. Tokyo: International Institute for Buddhist Studies, 1987.

Schopen, Gregory. *Buddhist Monks and Business Matters: Still More Papers on Monastic Buddhism in India*. Honolulu: University of Hawai'i Press, 2004.

Schwartz, Benjamin. *In Search of Power and Wealth: Yen Fu and the West*. Cambridge, MA: Belknap Press, 1964.

Scott, David. "William James and Buddhism: American Pragmatism and the Orient." *Religion* 30, no. 4 (2000): 333–52.

Seibt, Johanna. "Process Philosophy." In *The Stanford Encyclopedia of Philosophy* (Summer 2023 Edition), ed. Edward N. Zalta and Uri Nodelman. https://plato.stanford.edu/entries/process-philosophy/.

Sellars, Wilfrid. "Foundations for a Metaphysics of Pure Process." *Monist* 64, no. 1 (1981): 3–90.

——. *Science, Perception and Reality*. New York: Routledge and Kegan Paul, 1963.

Sen, Amartya. *The Argumentative Indian: Writings on Indian History, Culture, and Identity*. New York: Picador, 2006.

Shah, Alpa. *Nightmarch: Among India's Revolutionary Guerrillas*. Chicago: University of Chicago Press, 2019.

Sharma, J. P. *Republics in Ancient India*. Leiden: Brill, 1968.

Shaver, Robert. "Egoism." In *The Stanford Encyclopedia of Philosophy* (Winter 2021 Edition), ed. Edward N. Zalta. https://plato.stanford.edu/archives/win2021/entries/egoism.

Shi, Shengkai 釋聖凱. *Fojiao xiandai hua yu hua xiandai* 佛教現代化與化現代 (The modernization of Buddhism and the Buddhicization of the modern). Beijing: Jincheng chubanshe, 2014.

Shields, James M. "Blueprint for Buddhist Revolution: The Radical Buddhism of Seno'o Girō (1889–1961) and the Youth League for Revitalizing Buddhism." *Japanese Journal of Religious Studies* 39, no. 2 (2012): 333–51.

Shino, Yoshinobu 志野好伸. "Testugaku no kyōkai kakutei: Kindai Chūgoku ni okeru Berukuson juyō no ichi rei" 哲学の境界画定—近代中国におけるベルクソン受 容の一例 (On drawing the boundaries of philosophy: A case study of the reception of Bergson in modern China). *Chūgoku testugaku kenkyū* 24 (2009): 146–62.

Siderits, Mark, Tom Tillemans, and Arindam Chakrabarti, eds. *Apoha: Buddhist Nominalism and Human Cognition*. New York: Columbia University Press, 2011.

Sosis, Alcorta R. "Signaling, Solidarity, and the Sacred: The Evolution of Religious Behavior." *Evolutionary Anthropology* 12, no. 6 (2003): 264–74.

Soucy, Alexander. "Individual and Collective Karma in the Works of Thích Nhât Hanh." *Journal of Vietnamese Studies* 19, no. 1 (2024): 77–108.

Stengers, Isabelle. *Thinking with Whitehead: A Free and Wild Creation of Concepts*. Trans. Michael Chase. Cambridge, MA: Harvard University Press, 2011.

——. *Cosmopolitics I*. Trans. Robert Bononno. Minneapolis: University of Minnesota Press, 2010.

Stepien, Rafal K. *Buddhism Between Religion and Philosophy: Nāgārjuna and the Ethics of Emptiness*. New York: Oxford University Press, 2024.

Stepien, Rafal K., ed. *Buddhist Literature as Philosophy, Buddhist Philosophy as Literature*. Albany: State University of New York Press, 2020.

Stone, Jacqueline I. *Original Enlightenment and the Transformation of Medieval Japanese Buddhism*. Honolulu: University of Hawai'i Press, 1999.

Storm, Jason Ānanda Josephson. *Metamodernism: The Future of Theory*. Chicago: University of Chicago Press, 2021.

——. *The Myth of Disenchantment: Magic, Modernity, and the Birth of the Human Sciences*. Chicago: University of Chicago Press, 2017.

Stueber, Karsten. "Empathy." In *The Stanford Encyclopedia of Philosophy* (Fall 2019 Edition), ed. Edward N. Zalta. https://plato.stanford.edu/archives/spr2018/entries/empathy.

Sullivan, Shannon, and Nancy Tuana, eds. *Race and Epistemologies of Ignorance*. Albany: State University of New York Press, 2007.

Surendran, Gitanjali. "'The Indian Discovery of Buddhism': Buddhist Revival in India, c. 1890–1956." PhD diss., Harvard University, 2013.

Táíwò, Olúfẹ́mi O. *Elite Capture: How the Powerful Took Over Identity Politics (And Everything Else)*. Chicago: Haymarket Books, 2022.

Taylor, Charles. *Philosophy and the Human Sciences*. Cambridge: Cambridge University Press, 1985.

——. "Social Theory as Practice." In *Philosophical Papers*, Vol. 2, *Philosophy and the Human Sciences*, 91–115. Cambridge: Cambridge University Press, 2012.

——. *Sources of the Self*. Cambridge, MA: Harvard University Press, 1989.

Tikhonov, Miller V. *Selected Writings of Han Yongun: From Social Darwinism to "Socialism with a Buddhist Face."* Leiden: Brill, 2008.

Tillemans, Tom. "Dharmakīrti." In *The Stanford Encyclopedia of Philosophy* (Spring 2021 Edition), ed. Edward N. Zalta. https://plato.stanford.edu/archives/spr2017/entries/dharmakiirti/.

Tsui, Brian. *China's Conservative Revolution: The Quest for a New Order, 1927-1949.* Cambridge: Cambridge University Press, 2018.

Tuck, Andrew P. *Comparative Philosophy, and the Philosophy of Scholarship: On the Western Interpretation of Nāgārjuna.* New York: Oxford University Press, 1990.

Turner, Alicia Marie, Laurence Cox, and Brian Bocking. *The Irish Buddhist: The Forgotten Monk Who Faced down the British Empire.* Oxford: Oxford University Press, 2020.

Tzohar, Roy. "The Buddhist Philosophical Conception of Intersubjectivity: An Introduction." *Sophia* 58, no. 1 (2019): 57–60.

——. "Imagine Being a *Preta*: Early Indian Yogācāra Approaches to Intersubjectivity." *Sophia* 56, no. 2 (2016): 337–54.

——. *A Yogācāra Theory of Metaphor.* New York: Oxford University Press, 2018.

Valmisa, Mercedes. *Adapting: A Chinese Philosophy of Action.* New York: Oxford University Press, 2021.

——. "We Are Interwoven Beings." *Aeon*, November 25, 2022. https://aeon.co/essays/in-classical-chinese-philosophy-all-actions-are-collective.

Van Norden, Bryan. *Taking Back Philosophy: A Multicultural Manifesto.* New York: Columbia University Press, 2017.

Voegelin, Eric. "The Growth of the Race Idea." *Review of Politics* 2, no. 3 (1940): 283–317.

Von Hinüber, Oskar. "The Buddha as a Historical Person." *Journal of the International Association of Buddhist Studies* 42 (2019): 231–64.

——. "Buddhist Law According to the Theravāda-Vinaya: A Survey of Theory and Practice." *Journal of the International Association of Buddhist Studies* 18, no. 1 (1995): 7–45.

Waldron, William. *Making Sense of Mind Only: Why Yogācāra Buddhism Matters.* Somerville, MA: Wisdom Publications, 2023.

Walker, Trent. "Cognition's Embrace: Yogācāra Themes in the Writings of Thích Nhất Hạnh." *Berkeley Student Journal of Asian Studies* 6 (2016): 109–37.

Walser, Joseph. "When Did Buddhism Become Anti-Brahmanical? The Case of the Missing Soul." *Journal of the American Academy of Religion* 86, no. 1 (2018): 94–125.

Walsh, Michael J. *Sacred Economies: Buddhist Monasticism and Territoriality in Medieval China.* New York: Columbia University Press, 2009.

Walters, Jonathan S. "Communal Karma and Karmic Community in Theravāda Buddhist History." In *Constituting Communities: Theravāda Buddhism and the Religious Cultures of South and Southeast Asia*, ed. John Holt, Jacob N. Kinnard, and Jonathan S. Walters, 9–40. Albany: State University of New York Press, 2003.

——. "Suttas as History: For Approaches to the Sermon on the Noble Quest (Ariyapariyesanasutta)." *History of Religions* 38, no. 3 (1999): 247–84.

Wang, Fansen 王汎森. *Zhongguo jindai sixiang yu xueshu de xipu* 中國近代思想與學術的系譜 (A genealogy of modern Chinese thought and scholarship). Expanded Edition. Shanghai: Shanghai sanlian chubanshe, 2018.

Wang, Hui. *China from Empire to Nation-State.* Trans. Michael Gibbs Hill. Cambridge, MA: Harvard University Press, 2014.

——. *China's Twentieth Century: Revolution, Retreat, and the Road to Equality.* New York: Verso, 2016.

Wang, Jessica Ching-Sze. *John Dewey in China: To Teach and to Learn*. Albany: State University of New York Press, 2007.

Wang, Zuoyue. "Saving China Through Science: The Science Society of China, Scientific Nationalism, and Civil Society in Republican China." *Osiris* 17, no. 1 (2002): 291–322.

Wangchuk, Dorji. *The Resolve to Become a Buddha*. Tokyo: International Institute for Buddhist Studies, 2007.

Ward, Larry. *America's Racial Karma: An Invitation to Heal*. Berkeley: Parallax Press, 2020.

Ward, Larry, and Julie Flynn Badal. "*America's Racial Karma*: Buddhist Teacher Larry Ward's New Book Invites Us to Heal from the Karma of Racism." *Tricycle*, September 22, 2020. https://tricycle.org/article/larry-ward-racial-karma/.

Weinstein, David. "Herbert Spencer." In *The Stanford Encyclopedia of Philosophy* (Fall 2019 Edition), ed. Edward N. Zalta. https://plato.stanford.edu/archives/fall2019/entries/spencer/.

Welch, Holmes. *The Buddhist Revival in China*. Cambridge, MA: Harvard University Press, 1968.

Westerhoff, Jan. *The Dispeller of Disputes: Nāgārjuna's Vigrahavyāvartanī*. Oxford: Oxford University Press, 2010.

——. *The Non-existence of the Real World*. Oxford: Oxford University Press, 2020.

Wong, David B. *Moral Relativism and Pluralism*. Cambridge: Cambridge University Press, 2023.

Wu, Xianwu 吴先伍. *Xiandaixing de zhuiqiu yu piping—Bogesen yu zhongguo jindai zhexue* 现代性的追求与批评—柏格森与中国近代哲学 (The quest and critique of modernity: Bergson and modern Chinese philosophy). Hefei: Anhui renmin chubanshe, 2005.

Xiang, Shuchen. *Chinese Cosmopolitanism: The History and Philosophy of an Idea*. Princeton, NJ: Princeton University Press, 2023.

——. "Decolonizing Sinology: On Sinology's Weaponization of the Discourse of Race." *Social Dynamics: A Journal of African Studies* 49, no. 2 (2023): 280–98.

Xu, Jilin. "Social Darwinism in Modern China." *Journal of Modern Chinese History* 6, no. 2 (2012): 182–97.

Yan, Joey Yiqiao. "Buddhist Monks, Lay Buddhist Local Elites, and Wartime Relief Activism in Chengdu and Chongqing, 1938–1945." MA thesis, Chinese University of Hong Kong, 2020.

——. "Karma as a Means of Wartime Political Mobilization: A Reading of Chinese Buddhists' Response to the Second Sino-Japanese War, 1937–1945." *Journal of Global Buddhism* 24, no. 2 (2023): 95–99.

Ying, Lei. "Huxley's Karma and Lu Xun's Ghosts: Rethinking the Secularist Assumption and Chinese Modernity." *Journal of Asian Studies* 83, no. 3 (2024): 533–52.

Yong, Ed. *An Immense World: How Animal Senses Reveal the Hidden Realms Around Us*. New York: Random House, 2022.

Yoshimura, Makoto 吉村誠. "Chūgoku yuishiki ni okeru mon kunjū ni tsuite" 中国唯識における聞熏習説について." *Journal of Indian and Buddhist Studies* 58, no. 1 (2010): 246–51.

——. "The Wéishì School and the Buddha-Nature Debate in Early Táng Dynasty." In Kragh, *Foundation for Yoga Practitioners*, 1234–53.

Yü, Ying-shih. "The Radicalization of China in the Twentieth Century." In *China in Transformation*, ed. Wei-ming Tu, 125–50. Cambridge, MA: Harvard University Press, 1994.

Yuan, Yuan. "Chinese Buddhist Nuns in the Twentieth Century: A Case Study in Wuhan." *Journal of Global Buddhism* 10 (2009): 375–412.

Zu, Jessica. "*Adhipati*, Yogācāra Intersubjectivity, and Soteriology in Kuiji's Commentaries." *Sophia*, June 5, 2024. https://link.springer.com/article/10.1007/s11841-024-01019-9.

——. "Collective-Karma-Cluster-Concepts in Chinese Canonical Sources: A Note." *Journal of Global Buddhism* 24, no. 2 (2023): 88–94.

——. "Karma, *Adhipati*, and Weapons of Mass Destruction: Wang Enyang's (1897–1964) Yogācāra Theory of Intersubjective Responsibility." *Journal of Buddhist Philosophy* 6, no. 1 (2025).

——. "Liberation Buddhology for Postracial Worldmaking." *Religious Studies Review* 50, no. 1 (2024): 119–29.

——. "Objective Humanities, Reflexive Humanities." *Religious Studies Review* 48, no. 4 (2022): 501–4.

——. "Ouyang Jingwu's *Must-Read Buddhist Classics for Laity*: Body Politics and Gendered Soteriology." *Journal of Chinese Religions* 47, no. 1 (2019): 61–86.

——. "Theorizing Social Consciousness: Lü Cheng (1896–1989) and the Rise of a New Buddhist Idealism in Modern China." PhD diss., Princeton University, 2020.

——. "Three Plays and a Shared Socio-spiritual Horizon in the Modern Buddhist Revivals in India and China." *International Journal of Asian Studies* 19, no. 2 (2022): 215–38.

——. "War, Piety, and Public Letters: The Making of a New Pure Land Patriarch in Modern China." *History of Religions* 63, no. 1 (2023): 75–119.

Index

Page numbers in *italics* indicate terms appear in tables.

Abhidharmic Reading of the Four Āgamas, An, *100*
Acclamation of the Holy Teaching, *100*, 156
action-oriented ethical training, 103
action-oriented ethics, 16–20, 97, 111, 114, 214n2
action-oriented moral reasoning, *8*, 20, 97, 98, 123
action-oriented moral training, 113
actions and coactions, 80, 97, 114; anchoring process of, 9; redefinition of humanity in terms of, 113; human interconditionality, 114; interwoven chains of, 80; mycelial meshwork of, 110; motivated patterns of, 3, 13; recurring patterns of, 20, 74; theory of, 19–20, 87, 135–36. *See also* coaction
actual (human) life (*xianzhuang rensheng*): at odds with the aesthetic life, 41; perpetuates this, 109; inequalities in this, 146; rekindle humanness in this, 148
actual society (*xianzhuang shehui*), 41; chief vice of the, 127; quest to transform this, 217n30
Acri, Andrea, 214n6
Adamek, Wendi L., 19, 110, 136, 194n59, 218n55, 219n72, 223n9, 235n89
adhipati, 14, 62, 192n42, 205n46, 212n47; karmic efficacy and, 85; intersubjective resonances as coming from, 89; to theorize genuine intersubjective coactions, 84; Wang Enyang's, 84–87; Wang Xiaoxu's, 89. *See also zengshang*
aesthetic antipathy (*meide fanqing*), 36
aesthetic awakening, 42, 106
aesthetic education (*meiyu*), 1–2, 21, 34, 41–43, 106, 197n39
aesthetic empathy (*mei de tongqing*), 36–39, 118
aesthetic life (*mei de rensheng*), 36–37, 41–42, 196n22
aesthetic resonance, 37, 121
aesthetic revolution (*meishu geming*), 1–3, 21, 24–25, 31, 33–34, 46, 110, 118, 195; uncanny resonances with Judith Butler's new imaginary, 41; seed community for, 127; seeds of, 105; structural resemblance to, 131
aesthetic translation, 38–40
agentless agency, 73, 87, 109, 110, 145
Ālambana-parīkṣā (analysis of the objective basis), 119, 156

ālayavijñāna, 72; conflated with *élan vital*, 92, 93; objective aspect of, 85; ripening consciousness, 78; stream of consciousness, 11–13, 83, 168; storehouse consciousness, 44–49, 155, 88–91, 184, 230n25; universalized, 71–72
Ambedkar, B. R, 66, 207n66–67
ameliorative project, 15, 94, 95, 106, 127, 129, 148, 181, 193n45
An, Yangming, 198n60
Anālayo, Bhikkhu, 175, 231n32, 235n101
Anesaki, Masaharu, 231n31
Andrews, Susan, 223n18, 226n45
Ansell-Pearson, Keith, 196n21
antirealism, 36, 47, 209n8. *See also* irrealism; realism
apoha (double negation; *zhequan*), 160, 232n47
anticaste, 62, 65, 66, 207n64
antinomy of the individual and the social, 31, 64, 74, 75, 202n21, 210n16
App, Urs, 218n40
as if (*ru*), 17, 74, 117–20, 128, 153, 169, 221n97
Asaṅga, 125, 129, 159, 221n95, 223n16, 224n25–26
aspiring bodhisattva, 95, 112, 116, 142; self-proclaimed revolutionaries and, 177; self-governed community of, 112, 128; trust their natural propensity toward awakening, 117
āśrayaparivṛtti, 31, *100*, 102, 104–9, 145, 162, 187n1, 215n22, 216n28; original quiescence and, 142. *See also zhuanyi*; revolutionizing consciousness
Aviv, Eyal, 205n48, 213n63, 217n33, 230n21
Awakening Faith (*Qixinlun*), 71, 92, 154, 198n61, 199n73, 213n63, 230n22
Ayyathurai, Gajendran, 207n64

Balkwill, Stephanie, 205n49, 226n45, 236n4, 236n10
Barnard, William, 198n56
Barth, Daniel, 200n2, 201n12
beauty and truth, 37, 43, 175
Behrent, Michael C., 196n23–24
Benn, James A., 205n49, 226n45
Bergson, Henri, 17, 44, 48, 49, 193n48, 198n56, 199n71, 200n82, 208n4; criticized Einstein, 45, 199n67; reception of, 44, 198n50, 199n62, 198n60; Zhang Taiyan and, 46, 48
Bergsonism, 46, 47, 49, 52; and New Confucianism, 73; and Yogācāra, 45, 52, 92, 198n60; moralized, 43–45; sinicized, 50, 198n50, 213n65
Besant, Annie, 202n21, 203n24
Bingenheimer, Marcus, 211n35
Blavatsky, Helena Petrovna, 56, 202n21, 203n24
Blum, Mark L., 114, 219n65
bodhicitta, 143, 160, 175, 232n56; commoners with awakened, 116; function of, 143; institutionalized, 163–64, 170
bodhisattva lineage, 134, 155
bodhisattva path, 114, 117, 120, 137, 175, 177; for aspiring learners, 174; gradualness of, 143; of co-liberation, 103, 144; independent, 157; philosophical-cum-soteriological independence for, 138; Yogācāra, 129, 130
bodhisattva precepts (bodhisattva vinaya, Mahāyāna vinaya, *pusa pini, pusajie, dachengjie*), 26, 125, 128, 137, 140, 144, 163, 164, 223n15, 223n16; 223n22, 224n23, 225n30; actualized communities guided by, 139; as guidelines for all actions leading to co-liberation, 137; as rules for democratic deliberation, 173; historical narrative about formation of, 130–31; historicity of, 135; independent lineage of, 125–35; institutional lineage of, 124, 128, 135; springhead of, 137; Yogācāra, 133–34, 139, 141, 224n28; unbroken institutional lineage of, 124, 125–35, 224n23
Bodhisattvabhūmi, *100*
Boucher, Daniel, 223n11
Boyd, Richard, 222n2
Brahmā Net Sūtra, the, 125, 130–31, 139, 223n18
Brindley, Erica, 211n32, 218n54
Bronkhorst, Johannes, 17, 18, 193n51
Brown, Mackenzie C., 203n26
Bru, Sascha, 195n7

Buddhability, 26, 112, 120, 214n3; interconditioning, 114
Buddhability-cum-humanity, 26, 95, 97, 98, 114, 117, 181
Buddhadāsa, Bhikkhu, 67, 207n70
buddhahood, 62, 97, 98, 112, 116, 117, 158, 180, 204n40, 205n47; foundation for a transpersonal and intersubjective oneness, 104; as intersubjective oneness, 137; intersubjective, 171; transpersonal or intersubjective, 26, 103
Buddha nature, 59, 108, 116, 155, 160, 179, 204n40; transformative force of, 117
Buddhisize (*fohua*), 69, 124, 181; Taixu on, 211n29; Zhang Ruzhao on, 180
Buddhisized critical thinking, 151, 163–64, 173, 183
Buddhisized human perfectibility, 97–98
Butler, Judith, 36, 41, 196n20, 212n44

Cai, Yuanpei, 21, 48, 72, 106, 147; on aesthetic education, 41, 43; on *ālayavijñāna*, 92–93, 218n45; on Bergsonism, 92, 199n71; on Wang Xiaoxu (Jitong), 64, 65, 92–93
Callero, Peter L., 219n74
Canales, Jimena, 199n67
Césaire, Aimé, 114, 219n70
caste, 17, 65, 146, 205n47; Brahmanical concept of, 59; Buddhist concept of, 57; unjust system of, 146; Yogācāra critique of, 204n39. *See also zhongxing; zhongye*
castism, 19, 59, 62, 146
caste-inspired view of human soteriology, 205n47
causal (karmic) efficacy, 4, 8, 13, 14, 74; and *adhipati*, 85; and propensity, 81; intersubjective corroboration, coherence, and, 86, 149, 165; seeds and their, 47. *See also* Yogācāra three Cs
civil society organizations, 25, 79, 111, 127, 181, 229n12
Chakrabarty, Dipesh, 190n14
Chakravarti, Uma, 193n53, 206n63, 208n75, 222n1
Chang, Ku-ming, 198n52
changing referents (*bianfa*), 4–10, 29, 95, 148
Chen, Duxiu, 2, 33, 187n1
Chen, Janet Y., 198n61
Chen, Zhenru, 118, 221n90
Cheng Weishilun (*Establishing consciousness-only*; *CWSL*), 78, 84, *100*, 166, 170, 234n76; Lü Cheng's edition of, 170; Taixu drew upon, 79
Cheng, Yinghong, 214n5
Chidester, David, 174, 235n95
Cho, Francisca, 20, 191n27, 214n2
Ciaudo, Joseph, 198n50, 198n60, 199n71, 213n65
coaction, 38, 42, 80, 113, 163, 185; democratic, 145; guidelines of, 137; intersubjective, 172; motivated, 13, 144, 174; new patterns of, 185; nonviolent, 87, 145; organizational, 26, 111, 123, 124, 135–41; peaceful, 79; paradigm, 19, 110, 136; society as intersubjective, 82–87. *See also* actions and coactions; copoiesis
coevolution, 120, 121
Collection of Six Perfections Sūtra, 101
collective karma (*gongye, tongye*), 54–57, 62, 71, 75–76, 86–87, 89, 205n46, 210n20, 211n27; Besant's, 202n21, 203n24; Blavatsky's, 56, 202n21; Halbfass on, 203n28; Hayes on, 203n29; of killing, 75; Theosophical concept of, 55, 203n24; Thich Nhat Hanh's, 236n20; Yogācāra, 62. *See also* similar karma; shared karma
co-liberation (collective liberation), 3, 26, 48, 49, 95, 120, 122, 182; actions leading to, 137; curriculum of, 108; democratic, 26, 151; nirvāṇa as, 110; path of, 103, 105, 109, 144, 158, 176; pedagogy for, 182; process of, 111; producing knowledge for, 99, 163; shared goal of, 26, 135, 181, 183
Commentary on the Four Hundred [Stanzas of Madhyamaka], 100
communism, 65, 135, 141; of Buddhist knowledge, 156; of knowledge, 163, 175; of soteriological knowledge, 130
comparative hermeneutics (*bijiao yanjiu fa*), 50, 108, 124, 152–56, 163, 169, 175; and Buddhisized critical thinking, 163, 173; as interconditioned rigor; evaluating truth claims with, 164; idiosyncratic method of, 125; to prove his unconventional claim, 155

compassion (*ci*), 85, 139, 144, 145, 147, 157, 160, 182; and interdependence, 112; as self-care strategy, 158, 161; care and, 94; critical thinking grounded in, 183; democratic communities of, 149; ecology of, 146; egalitarian, complex society grounded in, 174; emotional norm of, 140; épistémè of, 112, 124, 164; idyllic flow of, 109; logic grounded in, 159; no-self, interdependence, and, 70, 136, 150, 225n34; rationality serves to harness the affective power of, 175; wisdom grounded in, 151
compassionate mind-heart (*cixin*), 159
Compendium of Abhidharma, 100
Compendium of Dharma, 100
Compendium of the Perfection of Wisdom, A, 100
Comte, Auguste, 61, 63, 204n43
Cook, Ramsay, 203n27
Coovadia, Imraan, 216n27
copoiesis, 19, 41, 79, 86; interconditioned, 108; intersubjective, 39; meshwork of, 80. *See also* coaction
cosmo-sociokarma, 55
critical thinking (*piping sixiang, piping jingshen*), 151, 157; as logic grounded in compassion, 159; Buddhisized, 163, 164, 173, 183; grounded in meditative absorption, 111
"Cultivating Compassion" (*Dafangguangfo huayan jing—xiucifen; Flower Ornament Sūtra--The Chapter on Cultivating Compassion*), *101*, 159–60
cultural death, 29, 121

Da zhidu lun (*Treatise on the Great Perfection of Wisdom*), 130
Dacheng fajie wu chabie lun (*Treatise on Non-Distinction in the Great Vehicle Dharma Realm*), 143
"Dachengjing bijiao dufa" ("Comparative Hermeneutics," the text), 152, 230n16, 230n24–25
Daji xukongzang suowen jing—juezefen (*Sūtra of the Questions of Bodhisattva Ākāśagarbha*), *101*, 160
Daoxuan, 112, 219n61
Darwinist competition, 31, 73, 121; antidote to, 87; dystopian myth of, 123; life corrupted by, 148; living hell of, 122
Darwinist struggle for survival, 76
Daswani, Rekha, 222n1
Dávid-Barrett, Tamás, 228n75
Davidson, Ronald Mark, 216n28
De Jong, Jan Willem, 189n11
decolonial, 5, 144, 149
Deeds of the Buddha, 101
Deleuze, Gilles, 199n67
democracy, 18, 52, 64, 68, 117, 139, 182, 185; bodhisattva, 125; bodhisattva of, 26, 124, 146, 181, 183; Buddhist, 133, 135–36, 140–41; deliberative, 140, 163, 175, 227n49; Dharmic, 26, 135–41, 146, 227n53; mass, 140, 146; noncoercive, 26; of the karmic tracks, 74, 77; processual philosophy of, 225n34; secular, 144; social, 140, 146; socially engaged, 124; tribal, 226n48; Yinshun on, 90
Denzin, Norman K., 6, 189n9, 190n15, 191n18, 191n21–23
Desmond, Matthew, 178, 235n2
destructive excitement, 145
Dev, Acharya Narendra, 66
DeVido, Elise A., 236n11
dévisagement réciproque (reciprocal scrutiny), 5, 145, 150, 163
Dewey, John, 17, 94, 145, 193n48; 208n4, 213n72
Dhammapada, *100*, 106–8, 137, 217n38, 218n41, 226n39
dharmakāya (dharma body), 103, 110, 141, 143, 155, 215n18
Dharmapāla, 17, 59, 104, 119, 167, 233n68, 233n70, 233n71
Diamond Sūtra, the, *100*
diffractive, 3; analysis, *8*, 15–16, 157, 193n45; method, 3, 15–16, 20, 32; question, 73
Dignāga (Chenna), 59, 160
Dikötter, Frank, 201n12
direct *ālambana* (direct objective basis, *suoyuanyuan*), 84, 85
discipline of Nirvāṇa, the, 102–4, 112–14, 117, 215n18
doctrinal oneness, 103, 156

Donzelot, Jacques, 196n24
Duara, Prasenjit, 207n72
Duiker, William, 197n39
Durkheim, Émile, 37, 52, 73, 195n14, 196n23, 200n5, 209n13
Duval, Kathleen, 228n69

egoism, 87; collective, 87; individual, 87; inherent, 73; moral, 74, 87, 127, 182, 185, 209n10; rational, 87; social Darwinist, 145; structural inequalities that abet, 127
Einfühlung (empathetic exchange, *ganqing yiru*), 36, 169
Einstein, Albert, 45, 199n67
Ekottara Āgama (*Zengyi ahanjing*), 179
élan vital (vital impetus), 38, 45, 168; conflated with *ālayavijñāna*, 92, 93; resemblance of *ālayavijñāna*, 44
Elstub, Stephen, 227n49
Eltschinger, Vincent, 17, 19, 193n50–51, 194n56, 204n39, 222n1
emptiness-cum-interdependence, 175
engaged Buddhism, 178, 181, 193n53, 206n63
épistémè, 4–6, 10, 13, 51, 188n6
épistémè of compassion, 112, 124, 164
epistemic domination, 150, 164, 178, 194n65
epistemology, 5–10, 157, 189n11, 194n53; academic, 10; Buddhist, 13; objectivist, 7, 26; of liberation; social, 26, 27, 151–52, 165, 173, 181; sociality of, 173; subjectivist, 7; transformative, 95, 105, 148–52, 165, 173, 174, 178, 181, 183; Yogācāra, 44, 45
Epstein, Brian, 195n14
equal conditions for liberation, 124, 129, 139
equal support for life and liberation, 172
equality (*pingdeng*), 26, 36, 64, 74, 146, 158, 161, 182, 185; and freedom, 41, 75; and justice, 75; institutional, 87, 137; interconditioned, 158; justice and, 227n56; lay-monastic, 130; quest for, 18; social, 41, 66, 81, 87, 164, 180, 193n53; spiritual, 66, 67, 81, 131, 179, 180–82; women's struggle for, 180
Essentials (*Zangyao*), 3, 22, 131, 142; relation with *Five Disciplines*, 99, 119, 129, 134, 140, 168–69
Eubanks, Charlotte, 224n19
evolutionism, 24, 54, 56; critics of, 43; encounters of karma and, 54, 201n11; encounter of Yogācāra with, 57, 59; fusion of Yogācāra karmic theory with, 55; science and, 43; social, 47; socio-, 93; socio-spiritual, 50; spiritual, 195; Yogācāra and, 57, 62
Explanation of the Investigation of Objective Bases, *100*
Extensive Pure Vinaya (*Vaipulya Sūtra of the Pure Vinaya*, the), *101*, 125, 128–29, 137, 223n15

family karma, 203n24
Fisher, Gareth, 201n19
Five Disciplines (*wuke foxue*, *wuke sanzhou*), 22, 220n87, 232n38, 235n86; and three phases, 98–102, 104–11; on bodhisattva vinaya, 125, 127, 128, 131, 134; on Buddhability, 112, 117, 121; on critical thinking, 151, 157, 159, 161, 162, 171; on Dharmic democracy, 137, 141, 142; on Discipline of Nirvāṇa, 102, 104
Fodi jinglun (*Treatise on the Buddha-Stage Sūtra*; *Buddhabhūmi-sūtra-śāstra*), 104, 215n18
Foucault, Michel, 188n6
Freire, Paulo, 182–83, 236n13
Frye, Marilyn, 194n65
Fundamental Verses on the Middle Way, *100*
Fukaura, Seibun, 231n37

Galtung, Johan, 219n70
Garfield, Jay L., 189n11, 192n41, 208n2, 208n4, 209n10, 210n14, 210n19, 234n80
gaige (reform), 1, 147, 162, 187n1
ganying (empathetic response), 79, 80, 110, 211n32, 211n35, 218n54
geming (revolution), 1, 33–34, 162, 187n1
Gemingjun (Revolutionary Army, The), 51–52
gendered soteriology, 177, 181
Ghanavyūha Sūtra (*Dacheng miyan jing*; *The Sūtra on the Invisible Splendor of the Mahāyāna*), *101*, 104, 230n24
Gildow, Douglas, 197n39
Girō, Seno'o, 67, 207n69
Gold, Johnathan C., 165, 233n63
Gombrich, Richard F., 229n13
Gong, Jun, 64, 203n30, 206n61, 206n63

Goodman, Russell, 213n70
Goossaert, Vincent, 195n2, 226n46
Great Cloud Sūtra—The Chapter on the Great Assembly, The, 101
great compassion, 145, 150, 157
Great Ornament Sūtra, The, 100
Great Perfection of Wisdom--The Mañjuśrī Chapter, The, 100
Graziano, Michael S. A., 219n74
Green, Adam S., 193n51–52, 228n69
Guan, Yici, 64, 65
Guba, Egon G., 189n9, 191n18, 191n21–23
guest dust (*kechen*), 106, 107, 111, 137, 217n34
Guyau, Jean-Marie, 36–38, 196n21, 196n23, 196n27–28, 197n31
Gvili, Gal, 198n54
Gyatso, Janet, 226n41

Halbfass, Wilhelm, 56, 203n23, 203n28
Hammerstrom, Erik, 195n15, 198n49, 198n52, 198n55, 206n52, 213n55
Han, Qingjing, 90–91
Han, Yongun, 66, 207n68
Haraway, Donna, 193n45
Harding, Frank James William, 196n23, 196n28, 197n31
Harrison, Peter, 189n11, 190n17, 209n11
Haslanger, Sally, 185, 186, 193n45, 213n69, 217n35, 237n23–24, 237n26
Heap of Jewels Sūtra (*Baoji jing*; *Ratnakūṭa-sūtra*), 58, 133, 134, 224n28
Heart of Abhidharma, the, 100
Helmholtz, Herman, 39, 197n33
Hengbao, 179–80, 181, 186
Hershock, Peter D., 16, 193n47, 214n2
hetuvidyā (logic; *yinming*), 102, 157–59, 161, 165
hierarchy, 130, 193n51; nondemocratic, 146; racial, 55; spiritual, 116
Hildebrand, David, 213n71
Hiragawa, Akira, 189n11
historical sedimentation, 154–55, 164
hooks, bell, 178, 181–85, 236n12–19
huguo baozhong (protecting the nation, preserving the race), 6, 25, 53, 83
Hu, Hsiao-Lan, 193n53, 201n16, 209n12, 214n2, 219n74, 228n76
Hu, Shih, 64, 65
Huang, Jusu, 118, 220n89
Huang, Max Ko-wu, 201n8, 201n10
Huayan (Avataṃsaka), 92, 143, 198n61, 199n69, 218n45
Huiyuan, 112, 219n61
Humanistic Buddhism (Renjian Fojiao), 76, 90, 181, 211n22
Huxley, Thomas Henry, 63, 73, 121, 201n11, 202n20, 202n21, 202n22; applauded the Buddha, 56; portrayed karma as energy-like magnetism, 56; read karma as individual, 55, 56, 58; Yan Fu translated, 24, 51, 53, 57, 203n31

icchantika (*chanti*, *yichanti*), 62, 204n40, 205n47, 220nn83–84; bodhisattva (*pusa*), 116, 117; voluntary, 116, 117
idealism (*weixin zhuyi*), 17, 85, 209n8, 233n71; and solipsism, 85; Berkeleyan, 16, 85; materialism and, 35; metaphysical, 168; refute, 73; social, 123; theological, 164; two extremes of, 71. *See also* antirealism; irrealism; materialism; realism
ignorance, 12, 138, 182; epistemological, 182, 185; mental afflictions of, 131, *132*, 182
impartiality, 7, 149, 173; benchmark of, 174; conflated objectivity with, 150, 164; scholarly value of, 7; social values of, 150
incommensurable ontology, 5
incommensurable research paradigm, 4, 6, 9, 189n9
incommensurable worlds, 12, 14, 192n42
incommensurable worldview, 4, 5
incommensurability, 13; of different worlds, 149
indirect *ālambana* (indirect objective basis, *shu suoyuanyuan*), 62, 87, 117, 120, 205n46, 212n46; and similar karma, 86; distinguishes Yogācāra from other idealisms, 85; functions to explain intersubjectivity, 84; objective aspect of *ālayavijñāna* gives rise to, 85; serves as the cornerstone of an intersubjective sociality, 117–18; Thusness as, 119; to describe scientific fundings, 84

individual karma, 59, 87, 89, 90; Buddhist, 58; Huxley's 55, 56; objective portrayal of, 57; Orientalist reading of, 51, 57, 58; Yogācāra, 60
individualism, 41, 195n14, 219n74, 224n26; as a cage, 42; birdcage of, 36; institutionalized, 139; rampant, 31, 121; secular discourse of, 78; Western, 57, 68, 123
Ingold, Tim, 136, 211n34, 226n36
inner learning (*neixue*), 142; social function of, 235n98; systemization of, 99; *yuanzheng zhi*, 153
Inner Learning (*Neixue*, the journal), 24, 152, 156, 220n88, 234n83
Inner Learning Institute, The (Neixue yuan), 21, 22, 24, 104, 133, 162, 179, 183, 199n73, 206n61; 213n61, 220nn88–89; as the model for a different kind of lay community, 112; students at, 93, 181; colleagues at, 123; core members of, 82; debate at, 118; leader of, 98; occupied a position of power, 181; officially dissolved, 162
Inquiry of the Householder Ugra, The, 101
interconnective stimulation (*jiaogan*), 110, 111, 114, 158
interconditionality, 214n2; and relationality, 68; karmic, 71, 74; nirvāṇic, 139; nonviolence grounded in, 79; social ethics of, 55
interconditioned, 106, 235n100; awakening, 216n29; behavioral pattern, 150; copoiesis, 108; equality, 158; liberation, 123; meditative realization as, 105; normativity, 150; rigor, 157; social change as, 216n27; social phenomena, 151; transformation, 173; unfolding, 149
interconditioning, 172, 214n2; Buddhability, 114; causally constitutive and, 110; copoiesis and, 41; human, 97, 114, 124, 215n22; intersubjective, 138; karmascape, 162; karmic, 127; mycelial meshwork of, 170; nirvāṇic, 103, 124; new patterns of, 148; ontology as the basis of both social arrangements and scholarly pursuits, 174
interdependence (interdependency), 19, 26, 41, 67, 70, 139; as a condition of equality, 36; compassion and, 26, 70, 112, 149, 150, 225n34; constitutive, 41; empathetic, 158, 160; equality grounded in, 18; equality premised upon, 41; equitable social imagination of, 75; irreducible, 171; karmic, 152; of lives, 36; radical, 25
interpretative matrix, 152–53
intersubjective agreement, 13, 14, 153, 160, 161, 165, 169, 170, 234n76; arising from shared karmic seeds, 81; as an epistemological outcome, 165; as a manifestation of consciousness-only, 169; as the proof of consciousness-only, 169; become the cornerstones of a communism of knowledge, 175; on seemingly objective existences, 84; on their shared natural environments, 86; sedimented, 157; shared karmic seeds generate, 166, 211n36. *See also prasiddha*; Yogācāra three Cs
intersubjective consensus. *See also prasiddha*; Yogācāra three Cs
intersubjective corroboration (*huzheng*), 4, 8, 13, 14, 83, 165; epistemological checks of, 86; epistemic standards of, 149; mediated by language, 86; of connected, aggregated karmic processes, 152. *See also prasiddha*; Yogācāra three Cs
intersubjective oneness, 38, 171, 172, 175, 197n33; as an aesthetic society, 103; buddhahood as, 104, 117, 137; cohered by aesthetic empathy, 118; quest for, 139; the social as, 162; transpersonal and, 104; Yogācāra, 153
intersubjective openness, 145
intersubjective resonance, 37, 84, 89, 166
intersubjectivity, 35, *72*, 81, 112, 192n42, 210n19, 233n73; and an agentless human agency, 145; genuine, 87; grounded in aesthetic resonances, 121; indirect *ālambana* functions to explain, 84; ontological primacy of, 168; philosophy of, 153; *prasiddha* could be used to establish, 165; problem of, 14, 168; producing, 15; question of, 83; theorize, 38, 82, 192n41; Yogācāra, 14, 31, 86, 87, 117–18, 149, 211n36, 212n47, 233n66. *See also adhipati*; indirect *ālambana*

intertextuality, 133–34
Introduction to Logic (*Yiming ruzhengli lun*, *Nyāyapraveśa*), *101*, 159
institutionalized bodhicitta, 163–73
irrealism, 81, 212n38. *See also* antirealism; materialism; realism
itthibhāva (femaleness), 179
Ivanhoe, Philip J., 212n40

James, William, 94, 193n48, 213n70, 213n72
Jenco, Leigh K., 5, 148, 190n13, 190n14, 229n1, 229n3, 229n4, 229n11
Jenkins, Katherine, 9, 10, 71, 191n24, 191n25, 208n5
Jessup, James Brooks, 226n46
Jewel-Arising Treatise on Establishing Consciousness-only, *100*
Jewels in the Hand Treatise, *100*
Ji, Zhe, 228n71
Jiang, Tao, 190n16
Jizang, 112, 219n61
jimie (relinquishment), 107
jijing (quiescence), 107
Jitiaoyin suowen jing (*The Inquiries of Jitiaoyin*), 129. *See also Pinaiye jusha fangguang jing*
Jones, Charles B., 228n72
Joshi, Maya, 207n66
Jullien, François, 18
just awakening (*zhengjue*), 36
"Just Awakening and Renunciation" (Zhengjue yu chuli), 23, 124, 128, 146, 217n30, 222n3
just society, 3, 36, 65, 78, 124, 206n63; decent and, 147; establishing, 88, 92, 201n15, 216n29; how to theorize a, 15; nonviolent and, 71; philosophy of a, 17; producing knowledge for, 149; theorization of, 77; to bring forth formations of, 79; to build, 36, 66, 91, 222n3; to imagine, 68, 123; quest for, 68, 70; vision of, 25; what constitutes a, 18, 36, 77

Kachru, Sonam, 11, 191n26, 191n27, 191n30, 192nn37,40,41; on cosmological individual, 11, 192n32; on the constitutive variety of worlds, 12, 191n33; on *jiwei* (elemental event), 192n38; on Vasubandhu's hermeneutics, 227n54; on virtual space, 192n39
Kang, Xiaofei, 236n10
Kapstein, Matthew T., 224n26
Karashima, Seishi, 220n83
karma-informed moral reasoning, *8*, 98, 123, 136
karmic confluence (*gongye*, *tongye*), 71, *72*, 75, 89, 90, 205n46, 210nn18–19; nation as, 77; misread as, 86; society as, 74, 81; society cohered by, 77
karmic seeds (*yezhong*; *karma-bīja*), 14, 25, 48, 53, 57–59, 62, 211n36; agentive, 46, 49, 74; as agentive potentials, 168; collective, 184; common, 78; fruits of, 89 in Abhidharma, 204n38; impure, 82; in *The Śūraṅgama Sūtra*, 204n35; pure, 82, 166; shared, 78–81, 86, 166; with common characteristics, 78, 166
karmic society, 74; country as a, 77; nation as a, 77; Yogācāra, 81
karmic web that is society, 175
karmically entangled, *8*, 12
Katz, Paul R., 195n2, 236n10
Keng, Ching, 192n41, 216n24, 220n84
Kerekes, Susanne, 201n17, 201n19, 225n33
Kern, Martin, 228n67
Keyes, Charles F., 201n14
Kiely, Jan, 206n59, 208n74
Kirylo, James D., 236n13
Kosambi, Dharmanand, 66, 207n65, 232n41
Kosuta, Matthew, 228n66
Kowner, Rotem, 200n2, 201n12
Kragh, Ulrich Timme, 204n40, 224n26
Kuiji, 14, 47, 84, 199n69, 216n29, 221n95, 229n6, 233n67; attributed this two-part interpretation to Sthiramati, 168; commented on *Triṃśikā*, 167, 169, 192n42, 205n46, 212n46, 212n47, 234n77

La Vallée Poussin, Louis de, 233n71
Lai, Huei-Yun, 199n62
Lai, Sufen Sophia, 201n12
Lai, Whalen, 220n83
Lam, Tong, 206n51
Lambourne, Lionel, 197n36

Laṅkāvatāra Sūtra, *101*, 117, 154, 220n82, 220n87, 223n18, 230n24
Lawlor, Leonard, 200n82
Li, An, 194n62, 230n16
Li, Jinxi, 44, *72*, 92, 93, 198n59, 198n61
Li, Jingjing, 192n41, 205n46, 212n46, 216n29, 233n68
Li, Shicen, 40, 43–45, 46, 197n40, 198n58, 198n59; introduced Yogācāra alongside the global flow of evolutionary theories, 50
lifeworld (*loka*), 49; incommensurable, 14; karmically connected, 14, 149; multiple, 4, *8*, 10–13, 215n22
Liang, Qichao, 62, 98
Liang, Shuming, 44, 62, 198nn59–60, 221n98, 230n26
liberation Buddhology, 15, 25–27, 95, 98, 117–18, 122, 148–51, 179, 181–83
liberation theology, 182, 236n13
Lin, Chen-kuo, 188n4, 198n53, 217n33, 230n21
Lin, Pei-ying, 223n18, 226n39
Lincoln, Yvonna S., 6, 189n9, 190n15, 191nn18–19
Ling, Trevor, 193n53, 207n71
Lipps, Theodor, 36–38, 196n29, 197n31
Liu, Ming-Wood, 220n83
Liu, Xinru, 193n53, 208n75, 222n1
livable future (world), 74, 79, 87, 97, 144
Loftus, Timothy, 207n67
Lotus Sūtra, The, *101*, 215n20
Lü, Cheng, after 1949, 146–47, 162, 173; biographical sketch of, 20–23; critique of Taixu's monastic reform, 223n6; on aesthetic revolution, 1–3; on Bergsonism, 44–49; on bodhisattva vinaya, 123–25, 127–35; on Buddhability and humanity, 97–98, 112–22; on Cai, Yuanpei, 41–43; on civil society organization, 127; on comparative hermeneutics, 152–57; on critical thinking, 151, 157–62; on Dharmic democracy, 135–45; on enchanting social relations with aesthetic empathy, 40–43; on *mātṛka*, 133–34; on moral agency, 45–50; on nirvāṇa, 102–4; on revolution of the mind-heart, 32–35; on revolutionizing consciousness, 104–11; on the social function of aesthetics, 35–38; on the social function of translation, 38–40; on sociality and Yogācāra intersubjectivity, 117–20; on vinaya studies, 126–27; on spiritual coevolution, 121–22; on Zhang, Taiyan, 44–45
Lü, Fengzi, 20
Lu Xun (Zhou, Shuren), 62
Lu-Adler, Huaping, 205n47, 225n34, 229n8, 237n25
Luo, Ning, 197n39
Lusthaus, Dan, 156, 168, 188n4, 191nn26–27, 192n41, 231n34, 233n72, 234nn75–76

Madsen, Richard, 226n47
Madhyāntavibhāga (*Bian zhongbian lun*, *MAV*), 107–8
Mahāparinirvāṇa Sūtra, 112, 115, 120, 219n65, 220n83; *Chapter of True Dharma, The*, *101*, 113, 114
Mahāyānasaṃgraha (*Compendium of the Great Vehicle*, *She dacheng lun*, *Msg*), *100*, 129, 142, 143, 221n95, 223n15, 227n59
Mahāyānasūtrālaṃkāra (*Dacheng zhuangyan jinglun*), 128, 223n12, 230n16
Maitreya (Cishi), 107, 125, 211n29; Buddhaghoṣa as, 232n41; collecting bodhisattva precepts, 131–34, 224n25, 224n26
Makeham, John, 188n4, 190n14, 205n48, 217n33, 230n21, 231n34
Marc, Joly, 210n16
materialism (*weiwu zhuyi*), 35, 64, 73, 208n7; and scientism, 44; excessive, 31, 121; historical, 35, 90, 164, 173; two extremes of idealism and, 71; philosophical idealism or, 164; rejection of, 44, 72, 73; scientific, 24, 88, 90; Western, 65. *See also* idealism
Mather, Richard B., 226n40
mātṛkā (underlying matrix; *benmu*), 132–33, 134, 152, 156, 157, 159
Marxism (*Makesi zhuyi*), 35, 65, 206n56; Kosambi's Buddhism and, 66, 207n65
McDermott, James P., 202n21, 203n23, 203n28
McLeod, Alexus, 229n7

meditation (*dhyāna*), 95, 131, 136, 145, 157, 199n64; and reasoning, 102; instructions for, 158–9; Lü's daily, 22, 23; perfection of, 144; Yogācāra, 158
meditative absorption (*samādhi*), 102, 111, 117, 144
meditative insight, 106, 109, 159, 161
meditative instruction, 158, 184
meditative methods, 158
meditative practice, 159
meditative realization, 105
meditative training, 102
Merton, Robert K., 151, 161–64, 229n14, 232n57, 233nn58–59
meshwork, 162; karmic, 80; mutually conditioning, 114; mycelial, 110, 133, 170
Metaphysical Institute, the, 162, 206n61
metamethodological, 3, 4, 9, 15
Metzinger, Thomas, 219n74
Minor, Robert N., 203n26
Mitsukawa, Toyoki, 234n80
Moore, Matthew J., 222n1, 226n44
Mukai, Akira, 156, 231n30
Murthy, Viren, 196n25, 198n49, 200n4, 205n49

Nāgārjuna, 130, 170, 175, 189n11, 192n44, 235n100
Nagel, Thomas, 188n6, 235n96
Nakajima, Takahiro, 229n11
Nālandā, 98, 99, 102, 104, 106, 214n6, 215n14; essential teachings of, 133; five disciplines of, 102; learning, 125, 133; modeled after, 99
Nanjing, 20–23, 213n61, 220n88, 228n70; Inner Learning Institute back to, 104; Inner Learning Institute in, 82; Republican government, 91
Nanjō, Bun'yū, 24, 59
national karma, 56–57, 61, 62, 203n24, 203n28; Wang Enyang frequently referenced, 86. *See also* collective karma; shared karma; *zhongye* (Yogācāra national/racial) karma
natural kinds, 11, 18, 80, 83, 165; as if they were, 17; mind-independent, 11, 74; scientific agreements about, 87; social kinds came to be equated with, 35;
neifan (Buddhist commoner), 115–16
Neufeldt, Ronald W., 201n14, 203n26
neutrality, 9, 151
New Confucianism (Xinrujia), 43, 73, 198n52, 198n60
New Culture Movement, the (Xinwenhua yundong), 2, 21, 34, 63, 64, 94
New Man, 98, 114, 214n5
Nhat Hanh, Thich, 178, 181–82, 184, 214n2, 236n20
nirvāṇa, 82, *101*, 115, 116, 122, 142, 159, 161, 179, 215n14, 215n22, 218n49, 235n89; as co-liberation, 110; as the cause of liberation, 105; as one true-reality realm, 170; as the outcome of liberation, 108; as the relinquishment of afflictions, 110; *dharmakāya* and, 215n18; discipline of, the, 102–4, 112–14, 117, 160; original quiescence and, 109; transitioning toward, 109
nirvāṇa-cum-buddhahood, 112, 117
nirvāṇa-cum-extinguishing-suffering, 142
nirvāṇa-cum-one-true-reality-realm, 142
Noble Sūtra of the Explanation of the Profound Secrets, 100
noncoercive, 75, 77; association of persons, 79; complex social formations, 78, 135; democracy, 26; reform, 87
nondual, 57, 58, 88, *101*, 209n9, 232n38; doctrine of, 31; equitable social imagination, 75; of saṃsāra and nirvāṇa, 215n22; nonviolence-based theorization, 81; processual teaching, 203n34; regarding the duality of individuality and society, 103; rejection of the subject-object structure, 189n7; ways of knowing, 71; worldview, 12, 55
norm, 6, 221n95; behavior, 163; disciplinary, 6–7; ethical, 148, 150; emotional, 140; nonviolent revolution as the, 145; of collective actions, 124; would emerge through a fair and civil process, 140
normativity, 140; interconditioned, 150

Ober, Douglas, 207n65, 207n67
Oldenberg, H., 56
objective certainty, 145

objective humanities, 165,
objective knowledge, 5, 7, *8*, 106, 121, 152; as the result of the historical sedimentation, 164
objective naturalism, 189n11. *See also* subjective naturalism
objective scholarship, 106, 157, 161
objective universe, 70
objectivist epistemology, 6, 7, *8*, 13, 26, 189n11
objectivity, 4, 13, 18, 31, 81, 149, 164, 165, 174; abstraction of, 9; academic standard of, 4; and science, 25; and universality, 149; as outcome of social practice, 149, 211n37, 229n5; as the benchmark of knowledge, 11; as a viable epistemic principle, 26; as convenient fiction, 83, 118; benchmark of, 152; challenge to, 10, 191n27; constructedness of, 151; danger of, 150, 229n8; dualism of, 25; dualistic reification of, 70, 168; naturalizing, 74; ontological claim of, 7; ontological divide between, 80; replacing, 13–15; scientific, 157. *See also* subjectivity
Ōishi, Masayoshi, 197n30
Okabe, Kazuo, 189n11, 217n37
Ohnuma, Reiko, 194n60
Olson Jr., Mancur, 225n34
Omvedt, Gail, 222n1
one true-reality (dharma) realm (one dharma realm, *yifajie*, *yizhen fajie*), *100*, 102, 103, 109, 110–11, 142, 215n18, 215n22, 217n32; Buddhisized as, 124; dependent arising of, 121; *dharmakāya* equated with, 110; interconnective stimulations to manifest, 111; learners bring forth, 160; nirvāṇa as, 170; remake the world into, 120; where sentient beings and buddhas are empathetically connected, 160
one objective world, 4, 6, 149, 160, 169, 188n6
ontic injustice, 9–10
ontological commitment, 6, 149
Oreskes, Naomi, 26, 150, 164, 229n10, 229n14
organized skepticism, 151, 228n64; as both a methodological and institutional mandate, 164; for establishing intersubjective accord, 175; grounded in compassion, 144; institutionalized bodhicitta and, 163–73; represented an essential self-correction mechanism, 163; social epistemology and, 150
Orientalism, 135, 190n14, 218n40; Amartya Sen on, 202n20
original enlightenment (*xingjue*), 143, 156, 230n26; in *Awakening Faith*, 154; lead to philosophical solipsism, 156; Lü's critique of, 227n60, 231n27
original quiescence (*xingji*, *zixing benji*), *100*, 102–3, 142, 145, 158, 215n20, 218n49; as the fundamental tenet, 107, 137; debates on, 217n33, 231n27; equivalent to original purity, 106, 153; function of, 108, 110, 215n20; in *MAV*, 108; insight into, 106, 161; leads to renewal, 156; realization of, 105–6, 108–9. *See also* original purity
original purity (*zixing benjing*), 103, 105; and the perfected nature, 153; appeared first, 155; relation with original quiescence, 107–8, 156. *See also* original quiescence
outcaste, 65, 180
Ouyang, Jingwu, 20–22, 152, 174, 199n69, 205n48, 206n61, 214n7; founded China Inner Learning Institute, 82; gendered soteriology of, 177, 179–81, 212n39; on *Awakening Faith*, 213n63, 230n21, 230n26; on co-liberation, 111; on multiple lifeworlds, 215n22; on *Msaṃ*, 142–43, 227n57, 227n59; on original quiescence, 105, 217n33; on *siyiren* (four kinds of humans as worldly support), 112–13, 219n61; on socio-soteriology, 82–83, 84; on state and politics, 207n73; on *tiyong* (foundation and function), 113; on Yuanxue, 98–99, 102
Owen, Alex, 43, 198n51

Paek, Sŏnguk, 66, 207n68
Palmer, David A., 195n2, 226n46
pāramitā (perfection), *100*, 137, 183; six, *100*, 122–23, 141–45
Park, Jin Y., 207n68
Park, Peter K., 225n34
Pater, Walter, 40, 197nn35–36

Path of Liberation, The, 101
peaceful, 4, 75, 90; and happy country, 79; and just world, 83; coaction, 79; utopia, 52
peaceful coexistence (*gonghe*), 63, 67, 68, 71, 88
Peking University, 21, 94
People's Bell (*Minduo*), 40, 45, 50, 92, 198n61
perfuming (*xun*, *xunxiu*, *vāsanā*), 58, 218n43, 218n49; through hearing (*wenxun*, *śrutavāsanā*), 107, 108, 109, 137, 218n45
personal karma (*ziye*, *bieye*), 75, 211n27
Phillips, Stephen, 192n36
Pinaiye jusha fangguang jing (*Vinaya Ghoṣa Vaipulya Sūtra*), 129, 223n16. *See also* *Inquiries of Jitiaoyin*
Pollock, Sheldon, 175, 235n99
positivism, 64, 66, 67, 74, 121, 129, 151, 174; Auguste Comte's, 61, 63, 204n43; critique of, 190n17; post-, 4, 5, 6–7, *8*, 18, 71, 189n11
pragmatism, 190n17, 213n72
praise oneself and slander others (*zizan huita*), *132*, 138, 173
prasiddha (intersubjective agreement; *jicheng*, *grags pa*), 14, 166, 169, 234n76; as an epistemological outcome, 165; as evidence for the ontological primacy of intersubjectivity, 168; as evidence of a reliable causal explanation, 170; as precarious linguistic conventions, 166; became a natural condition, 166; collective karmic unfolding of establishing, 173; dual function of, 165; *loka*-(*shijian*), 166; social turn of, 166; *yukti*-(*daoli*; *rigs pas*), 166, 234n82
prātimokṣa (code of discipline; *suishunjietuo*; *biejietuo*), 123, 126, 127, 128, 223n5
process (processual) philosophy, 17, 71, 80, 87, 115, 117, 193n46, 211n33; Buddhist, 16–20, 110; of democracy, 225n34; pre-Whiteheadian, 208n4; social, 16, 18, 19, 71, 97, 117, 123, 135, 165, 222nn2–3; Whiteheadian, 208n4
propensity, 81, 115, 170, 202n21; human, 97; natural, 109, 117; of kindness, 97; preordained, 116; toward awakening, 117
Prueitt, Catherine, 192n41, 210n14, 210n19, 211n36
Pusey, James Reeve, 200n7

Qingyi Jushi, 65, 180
Queen, Christopher S., 206n63
Quine, Willard van Orman, 10–11, 191n29, 210n15
qunxue, 60. *See also* sociology

racial karma, 184, 237n21, 237n22. *See also* collective karma; national karma; *zhongye*
raciology, 56, 60, 205n47, 225n34
Radich, Michael, 216n23
Rajapakse, Vijitha, 202n22
realism, 40–43, 50, 165, 208n7, 235n100; and scientism, 43; critical, *8*; idealist, 91; linguistic, 165; naïve, 149; ontological, 81, 88, 91; philosophical, 164; scientific, 37, 152, 164, 175; social, 123. *See also* antirealism; irrealism; materialism
Reat, N. Ross, 203n34
reflexive humanities, 165, 178,
relation-centered ethics, 20, 82
relational accountability, *8*
renunciation (*chuli*, *chushi*), 23, 124, 128, 146, 162, 217n30, 222n3
republicanism, 37, 53, 151; action-oriented, 26; *gonghe*, 63; in Buddhist saṅgha, 123, 146, 222n1; monastic, 135, 139, 140, 141, 227n53; spiritual, 228n76
research paradigm, 4, 189n9, 189n11; Buddhist, 66; competing, 4–10; incommensurable, 4, 6, 9; indigenous, 7; positivist, 66, 67; Yogācāra, 7, *8*, 10, 17, 23, 70
revolution of consciousness, 109, 123, 161, 214n3. *See also* revolutionizing consciousness; *āśrayaparivṛtti*; *zhuanyi*
revolutionary fervor, 24, 66, 68, 206n63
revolutionary nonviolence, 3, 25, 104, 105, 109, 111, 119, 121, 124, 145, 150, 186, 216n27
revolutionizing consciousness, 42, *100*, 102, 103, 159, 175, 187n1; Buddhological project of, 21; in three phases, 104–11; new path of, 173; vital force in, unyielding effort in, 143;

Yogācāra project of, 161, 222n3. *See also* *āśrayaparivṛtti; zhuanyi*
Rhys Davids, T. W., 56, 135, 225n32, 228n68
Rice Seedling Sūtra (*Daoganjing*; *Śālistambasūtra*), 58, 203n34
Ritzinger, Justin, 201n19, 206n62, 211n29, 226n43
Root Verses of Abhidharma-kośa-bhāṣya, *100*
Root Verses of Mahāyānābhidharmasūtra, *100*
Root Verses of Resources for Bodhi, *100*

Said, Edward, 190n14
Sakuma, Hidenori S., 133, 224n26
Salice, Alessandro, 196n29
Salomon, Richard, 218n41
Saṃyuktāgama (*Za'ahanjing*), 156, 230n16
Sankrityayan, Rahul, 66, 207n65, 207n66
saṅgha jewel (*sengbao*), 113–16
saṅgha reform, 126, 127
Śāntideva, 227n56, 229n13
Sasson, Vanessa R., 178–79, 236n3
Satō, Taijun, 152, 230n16
Schlosser, Markus, 212n54
Schmithausen, Lambert, 230n25, 231n35
Schopen, Gregory, 205n49
Schwartz, Benjamin, 200nn6–7
science, 18, 70, *72*, 74, 148, 164, 191n29, 197n33, 209n11, 219n74, 229n12; agency and, 73, 81, 91; and evolutionism, 43; and democracy, 52; and revolution, 91; and social Darwinism, 50, 73, 80; and society, 81; as a product of social processes, 164, 211n37, 229n5; Bergsonian, 47; Bergson's critique of, 44; Buddhism and, 89, 93, 161, 191n27, 195n15, 206n52; compatibility of Buddhism and, 66; contested perceptions of, 45; higher, 64; moral system of, 44; normative structure of, 163, 229n14, 233n59; redefined as, 25, 151; religion and, 65; verified by, 41; Western, 18, 64, 93, 150, 210n17
secular, 32, 64, 71, 76, 135, 202n20; Confucianism, 212n40; democracy, 144; discourse, 78, 151; nation-state, 79, 93; paradigm, 32, 52, 77, 135, 189n11; rationality, 189n11; society, 79; socio-soteriology, 83; subtraction, 56; symmetry, 82, 91
secularism, 32, 71, 88, 91; expansion of, 208n6; humanity, relationality, and, 71; methodological, 189n11; superscription of, 88
Seibt, Johanna, 18, 193n46
Selected Passages from Compendium of Validities, *101*, 160, 232n45
Selections from Establishing Consciousness-only, *100*
Selections from Kathāvatthu, *100*
Sellars, Wilfrid, 208n2, 210n14; on process ontology, 208n4
Sen, Amartya, 32, 189n8, 195n3; on forms of orientalism, 202n20; on secular symmetry, 82, 208n6, 212n40
Seven Selected Chapters from the Avataṃsaka Sūtra, *100*
similar karma (*gongye, tongye*), 14, 62; indirect *ālambana* and, 86; new moral frame of, 77; Ouyang believed, 83; produced through, 88. *See also* collective karma; shared karma
Six Doors of Teaching Dhyāna, *101*, 158–59
siyiren (four kinds of humans as worldly support), 105, 112–17, 219n61, 219n68
Shah, Alpa, 228n76
shared karma (*gongye, tongye*), 62, 146; civil society organizations bounded by, 181; Yogācāra notion of, 81, 185. *See also* collective karma; similar karma
Sharma, J. P., 222n1
Shaver, Robert, 209n10
Shang, Xiaoyun, 65
Shanghai, 2–3, 21, 22, 33–36, 65, 76, 226n46
Shi, Shengkai, 208n74
Shields, James M., 207n69
Shino, Yoshinobu, 199n66
Shizhu piposha lun (*Daśabhūmikavibhāṣa*), 130
Siderits, Mark, 232n47
sikkhāpada (points of learning; *xuechu*, *jie*, *lü*), 128, 132
śīla (moral discipline; *jie*, *lü*), 127–28, *132*, 136–41, 144; *adhi-*, 129; *kuśalā-dharma-saṃgrāhaka-*, 130; *saṃvara-*, 129; *trividhāni śīlāni*, 129; *sattvārtha-kriyā-*, 130

sishi (four kinds of nutriment), 171–72, 235n85
social Darwinism, 37, 44, 53, 54, 67, 214n5; alternatives to, 44; and Bergsonian evolution, 92, 152; antidote to, 24; encounters of Yogācāra with, 29, 51; critique of, 43; grievance against, 80; logic of, 37; science and, 43, 50, 73, 175; Spencer's and Huxley's, 73, 121; Yogācāra and, 24, 92
social epistemology, 26, 27, 151, 165; decentralized, 181; feminist theorizing of, 150; institutionalize the three Cs into, 150; Lü Cheng's, 152, 173
social justice, *8*, 9, 71, 184; Buddhism, science, and, 66; co-awakening to, 3; peace and, 222n3; spirituality and, 182; Yogācāra quest for, 18
social kinds, 9–11, 18, 64, 80, 81, 83, 87, 88, 124, 191n20, 193n25, 225n33; idealist and materialist interpretations of, 35; mind-independent, 17, 74; naturalization of, 4; process-cluster account of, 222n2
social knowledge, 27, 90, 149, 164, 211n37
social sciences, 4, 5, 9–10, *72*, 80, 210n16; natural sciences and, 88; paradigm wars in, 7; physics envy in, 11; state and, 17
social structure, 25; just, 142; unjust, 127
socialism, 56, 64, 207n65, 207n68; Dhammic, 67, 207n70
sociality-cum-intersubjectivity, 84, 87, 117
society-cum-collective-karma, 81
society-cum-karmic-confluence, 74, 75, 80, 87
sociokarma, 55, 57, 210n18
sociology, 53, 60, 61, 72, 206n51; Durkheimian, 37, 73, 209n13, 219n74; evolutionism and, 55; institutionalization of, 67; of aesthetics, 36; philosophy and, 65; reflexive, 19; science and, 80; social Darwinism and, 51, 54. *See also qunxue*
socio-national karma, 86
socio-soteriology, 3–4, 15, 23, 50, 93, 178, 181, 192n43; as superscription of secularism, 88; Buddhist, 70; lens of, 32, 66, 94; Lü Cheng's, 4, 25–29, 51, 98, 104–11, 114–17, 122, 145–47, 165, 173; Ouyang's, 82–83; promise of, 68; Taixu's, 78–82, 211n31; to diffract constructed binaries, 32; to refocus scholarly attention, 68; Wang Enyang's, 83–87; Yogācāra, 3, 5, *8*, 24, 50, 81
socio-spiritual horizon, 52, 54, 62
solidarity, 37, 147
Soma, Therī, 179–81, 236n6
Sosis, Alcorta R., 228n75
Soucy, Alexander, 207n65, 236n20
Spencer, Herbert, 53, 57, 63; on raciology, 60–61; on social Darwinism, 73, 121, 204n43; *Study of Sociology, The*, 24, 51, 57, 60, 204n41; *Social Statics*, 204n42
śrāvaka vinaya (śrāvaka precepts), 127, 128, 134, 137, 138, 155, 223n15, 224n21
Śrāvaka Prātimokṣa, 125, 131, *132*, 138
Stanzas from the Treatise of the Ultimate One-Vehicle Jewel Lineage, 101
Stengers, Isabelle, 193n48, 211n37
Stepien, Rafal K., 15, 189n11, 192n44, 229n7
Sthiramati, 168–69, 233n66
Stone, Jacqueline I., 230n26
storehouse consciousness. *See ālayavijñāna*
Storm, Jason Ānanda Josephson, 201n9; on politics of compassion, 150; on the processual paradigm, 19, 136, 150, 191n20, 222n2
structural violence, 114, 172, 219n70
Stueber, Karsten, 196n29
subjective imposition, 6, 152–53
subjective naturalism, 189n11. *See also* objective naturalism
subjectivity, 4, 7, 31, 198n53; abstractions of, 9; as convenient fiction, 83; dualism of, 25, 168; naturalized, 7, 74; ontological divide between, 80; reification of, 70. *See also* objectivity
Śūraṅgama Sūtra, The, 77; in Yan Fu's translation 58, 204n35; related to universalized *ālayavijñāna* 71
Surendran, Gitanjali, 207n67
survival of the fittest, 25, 41, 68, 145; dangerous reifications of, 81; deadly myth of, 109; instructive lesson of, 63; Yan Fu's translation of, 53–54
Sūtra of the Lion's Roar of Queen Śrīmālā, The (Śrīmālādevī Siṃhanāda Sūtra), 101, 114, 156, 230n24

Sūtra of the Questions of Bodhisattva Ākāśagarbha—The Section on Deciding and Selecting, *101*, 160
Sūtra on the Great Perfection of Wisdom, The, *100*
Sūtra on the Invisible Splendor of the Mahāyāna Treatise on the Buddha-Stage Sūtra, *101*, 104
systems of domination, 172, 178, 183, 185

Tagore, Rabindranath, 65
Táíwò, Olúfẹ́mi O., 41, 197n41, 197n46
Taixu, *72*, 83, 86, 88, 90, 111, 124, 126, 181, 198n61, 199n73; influence on Thich Nhat Hanh, 236n11; on karmic society, 76–80, 185, 207n73, 211n31; preference for Yogācāra bodhisattva precepts, 139
Tang, Zhean, 197n34, 197n37
tathāgatagarbha, 103, 153–56, 230n24; from original purity to, 108; weak reading, 103, 216n24
Taylor, Charles, 97, 209n11, 214n4; on social theories, 148, 229n2
Thass, Iyothee, 66, 207n64,
Theory of Heavenly Process (*Tianyan lun*), 57, 60, 204n37
Tikhonov, Miller V., 207n68
Tillemans, Tom, 199n65, 232n47
tiyong (foundation and function), 113
Tongmenghui (the United League), 91
transformative epistemology, 95, 148–51, 165, 173, 183; Buddhability-cum-humanity, bodhisattvas of democracy, and, 181; goal of practicing, 178; scholarship, self-cultivation, and, 105; serves as a mirror, 174
transformative interrogation, 27, 151, 164, 183, 186
Treatise on Entering Abhidharma, *100*
Treatise on the Four Noble Truths, *100*
Treatise on the Great Perfection of Wisdom, *100*
Treatise on the Nonduality of Mahāyāna Dharmadhātu, *101*
Tsui, Brian, 228n70
Tuck, Andrew P., 189n11
Turner, Alicia Marie, 207n70
Tzohar, Roy, on intersubjectivity, 192n41, 210n19, 211n36, 233n66, 233n73; on subsequent awarness, 221n95

U Dhammaloka (William Colvin), 67
uncommon karma, 87
universal beauty, 32, 39, 42, 119, 170
upalabdhi (*liaojing; rig par byed pa* or *yul rnam par rig pa*), 234n74

Valmisa, Mercedes, 19, 136, 194n58, 209n10, 211n32–33, 211n34, 218n50
Van Norden, Bryan, 208n2
Vasubandhu, 12, 55, 66, 78, 84, 107, 159, 192n39, 200n79, 213n62; Asaṅga and, 221n95, 223n16; inspired by, 141; Maitreya, Asaṅga, and, 224n26; offers an answer to four objectivist challenges, 13–15; on hermeneutic theory, 227n55; weak reading of *tathāgatagarbha*, 216n24
Verses Distinguishing the Middle and the Extremes, *100*
vibhaṅga (commentary on vinaya rules), 223n5
vijñapti (*liaobie*), 168, 170, 234n74
vijñaptimātra (*vijñānamātra*, *weishi*, *weiyan*, consciousness-only), 31, 55, *100*, 142, 160, *167*, 170, 198n52, 237n77; and the Buddha-Nature debate, 204n40; centrality of, 120; coherence of, 13, 14; in Thich Nhat Hanh, 236n20; Lü Cheng on Bergsonism and, 47, 198n59; school of, 3, 62, 145, 170; Taixu on, 78; truth of, 47, 48, 124, 143, 166, 169, 170; Wang Enyang on, 84, 212n45; Xiong Shili's, 230n26; Xuanzang's and Dharmapāla's, 233n70
vikalpa (*fenbie*, discrimination), 86, *167*, 169173
vikalpita (*suo fenbie*, discriminated), 167
Vimalakīrti Sūtra, *100*, 138, 198n61, 226n40
Viṃśika (*Twenty Verses*), 84, 170, 227n55, 234n81; critique of mind-independence, 13–15; Wang Enyang's commentary on, 84, 212n46
Voegelin, Eric, 201n13
voluntary participation, 26, 116, 130
Von Hinüber, Oskar, 226n48, 227nn52–53

Waldron, William, 189n7, 209n9, 231n33, 233n73; on modal of analyzing causal relations, 235n87
Walser, Joseph, 122, 221n102

Walters, Jonathan S., 55, 77, 201n15; on Buddhist studies methods, 223n8, 226n48; on early scholarship of individual karma, 202n21, 203n28; on karmic confluence, 210n18
Wang, Enyang, *72*, 83, 84, 210n17, 212n42, 212n51, 221n94; on *adhipati* and collective karma, 85, 86–87, 192n42, 205n46; on Berkeley's idealism, 85, 212n50; on indirect *ālambana*, 85, 87, 118, 221n98
Wang, Fansen, 195n5
Wang, Hui, 120, 200n1, 221nn99–100
Wang, Jessica Ching-Sze, 213n72
Wang, Xiaoxu (Jitong), 64, 65, *72*, 91, 124, 208n1, 213n61; on subjectivity and objectivity, 70; on Yogācāra social philosophy, 88–89
Wang, Zhixin, 156, 161, 231n28
Wang, Zuoyue, 229n12
Wangchuk, Dorji, 232n56
wangguo miezhong (national demise and racial extinction), 53, 84
Ward, Larry, 178, 181, 237nn21–22; on Yogācāra racial karma, 184–85
Warren, Henry Clarke, 232n41
Weinstein, David, 204n43
Welch, Holmes, 162, 205n48, 232n52
Westerhoff, Jan, 209n9, 210n15, 212n38, 234n80, 235n100
wisdom (*ñāṇa*, *prajñā*, *zhi*, *hui*), 85, 136, 151, 157, 182; and knowledge, 232n38; conventional, 112, 116; of emptiness, 174, 175; eyes, 219n68; perfection of, 144; received, 24; shared, 163; supreme, 161; true, 108, 116; unobstructed, 144
Wong, David B., 20, 194n61
World War I, 20, 21, 24, 63, 121
World War II, 65, 70, 121
Wu, Xianwu, 198n60

Xiang, Shuchen, 201n12, 203n25, 209n11
xin xiangxu (continuity of the mental stream), 103, 159, 217n32
Xinhai Revolution, 32, 52, 53, 63, 91
Xiong, Shili, 156, 221n98, 230n26, 231n27
Xu, Jilin, 214n5
Xuanzang, 14, 47, 105, *167*, 214n6, 216n29, 221n95, 233n67, 234n80, 235n86; Lü on Xuanzang's translation, 233n70; on *adhipati*, 212n47; on authorship of *Yogācārabhūmi*, 224n25; on indirect *ālambana*, 84, 117, 212n46; on *icchantika*, 116; on karmic seeds with common characteristics, 78; on model of consciousness, 168, 200n79, 233n68, 234n77, 234n81; on one reality realm, 110; on perfected nature, 218n52; on perfuming, 218n43; on *prasiddha*, 166, 169–70, 234n76; on precepts, 224n21; on Southern Yogācāra, 159; pivotal in transmitting Nālandā learning, 98, 104, 131–32

Yan, Fu, 24, 51, 93, 121, 200n7, 203n31, 204n35, 204n37, 204n41, 204n43; on Spencer, 53–54; on *zhongye*, 25, 57–63
Yan, Joey Yiqiao, 201n19; 210n21
Yang, Wenhui, 60
Yao, Binbin, 198n59, 213n64
Yijing, 98, 119, 132–33, 214n6
Ying, Lei, 62, 201n11
Yinguang, *72*, 76–77, 86, 206n59, 211n26
Yinming ruzhengli lun (*Introduction to Logic*; *Nyāyapraveśa*), *101*, 159
Yinshun, *72*, 90, 213n60, 222n4, 231n32
Yoga Bodhisattva Prātimokṣa, 95, *101*, *132*, 139, 173, 224n28; and *Śrāvaka Prātimokṣa*, 131, 138; as communal rules for democratic participation, 123–24, 130; as only authentic lineage of Mahāyāna vinaya, 125–26; in terms of structural analysis, 144
Yoga Bodhisattva Karman, *101*, 125, 131; mirroring the monastic biweekly assembly, 140
Yogācāra, Northern transmission of, 158
Yogācāra, Southern transmission of, 158, 159
Yogācāra causal enframing/framework (*weishi yuanqi*), 25, 46–47, 81, 120, 199n69; as social coevolution, 121; as only antidote to, 50; Xuanzang's, 170; to change the terms of the modern debate, 114; to justify the

relation between scholarship and activism, 235n86
Yogācāra karmic/causal theory, 47, 81, 85, 121, 162, 175, 184; as ever-expanding process of interconditioned transformation, 173; as philosophical framework, 123; as philosophical foundation, 165; as antidote to, 24; fusion of, 55; linked evolution of life with, 50; of the perceptible world, 152; to defend *correctness*, 74; subsumed Western sciences into, 18; to theorize civil society, 135; Xuanzang's, 235n86
Yogācāra social philosophy, 24, 52, 55, 171
Yogācāra three Cs, 4, 11, 25, 26, 149; and organized skepticism, 164; reinvented "scientific method" in terms of, 151; replacing objectivity, 13–15; systemized, 152
Yogācārabhūmi, 132, 166, 224n28, 225n30, 231n35; authorship of, 224nn25–26; diffractive analysis of, 157; intertextual practices of, 133–34, 156, 231n32; on Buddha nature, 204n40; on four kinds of nutrient, 235n85; on *zhongxing*, 204n38
Yong, Ed, 12, 192n34
Yoshimura, Makoto, 204n40, 218n45
Yü, Ying-shih, 196n26
yuanqi (conditioned coarising), 46, 110, 173, 199n69, 222n3
Yuanxue (the Institute's Learning), 98, 105–6, 108, 113, 161, 214n7, 215n11; Chinese translation and, 107; the essence of, 117; grounded in original quiescence, 158, 215n20; inaugurated a nonviolent means, 164; Yuanxue and a systematic integration of Buddhology into soteriology, 99; resembles Mertonian normative structures of science, 163
Yuan, Yuan, 179, 236n5
Yuanying, *72*, 77, 86, 211n27
Yuanzhao, 112, 219n61

zengshang (activating and amplifying influence), 14, 146, 220n76; *jiexue*, 129; *li*, 84; *waiyuan*, 115; *xiangzi*, 159; *yuan*, 62. *See also adhipati*
Zhang, Ruzhao, 180–81, 186
Zhang, Taiyan, 21, 52, 62, *72*, 198n61, 199n64, 200n4, 205n49; and "scientific" Yogācāra, 43–45; Lü's criticism of, 46, 47; on universalized *ālayavijñāna*, 92–93
zhenru (Thusness), 118–20, 216n24, 221n94
zhijue (intuition), 43, 44, 48, 49, 198n50, 198n60
Zhongguo Fojiao xiehui (Buddhist Association of China), 146
zhongxing (caste/birth/family), 57–59, 62, 116, 204n38. *See also* caste; *zhongye*
zhongye, 24–25, 57, 203n31, 204n38; as Yogācāra individual karma, 57–60; as Yogācāra national/racial karma (*zhongye*), 60–63, 64
zhongzu (family, clan, race, species), 59
Zhou, Shujia, 90–91
Zhou, Zuoren, 62
Zhu, Feihuang, 90–91
zhuanshi (remaking the world), 105, 120, 124, 162
zhuanyi, 102, 104, 161, 187n1; a new path of, 173; as a new paradigm of liberation, 105; as social evolution-cum-revolution, 31, 222n3; linked to social reform, 217n30. *See also āśrayaparivṛtti*; revolutionizing consciousness
Zou, Rong, 51–54, 200n3
zuoyi (intellectual analysis), 158, 159

GPSR Authorized Representative: Easy Access System Europe, Mustamäe tee 50, 10621 Tallinn, Estonia, gpsr.requests@easproject.com

www.ingramcontent.com/pod-product-compliance
Lightning Source LLC
Chambersburg PA
CBHW031237290426
44109CB00012B/329
9780231216043